Organizational Change

Organizational Change

Views from the Edge

Robert J. Marshak

The Lewin Center
Bethel, Maine

For information:
The Lewin Center
P.O. Box 68
Bethel, ME 04217

Printed in the United States of America

Library of Congress Cataloguing-in-Publication Data

Organizational change: views from the edge
Robert J. Marshak, author
Includes references and index.

ISBN number: 978-0-615-23059-7

Catalogue number: 2008939663

This book is printed on acid-free paper.

07   08   09   10   11   10   9   8   7   6   5   4   3   2   1

Managing Editor:	Patricia Millar
Copy Editor:	Mary Lyon Millar
Indexing:	S. Anne Fifer, Graffito, USA
Typesetter:	Charles Raywood, Profile Direct, Canada
Printer:	Jean Schroeder, Sheridan Books, USA

To HM, MBM and ABM

Contents

Introduction from the President, The Lewin Center

Charles Seashore

Organizational Change: Views from the Edge was an idea that emerged from a two hour consultation and conversation I was having with Bob Marshak. We were talking about the kind of inquiry and research that our Board wanted to highlight in our initial definition of The Lewin Center for Social Change, Action and Research. In the course of talking, we explored the values and the guiding principles including, of course, our choice of Kurt Lewin as the driving force at the core of our profession.

We thought we were talking about a research agenda but it suddenly morphed into a conception of a product that would illustrate and demonstrate our vision—a product that would exemplify our focus on the intersection of social action theory and practice. Knowing how daunting it is to start a book from scratch, we quickly turned to the idea of pulling together the broad collection of Bob's articles that were already published but not easily available in one place.

We somewhat foolishly thought that it could be done in a relatively short period of time with a minimum of effort and yet provide a reference point to our many colleagues who have aspirations to be scholar-practitioners. We now know that putting together materials from different formats, table constructions and font variations requires a team of people, scratching their heads around a demanding task where errors are more frequently introduced than removed in the process. So it is with great pleasure that we share the fruits of our work with you, the interested and passionate reader that we have conjured up in our minds.

However, the story began for me a long time before the conversation with Bob. As a third generation psychologist, I have been blessed with the opportunity to grow up with access to my grandfather Carl's home and psychological laboratory in Iowa City and my father's shop in the basement of the psychology building at Northwestern University—experimental psychologists are crazy about apparatus and anything that promotes the ability to test out ideas in action. I came to appreciate the connection between ideas and action at a deeper level later, after deciding to major in psychology at the University of Colorado. It was there I became aware that my grandfather, as Dean of the Graduate School, played a key role in recruiting Kurt Lewin to the University of Iowa to join colleagues in the development of the Iowa Child Welfare Research Station. It was there that Lewin became the mentor of Ron Lippitt and the catalyst for the field research that became Ron's dissertation. This was the famous study of autocratic, democratic and laissez-faire leadership in children's groups, an early marking point in the adventure of action research in social psychology, particularly the study of groups in the context of a democratic society.

The Founding Board of The Lewin Center was made up of seven colleagues who all came into our full personal and professional development through our involvement with the NTL Institute, initially known as the National Training Laboratory in Group Development. Kurt Lewin was a part of the planning for that first conference but died in the spring of 1947, just months before the first group of participants arrived for a three week learning laboratory focused on group process, the dynamics of change and the use of experiential learning as a powerful design in adult education. All of us knew the colleagues of Lewin—Lee Bradford, Ron Lippitt and Ken Benne—but none of us actually had the good fortune to meet Lewin. But we, along with whole generations of colleagues in the fields of group process, social psychology and organization development, have experienced the powerful influence of his work. His phrase that "nothing is as useful as a good theory" combined with the deep convictions of the importance of the pursuit of social justice through experiential learning and action research has meaning far beyond those few words. Our lives have been permanently transformed by taking the path laid out by those pioneers.

Thus, when the opportunity arose in the late summer of 2005 with the announcement that the NTL Founders House in Bethel was going to be sold, we leapt at the opportunity to contribute to the next generations by forming The Lewin Center. We had 60 years of history of NTL in Bethel to inspire our work. It was formed in May, 2006 and we took occupancy of the beautiful Victorian home, originally the Gehring Clinic in September, 2006. We had two purposes in mind. We wanted to honor the legacy of the NTL's past and hope to help shape the future of applied behavioral science in the service of social justice.

We have had the powerful support of many of our colleagues and citizens of Bethel, Maine in launching our enterprise. It is a location where thousands of participants have come from all corners of our planet to explore the dynamics of human interaction. It is the creative center where hundreds of our colleagues have invented a field at the intersection of theory and practice. The focus was on the development of understanding by creating settings in which staff and participants jointly constructed a laboratory for experimentation and innovation in the pursuit of social justice which would lead to better and better theory.

The original passionate exploration of the dynamics of groups emerged from the aftermath of World War II. It was fueled by the desire to explore alternative models of power and participative leadership that would inform citizen actions in every community and institution, both here and abroad. We hope that The Lewin Center can look ahead and be a part of addressing the critical issues now confronting the world.

We have chosen Bob's work as a means of getting started on our task. We hope that you, the careful reader and discerning practitioner, can pick up the powerful underlying themes that tie together these many articles. We think they speak to the immutable connection of idea and action. We hope that they will inspire you to generate new ideas and bold new actions. We are counting on you to take on the daunting task that Lewin inspired in us, to use our intellect and our energy to make a much better world together.

On behalf of the current Board of Directors of The Lewin Center, which includes Argentine Craig, Brenda Jones, Lennox Joseph, Fred Nader, Edie Seashore and me, and in memory of Don Klein whom we still miss dearly, I commend this book to you and your colleagues.

Charles Seashore, President of The Lewin Center
February, 2009

A Note from the Managing Editor

Patricia A. Millar

Since 1992, I've worked as an organization development (OD) practitioner, as a business owner and as an employee. I've supported diverse clients and seen the benefits and limitations of various platforms for this evolving profession: mid-size consulting company, sole proprietor, small boutique shop, and internal practice within a large multinational. Throughout the evolution of my life-work, a passionate desire to fully realize human and organizational potential has motivated my efforts. I've had the pleasure of working with incredible colleagues and an array of amazing clients.

Prior to my corporate and consulting work, in the 70s and 80s, I supported international students, refugees, and local community development projects. Recently, a renewed desire for sustainable development and social justice permeates my intentions and informs my choices. A deep recognition of the embeddedness of human actors in their environment and in interaction with other parts of a systemic whole has come to be a matter of serious reflection for me.

This collection by a senior practitioner and scholar has given me greater clarity about the relationship of the parts to the whole, about the history and evolution of our profession, about the contexts and cultures within which we work, and about the questions we must ask ourselves to realize the aspirations of our calling. I believe it is essential for those entering and continuing in the field of human and organizational development to find ways to become grounded in what and who have gone before. It is equally important to cross borders into unexplored territories.

Like me, Bob is a border crosser. In this collection, he takes us on a journey to the past for a look at the origins of OD, and then forays into the Oriental mind and culture while inquiring into the fundamental assumptions of a Western worldview. He invites us to moments of intense reflection on the purpose of our work and our ways of being as practitioners. The deeper implications of theoretical stances, belief systems, and strategies for client engagements become clearer as he draws distinctions for consideration in his clear, succinct prose.

Bob's writing is engaging and develops well, so readers can easily follow the logic of his thinking as he weaves his way through complex topics. He illuminates situational dynamics with case studies and examples, and offers plenty of organizing frameworks and summaries along the way to reinforce key points.

I believe the OD profession is at a critical juncture, a time when it is vitally important for us to bring into conscious awareness the many factors influencing our decisions, traditions, and new directions. Bob Marshak is a proficient guide, one who has never ceased from reflective practice and scholarly inquiry. I am delighted to have taken part in bringing his published work over 25 years to all of you, in a single volume.

Preface from the Author

Robert J. Marshak

It is an honor to be the first publication of The Lewin Center both in terms of the Center's purposes and the rich traditions of people, scholarship, and thoughtful action it embodies.

The present volume encapsulates twenty-five years of my thinking about organizational change originally published in a variety of scholarly and practitioner journals. The essays are organized thematically, although there is a rough chronology within each of the themes reflecting in some cases the development of my thinking over the years. The main topic headings are: Organization Development: Past, Present and Future; Cross Cultural Views on Organization Development; Metaphors, Language, and Change; and Insights for Organization Development Practitioners. Each of these topical sections has a brief introduction that provides a snapshot look into some of the thinking and/or events that led to the specific publications. Finally, the whole collection is preceded by a short essay that fittingly notes the continuing influence of Kurt Lewin.

In putting together this collection I had a chance to reflect on whether or not there were any themes that recur throughout my work. I'm sure others may discern more themes or sub-themes than me, but somewhat to my surprise several themes do seem to run through my writings from beginning to end. These include:

1. The topic of organizational change. I suppose this is somewhat obvious given the title of the book, but it was nonetheless striking to me in retrospect that virtually everything I have ever written relates directly to the topic of organizational change in terms of underlying theories, assumptions, practices, and consulting roles.

2. Viewing things from the dual perspectives of "inside looking out" and "outside looking in." That is what is meant by "views from the edge." My orientation or stance tends to be a combination of both insider and outsider to whatever topic I am addressing. I suppose in one sense this is a reflection of marginality and the classic role of the consultant as needing to be on the margin of whatever system one is working with. In another sense it is consistent with a participant observer research stance. In my case it also seems related to a consciousness of boundaries such that for any phenomenon or concept there is always an awareness of the limits of what is and the possibilities that lie beyond the edge of prevailing thinking. This also turns up in my writing style as noted next.

3. In terms of methodology or style, my writings tend to elucidate ideas by contrasting ideal types and exploring polarities. As mentioned above, this may relate to a lifelong orientation towards noting both "what is" and also "what is not." Each reveals the other, thus in my writings I will frequently describe what something is

not as a way to illuminate what it is; or describe what it is in ways to make clear what it is not. This orientation, or view from the edge, will tend to err on the side of contrast, as readers who prefer to understand things through similarity will undoubtedly notice. I recall hearing somewhere that people tend to learn and understand things predominately in one of three ways. One way is by noting how things are similar or alike each other. Another is how things are different or differ from each other. The third way is by noting categories of things that are like each other on one dimension and different from each other on another dimension. For example, one could look at the various schools of psychology (e.g., analytical, behavioral, humanistic, cognitive, etc.) and understand them as being alike in that they are all theories about human psychology. One could also note the ways in which they differ from each other along one or more important dimension. Finally, one might place them in different categories as a way to understand both the similarities and differences among them and/or how they are similar to or contrast with other social science theories. In reflecting on my own preferences I clearly understand things first by noting differences and secondarily by categorizing things. This tendency should become clear in the writings that follow. I also sometimes wonder if my inquiry into yin-yang philosophy, described in the section on Cross Cultural Views of Organization Development, isn't also connected in some ways to this orientation.

4. Another dominant and recurring theme in my thinking and writing is an implicit and explicit cognitive orientation that manifests itself in a number of ways. First, there is an interest in alternative cognitive structures and realities that may take the form of different consciousnesses, cultures, cognitive schemata, philosophical systems, formal and informal theories, and so forth. This, of course, goes along with my orientation towards both what is, according to prevailing assumptions or thought, and what lies beyond that edge. Second, an interest in how these alternative "mental models" can mediate experience, interpretation, and action taking. In other words, how thought and action are dependent on the boundaries of current and sometimes unthinking beliefs, assumptions and cognitive constructs. Furthermore, how possibilities for change or innovative action may be revealed by seeing beyond the edge or limits of prevailing thought. Third, although not formally educated in cognitive psychology or cognitive linguistics, a lifelong orientation that language and metaphor may shape and reveal inner patterns of thinking. In other words, how what someone says may reveal inner, and sometimes subconscious, ways of thinking and knowing. Lastly, a recognition of the power of being able "to step into" another's way of experiencing the world while holding your own as a method that allows for empathy, connection, understanding, and also the exploration of new or reframed possibilities. In order to be able to do this one needs to be able to stand at the edge or boundary of one's own and another's cognitive framings.

5. Finally, connected to all of the above orientations, the theme of how language, thought and action are inextricably intertwined runs through virtually all of my

work whether intended for practitioners or academics, and whether or not it was the main focus of the article. What I personally found interesting and surprising was the degree to which this theme appears from the very beginning even before I had developed and refined my thinking through various academic and applied explorations.

I hope the reader finds something of interest here whether from a practitioner or scholarly perspective. Naturally, I stand at the edge of both, neither totally inside nor outside either. I hope this perspective and background adds to the texture and taste of the various essays and ideas.

Acknowledgements

I wish to thank the Board of The Lewin Center for approaching me with the idea of compiling this book. It is a wonderful (and also a bit daunting) opportunity to be able to put such an extensive range of one's work into a single volume so that people can read the development of one's thinking over an extended period of time. In particular, I want to thank Dr. Charles Seashore, President of The Lewin Center, for initiating and supporting this project and the vision and ideals of the scholar-practitioner it is intended to exemplify.

I also wish to thank Ms. Patricia Millar for her wonderful work as managing editor for this volume. In addition to all the logistics involved, Patti helped to shape the final contents and form of the book, and worked tirelessly to ensure all the moving pieces came together. Without doubt this book would not have happened without her caring and tireless efforts. Special thanks also to Dr. Ruth Scogna Wagner who helped early on to get this project off and running and also helped encourage me to write the introductions to each section.

Finally, thanks also go to my wife, Allison Binder Marshak, for understanding and supporting my introverted "hobby" of writing articles and book chapters in between my consulting and teaching assignments. She has always encouraged my writing efforts and been delighted whenever something ended up in print.

Robert J. Marshak, Ph.D.
Reston, Virginia
July 1, 2008

Prologue: Commentary on Kurt Lewin's Heritage

Kurt Lewin seems to be one of those unique individuals whose influence extends in many directions, partially through his own work but, importantly, through the work of others who have been informed or inspired by one or more of his seminal ideas. Lewin's ability to have impact far beyond his native Germany, or even his adopted home the United States, is worth noting and will be discussed below. Participatory research is yet another example of this continuing influence across time and space.

Participation versus Hierarchy in Research

Participatory research (Wennberg & Hane, 2005) places emphasis on the imperative for participation as opposed to elitism or hierarchy in actionable research or, in other terms, on the democratization of knowledge generation and application. This is one of the important dimensions of Lewin's famous advocacy of an "action research" orientation.

Partially owing to this emphasis on participation, both action research and participatory research are open to a range of questions and issues about their legitimacy and ethics as research – as opposed to action – strategies. A flavor for the ongoing controversy, and concerns about action research will be summarized below as a way of adding to the participatory research discussion. Given the Northern European origins of participatory research, some preliminary questions about the cross-cultural implications of participatory versus hierarchical approaches to knowledge generation and application also will be discussed, followed by a brief historical update on the global scope of Lewin's personal impact. Finally, the Gestalt aspects of Lewin's advocacy of action research and a participatory approach will be reviewed briefly.

Some Research Questions about Participatory Research

Ongoing concerns about the action research approach and, therefore, participatory research, as research endeavors, include: low reproducibility of settings and findings, limitations on the means of collection and documentation of data, and the manner in which the personal interests, knowledge, and competencies of the researcher(s) may influence the research (Huxham & Vangen, 2003). For some, these are severe enough limitations to question whether the term "research" should even be applied to such approaches. Of course, these limitations apply, to some extent, in any research effort or approach. What matters, therefore, is to document as much relevant data as possible, as accurately as possible; to apply or induce some framework(s) to the data; and to arrive at valid insights that contribute to knowledge in some significant way.

There are also a number of ethical dilemmas that are often raised, especially by critics, about this type of approach to "research." These include dilemmas associated with participant selection, possible divergences in the needs and interests of actors and researchers, and anonymity and confidentiality of the information provided (Walker &

Slightly edited from Marshak, R. J. (2005). Commentary on Kurt Lewin's heritage. *Gestalt Review, 9*(3), 281-285. Republished with permission.

Haslett, 2002). The dual purposes of an approach that combines social interventions with research is also questioned by some commentators, but certainly not all (Huxman & Vangen, 2003). As participatory research endeavors are expanded and reported in the literature, these kinds of questions will surely be raised and, I'm equally sure, be addressed just as they have been about action research.

Cross-Cultural Questions about Participatory Research

Both action research and participatory research place a strong emphasis on the involvement of people beyond an elite or hierarchy to address social issues and concerns. This is consistent with aspects of Northern European and North American cultures, but not all cultures. A number of years ago, I commented on the Western biases of Lewin's linear model of change as contrasted with the cyclical model inherent in Confucian and Taoist philosophy (Marshak, 1993). There are also cultural differences with respect to participation and hierarchy: many cultures, especially East Asian cultures, place greater emphasis on deference to superiors. In such settings, hierarchy and harmony go together, and too much "participation" can be experienced as a form of anarchy (Marshak, 2004). It will be interesting, therefore, to follow how participatory research will be interpreted and carried out in non-Scandinavian contexts.

Of course, Lewin's ideas are widely known in East Asia and, as the following anecdote to update the historical record will attest, his personal influence in that part of the world may be far greater than is presently known in the West.

Lewin's Personal Reach

Lewin emigrated to the United States in the early 1930s as the Nazis came to power in his native Germany. His personal influence on leading American and European psychologists and social scientists is widely known. Less widely known, owing to the Cold War, is his influence on Russian and Eastern European psychologists through his former colleagues and students at the Berlin Institute, such as Bluma Zeigarnik.

More as a footnote, it has also been documented that Lewin had some personal influence on psychologists in Japan, again as a result of his contacts at the Berlin Institute. In 1933, following his lecture at Stanford University, Lewin:

> ...decided to return by way of the Pacific, so that he could make stops in Japan and Russia, where he had been invited to lecture. Leaving Japan, he would proceed by way of the Trans-Siberian Railroad across the U.S.S.R. to Moscow and continue later by train to Berlin. (Marrow, 1969, p. 67).

What is not documented anywhere, as far as I know, is that Lewin also may have visited and influenced the field of psychology in Korea. This came to light during a trip I made to Korea in 1997 with the then President (Lennox Joseph) and a former President (Edith Whitfield Seashore) of NTL Institute for Applied Behavioral Sciences. During a dinner in Seoul overlooking the Han River, one of the attendees, a very elderly Korean psychology professor, asked if it were true that Kurt Lewin was the founder of NTL Institute. After hearing the translated explanation that Lewin died in 1947, shortly before NTL Institute was created, we were then asked if we knew that, "Kurt Lewin visited and helped establish the Department of Psychology at Seoul National University." While my two colleagues looked at each other with some disbelief, I recalled that Korea had been annexed by Japan in 1910, and that there was no Korean national identity until after the defeat of the Japanese in World War II. With this background, I replied, "That would have to have been during the unfortunate period of the Japanese occupation and Seoul National University would have had a Japanese name." My conjecture was confirmed when I was congratulated on my knowledge of Korean history and told that it was in fact during the early 1930s that Lewin had visited Seoul. A quick look at any map of Northeast Asia will also confirm that if one were traveling from Japan via the Trans-Siberian Railroad back to Moscow and Berlin, one would presumably travel through what is now present-day South and North Korea, and was then considered part of Japan.

Gestalt Aspects of Participatory Research

Finally, it is worth noting the Gestalt aspects of action research and presumably of participatory research. Lewin was an associate of Kohler and Wertheimer at the Berlin Institute, and was impressed by Gestalt holism:

> Though he was never a completely orthodox Gestaltist, he did become a vital force in the new movement and contributed to it his own special insights. To Lewin Gestaltism seemed closer to actual experience than did piecemeal analysis, which had prevailed in psychology during his prewar student days (Marrow, 1969, p. 13-14).

Specifically, action research and participatory research involve contextualized and live social and organizational settings, rather than segementalized laboratory experiments and surveys. This supports integrative and practical-oriented approaches to research consistent with Lewin's original intentions (Lewin, 1947). Lewin intended that action research help address the inherent limitations of studying complex social events in a laboratory, as well as the artificiality of separating out single behavioral elements from an integrated system (Foster, 1972). Furthermore, Lewin advocated the study of social dynamics "...not by transforming them into quantifiable units of physical actions and reactions, but by studying the intersubjectively valid sets of meanings, norms and values that are the immediate determinates of behavior" (Peters & Robinson, 1984, p. 115). Thus action research and participatory research are both more participatory than elitist and more Gestaltist than reductionist in their approaches to knowledge generation and application.

References

Foster, M. (1972). An introduction to the theory and practice of action research in work organizations. *Human Relations*, 25, 529-556.

Huxham, C., & Vangen, S. (2003). Researching organizational practice through action research: Case studies and design choices. *Organizational Research Methods, 6,* 383-403.

Lewin, K. (1947). Frontiers in group dynamics: Channels of group life: Social planning and action research. *Human Relations, 1,* 143-153.

Marrow, A. J. (1969). *The Practical Theorist: The Life and Work of Kurt Lewin.* New York: Basic Books.

Marshak, R. J. (1993). Lewin meets Confucius: A re-view of the OD model of change. *Journal of Applied Behavioral Science, 29,* 393-415.

Marshak, R. J. (2004). Organization development and post-Confucian societies. In P. F. Sorensen, T. C. Head, T. Yaeger, & D. Cooperrider (Eds.), *Global and International Organization Development, 4th edition.* Champaign, IL: Stipes Publishing, 295-311.

Peters, M., & Robinson, V. (1984). The origins and status of action research. *Journal of Applied Behavioral Science, 20,* 113-124.

Walker, B., & Haslett, T. (2002). Action Research in management-ethical dilemmas. *Systemic Practice and Action Research, 15,* 523-533.

Wennberg, B., & Hane, M. (2005). Kurt Lewin's heritage: A possible breakthrough? *Gestalt Review, 9*(3), 245-270.

PART I:
Organization Development:
Past, Present and Future

Introduction
Robert J. Marshak

I first became aware of organization development (OD) in 1972 after returning to my graduate studies that had been interrupted by required military service during the Vietnam War. I recall reading some references to it and then taking a course offered for the first time in the Fall of 1972 called "Small Group Dynamics" which included a T-Group experience. After that I continued to read about OD and take additional graduate courses related to it as I finished my masters and doctoral degrees. I also began trying to put some of the ideas I had been reading about in class into practice in my fulltime job as a management analyst in a US Government research agency. I also had to figure out how to use OD ideas, models, and technologies within an agency setting that was decidedly not "touchy-feely" and valued "expert knowledge." That, plus my own ways of learning and knowing, invited me to discern the contours of this thing called OD. In short, to search for the edges or boundaries of this social science technology to help me to understand both what it was, and, equally important to me, what it was not.

Over the years of learning about organization change and OD methods and theories, I never lost my sense that, although notoriously difficult to define, there were some fuzzy boundaries to OD such that there was an "in" and an "out" that could be described and explored. I even found myself then, and now, describing myself as "someone who does OD… and also other things." By that I mean that OD is not everything and that it is meaningful, i.e., it works under a set of assumptions and conditions that when not present may call for different assumptions, technologies, or approaches.

The articles presented in this and other sections of the book reflect this orientation of being on the edge; both looking inward at OD and its core assumptions, while also considering what might lie outside in the form of different assumptions, conditions, theories, and so forth.

The first selection on *Organization Development as a Profession and a Field* was written late in my thinking and more inward than outward looking. It was my attempt to describe what I considered to be the defining characteristics of traditional or classical OD. In short, more about what OD is or has been, than what it is not or might be becoming outside of its traditional "edge" or boundaries. It also clearly emphasizes my belief that the glue that holds the OD enterprise together is more about its underlying values or ideology than tools or techniques.

Managing in Chaotic Times was a short outward looking discussion describing what I was noticing in the early 1990s as a change in the landscape of organizational change. It struck me that the paradigm developed for industrial age organizations was changing and that we were entering at the end of the 20th century a transition period between what had been and what was still to fully emerge. This also meant that our assumptions about managing change needed to shift as the organizational circumstances and contexts were moving through a transition period that could feel like "chaos." The theme of shifting paradigms and contexts of change is one that continued to run through a number of my later articles, but this was my first "take" on the subject.

Reinventing Organization Development Theory and Practice was written with my long-time collaborator Judith H. Katz. It was intended to reflect our growing belief that the contours of traditional organization development were too restrictive for what we were observing as emerging practices and needs. It was a beginning attempt to enlarge what might be considered "in" versus "out" in organization development theory and practice.

Contemporary Challenges to the Philosophy and Practice of Organization Development is probably my most comprehensive assessment of the past, present and emerging state of organization development. It sits squarely on the edge describing what I have seen, experienced and thought about the contributions and limitations of organization development over a thirty year period beginning in the early 1970s. It is the first place I began to talk in terms of a traditional or "classical OD" as distinct from other, emerging forms. In a continuing theme, the central role of assumptions and values in defining OD versus other forms of organizational change, such as "change management," is also prominently discussed.

Returning to the theme of changing contexts and constructs of change, *Morphing: The Leading Edge of Organizational Change in the Twenty-first Century* ponders whether or not we have the language and concepts to deal with continuous change versus the traditional "start-stop" models of change prevalent in OD. It also raises the concept of continuous transformational change, dubbed "morphing," to deal with the hyperactive environments experienced in some twenty-first century business environments such as the Internet and electronics.

Finally, this section closes with a discussion of *Emerging Directions: Is There a New OD?* This was written as a follow-up and elaboration of ideas first introduced in Contemporary Challenges to the Philosophy and Practice of Organization Development. In brief, it asserts that there is a set of assumptions and practices that helped define traditional or "classical" OD, and a range of newer practices based on differing assumptions, theories and practices, loosely labeled "new" OD. I wrote this partly as a way to put the possibility of multiple ODs on the table for discussion, mindful of the tendency within the OD community to somehow be inclusive of everything such that there is nothing new or different, but instead only continuations and permutations of what has always been. From my perspective on the edge this did not and does not make sense, especially in terms of fostering and encouraging innovation in OD theory and practice.

1
Organization Development as a Profession and a Field

Organization development (OD) has been around since the late 1950s and early 1960s, but it still proves difficult to explain what it is, what it does, and why you might want it or need it. The reasons for this seem twofold. First, it is still an evolving field of practice and is therefore difficult to pin down. Second, it requires an understanding of a synthesis or integration of several sets of knowledge united by an underlying philosophical belief and value system(s). Consequently, the range of definitions offered over the years all sound somewhat similar, and they also seem to miss the mark in explaining to outsiders, "So, what exactly is OD?"

Consider these definitions:

Organization development is an effort (1) *planned,* (2) *organization-wide,* and (3) managed *from the top,* to (4) *increase organization effectiveness* and *health,* through (5) planned *interventions* in the organization's "processes," using behavioral science knowledge. (Beckhard, 1969, p. 9)

Organization development refers to a long-range effort to improve an organization's problem-solving capabilities and its ability to cope with changes in its external environment with the help of external or internal behavioral-scientist practitioners, or change agents, as they are sometimes called. (French, 1969, p. 24)

Organization development is a planned process of change in an organization's culture through the utilization of behavioral science technology, research, and theory. (Burke, 1982, p. 10)

Organization development is a system-wide application of behavioral science knowledge to the planned development and reinforcement of organizational strategies, structures, and processes for improving an organization's effectiveness. (Cummings and Worley, 1997, p. 2)

Now, at this point in most discussions of "what is OD?" the author offers his or her or their definition of OD, intended to make clearer what it is and what it does. No such effort is expended here. Instead, the intention of this discussion is to go behind the words to the underlying ideas and values that not only give definition to organization development but make it both a field and a profession distinct from other forms of management and organizational consulting or training. First, the underlying knowledge and philosophical systems that help define what is and is not the field of OD are described. Next, some of the implications for the professional practice of OD are explored. Finally, some of the current and emerging issues confronting OD are enumerated.

Marshak, R. J. (2006). Organization development as a profession and a field. In B. B. Jones, & M. Brazzel (Eds.) *The NTL Handbook of Organization Development and Change.* San Francisco: Jossey-Bass/Pfeiffer, pp.13-27. Republished with permission.

The Field of Organization Development

There are some who would not describe OD as a field, partly because it draws from many academic fields and disciplines and partly because it is a field of practice more than a field of academic inquiry. Nevertheless, OD practice is informed and defined by a more or less integrated set or sets of theories, ideas, practices, and values and therefore qualifies as a field of applied knowledge. Consequently, to understand what OD is and what it does, we must first understand the dimensions of knowledge, ideas, and values that in combination produce practices that are labeled as organization development.

There are three primary sets of knowledge and an underlying value system that lead to what is called organization development. The discussion that follows errs on the side of attempting to simplify and present essential characteristics. No attempt is being made to elucidate the full characteristics and nuances involved. In this sense, the discussion aspires to make clear some of the fundamentals for understanding organization development at the risk perhaps of appearing to be too simplistic or leaving some important dimension(s) out of the discussion. Finally, in this discussion the reader is reminded that the focus of the field follows its name: the development of organizations. Diagnostic and intervention activities may involve individuals, pairs, and teams, but these efforts are presumed to be part of a systemic effort to enhance the functioning of an organizational system.

Understanding Social Systems

The first set of knowledge, at its simplest level, is understanding the potential subject(s) of an intended development or change effort. Because OD seeks to foster the improved effectiveness of organizations and other social systems, a range of knowledge pertaining to the functioning of individuals, groups, organizations, and communities – separately and as integrated systems – is required. Thus organization development draws on a number of theories and ideas predominantly from the behavioral or social sciences (psychology, social psychology, sociology, anthropology, political science) but also to a lesser extent from economics, religion, and even the hard sciences of physics and biology. However, as is explained in more detail later, OD does not draw equally from all types of theories and ideas about human behavior in organized social settings. Instead it tends to be based in those theories and ideas that are consistent with its underlying, and sometimes unarticulated, philosophical value system. So, for example, most organization development practices are predicated on the assumption that people are motivated by factors beyond purely economic incentives.

Understanding the Hows and Whys of Change

A central aspect of OD is fostering planned development and change in social systems. This means that the bodies of knowledge that help explain how individuals, groups, organizations, communities, and even societies change are all pertinent to organization development. How do we go about inducing, supporting, or facilitating change in a manager, in a team, in an organization, in a network of organizations? The range of ideas about change and development coming from, for example, education, training, economics, psychology, social psychology, sociology, and anthropology is all potentially relevant to OD practice. Again, however, not all ideas about change are embraced by the underlying OD value system. For example, we might be able to force or coerce people to make certain changes, but this would not be considered organization development (and would in fact be refuted by OD practitioners).

Understanding the Role of a Third-Party Change Agent

The final set or sets of knowledge helping define OD pertain to the role of the OD practitioner. When working with an organization to help bring about a desired change, the OD practitioner is not the person in charge. Instead the OD practitioner is a third-party change agent aiding the person or persons in charge as well as the system itself to bring about the desired changes. An OD practitioner, whether internal or external to the subject system, must understand the issues, politics, psychological processes, and other dynamics associated with being a third-party change agent or practitioner working with people called clients in complex social systems. Here too, not all theories and ideas about the third-party role are endorsed or embraced by organization development. Once again, it is those ideas and practices that are consistent with or congruent with the underlying values and philosophy of OD that become part of the theories and practices associated with the proper role and responsibilities of an OD practitioner. For example, a third-party role wherein an expert tells people what they should do is an accepted if not essential part of a great deal of management and other types of consulting but is rejected in organization development as a general mode of practice.

These three sets of knowledge about (1) social systems, (2) how to change social systems, and (3) third-party change agent roles are the essential areas of expertise for an effective organization development practitioner. They are also insufficient to fully understand the theory and practice of OD as distinct, for example, from other forms of consulting and training intended to foster or induce development or change in organizations or other social systems. To make this distinction requires understanding the underlying philosophy of organization development and how it links and integrates selective aspects of each of the main bodies of knowledge making up OD practice.

Understanding the Underlying Values and Philosophy of
Organization Development

Organization development is often referred to as a values-based or normative field of practice. This is true, although not always fully understood. Furthermore, it is difficult to precisely enumerate the exact values that are the essential ingredients making OD more or less uniquely OD. It is, however, possible to describe some of the defining characteristics of the underlying value system and some of the ways in which this value system is evolving over time. At some considerable risk of oversimplifying or leaving out something important, four key value orientations help form the underlying philosophy of organization development:

1. A humanistic philosophy
2. Democratic principles
3. Client-centered consulting
4. An evolving social-ecological systems orientation

A Humanistic Philosophy. Organization development not only accepts but also promotes a humanistic orientation to social systems. This includes beliefs that people are inherently good, not evil; that they have the capacity to change and develop; and that through the exercise of reason and judgment they, not outside forces or inner drives and emotions, are capable of empowered action in the best interests of the enterprise. This orientation also affirms the value and dignity of each person. Furthermore, to be effective, social systems should not restrict, limit, or oppress people regardless of their role in the organization or their demographic background. In organization development the human side of enterprise is always a central consideration, along with other aspects such as economics, technology, and management practices and principles. Historically, this orientation in OD has been expressed by the assertion that an organization that empowers its people is also a more effective organization.

Democratic Principles. Partly because of its humanistic philosophy and the roots in World War II of many of its founders, organization development also advocates democratic principles – meaning, involvement in decision making and direction setting should be broadly rather than narrowly delineated. Another way of saying this is that OD tends to reject the notion that there are elites who possess superior knowledge and who alone should make decisions on behalf of others. Instead, OD believes and advocates that important and relevant knowledge is more broadly distributed and that more rather than fewer people are capable of and should be involved in making inputs or in the actual process of decision making. In this regard, organization development is in the tradition of the British philosopher John Locke (1632–1704) and Anglo-American liberalism in general, rather than that of Thomas Hobbes (1588–1679), who justified autocracy and an absolute monarchy as required to protect people from their baser instincts. In practice therefore organization development advocates more democratic processes not simply as a way to get buy-in (although buy-in is famously associated with involvement) but because there is a belief that the resulting decisions are also superior, implementable, and more relevant to important audiences and stakeholders.

Client-Centered Consulting. Consistent with humanistic and democratic values, organization development believes that change efforts should be client-centered, not practitioner-centered. This expands on humanistic and democratic values and assumptions and asserts that human systems are capable of self-initiated change and development when provided with appropriate processes and supportive conditions. The role of the OD practitioner is therefore to partner with the client system in self-directed change efforts operating from a third-party change agent role. In carrying out this role, the practitioner uses knowledge and skills about how social systems function and change in order to support, educate, facilitate, and guide the client system in its work. The role of the practitioner in client-centered consulting is neither to impose or enforce an unwanted change agenda on the client system nor to furnish "expert" answers to the client's issues. It is, however, acceptable and appropriate for an OD practitioner to constructively confront blind spots in a client system and to engage in education or awareness-raising interventions should a client system be operating from incorrect or incomplete information. Therefore a primary intervention by an OD practitioner is often to suggest and facilitate participative processes for diagnostic data gathering, informed decision making, and building client-system commitment for change.

An Evolving Social-Ecological Systems Orientation. A social-ecological systems orientation is, perhaps, a more recent or emerging aspect of the underlying organization development values and beliefs. In its simplest form, it means that ends should not be defined in terms of an individual, group, or organization alone. Rather, a perspective of the much larger and broader social, economic, and environmental system(s) must be held, and ends should be considered in terms of their impact on the broader, even global, system – not, for example, on a specific organization. Thus, if maximizing the profits of a specific organization might threaten the environment or negatively affect a community or country on the other side of the planet, it should be avoided in favor of outcomes that take into account the broader global or ecological system of which everyone is a part. On the basis of this orientation, it could therefore be a legitimate role for an OD practitioner to help an organization understand the full range of impacts of its choices, beyond perhaps what was considered in the past. This orientation might also lead an OD practitioner to seek to help a client system rethink or reposition projects or endeavors that are intended to contribute to a specific organization's success but could ultimately be harmful from a broader social, economic, or ecological perspective. A summary depiction of the three core knowledge areas and the underlying values and philosophy of OD are in Figure 1.1.

Figure 1.1
Core Knowledge Sets and Underlying
Philosophy of Organization Development

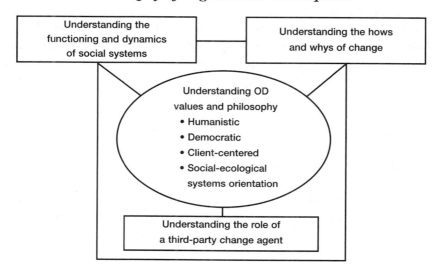

Organization Development Results from an Integration of Ideas and Ideals

What is called organization development results from putting into practice these three sets of knowledge and skills, integrated by the underlying normative value system(s) and intended to enhance an organizational system. This integration defines what OD is and also what is not OD. Thus change activities aimed at, for example, individual performance alone, or based on prescriptive methods, may be important forms of coaching, training, and consulting but are not considered to be organization development. To help illustrate these important points, a few simple examples will be given as stand-ins for a more thorough and complex discussion.

OD and Social Systems

First, let us consider that there are numerous theories and ideas about human nature. In psychology, for example, psychoanalytic theories such as those advanced by Freud and his followers postulate that individual behavior is influenced, if not controlled, by basic inner drives and that individual behavior can be controlled by unconscious and nonrational processes. In contrast, behavioral theories such as those associated with B. F. Skinner consider the positive and negative reinforcements coming from an individual's environment to be the determinants of behavior. Partly in response to the more limited or limiting view of human nature advanced by these two schools of psychology, a third school, called humanistic psychology, emerged in the 1950s and suggested that individuals were inherently capable of higher-order functioning, that they could determine for themselves how to develop and behave, and that individuals were capable of transcending narrow self-interest in service to themselves or others.

In general, it was the ideas of the pioneering humanistic psychologists, notably Abraham Maslow (hierarchy of needs), Douglas McGregor (Theory X and Theory Y), Carl Rogers (unconditional positive regard), and Chris Argyris (congruence of individual and organizational needs), that helped define the field of organization development by implicitly contributing to its strong, underlying humanistic value system. Consequently, in practice humanistic theories of human behavior have a central or prominent role in how OD practitioners think about and diagnose human systems, even though they augment those theories with an eclectic array of other theories and belief systems, including, at times, those of Freud and Skinner. Similarly, given the range of theories about groups and organizational behavior, OD tends to reject, for example, those theories and ideas that postulate the need to provide economic incentives (alone) or closely monitor and control people. The need for more autocratic management based on Theory X assumptions is rejected as unwarranted and ultimately counterproductive.

OD and Change in Social Systems

Just as there is an array of theories about individual, group, and organizational behavior, there are also theories about how individuals, groups, and organizations change and develop. Staying at the individual level of behavior and again contrasting psychoanalytic, behaviorist, and humanist schools, one confronts varying ideas and emphases about how change and development occur. For example, from a behavioral orientation one would seek to condition new behavior through manipulation of the environment of rewards and punishments resulting from an individual's behavioral choices. From a more humanistic perspective, one might assume instead that people are capable of rational, self-directed learning and growth, especially in a supportive environment that treats them with dignity and respect. Thus change theories and practices that might suggest or support the notion that people must be forced, coerced, manipulated, or ordered to change tend to be rejected in favor of theories and practices that assume people can, on their own, rationally assess the need to change and are capable of changing, especially when given the appropriate data or feedback information.

Although OD draws on a variety of theories and ideas about individual, group, and organizational change and has a range of methodologies and practices, all or almost all OD practices are predicated on more positive and humanistic ideas about change in human systems. For example, action research, which is one of the fundamentals of organization development, is based on the assumption that people can and will change when involved in a process of rational inquiry into their present situation to determine new courses of action. This orientation is so strong in organization development that some would include an action research orientation as part of its core values. Others include it as one of OD's preferred theories of change along with others supported by rational, humanistic, democratic, and client-centered assumptions and values. These theories of change and supporting values and assumptions about change lead to OD practices that tend to emphasize giving the involved or affected people supportive processes wherein they can rationally assess their situation and develop new actions, behaviors, and directions. Theories and practices predicated on somehow forcing people to change, or developing answers for them because they are somehow incapable of doing so themselves, are not part of the accepted change philosophy and practices in organization development.

OD and Third-Party Roles

In organization development, the third-party role of the practitioner is defined, in many respects, by its underlying values and supporting theories about the nature of change in social systems. If we assume that most people are capable of self-directed growth and development, especially when given appropriate feedback or information in a supportive environment, then the role of the third-party OD practitioner becomes clear.

Specifically, the role of the OD practitioner is to collaborate or partner with the subject system by facilitating, coaching, or otherwise supporting self-directed change. This is done by suggesting and facilitating processes that encourage and support inquiry, discovery, and motivation to change, while establishing and reinforcing new behaviors, actions, or directions. An assortment of skills, interventions, and practices is required to successfully carry out this role, but the first and most essential ingredient is to operate from a client-centered, collaborative, and facilitative mind-set. If instead one were to assume that people were not capable of changing on their own, or were totally governed by narrow self-interest, or were lacking somehow in intelligence or capability, then quite different third-party roles could be justified as necessary and appropriate. After all, why would you want to involve people in working on a change initiative if you think they are somehow incapable of developing a good or appropriate answer to whatever the situation is under consideration? Might you not instead be more helpful by offering them the right answer to implement based on your neutrality or your superior knowledge or information? Because organization development tends to reject this set of assumptions and resulting reasoning, it also tends to reject the expert third-party role in favor of a more collaborative or facilitative one – recognizing, of course, that within an overall collaborative or facilitative role OD practitioners can and should suggest to ("tell") clients what are considered to be successful practices and processes on the basis of their knowledge and expertise in facilitating change.

In sum, then, organization development is an applied field whose practitioners draw on knowledge about how social systems function and change while working from a third-party collaborative and consultative role based on and integrated by humanistic, democratic, client-centered, and more recently, social-ecological values and principles. Organization development practices are applied in organizational and community settings where the responsible managers, executives, and leaders wish to enhance the functioning and effectiveness of their organizational unit or enterprise. Organization development is usually more successful when applied in a setting where the responsible parties are in at least minimum agreement with, or ideally wish to advance, its underlying normative values and principles. Thus settings where leaders and managers are more in agreement with Theory Y versus Theory X assumptions, or believe most people are willing and able to develop new organizational practices and behaviors if given a supportive, data-based, facilitated process of inquiry, may be more conducive for organization development than others.

The Professional Practice of Organization Development

In the early days, developing and advocating application of sound humanistic and social science theories and principles to help improve organizations was at least partly an *avocation* or calling of the early pioneer practitioners of what became known as organization development. Many, but not all, were university-based or university-trained, and most or all believed that the World War II triumph of democratic values combined with advances in the social sciences could improve the functioning of the highly bureaucratic organizations typical of that era. They also believed they could improve and enhance the human condition in organizations (and in general) by incorporating into organizational functioning the latest humanistic and democratic theories, principles, and values. Over time, the ideas and practices of the often part-time and usually externally based OD advocates became accepted in varying degrees and incorporated into a range of full-time, internally and externally based OD practitioner roles. There has also developed a number of OD-related professional associations or divisions of associations; a substantial and still-evolving practitioner and academic literature; and certificate, master's, and doctoral degree programs. From an avocation of the pioneers, organization development in the twenty-first century is now an established – although not licensed – *vocation* or profession.

Professional Roles

The discussion of the three knowledge bases and underlying philosophy of organization development suggests the range of knowledge and skills required for the professional practice of OD. This is compounded by the multiple roles an OD practitioner may need to play in engaging with a client system. Various descriptions of OD practitioner roles have been advanced over the years emphasizing the need to be proficient in many skills and practices. Several of the most critical roles are highlighted here. For example, an OD practitioner needs to be:

- A skilled *professional practitioner* able to initiate, negotiate, and maintain a collaborative consulting relationship with managers, executives, and leaders over the life of an engagement. This also includes knowledge of and ability to manage or facilitate the phases and processes associated with an organizational change effort.
- A skilled *diagnostician* capable of reading and understanding the behavioral dynamics of individuals, teams, organizations, and even larger social systems.
- A skilled *social scientist researcher* capable of designing and conducting various data-gathering and data-analysis methodologies, including interviews, questionnaires, focus groups, and so on.
- A skilled *interventionist* knowledgeable about a range of participative methods and processes that enable and encourage people to collectively engage or explore important issues and opportunities.
- A skilled *educator or trainer* able to communicate new ideas and skills to system members to better prepare them to address their issues, opportunities, and concerns.
- A skilled *facilitator* of small and large group participative processes capable of dealing with such difficult dynamics as those associated with issues of power, authority, leadership, conflict, diversity, resistance, and the like, as well as able to keep participants engaged and on track.
- A skilled *coach* able to advise, support, and when appropriate constructively confront client system managers, executives, and members to encourage and help develop the skills, behaviors, and attitudes necessary for their success and that of the overall change effort.

Each role requires in itself a depth of knowledge and skills, but successful OD practice demands integration and appropriate application of all of these roles. The ability to effectively perform some or a subset of these roles using OD practices can be valuable, but it should not be mistaken for full professional practice of organization development.

Professional Values and Ethics

Finally, although organization development has neither a governing body nor an officially recognized and enforced code of conduct, it does have a set of generally recognized values and ethics that are based on its underlying philosophy and principles. (See for example, Gellermann, Frankel, and Landenson, 1990.) In this sense, organization development practitioners form a values-based community of practice. In a way, what helps define someone as an organization development practitioner, as opposed to another type of change practitioner, is belief in and adherence to a significant portion of the underlying humanistic, democratic, client-centered, and social-ecological values and principles.

Tensions within Organization Development

Primarily because of its strong values-based orientation, there are a number of tensions and ongoing discussions within the field of organization development. This includes whether or not OD focuses too much on "soft" people issues; whether it should address diversity and multicultural dynamics, including considerations of the degree of applicability in all countries and cultures; and issues related to dealing with lack of readiness for change.

OD is Too Touchy-Feely

Almost from its inception, OD was labeled by some as too touchy-feely. This reflects its strong humanistic and developmental orientations, as well as the psychological and social-psychological knowledge and methodology bases. Balancing humanistic values with more technological or business-oriented goals, such as economic efficiency, can be difficult. Holding humanistic values and assumptions while addressing challenges from "pessimistic" economic assumptions about human nature and motivation can also be difficult without coming across as too strident or doctrinaire. If the balance struck appears too rooted in human development or humanistic values, perhaps as opposed to economic values and objectives, then organization development or the OD practitioner can be labeled too touchy-feely. On the other hand, if the core values of organization development are ignored or subjugated to a great degree, the practitioner is likely to be accused of not practicing OD. This is made especially difficult by the absence of clear criteria about what is too much or too little. These tensions are also revealed in the ongoing discussion within the field about the importance of "our values" as well as among those who on the one hand wish to adopt a more pragmatic values orientation and those who by contrast wish to remain strongly centered in the traditional orientation (Worley and Feyerherm, 2003). These discussions and periodic challenges to the field raised in journals, at conferences, and by clients are inherent in a strongly values-oriented field, especially if the values are not taken for granted by everyone or by all managers and organizations. The challenges also become an opportunity for the OD profession and individual practitioners to periodically reassess, rebalance, and rededicate themselves to a set of core values and principles that define the field of practice.

Addressing Multiculturalism and Diversity

Organization development promotes a range of values (for example, respect, inclusion, democratic principles, and empowerment) as core aspects required for effective functioning of groups, organizations, and communities. Since perhaps the early 1980s, if not earlier, this has led to a number of challenges and tensions within the profession, notably whether organization development is applicable in all countries and cultures and whether addressing issues of diversity or social justice should be a central aspect of the professional practice of OD.

First, in terms of multiculturalism, there has been continuing commentary over the years questioning whether a field of practice based so strongly on Western, liberal-democratic, and humanistic values can be equally applicable in all countries and cultures (see, for example, Jaeger, 1986). Others assert that with multicultural sensitivity and some adaptation OD is applicable in all cultures and contexts. This is a discussion fueled in recent years by globalization and the increasing number of OD practitioners working in multinational or transnational organizations. Although sensitivity, balance, and flexibility are called for, OD is also predicated on a core set of values; the choice therefore, in some settings, may be whether to use OD premises and methods at all, rather than trying to adapt or downplay some dimensions or practices.

Since the 1980s, interventions to help organizations deal with and effectively incorporate an increasingly diverse workforce located in many cases around the world has become commonplace. Interventions range from multicultural awareness training to transforming organizations with the intent of ridding them of hidden but institutionalized barriers to the full inclusion of all people. This set of practices, in the United States, is often called dealing with diversity, and its practitioners diversity practitioners. Many but not all might also consider themselves to be organization development practitioners. The tension within the field and among practitioners is whether or not diversity is a separate or semi-separate field of practice or an inherent aspect of organization development. If the latter, then it would be expected that all professional practitioners will be knowledgeable, adept, and required to deal with diversity and social justice dynamics and issues. If it is not an inherent aspect of the field, then although OD practitioners should of course be sensitive and aware of the requirement to address such issues in some fashion, it would be optional as a matter of professional practice and responsibility.

At this point, whether organization development practitioners should address the multicultural dynamics of groups, organizations, and communities seems no longer open to serious question or debate. Given the core values of OD and the increasingly diverse and multicultural organizational settings for its practice, it is clear that all professional practitioners need to fully understand and as appropriate address multicultural and diversity issues and dynamics as they present themselves, just as they would need to address any other set of issues and dynamics central to the theory and values orientation of OD. Exactly what this means in practice, as well as divergent views about how to best address these issues, will remain ongoing areas of discussion and reflection among practitioners.

Change and Readiness for Change

Organization development is about change in human systems, but not just any change under any circumstances. Instead, OD theory and practice assumes and even promotes several key criteria related to change efforts:

- Change(s) should be directed toward enhancing or developing individual, group, and organizational capabilities, as well as the conditions under which people work and contribute. It is assumed that this is a primary determinate of higher performance in organizations.
- Change(s) should be carried out in a way consistent with social science knowledge about human systems and how they change, as well as a generally optimistic set of values and assumptions about human capability and potential.
- Change(s) should be initiated and led, to the greatest extent possible, by the people involved; it should also be based on their assessment and concurrence with the need to change.
- Change efforts should not only lead to the desired change but also leave a client system with increased capabilities and skills to address future situations and needs.

A dilemma and discussion in organization development is what to do when one or more of these criteria is absent. Consider, for example, corporate downsizing, which has been going on since the late 1970s. In its early days, many OD practitioners felt it was inappropriate or even unethical to be involved in downsizing change efforts that did not seem to match any (or very many) of the implicit criteria needed for an OD change effort. In later years, as downsizing was redefined as "rightsizing" to enhance corporate competitive capabilities, more – but not all – OD practitioners felt using OD technology in rightsizing redesign efforts was workable and acceptable.

Another aspect of this ongoing tension relates to the concept of readiness for change. In organization development it is not simply a matter of there being a call or demand for change; there must also be readiness for change in the system. Because of the values, assumptions, and criteria guiding OD change efforts, unless there is a felt need or readiness for change in the system OD interventions may not work. Simply put, it would not be possible to enter into a client-centered, collaborative change effort intended to enhance the capabilities of the organization on the basis of social science theories and practices and guided by humanistic and democratic values if the client system were not ready and willing to do so at some level. Instead, initial interventions such as education or diagnostic action research would be needed to develop readiness for change, particularly readiness for OD change methods. In many contemporary organizations, however, OD practitioners (especially internal practitioners) are asked to conduct change interventions whether the target system is ready or not, and with little or no time to create readiness. This sometimes places the OD practitioner in the position of trying to carry out interventions under conditions where the premises for success are not fully met or else risk appearing to be unresponsive or unable to help.

Exactly how to handle such dilemmas is an important discussion within the professional practice of organization development because of its philosophy and values about change. As new situations present themselves, the field and individual practitioners must adapt and adjust to be responsive within the broad framework of the principles and practices of the profession.

Conclusion

Organization development is at once a simple and complex field of professional practice. Initially learning the many knowledge bases, roles, and skills required for professional practice and then integrating and internalizing how they all fit together according to an extensive, but sometimes only implied, value system or philosophy can be both challenging and confusing to would-be practitioners and clients alike. Once the sets of values, knowledge, and skills are understood and mastered, the practice of OD becomes much simpler and more straightforward. It is indeed the requirement to know an extensive range of knowledge and methodologies integrated by a philosophical system that makes organization development a worthy field of professional practice.

References

Beckhard, R. (1969). *Organization development: Strategies and models.* Reading, MA: Addison-Wesley.

Burke, W. W. (1982). *Organization development: Principles and practices.* Boston, MA: Little, Brown.

Cummings, T. G., & Worley, C. G. (1997). *Organization development and change,* 6th ed. Cincinnati, OH: South-Western College Publishing.

French, W. (1969). Organization development: Objectives, assumptions and strategies. *California Management Review.* 12(2), 23-34.

Gellerman, W., Frankel, M. S., & Ladenson, R. F. (1990). *Values and ethics in organization and human systems development.* San Francisco: Jossey-Bass.

Jaeger, A. M. (1986). Organization development and national culture. Where's the fit? *Academy of Management Review.* 11(1), 178-190.

Worley, C. G., & Feyerherm, A. E. (2003). Reflections on the future of organization development. *Journal of Applied Behavioral Science,* 39(1), 97-115.

2
Managing in Chaotic Times

Things aren't what they used to be. Sound familiar? In every age, of course, people say the same thing as they face the continual processes of change. New ideas and new technologies replace established ones. There is initial resistance, but if the new really is superior to the old, then, eventually the old is swept away in the path of the new. Yet something, somehow, *does* seem different about the changes managers and leaders around the world are facing today. What's different?

What's different today is not the *process* of change, but its *depth* and *breadth*. All available signs point to the conclusion that we are in the midst of a change in *eras*, a change of historical magnitude, the kind that comes along every 500 years or so. We are living through and witnessing the dusk of one age and the dawn of another. That's why today's change *is* different from yesterday's – and tomorrow's. Today's change stems not just from the introduction of new technologies, new markets, or new competitors, or even from the collapse of communism in Eastern Europe and the former Soviet Union. Rather, it is an epochal change at the deepest social, political, economic, technological, religious, and philosophical levels, occurring simultaneously and globally.

Unlike the transition from horse and buggy to the automobile, the current shift is more akin to the depth of changes in all institutions and beliefs that demarcated the Middle Ages (500-1500 AD) from the Modern Age. Table 2.1 shows eight great inventions: four that helped usher in the Renaissance and thus the Modern Age, and their four contemporary counterparts.

Table 2.1
Era-Changing Inventions

Era Shift	Middle Ages to Modern Age	Modern Age to Postmodern Age
Inventions	Gunpowder	Atomic bomb
	Printing press	Television
	Magnetic compass	Space satellites
	Mechanical clock	Computer
Cumulative Impact	Contributed to the rise of nation-states and secular over religious authority	Threat of global destruction increased awareness of global interdependence
	Expanded communication of ideas linked distant and disparate people	Instantaneous verbal and visual communication with anyone, anywhere, anytime created global village
	Global explorations led to discovery of "new worlds"	Galactic explorations led to new theories of humanity and the universe
	Human-made machines replaced reliance on nature	Human-made computers replaced reliance on human reason
	Belief in the unlimited potential of individual human reason	Belief in the unlimited potential of harmony, partnership, and cooperation

Marshak, R. J. (1995). Managing in chaotic times. In R. A. Ritvo, A. H. Litwin, and L. Butler (Eds.), *Managing in the Age of Change*, Burr Ridge, IL: Irwin Professional Publishing, pp. 58-66. Republished with permission.

What ultimately changed, then, was not only what people did, but how they thought about what they did across the full spectrum of social experience. Consequently, it seems safe to assert that we are now living in the transition period between the Modern Age (1500-1950 AD) and a yet-to-be-named postmodern age. More specifically, we seem to be caught in midair between the outdated principles and practices of industrial organization and management and the embryonic postindustrial principles and practices.

A Time of Chaos

The result of this change is a growing sense of disorder, confusion, and loss of control as established ways of thinking and acting collapse almost overnight. Interestingly, this is also a period of great innovation and creativity as the collapse of old orthodoxies clears the way for the creation of new insights, ideas, and innovations that were previously unthinkable.

Table 2.2
The End of Industrial Organization and Management

	Principles	
Aspect	**Collapsing**	**Emerging**
Markets	National	Global
Structures	Mechanistic	Adaptive/organic
Processes and technologies	Sequential	Simultaneous
Focus	Segments	Wholes
Coordination method	Rules/plans/orders	Values/visions/interactions
Relationships	Independent	Interdependent
Success criteria	Certainty	Flexibility
Dominant metaphor	Machine	Computer

Consequently, we live in a time of chaos, the paradoxical state that is entered through collapse and exited through creation. Trends and directions become clearer each year, even as the specifics of what to do remain elusive (see Tables 2.2 and 2.3). It is the blessing of this in-between period that we can create the new paradigms, principles, and practices that will define post-modern organization and management. Its curse is that we have few established models or certainties to turn to.

History will record that the defining characteristic of organizations and management at the dawn of the 21st century was handling the decline and fall of the old established ways of working and, out of that disorder, the simultaneous creation and rise of new ways of working. For that reason, navigating through the chaotic abyss will be the quintessential skill needed by leaders and managers in all institutions.

What to Expect

During our journey through the tumultuous passageway between the old and the new order, we should not be surprised to encounter any or all of the following:

Table 2.3
Organization and Management Success Characteristics

Collapsing	Emerging
Steady responses	Fast(er) responses
Stable operations	Flexible operations
Broad/multiple directions	Focused directions
Hindsight analysis	Foresight and intuition
Tall hierarchies	Flat(ter) networks
Structured channels	Fluid flows
Fat, frills, and fads	Fundamentals
Action lists	Follow-through on actions
Command and control	Freedom and dignity
Impersonal relationships	Friendly relationships
Smooth over issues	Face issues
Risk averse	Forgiving (enough for innovation)

1. Expect to be in the passageway for another 10-20 years before clear concepts and conditions upon which to build a postmodern organization begin to appear. Confusion and constant change will be your traveling companions.

2. Expect to feel constantly behind the curve as the cumulative and interactive effects of the new era compound until they reach the critical mass that will begin to clearly define the new organizational and managerial system(s).

3. Expect to find that many of the methods and skills you have used until now won't work well anymore. Don't expect anyone to be able to tell you exactly what to do.

4. Expect things that previously seemed impossible or unimaginable to happen, to make sense, and to pave the way for even more dreamlike realities.

5. Expect the answers to come from newcomers or outsiders, not from established managers or consultants. Beware of people who say they've seen it all before or that this is just a passing fad.

6. Expect strong emotions from everyone, due to confusion, disorientation, fear, and feelings of impending loss.

7. Expect people to be immobilized sometimes as they wish for a heroic figure who will provide direction, restore order, and help them move forward, all in a matter of weeks.

8. Expect to be tempted to play the part of the heroic figure. Don't.

9. Expect excitement, creativity, and a burst of energy when people discover new ways to solve problems.

10. Don't expect an easy, quick trip.

What to Do

To successfully manage oneself and others through these chaotic times, any or all of the following would be helpful:

1. Confront the strong emotions associated with fear and impending loss with even stronger emotions related to faith, hope, and inspiration. Be positive and engaging. This is not a time to confront negative emotions with cool, calculating reason.

2. Provide people with:
   - *Visions* of the new ways of working, to give them a destination.
   - *Vectors* to move along, to give them a sense of direction.
   - *Values* to inform their actions, to give them inner guidance and a source of strength and comfort.
   - *Valences* to the journey, to give them hope, capacity, and enough interest in the outcome to work together to achieve it.

3. Seek successes and innovators wherever you can. Develop and move them throughout your system. The magnitude of the change is too great to happen through one grand plan or person. It's hard to know now what will be most central, or where. Movement in the right direction is what counts.

4. Be a stabilizing force as well as a change agent. You won't need to create change so much as you will need to channel and direct its forces while providing enough stability to keep your people and operations afloat. Your imperatives are paradoxes: destroy and create, change and stabilize. To help provide enough stability for people to stay functional without getting frozen in fear or resistance, consider the following:

   - *Prepare for a chaotic journey.* Tell people what to expect, train them in survival skills, and clarify what's important and what's not. Tell them the truth. This is not the time to treat others like frightened children, even if they behave that way and/or it makes you feel stronger and more powerful.

- *Provide balance.* Don't overdo, overstress, or overwhelm anything or anyone. Lead, but don't get so far ahead of people that they feel lost or abandoned. In short, navigate so that neither you nor they go "overboard."
- *Preserve the core of the future, whatever it may be.* On a long, rocky, winding journey you don't want to be overloaded, nor do you want to confuse people with too many nonessential things. Remember: Focus everyone on the core of the future, not the past or present. Everything but the core can be lost or forgotten. The core can provide a source of stability and strength.
- *Periodically find a lull.* Linger long enough to re-group, re-energize, and refocus; then move on. People really are capable of doing amazing things under impossible conditions for long periods of time – but not forever. Even a short breather helps; this is a marathon, not a sprint. If necessary, create an "eye of the hurricane" retreat. Instead of planning what and how to change, devise ways to support each other, work together, and stay focused.
- *Plan to zigzag and to travel rarely in a straight line.* A straight line may be the shortest route between two points, but things will move so fast you won't have time to think and react. If you zigzag, you'll buy yourself extra reaction time, better visibility of what's ahead, and better maneuverability. Just don't lose sight of your destination; otherwise you may zag when you should have zigged.

5. Because you and your organization are in for a period of "permanent white water" in the economic river, manage as though you are shooting the rapids. That means:

- Strip down your organization to its bare essentials. Avoid being top-heavy or lopsided; balance the load.
- Increase the handling ease and maneuverability of your organization and management team. Redesign and/or adapt as you go.
- Work to achieve faster response and reaction times. Don't slow your communication and decision-making systems with "nice-to-know" information. Only the minimum essential information is needed.
- Stay alert. Everyone needs to look out and watch out. Send scouts ahead. Otherwise, constantly anticipate.
- Learn as you go. Don't make the same mistake twice. Experiment to discover better ways of handling difficult situations. Adapt, adjust, and innovate.
- Don't overplan; steer. You won't be able to stop to plan, nor plan to stop. Definitely set a course and prepare for the journey, then steer and navigate.
- Maintain everyone's balance, sense of direction, and anticipation. Minimize boat rocking and instability. Lead by example.
- Develop ways to recover people and things that fall overboard. Also, develop ways to put people safely ashore who need to get off. Jettison any *thing* that is not needed or gets in the way.
- Inspire, challenge, and encourage everyone to pull their weight. You can't afford hangers-on.
- Always remember: Your job is to get your organization and its people through the rapids, not to attempt to escape the rapids by going ashore.

- Finally, build trust in yourself, your people, your organization. Make courage, faith, hope, and inspiration your watchwords. And, oh yes, look out for rocks!

As the leader/manager, you also have some special responsibilities. You will need to:

- Prepare by getting your own act together.
- Let go. Start out. Keep moving.
- Be bold. Take calculated risks.
- Focus on outcomes, not problems.
- Be visible. Communicate constantly. Inspire.

These are the best of times and the worst of times. Great challenges lie ahead. New worlds are being created; old ways are passing. Fear, hope, malaise, and excitement are in the air. It's time to get up, let go, and move out. Good luck!

3
Re-inventing Organization Development Theory and Practice

Many organizations are recognizing the need to transform themselves to remain competitive in a world of complex technological change, increased global competition, growing interdependencies and major shifts in the marketplace. Just as organizations are being challenged to undergo revolutionary change and abandon many of the traditionally held assumptions, structures and practices that once led to success, a similar challenge exists for the field of Organization Development.

We cannot rely on our past successes and proven practices to maintain our future viability. It is time to rethink, recreate and reinvent our profession, theories and practices. We must be willing to develop new approaches as we explore some tough questions about the very basics of Organization Development theory and technology:

- How do the underlying Organization Development assumptions about change, diagnosis and intervention developed in the 1940's, 50's and 60's fit in today's Information Age?
- What is the role for Organization Development "change" agents in organizations facing constant change?
- Do Organization Development practitioners have the frameworks, capabilities and skills to diagnose and respond to issues in complex multicultural global organizations?
- Does Organization Development have the technology to work more rapidly with large complex systems and groups and still be effective?
- How well are Organization Development practitioners dealing with the dynamic tension between the need to retool and feelings of confusion, ambiguity, loss, and incompetence as they learn to work differently?

Recently, Organization Development practitioners, educators and professionals have begun exploring some of these core questions. These include identifying the underlying values of Organization Development (Hurley, Church, Burke & Van Eynde, 1992); examining the limits of traditional methods (Reddy & Phillips, 1992); exploring the nature of change (Land & Jarman 1992; Marshak, 1993a; Vaill, 1989); reassessing methods for diagnosis (Marshak & Katz, 1992); and, creating new models for large scale intervention (Bunker & Alban, 1992; Dannemiller & Jacobs, 1992; Levine, 1989; Weisbord, 1989).

Today, almost every cornerstone of Organization Development is being challenged. If Organization Development is to continue to help organizations in the future, it must create new methodologies while redefining, redesigning and rethinking its role. This cannot be accomplished by Organization Development doing the same things it is currently doing, nor by merely tinkering around the edges. We must re-examine the WHAT, the WHY and the HOW of Organization Development practice. What is called for is total systems change: Reinventing Organization Development.

Katz, J. H., & Marshak, R. J. (1995). Re-inventing organization development theory and practice, *Organization Development Journal, 13*(1), 63-81. Republished with permission.

Moving Toward Redefinition and Reinvention

In order to reinvent the profession several fundamental dimensions of Organization Development must be addressed. These include the theories, methods, and practices related to: 1) change; 2) clients; 3) diagnosis; 4) intervention; and, 5) work styles. Our analysis suggests that the parameters to guide such a reinvention effort must include _all_ of these dimensions and that the desired solutions must reflect an increase in our competence and capacity. In short, the "New Organization Development" must be more comprehensive, better integrated, and capable of incorporating dimensions that have been previously excluded or defined out of the mainstream of theory and practice. Current and emerging practices must be successfully combined to create the next generation of Organizational Development.

Table 3.1
Redefine Change: An Ongoing Process

Current Orientations	and	Emerging Orientations
Developmental and Transitional Change		Transformational Change
Linear Change		Cyclical Change
Create Disequilibrium to Initiate Change		Create Balance and Harmony
Plan and Implement Change		Align with Ongoing or Emerging Changes
Start and Stop Change		Manage the Flow of Change

Redefining Change

Table 3.1 contains some of the current and emerging orientations towards change which must be jointly integrated in order to reinvent Organization Development. Most traditional Organization Development methods have been built on an assumption of the need to create planned change in "frozen" systems (Lewin, 1947). Today, our work must be based on an understanding of change not only as linear movement from one static position to a predetermined end point, but also as an ongoing process that may be cyclical in nature (Land & Jarman, 1992; Marshak, 1993a).

The challenge is to help organizations thrive, not merely survive, as they deal in an environment of "permanent white water" (Vaill, 1989). Gone are the old days of relative stability and calm (Marshak, 1995). The issue is not about doing the same things faster or that change has accelerated. Practitioners need to understand the complexity of change, and the implications of constant change that call for a redefinition of the role of "change" agents. It means planning and implementing change as well as managing and navigating the flow of change. It also means thinking of change in transformational, as well as developmental and transitional ways (Marshak, 1993b).

Many Organization Development interventions were designed to achieve a future vision. Once the end point was clearly identified, progress could be measured to establish success. Such change efforts were believed to take 5 years minimally. Today it is clear that there are no final end points and that few organizations can afford to wait 3-5 years to achieve results. Continuous improvement has gone from a buzzword to a way of life.

New road maps for negotiating change and new measures of progress that reflect change as an ongoing process are needed. The real challenge is to establish processes, structures, behaviors and approaches that assist the organization to respond more rapidly and with greater flexibility to a context that is in constant flux. Organization Development must focus on implementing visible results more quickly. Goals and success indicators must be aligned with continuous improvement measures of learning and increased effectiveness which recognize that change is both a destination and an ongoing journey. Organization Development efforts must focus on helping organizations capitalize on change versus being held captive to it.

Table 3.2
Reassess Clients: Working with Multiple Clients

Current Orientations		and	Emerging Orientations
Top	Up		Inside ▶ Out
▼	OR ▲		AND
Down	Bottom		In ◀ Outside
Address Hierarchy and Power			Address Relationships and Inclusion
Intervene by Levels and Stovepipes			Intervene Horizontally and with Concentric Wholes

Reassessing Clients

The ideal in most traditional Organization Development interventions has been to work with top leadership as the primary client and then cascade down through the rest of the organization (see Table 3.2). This is often done through each functional unit with each higher level manager serving as the "linking pin" to the next level lower in the organization. Today, as many organizations work to achieve empowerment, move to self-managed teams, eliminate levels of management, and create horizontal structures, working from "top to bottom" may ignore important leverage points.

Organization Development practitioners must reassess how they work with "the client" and broaden their approaches to include multiple clients and stakeholders at all levels. They must identify and develop interventions that respond to a wider range of clients. They must be able to enlist the involvement and ownership of not only the top, but also seek ways to enroll champions, develop horizontal and concentric involvement and include key stakeholders both inside and outside the organization. In short, Organization Development must move from the notion of a singular client who resides at the top to one of multiple clients identified through various stakeholder interrelationships, at multiple levels, throughout the organization.

Table 3.3
Redesign Diagnosis: Moving Toward a More Holistic View

Current Orientations	and	Emerging Orientations
Literal		Symbolic
Objective		Subjective
Rational		Emotional
Analytic		Intuitive
Overt		Covert

Redesigning Diagnosis

A major problem for Organization Development today is its limited ability to diagnose complex systems on multidimensional levels (see Table 3.3). Data collection and diagnostic processes often have a singular focus or approach, based primarily on collecting objective rational data. This is supported by the implicit belief that once data are collected they must be "published" and "owned" before they can be "worked" (Marshak & Katz, 1992). Equally important, and often lacking, are the means and methods to identify, surface and address the more covert, subjective and symbolic data not easily presented through verbal discourse or rational analysis (Marshak & Katz, 1988; 1991).

Organization Development must develop mechanisms for diagnosis that are more holistic and extend beyond a rational linear approach (Marshak, 1994). Diagnosis must take into account multidimensional data, the symbolic as well as the literal; the overt and the covert; the rational and the emotional. Data must be collected and analyzed with a wide enough lens to see the big picture and to understand complex and interdependent variables and dynamics. Diagnosis methods must provide information that encompasses the whole system and that integrates the rational, emotional, and psychological aspects of the system.

Restructuring Interventions

Organizations today are undergoing a major overhaul, striving for integration at all levels – mission, values, task and process. Many leaders understand the need to provide the necessary linkages between the rational, emotional, and spiritual aspects of the business and to support the development of technical, business and people skills for greater effectiveness. If Organization Development is to continue to help organizations in the future it must conduct a similar overhaul (see Table 3.4).

Table 3.4
Restructure Interventions: Connecting the Whole

Current Orientations	and	Emerging Orientations
Interpersonal and Small Group		Intrapersonal and Large Group
Emphasis on People Dimensions		Emphasis on All Dimensions
Segmented Focus		Integrated Focus
Address Parts and Levels		Address Inter-relationships
Need for Long-term Change		Need for Ongoing Change

In short, our ability to be effective implies the need to develop more integrative and collaborative approaches that address multidimensional dynamics in complex systems. Although Organization Development has always defined itself as bringing about total systems change we find, in effect, that many of our current practices work against achieving such results. First, Organization Development's traditional methods stem largely from small group and interpersonal approaches. Second, we find more and more Organization Development initiatives segmented into specialized niches ranging from quality to empowerment, high performance to diversity, socio-technology to customer service. Within these initiatives there is little attention to the whole or the systemic interconnections. As a result, much slips through the cracks or ends up disjointed. This, in many ways, reflects a traditional stovepipe approach to intervening. Also most Organization Development interventions tend to reflect a time orientation that was appropriate in the 1950's and 1960's but that is increasingly inconsistent with the pace of today's Information Age.

Although we are beginning to see a shift to large scale interventions, we have not, as yet, developed mechanisms to integrate and leverage multiple change initiatives. Nor have we drawn very heavily upon methods that address the deeper psychological dynamics of a system. To increase Organization Development effectiveness will require expanding its scope and focus to a larger conception of the whole. Restructuring and reengineering cannot be addressed separate from people; self managed teams must be linked with quality, diversity, leadership and empowerment. We must work faster, deeper, wider, smarter, and with larger numbers of more diverse people than ever before.

Reconnecting with Others

Many organizations are undergoing dramatic efforts to restructure all aspects of their business, creating cross-discipline and cross-functional teams including a wide range of constituents, customers, and stakeholders. They are creating teams that include individuals from all aspects of their business: research to sales, engineering, manufacturing, customer service and often the customers themselves. Despite these trends towards integration and cross-discipline teaming, many Organization Development professionals go about their work alone or with a unidimensional focus. Yet the need to collaborate, to find interdependencies, to use others as resources, and to seek support systems is more essential than ever (see Figure 3.5).

Table 3.5
Reconnect with Others: We Can't Do It Alone

Current Orientations	and	Emerging Orientations
Lone Practitioner		Teams and Groups of Practitioners
Singular Specialty		Multiple Specialties and Alliances
Independent Facilitator		Interdependent Stakeholder
Neutral and Separate from the System		Involved and Part of the System

Times and the scope of change have changed. No individual practitioner can undertake efforts of the magnitude needed today. Ways to connect Organization Development work with the work of others must be encouraged. As new methodologies are developed, Organization Development practitioners must learn from others and share with others. The days of the lone practitioner may be gone. Organization Development practice must rely more and more on developing partnerships that bring together diverse individuals who as a team can maximize diverse skills, perspectives, disciplines and experience (Katz & Miller, 1993). We can no longer adopt the stance of the outside "catalyst," but must become more of an interdependent stakeholder with the system.

Facing the Future of Organization Development: The Fear and the Promise

The need to expand and reinvent Organization Development is great. And yet, it is also frightening. In order to be effective we must, like our clients, address issues about our own role and competence. We too must move out of our comfort zones. Sustaining the courage and facing the fears as we work toward reinventing our profession, we are, in essence, simultaneously reinventing ourselves and what we can be. We may also find ourselves reconnecting to a greater dimension of growth and discover a new wellspring of energy and creativity. As we move toward reinventing our profession, we have the potential to rediscover the real core of Organization Development; namely, unleashing the full human spirit and potential in us all.

References

Bunker, B., B. & Alban, B. T. (Eds.) (1992). Special issue: Large group interventions. *The Journal of Applied Behavioral Science, 28* (4).

Dannemiller, K. D., & Jacobs, R. W. (1992). Changing the way organizations change: A revolution of common sense. *The Journal of Applied Behavioral Science, 28* (4), 480-498.

Hurley, R. F., Church, A. H., Burke, W. W., & Van Eynde, D. F. (1992). Tension, change and values in OD. *The OD Practitioner, 24* (3), 1-5.

Katz, J. H., & Miller, F. A. (1993). High performance and inclusion: A new model for teams. *The Diversity Factor, 2* (1), 2-6.

Land, G., & Jarman, B. (1992). *Breakpoint change and beyond.* NY: Harper Collins.

Levine, D. B. (1989). *The team planning methodology: Shaping and strengthening development management*. Working Draft 4A. Development Management Center, Office of International Cooperation and Development, US Dept. of Agriculture.

Lewin, K. (1947). Frontiers in Group Dynamics. *Human Relations, 1* (1), 5-41.

Marshak, R. J. (1995). Managing in chaotic times. In R.A. Ritvo, A. H. Litwin, and L. Butler (Eds.), *Managing in the age of change*. Burr Ridge, IL: Irwin Professional Publishing, 58-66.

Marshak, R. J. (1994). The Tao of Change. *The OD Practitioner, 26* (2), 18-26.

Marshak, R. J. (1993a). Lewin meets Confucius: A review of the OD model of change. *Journal of Applied Behavioral Science, 29* (4), 393-415.

Marshak, R. J. (1993b). Managing the metaphors of change. *Organizational Dynamics, 22* (1), 44-56.

Marshak, R. J., & Katz, J. H. (1992). The symbolic side of OD. *The OD Practitioner, 24* (2), 1-5.

Marshak, R. J., & Katz, J. H. (1991). Keys to unlocking covert processes. In M. McDonald (Ed.), *Building ourselves ... Our work ... Our organizations ... Our world: Organization Development Network Conference Proceedings*. (pp. 65- 71). Portland, OR: Organization Development Network.

Marshak, R. J., & Katz, J. H. (1988). The covert processes model™. Unpublished manuscript.

Reddy, W. B. & Phillips, C. (1992). Traditional team assessment: The way of the dinosaur. *The OD Practitioner, 24* (4), 1-2.

Vaill, P. B. (1989). *Managing as a performing art*. San Francisco, CA: Jossey-Bass.

Weisbord, M. R. (1989). *Productive workplaces: Organizing and managing for dignity meaning, and community*. San Francisco, CA: Jossey-Bass.

4
Contemporary Challenges to the Philosophy and Practice of Organization Development

For more than a decade there have been consistent concerns and questions raised in the academic and practitioner communities about the state of organization development (OD). The main observation has been that OD is not playing a central role during a time of extensive organizational change worldwide. In his 1993 Distinguished Speaker Address to the Organization Development and Change Division of the Academy of Management, Robert E. Quinn lamented: "We are in an interesting situation. We live in a world where organizations are struggling as never before to make change. The demand is enormously high. Meanwhile we have a discipline supposedly centered on the issue of how to make change, and we seem to have little influence. Something is wrong." (Quinn, 1996, p. 4)

Those most concerned point out that in its early years, OD was at the forefront of organizational change, inventing the foundational terminology, theories and techniques still used today. In those years, OD practitioners worked closely with CEOs and heads of major divisions to bring change to highly bureaucratic organizations. Now, the story goes, all that has changed. Today, most (but not all) OD practitioners find themselves left out of working at the highest levels on the major changes that have been transforming organizations and industries for the past ten to twenty years. Instead, OD is viewed by a few as dead, and by many others as having become marginalized or even irrelevant to the central change issues facing CEOs of contemporary organizations. Concurrent with the perceived decline of organization development has been the rapid ascendance of another organizational change practice called "change management" that has been spearheaded by the major global management consulting companies such as Accenture (formerly Andersen Consulting), BearingPoint (formerly KPMG), Cap Gemini Ernst and Young, and IBM Business Consulting Services (which acquired PricewaterhouseCoopers Consulting). It is the practitioners of change management who now work closely with CEOs and heads of major divisions on transforming the world's corporations. The practitioners of organization development are left wishing to be involved, but working mostly at lower organizational levels on less central issues, and/or with smaller organizations, associations and not-for-profits.

It is the intent of this discussion to look more closely at this situation, attempt to discern and describe some of the dynamics that may be involved, and to conclude by offering a few suggestions about possible future directions for organization development. The presentation begins with an extended discussion of some of the major challenges and controversies confronting OD. These include issues related to the underlying humanistic philosophy or ideology of organization development, its relative inability to respond to a range of business trends since the 1980s, and some implications of the emergence and influence of postmodernism and the new sciences for OD theory and practice. Next, the shifting demographics between 1986 and 2001 are reviewed along with some reflections on the possible consequences. Finally, initial ways to begin to address the questions and issues raised in the presentation are discussed, including the need to begin to differentiate at least three types of OD.

Marshak, R. J. (2005). Contemporary challenges to the philosophy and practice of organization development. In D. L. Bradford and W. W. Burke (eds.) *Reinventing Organization Development* (p.19-42). San Francisco: Jossey-Bass Publishers. Republished with permission.

Challenges and Controversies

There are a number of interdependent considerations for trying to understand the present state of organization development. They form something more like a tapestry of interwoven challenges and controversies than a set of independent, causal variables. A central consideration throughout is the ongoing challenges and controversies since the 1980s to the underlying philosophy or ideology of organization development. This is discussed in some detail here, followed by briefer discussion of other related controversies and challenges.

Humanistic or Business Orientation

One good way to help reveal the underlying philosophy or ideology of OD is to compare it to another related philosophy of organizational change called change management. To begin the discussion we must first recognize that despite the generic qualities about the names *organization development* and *change management*, both are jargon or even marketing or brand names used to describe a certain set of organizational change practices. It is also argued that they are terms representing ideological views on the processes and purposes of organizational change.

Briefly stated, the term *organization development* came into use in the late 1950s and early 1960s to describe a set of practices rooted in the behavioral sciences to create planned change in organizations (Burke, 1987; Cummings & Worley, 1997). Early practitioners of what became known as OD were heavily influenced by ideas and normative values based in social psychology and humanistic psychology – for example, the work of Lewin, Lippitt, Maslow, McGregor, Argyris, and the NTL Institute. The term *organization effectiveness* has also been used to describe basically the same practices.

In the 1980s, the major accounting/management consulting companies expanded their traditional practices to include "reengineering" or "business process reengineering" services. This ultimately led to the naming, or branding, of these new practice areas as *change management.* Thus, for a while at least, reengineering and change management were virtually synonymous. As a practicing organizational change consultant at that time, I quickly learned from discussion with potential clients that I needed to carefully explore what they meant, and therefore what services they were seeking, when they used the term change management. In the early 1990s, in almost all cases, when I was asked if I did change management, what they really meant to ask was if I did reengineering. Additional background about, and a more detailed comparison of, organization development and change management is in Worren, Ruddle & Moore (1999).

In change management, the assumption tends to be that specific changes can be identified and implemented using planning and project management techniques, while employing participative processes as a way to secure buy-in and support for the changes. Needed changes are identified, planned and led by managers and executives using consultants as agents and resources to help direct or steer the change(s). These changes are almost always intended to advance the competitive and therefore economic and financial well being of the organization and its shareholders. Other outcomes of the change may be important, but secondary to the economic objectives. From this interpretation, change management might also be considered ideologically to mean, "engineering organizations for economic gain."

In organization development, in contrast, the assumption is that changes cannot be successfully identified, let alone implemented, without the true involvement of those responsible for doing the actual work. The purpose of involvement is to secure the best ideas and information to address the situation, with buy-in a side benefit. It is also usually assumed that there will be interdependencies and dynamics that cannot be fully anticipated or planned for, requiring an interactive process open to new developments and outcomes. Emphasis is therefore on identifying and facilitating effective change processes assuming that the proper process(es) will lead to the best outcome(s). Finally, organization development envisions that change processes should lead to more humanistic organizations where greater emphasis on human development, freedom, creativity and empowerment will produce greater organizational efficiency, effectiveness, and economic return. For example, in the introduction to their seminal discussion of planning change, Bennis, Benne, Chin and Corey (1961) assert, "The predicament we confront, then, concerns method; methods that maximize freedom and limit as little as possible the potentialities of growth; methods that will realize man's dignity as well as bring into fruition desirable social goals" (p. 2). From this interpretation, OD might also be considered ideologically to mean, "facilitating human development for social and organizational gain." A short summary comparison of change management and organization development appears in Table 4.1.

Table 4.1
Comparison of Change Management and Organization Development

Change approach	Emphasis on	Methods	Dominant values	Management of change as
Change Management	Outcomes	Elite processes	Economic	Engineering and directing
Organization Development	Processes	Participatory processes	Humanistic	Facilitation and coaching

Another way to quickly compare the underlying ideologies of OD and change management is to consider the everyday language and values associated with each. Despite the fact that both address how to create or manage organizational change, and in many cases advocate similar principles and practices, the core emphasis is different. What is figure for one is ground for the other, and vice versa. The language and values, and therefore normative orientation, of OD are very much based in the language and values of humanism and social psychology. The language, values and normative orientation of change management are very much based in the language and values of economics and business. See Table 4.2 for a quick summary to illustrate the point.

Table 4.2
Language and Values of Social Psychology
and Humanism versus Economics and Business

Dimension	Social Psychology & Humanism	Economics & Business
Highest value	Human development	Financial return
Instrumental agent	Awareness	Money and resources
Image	Self-actualization	The bottom line
Location of values in action	Inner self	The marketplace
Icon	Enlightened and empowered self	Entrepreneur and business executive
Theme	The individual:	Business and markets:
	• Freedom	• Competitive strategy
	• Dignity	• Profit and loss
	• Empowerment	• Productivity
	• Emotions	• Return on investment
	• Spirit	• Efficient use of resources
	• Holistic integration	• Economic wealth

Ideologically, from an OD perspective change management is incomplete or misdirected because virtually by definition a directed, engineering approach to securing primarily economic ends does not fully achieve the real purposes of organizational change. If real organizational change should include human as well as economic processes and purposes, then engineering change is inherently incomplete. One cannot engineer human development, dignity, freedom, creativity, artistry, and so on. Consequently, change implicitly or explicitly intended to create those purposes cannot exclusively use an engineering-for-economic-gain approach. In this sense, change management is an incomplete approach to organization change because it cannot create the normatively envisioned humanistic organization that should result from an OD effort.

However, from a change management perspective OD is also incomplete, or at least some form of contradiction or confusion, because OD seems to advocate *individual* development over *organizational* performance. The traditional OD response to this basic question of individual versus organizational needs and interests is to assert that in essence if you create a humanistic organization it will inherently be a high performing organization.

Touchy-Feely and Bottom-line Orientation

Given the language, values and ideological orientation of OD, it should not be surprising that it has been labeled by its critics as "too touchy-feely" almost from the very beginning. For as long as I can remember, I have heard that approbation applied to OD along with requests to be more bottom-line oriented, or to be less "airy-fairy" and deal more with the "nitty-gritty." Although these labels or epithets have been around for as long as OD there is an important difference today. In the 1960s and 1970s the broader society was more liberal, more valuing of individual development and expression. Social values and business conditions were leading people to question the efficacy of the machine-like bureaucratic model of organization. OD was potentially both a value system and a way to free locked-up human and organizational potential. Forty years later, conditions have changed. Globally, most societies have become more conservative (or "moved more to the center"). Global competition and relentless cost cutting and job elimination have elevated the needs of the organization for competitive success over the needs of individuals. Ask not what your organization can do for you, ask what you can do for your organization … and be grateful you have a job. A more conservative orientation wherein organizational success allows for the possibility of individual accomplishment is more the norm in most organizations I encounter today. As a consequence, the ideological orientation and emphasis of OD is more marginalized today than ever before. This is not just in terms of the values and orientations of today's managers and executives, but also of newer generations of would-be OD practitioners. As one Generation X-er commented in a plenary session at an OD conference held in the mid-1990s, "Do you have to be a hippie from the sixties to be an OD consultant?" An important issue facing OD therefore is the compatibility of the philosophical or ideological orientation developed in the 1960s with current conditions. Just as most liberal ideologies, whether they be liberal democratic, socialist, or communist, have had to adjust their philosophies in the past forty years, so too might OD need to adjust its underlying premises and values in some ways and to some degree.

Challenges from Downsizing, Reengineering, and Change Management

Serious challenges to the ideological orientation and practice of OD emerged in the late 1970s and early 1980s in the form of the downsizing and reengineering movements. The inability of OD to effectively respond to these business trends helped create a void that was ultimately filled by change management practitioners.

First, let us consider the OD response to downsizing. As an example, I will use my experiences in the late 1970s. At that time, President Jimmy Carter began efforts to reduce the size of the federal government, including the agency where I worked as a full-time internal consultant. At the time there was little written about downsizing, and nothing to provide guidance on how to do it. Over the ensuing three to four years, and continuing under President Ronald Reagan, I was involved in multiple efforts to downsize thousands of employees from my agency, eventually leading to the elimination of my own job and staff. That's when and how I became an independent consultant! During that time period there never developed an OD position on downsizing, nor any methodologies, approaches or interventions to address it. Many of the OD colleagues I interacted with at the time felt it should not and could not, as a matter of principle, become involved in eliminating jobs and careers. This reminded me of earlier debates at NTL-sponsored OD workshops in Bethel, Maine toward the end of the Vietnam War when the majority of participants generally felt that it would be immoral to provide OD services to the military. Today, more than twenty-five years later as downsizing efforts continue unabated, there is still no OD position on whether or not it is acceptable to be involved in downsizing, nor (if acceptable) are there any specific OD methodologies, approaches or interventions to guide how to address it (Worley & Feyerherm, 2003). Also, there was and still is some question whether or not the principles and practices of organization development will work during the more conflictual, self-protective, and trust-destroying dynamics often associated with downsizing efforts. As a colleague remarked to me in 1979, "OD practices work when organizations are growing, not when they are in decline."

Next, consider what happened regarding reengineering and OD. In the late 1970s and 1980s I had many OD colleagues who were heavily involved in workplace redesign efforts primarily using socio-technical systems (STS) design principles and methods. At that time STS was an accepted, if not dominant, aspect of OD practices. By the 1990s OD practitioners working on work redesign efforts using STS principles had largely disappeared. What happened is a revealing story. First and foremost the market for workplace redesign efforts was successfully taken over by the major accounting and management consulting companies. Prior to their entry into the market, individual or small groups of OD-oriented practitioners provided craft-like redesign services, usually emphasizing the "socio" as much as or more than the "technical" dimensions of organization design. The major consulting companies entered the market in the mid-1980s offering standardized business process reengineering services, typically emphasizing technical over social dimensions, while still using many of the same STS principles and methodologies. They also offered their services in a more ideologically friendly package and on a scale (thousands of consultants) impossible for the mom-and-pop OD practitioners to match. At the same time, many (but not all) OD practitioners were openly skeptical or opposed to reengineering interventions, considering them to be or having become nothing more than thinly disguised ways to justify and carry out further downsizing rather than enhancing the capabilities of an organization and its workforce. Concurrent with this trend, fewer and fewer new OD practitioners were being trained in work redesign or STS principles and practices. By the 1990s presentations related to work redesign had vanished from OD conferences and STS theory was largely absent from the major OD degree and certificate programs that were training record numbers of new practitioners (e.g. AU/NTL, Bowling Green, Case Western, Columbia, Fielding, Pepperdine, NTL, and so on).

Finally, in many ways change management was spawned in the mid-1980s by the major accounting and business consulting companies responding to the downsizing and reengineering movements. By the 1990s it could be argued that change management, not organization development, had become the dominant brand of organization change in most large corporations. In addition to the different ideological orientation of change management, it also strongly incorporated and integrated business strategy and information technology along with the traditional business disciplines into its principles and practices. Many of the people-involvement change practices used in OD also became a part of change management, but to a lesser extent and with a different ideological focus, as previously discussed. In the meantime, OD practitioners, (with some exceptions) never really embraced or integrated strategic planning, information technology, or the business disciplines into their practices. Instead they opted to continue advancing and refining their ideas and techniques related to the "softer-side" of change: organizational culture, diversity, large group methods, organizational learning, mental models, and appreciative inquiry.

The net result of these and other factors, along with the fact that most corporations were now confronted with requirements to restrategize their businesses and incorporate information technology to increase productivity and cut costs (including people costs), meant that by the 1990s change management had become the organization change approach of choice in the executive suites of most major corporations. Certainly some OD practitioners were, and still are, involved in important change efforts at the highest levels of major corporations, but they have become more the exception than the rule and never as comprehensively involved as the major change management consulting companies.

Challenges from Human Resources, Executive Coaching, and Extra Lean Organizations

In OD, the role of the consultant is to partner with responsible managers and involve those impacted by any potential change(s) in processes that lead to improved results or relationships. The managers and employees are expected to assume ownership of the change by learning new skills and behaviors and by doing the change work themselves, while the OD consultant suggests and facilitates the process. In operationalizing this approach, early OD practitioners were advised to start at the top and cascade efforts down through the organization. Unfettered access to the top of an organization was considered to be critical, and early internal OD staffs positioned themselves to be independent of the Personnel Department and report directly to the CEO. When I worked as an internal consultant in the 1970s, my staff was called the Organization and Management Development Staff; we were a staff division separate from and equal to the Personnel Division. Today, there are many more internal OD staffs and capabilities than thirty years ago, but few if any report to the CEO. Most, in fact, are part of the Human Resources Division and usually exist in some combination with training, executive or leadership development, or succession planning, thus blurring and confusing the difference among OD, training, and HR planning. Despite what is asserted in theory, OD in practice in many organizations has become, and is thought of as, a human resources function with all the limitations and expectations associated with that.

Another challenge to OD comes from the recent exponential increase in executive coaching. In OD, a consultant might coach an executive or manager incidental to his or her joint work on a change effort that could include multiple two- or three-day retreats and workshops. Now that same executive can meet alone for one or two hours in the privacy of his or her own office to discuss how to develop themselves, work more effectively with others, and improve their area of responsibility. Though not the same as OD, executive coaching offers a viable service and consequently a substitute addressing human and psychological dimensions. It also can be consumed in smaller and less demanding time increments, in the comfort of one's own office, and where the manager has more control than would be possible in a facilitated group setting. In that sense, regardless of whatever else one may think of the recent explosion in executive coaching, it has taken market share away from organization development. In fact, partially because both heavily involve psychological and people dimensions, many OD practitioners today also market themselves as executive coaches as a way to take advantage of the market boom in coaching.

Finally, the trend since the 1980s toward very lean organizations may also have some consequences for OD. In most of the organizations where I consult, people are extremely busy, working long hours with little or no slack time or resources. What they want is someone under their direction to do the work for them, or to provide a more or less turn-key operation. This extends to change efforts as well. Following the OD principle of getting the client fully involved and learning the skills to manage change themselves is sometimes experienced as simply too time-consuming and requiring too many scarce resources to be a realistic option to an overworked and understaffed executive. The classic interpretation, of course, is that this is a form of resistance. It might also just be a form of reality in today's high-pressured, twenty-four/seven, very lean organization. From a harried executive's point of view it may sometimes be better to hire your own virtual organization change staff to manage the change, under your auspices. Thus an additional way to look at the ascendancy of change management consultancies is that they offer themselves as temporary, virtual change management staffs to busy executives managing very lean organizations.

Modern to Postmodern Controversies

Among the many streams contributing to the original formulation of OD was a strong positivist orientation rooted in mid-twentieth-century social science research methodologies. The whole premise of data-based change (for example, action research and survey research methods) presumes the existence and validity of an objective, discernable reality. By the 1980s, however, constructionist and postmodern approaches were beginning to heavily influence the social sciences with ideas about multiple realities and the inherent subjectivity of experience (Bergquist, 1993). Whether intended or not, these ideas seem to have influenced and/or been incorporated into OD thought and practice since the mid- to late-1980s. Whereas change management was integrating ideas predominantly from the objective business sciences, OD practitioners began incorporating more constructionist and postmodern ideas from the behavioral sciences, especially psychology, sociology, linguistics, and anthropology. The development of appreciative inquiry in the 1980s, based in part on social constructionist premises, is but one example of this trend. There has also been increased interest in multicultural realities and the influence of consciousness and mental models on organizational behavior. OD practitioners also seemed much more interested in the "new sciences" (Wheatley, 1992) than the traditional ideas from physics and biology that had helped shape the original formulations of OD theory. A partial listing of a new series of practitioner-oriented books published by Pfeiffer since 2001 is shown in Table 4.3 to help illustrate my point.

Table 4.3
Some Early Titles from the Practicing Organization Development Series

Title	Focus
Appreciative Inquiry: *Change at the Speed of Imagination*	In a constructionist world, the power of a positive (rather than a deficit) consciousness
Beyond Change Management: *Advanced Strategies for Today's Transformational Leader*	Transformational change requires transforming the consciousness of leaders
Facilitating Organization Change: *Lessons from Complexity Science*	Application of the new sciences to organizational change
Guiding Change Journeys: *A Synergistic Approach to Organization Transformation*	A cross-cultural guide to psychological or archetypal transformation
The Conscious Consultant: *Mastering Change From the Inside Out*	Clarifying one's consciousness and choices to better influence change

Although certainly not monolithic, this shift in interest and emphasis places contemporary OD and its practitioners sometimes at odds with traditional OD and with most business executives who still adhere to the premises of an objective, quantifiable, and measurable world. The increased emphasis on transforming consciousness, operating from multicultural realities, and methods that tend to be more about creating common social perceptions and agreements than data-based analysis, all contribute to distinguishing a significant range of contemporary OD from its traditional roots.

This shift potentially exacerbates (or perhaps helps define) the differentiation between early and recent adherents of OD. It also raises the legitimate question of whether or not contemporary OD is becoming philosophically as well as methodologically different from traditional OD. Since many of the postmodern ideas influencing contemporary OD come from scholars based outside of most business schools, the shift may also be contributing to the increasing distance between some academics and business executives on the one hand and many (but certainly not all) contemporary OD practitioners on the other. When this shift is combined with the advent of change management, both trends beginning in the mid-1980s, it is perhaps no wonder that by the end of the 1980s and early 1990s, business school OD academics were beginning to declare OD dead or ineffectual.

Shifting Demographics of OD Practitioners

So far this discussion has highlighted some of the shifts from traditional to contemporary OD and the advent of change management, all beginning in the early to mid-1980s. Concurrent with these changes there has also been a significant shift in the demographics of OD practitioners. Although precise data are not available, a recently published summary of the changing demographics of membership in the OD Network is a revealing proxy. Table 4.4 summarizes some of the key shifts between 1986 and 2001 in who identifies with being an OD practitioner.

Table 4.4
Shifts in OD Network Membership from 1986 to 2001

Category	1986	2001
Total membership	1, 938	3,960
Women	39%	55%
Men	61%	45%
Median age	44	50
Over 50	25%	48%
Doctoral degrees	28%	7%
Race	Predominantly white	Predominantly white
Roles	No data available	Internal 41% External 41% Academic 3%

Sources: Minahan, 2002 and Minahan, Hutton & Kaplan, 2002

During this period there was an increase of more than 100 percent in the number of OD Network members, potentially reflecting the growing market for organizational change consultants. A majority of these practitioners are now women whereas in 1986 more than 60 percent were men. Practitioners are also older, are equally likely to be internal as external, and have significantly fewer doctoral degrees, but are still predominately white. Finally, only 3 percent of practitioners belonging to the OD Network in 2001 identified themselves as full-time academics. This dramatically reflects the ongoing differentiation between scholars and practitioners of OD, at least in this particular association. The original OD scholar-practitioner ideal, it seems, has differentiated into either mostly scholars or mostly practitioners of OD with fewer and fewer scholar-practitioners.

Considered separately or as a whole, these shifts raise a number of questions and invite speculation about their meaning and potential impact on the practice of organization development. The shift from OD practitioners being mostly men to mostly women is perhaps most notable. Has this happened because a greater percentage of women in recent years have been attracted to or been "allowed" to enter the field? Is it because men are now less attracted to OD and/or are seeking opportunities elsewhere?

These questions leave us with a sort of chicken-and-egg causal quandary. Is the increase of women in OD at least partially a reflection of men leaving or avoiding a perceived-to-be-declining field of practice, or is the perceived decline or marginalization of OD a reflection of the increasing number of women practitioners since the mid-1980s?

Regardless of the reasons, if the historic biases towards women in the workplace continue to any degree, then a field of practice dominated by women could be susceptible to the same biases and stereotypes. For example, women and OD are too emotional and touchy-feely, women and OD don't have what it takes to address the tough issues, women and OD contribute best in supportive roles dealing with relationships and feelings, women and OD belong in housekeeping functions, such as human resources. Of course, if any validity is given to these stereotypes, then the interpretation that OD is too "soft" and less relevant to contemporary business issues precisely because it has become a field mostly of women gains credence. Not surprisingly, I have heard both views expressed. This alone suggests that the valuing and roles of women and OD in contemporary business organizations are not entirely independent phenomena. It also makes one wonder if the majority of change management consultants are men or women.

The decrease in doctoral-level practitioners from more than one in four to less than one in ten raises a similar chicken-and-egg quandary. Is the increase in academic concerns about the current state of OD a reflection of the decline in doctoral-level practitioners, or is the decrease in doctoral-level practitioners a reflection of the decline in OD? There is also the question of the potential impact resulting from having fewer doctoral-level practitioners. The early books and articles that helped create and give legitimacy to organization development were written mostly (but not exclusively) by scholar-practitioners who implicitly called for consultants well versed in objectivist behavioral science theories and methodologies in order to facilitate action research interventions with client systems. The decline in OD practitioners trained in social science research and methodology, the hallmark of most traditional doctoral programs, could therefore be a contributing factor to the shift away from a more or less "pure" action research approach to a wider variety of facilitated programs, events, and interventions. This shift could also be manifesting itself in the developing body of OD publications where the orientation is more about "how to do it," than "the theory of how to do it." All this could end up increasing the relative distance between OD practice and established social science research, theory and methodology, thereby contributing to the ongoing differentiation between scholars and practitioners of OD.

The aging of OD practitioners (at least OD Network practitioners) where almost one in two is over fifty may have some values-based and/or generational implications. As previously noted, OD came of age in the 1960s and classically reflects the liberal values and mores of that period. Thus the values and orientations of traditional OD may be more attractive to the baby-boomers who came of age in that era than to following generations. The comment, "Do you have to be a hippie from the 60s to be an OD consultant?" succinctly conveys the intergenerational tension. Some of the differences between traditional and contemporary OD may, therefore, reflect tensions between older and younger practitioners over what should be the controlling values and orientations of organization development.

Finally, we must wonder about the combined impact of these shifts on the acceptance and practice of OD in today's business organizations. In the 1960s the OD consultant knocking on an executive's door was likely to be an externally based white male with perhaps a doctoral degree. Today the OD consultant is likely to be a white woman without a doctoral degree who is perhaps an internal HR employee. Exactly how this shift in demographics, in a field notoriously known as being too touchy-feely, impacts the perceptions about and practice of OD is open to further inquiry and debate. However, in any consideration of what has happened to OD, the changing demographics of practitioners needs to be an integral part of the discussion.

Paths Forward for OD

Clearly there are many challenges and questions confronting contemporary OD. What, if anything, should be done is also full of controversy and conjecture. Based on the discussion so far, however, there seem to be a few givens and two types of options.

First, something needs to be done about definitions and terminology. When practitioners, academics or managers talk about OD are they referring to traditional OD, contemporary OD, human resources OD, and/or something else? When people say OD is dead or irrelevant, which OD are they talking about? What is needed is some form of taxonomy to define, compare and contrast the variations of OD that have developed over the years. On the basis of this discussion, three types of OD that might profitably be distinguished are summarized in Table 4.5.

1. *Classical OD*, based on the original humanistic values, principles and premises developed in the 1950s, 1960s and 1970s combined with objectivist, action research methodologies (for example, data-based interventions focused predominantly on behavioral processes such as data feedback team development)

2. *Neo-classical OD*, which maintains a primarily action research orientation but augments or amends the original humanistic values with both more emphasis on business values as well as on contemporary business issues and processes (for example, system redesign or transformation efforts that might include "right sizing" to help configure an organization for competitive success)

3. *Social Interaction OD or New OD*, which presently ranges from humanistic to both humanistic and business values but has been heavily influenced by postmodern constructionist and new sciences orientations (for example, appreciative inquiry which is based on a constructionist worldview)

Table 4.5 Three Types of OD

Orientations	Modern, Objectivist	Postmodern, Constructionist
Dominantly humanistic with some business values	Classical OD	New OD
Humanistic with more business values	Neoclassical OD	New OD

As an additional reference point, the values-based distinction suggested here between Classical and Neoclassical OD is similar to the difference Worley and Feyerherm make between the "traditionalist" and "pragmatist" camps of OD (2003). They do not, however, differentiate between modern- and postmodern-based OD.

One difficulty among many in creating such taxonomies is that establishing typologies is typically the work of academics, and it is unclear who might do such work given the distance between today's OD scholars and practitioners. Convening a group of academics and practitioners to jointly explore classification schemas concurrent with an academic or practitioner conference might be a first step. Some organizational change typologies already exist in the literature, but do not focus on differentiating the various types of OD. Instead they classify OD as but one of many different approaches to organizational change (Huy, 2001; Palmer & Dunford, 2002). Until and unless there is better and more established philosophical and conceptual clarity about what we are talking about, it will be difficult to do anything about the current state of organization development. Another benefit of such clarification, of course, comes in the marketplace. Right now there is enormous brand confusion about what ideologies and services are provided by people calling themselves OD consultants. Classical, Neoclassical and New OD consultants all claim they are doing something called "organization development" yet may offer widely different services and types of expertise.

Another set of issues worth exploring requires further research. These issues include what exactly dead or marginalized means, and who is practicing what type(s) of OD and with what impact? With respect to what is dead or marginalized, there are several important dimensions worth clarifying. For example, are OD principles, or practices, or philosophy dead or marginalized? From my observations a great many of the practices and even principles of Classical OD are now routinely incorporated in change management and even in the everyday lexicon and behavior of most managers (although not Classical OD ideology). If OD principles and practices, but not necessarily ideology, are incorporated in whole or part into everyday management, coaching, change management, knowledge management, training, and so on, should we consider Classical OD to have been an enormous success or a marginalized failure?

In terms of who is practicing what types of OD, it might be revealing to find out who was an advocate of Classical, Neoclassical and/or New OD. This might help clarify why there are such different perspectives on whether or not "OD is in trouble," and could help create a conceptual bridge to foster more effective dialogues among academics, executives and consultants. Another set of questions worth closer study relates to the changing demographics of OD practitioners. Exactly who and what has been marginalized? Have the principles and practices of OD been marginalized or just women practitioners of OD? Is an OD practitioner with an advanced degree perceived differently than another practicing OD? Do they use different approaches and methods or get disparate results? These and other related questions are all worth exploring to help determine what, if anything, needs to be addressed.

Given this armchair analysis, and absent the research I've described, I offer two intentionally contrasting "ideal type" options for the OD community to ponder. Pursuing both simultaneously without conscious intent, as seems to be happening now, is likely to obscure the issues and confuse the marketplace.

One option is the *intentional creation and legitimization of a Neoclassical OD.* This would require updating and rebalancing classical organization development in ways that would ultimately make it closer to, but not identical with, change management. First and foremost, this involves rebalancing the ideology of OD to be less exclusively and stridently humanistic while incorporating more economic and organizational values. The classic formula that a humanistic organization would inherently be a high performing organization would need some rethinking and rebalancing of values and beliefs. At the same time, the core humanistic values of OD cannot be abandoned or subjugated. This is philosophical work of an order similar to Chester Barnard's famous declaration of faith at the end of *The Functions of the Executive*: "I believe that the expansion of cooperation (the organization) and the development of the individual are mutually dependent realities, and that a due proportion or balance between them is a necessary condition of human welfare" (1938, p. 296).

In addition to a rebalanced ideology, Neoclassical OD would maintain an action research orientation while incorporating and integrating into its principles and practices the latest developments in the business disciplines and information technology – not totally or exclusively, but to a much greater extent than is the current situation. This also means that the presumed competencies and education of Neoclassical OD practitioners would need to be modified to reflect these additional knowledge and skill areas. The amount of education and knowledge required to be a proficient Neoclassical OD practitioner would also increase, reflecting the new mix of principles and practices. Given that many of the practitioners of change management have an MBA or other advanced degree, it would be reasonable to assume that a master's degree with additional training in people and/or business disciplines would be minimally required. None of this, however, will be possible until someone or some process is able to cogently and persuasively present a renewed ideology for organization development. This will not be easy, but it is essential.

The second option is to *more purposefully articulate and legitimate a "New OD."* The New OD would or could be ideologically similar to Classical OD, but more self-consciously based in postmodern, constructionist approaches in the social sciences, as well as the latest developments in the "new sciences," such as chaos theory and complexity science. The New OD might have an even greater emphasis on the psychology of consciousness or mind-sets, as well as how to use social interaction, in large and small groups, to create meaning and reality. Its core methodologies would be based more on constructionist social and symbolic interaction rather than on problem solving, objectivist action research. Such an emphasis would not necessarily negate other OD practices, but would ultimately require them to be practiced in a way consistent with the philosophical premises of the New OD. This too would require modification of the education and competencies of New OD practitioners and might also require the equivalent of a master's degree with some additional training.

A conscious choice to be a New OD practitioner would also most likely be a conscious choice to be at the margin for most major, for-profit organizations. This would not necessarily be a bad thing. Historically, OD practitioners and academics have operated at the margin where they could impact but not be incorporated into the system. It is only recently, with the success of change management, that very many OD practitioners have wanted to be incorporated into mainstream business. Focusing on New OD would also allow academics and practitioners opportunities to discover and invent new social technologies, which in time could become mainstream practices, just as was the case with Classical OD.

Is Classical OD dead or dying? Perhaps, although it is certainly practiced and preached by some practitioners and most academics. Are Neoclassical OD or New OD the only choices? No; both could be pursued, but probably not by the same person. In fact, it could be argued that right now all three forms of OD are being practiced. Unfortunately, all three are using the same brand name, creating confusion in the marketplace and an inability within the OD community to make choices and create clear focus and alignment around change ideologies and methodologies. OD is not at a crossroads; that point was passed in the 1980s. It is currently on multiple, unnamed paths without a clear sense of direction for any of them and formidable competitors in the marketplace. The paths need to be named, the requirements spelled out, and clear choices made.

References

Barnard, C. I. (1938). *The functions of the executive.* Cambridge, MA: Harvard University Press.

Bennis, W. G., Benne, K. D., Chin, R., & Corey, K. E. (Eds.). (1961). *The planning of change.* New York: Holt, Rinehart and Winston.

Bergquist, W. (1993). *The postmodern organization: Mastering the art of irreversible change.* San Francisco: Jossey-Bass Publishers.

Burke, W. W. (1987). *Organization development: A normative view.* Reading, MA: Addison-Wesley Publishers.

Cummings, T. G., & Worley, C. G. (1997). *Organization development and change* (6th ed.). Cincinnati, Ohio: South-Western College Publishing.

Huy, Q. N. (2001). Time, temporal capability and planned change. *Academy of Management Review, 26*(4), 601-623.

Minahan, M. (2002). OD network: Our evolution and growth. *OD Practitioner, 34*(2), 50-54.

Minahan, M., Hutton, C., & Kaplan, M. (2002). What OD practitioners want and need for success. *OD Practitioner, 34*(2), 55-60.

Palmer, I., & Dunford, R. (2002). Who says change can be managed? *Strategic Change, 11*(5), 243-251.

Quinn, Robert E. (1996, Winter). The legitimate change agent: A vision for a new profession. *Academy of Management ODC Newsletter,* 1-6.

Wheatley, M. J. (1992). *Leadership and the new science.* San Francisco: Berrett-Koehler Publishers.

Worley, C. G., & Feyerherm, A. E. (2003). Reflections on the future of organization development. *The Journal of Applied Behavioral Science, 39*(1), 97-115.

Worren, N. A. M., Ruddle, K., & Moore, K. (1999). From organization development to change management. *The Journal of Applied Behavioral Science, 35*(3), 273-286.

5
Morphing: The Leading Edge of Organizational Change in the Twenty-first Century

A central preoccupation of organization development is dealing with organizational change. Over the years, organizational theorists and organization development consultants have advanced a wide range of theories about organizational change. Most of these theories and ideas are based on concepts and assumptions about change that are rarely examined very closely. Many of these implicit beliefs, however, are now being challenged by the emerging dynamics and contexts of the Information Age. The difficulty is that many of our historical ways of thinking about organizational change may now be limiting our ability to fully address the new conditions and contexts confronting contemporary organizations. For example, many organization development models of change implicitly assume that organizational change is something that can be started and then stopped or stabilized. The whole idea of planned change assumes, in essence, that it is possible to determine rationally how to initiate and implement actions to achieve and then maintain a predetermined, desired future state. Peter Vaill, when first introducing the metaphor of "continuous white water" to describe emerging change dynamics, observed: "The present environment of chaotic change requires a response so different from the traditional managerial approach of diagnose-plan-implement-evaluate that perhaps I should not even use the simple word change to refer to the kinds of events contemporary managers are facing" (1989, p. xiv).

To the degree that some contemporary organizations may be finding themselves dealing with needs to engage in comprehensive and continuous change, then "start-stop" models of change may be helpful to some degree, but are ultimately insufficient to address the real change dynamics these organizations are facing. The remainder of this discussion will seek to articulate and justify this conclusion, offer the concept of "morphing" as an additional way to think about the change dynamics confronting organizations in certain types of environments, present some ideas and principles for how to guide organizational morphing, and conclude with a discussion of the implications for the theory and practice of organization development.

Organizational Change Is Changing

In recent years, as we entered the Information Age, the scope, speed, and even nature of change seem to have changed. The new information technologies of the past 50 to 60 years have created a new era, marked by the ability of people to access and share information with virtually anyone, anywhere, anytime about anything on a continuous, interactive and unrestricted basis. These new capabilities have altered both the organizational game and the rules of the game. "Connectivity, Speed, and Intangibles – the derivatives of time, space, and mass – are blurring the rules and redefining our businesses and our lives" (Davis & Meyer, 1998, p. 6). The result of these shifting conditions and capabilities is the emergence of a new context that invites different organization and management principles from those most applicable in the Industrial Age. Table 5.1 summarizes some of these shifts.

Marshak, R. J. (2004). Morphing: The leading edge of organizational change in the 21st century, *Organization Development Journal*, 22(3), 8-21. Republished with permission.

Table 5.1
Shifting Contexts and Paradigms

Industrial Age	Information Age
Communication Capabilities:	**Communication Capabilities:**
Some people can communicate at some times about some things to some places on a delayed basis in a sequential and/or restricted way using stationary equipment.	Anyone can communicate at anytime about anything to anywhere in an immediate, continuous, interactive and unrestricted way using mobile equipment.
Organization and Management Principles	**Organization and Management Principles**
National & international orientation	Global & transnational orientation
Vertical orientation	Value chains
Own versus buy	Virtual organizations & outsourcing
Standardize	Customize
Specialize & segment	Multi-functional & end-to-end
Vertical hierarchy	Horizontal networks & teams
Command & control	Commitment & collaboration
Rules & regulations	Values & vision
Focus on "hard" extrinsic aspects	Focus on "soft" intrinsic aspects
Use historic data ("lag time")	Use real time data ("no time")
Keys to Success	**Keys to Success**
Productive or technological capacity	Market or customer orientation
Analysis, certainty & stability	Speed, flexibility & innovation
Independence & autonomy	Interdependence & partnership

Whether or not there is a direct correlation, there has also been a shift occurring in organizational change dynamics. Two major indicators that a shift is occurring are the beginning changes in organizational change emphasis: first, from addressing parts/ segments of an organization to addressing more encompassing patterns/wholes; and second, from thinking in terms of episodic change to thinking in terms of virtually continuous change. For example, since the 1990s both practitioners and researchers have suggested that whole-system, rather than part-system, change is more likely to lead to successful organizational performance (Bunker & Alban, 1997; Jacobs, 1994; Macy & Izumi, 1993; Whittington et al., 1999). Similarly, others argue that continual not episodic change is required to deal with the increased speeds of the new business context. "Moreover, in high-velocity industries with short product cycles and rapidly shifting competitive landscapes, the ability to engage in rapid and relentless continual change is a crucial capability for survival" (Brown & Eisenhardt, 1997, p. 1).

When we combine the dimensions of parts-wholes and episodic-continuous into a matrix, the emerging nature of contemporary organizational change is suggested. The four change scenarios that are created by this matrix are shown in Table 5.2. Periodic Operational Adjustments are episodic changes to parts or segments of an organization; for example gap analyses and "fix-its" to some aspect of strategy, structure, processes, etc., but not to all at the same time. This was, implicitly, one of the dominant approaches to organizational change in past years, memorably captured in the phrase, "If it's not broke, don't fix it."

Continuous Operational Adaptations also focus on parts or segments, but do so on an ongoing basis. Continuous improvements, *Kaizen*, or TQM reflects this approach to organizational change. Periodic Systemic Re-Arrangements address organizational patterns or wholes, but on an episodic basis. Reengineering and systemic redesign efforts are examples of this approach to organizational change. Finally, Continuous Systemic Alignments call for ongoing changes to the whole organization; for example, virtually simultaneous and continuous changes to an organization's strategies, structure, processes, culture, and so on.

Table 5.2
Four Change Scenarios

Dimensions	Focus on Parts / Segments	Focus on Patterns / Wholes
Episodic Change	Periodic Operational Adjustments	Periodic Systemic (Re)Arrangements
	Gap-analyses	Reengineering
	Fix-its	System redesign
Continuous Change	Continuous Operational Adaptations	Continuous Systemic Alignments
	On-going improvements	On-going organizing
	Kaizen, TQM	Morphing

Although we have some experience and concepts to help us deal with the first three scenarios, we have little to adequately address the last one. Yet the need for virtually continuous change of whole systems is now the context confronting some organizations, or at least those in "high-velocity" industries such as electronics and the Internet. The difficulty of dealing with continuous whole-system change extends beyond a lack of experience with new capabilities and contexts. The difficulty also includes the absence of theories and concepts to appropriately describe and explain this emerging type of organizational change dynamic. For example, the concept of "transformational change" typically presumes an *episodic* transformation that is preceded and then followed by a more "normal" and stable period of development. This concept is consistent with the punctuated equilibrium paradigm of change wherein equilibrium states experience a radical or revolutionary disruption and shift before returning again to a new equilibrium (Gersick, 1991; Romanelli & Tushman, 1994). While organizational change theorists have historically commented on the differences between evolutionary, incremental or developmental change as contrasted with revolutionary, radical discontinuous or transformational change (for example, Greiner, 1973), and more recently on the differences between episodic and continuous change (Huy, 2001; Pettigrew et al., 2001; Weick & Quinn, 1999) discussions of continuous "transformational" change of whole-systems have been relatively rare or absent.

Consequently, within the context of the Industrial Age and the punctuated equilibrium paradigm of organization transformation, a suggestion that there could be *continuous* transformational change of whole systems might sound unrealistic or unbelievable. Nonetheless, some contemporary organizations are now confronting just such contexts. Because so many of our existing ways of thinking about organizational change are encumbered with concepts developed in a different time and context, we need to develop new ideas to help managers and consultants think about organizational change in new ways.

Many of Our Current Concepts of Change Are Limited by Implicit Fundamental Assumptions

Our current concepts of change are not only challenged by contemporary change dynamics, but they are also limited by powerful implicit assumptions about the fundamental nature of change. These implicit assumptions are rooted in the dominant philosophical worldviews of the Industrial Age. What are some of these assumptions and why are they so limiting?

We begin first with the Greek philosophers who helped shape the Western worldview. From Plato and Aristotle we inherit two basic assumptions that critically impact how we think about change. The first is that permanence and stability are in all cases preferred over chaos and change. This assumption creates an implicit bias that there is something "wrong" with continuous change or chaotic conditions and that they should be avoided if at all possible.

If the world is beautiful and its maker good, clearly he had his eye on the eternal: if the alternative (which it is blasphemy even to mention) is true, on that which is subject to change. (- Plato, *Timaeus*, 29)

God, therefore, wishing that all things should be good, and so far as possible nothing to be imperfect, and finding the visible universe in a state not of rest but of inharmonious and disorderly motion, reduced it to order from disorder, as he judged that order was in every way better.(– Plato, *Timaeus*, 30a)

Plato and Aristotle also equated change with motion and asserted that motion/change must have a cause. "For Aristotle... change is motion, and every motion has to result from a causal force" (Hall & Ames, 1995, p. 378). In both cases the ideas of Plato and Aristotle prevailed over the earlier views of Heraclitus who claimed that the world is an "everlasting fire" in a state of continual change (Wagner, 1995). The two basic assumptions that stability is desirable and change must be caused tend to implicitly support thinking about organizational change as desired states of stability interrupted by unfortunate episodes of "forced" change, or, even worse, chaos.

The metaphorical linking of change with motion also links assumptions about change to the Newtonian worldview that helped create and shape the Industrial Age. Thus concepts related to the movement of objects, including the laws of motion, causal forces, inertia, resistance, mass, momentum, paths, end states, and so forth are all likely to be implicitly invoked in any discussion of organizational change. This is the language of planning, managing, and engineering change.

Unfortunately, however, theories and practices of change embedded with implicit assumptions of a universe where permanence, order, and stability are preferred, chaos is feared, and change results from forced movement may limit our ability to think about and address continuous whole system change in contemporary organizations. "The dominant paradigms in organization theory are based on stability seeking and uncertainty avoidance ... these paradigms are inadequate for global hyper-competitive environments, although their replacements are not clear yet" (Ilinitch et al, 1996, p. 217). See Table 5.3 for a summary of some of the key historically embedded assumptions about change.

Table 5.3
Historically Embedded Assumptions about Change

1. Permanence and stability are preferred to change and becoming
2. Change must have a cause
3. Change is motion
4. Deliberate acts are necessary to create order out of disorder or chaos
5. Order is always preferred to disorder or chaos

Morphing

Clearly we need some new concepts less encumbered with historical assumptions to help us address certain aspects of the change dynamics of the twenty-first century. Such conceptualization will require a change in the consciousness or mindsets of both managers and consultants. The new mindsets will need to embrace the ideas of fluidity and continuous change rather than stability and certainty. Because so many of our existing terms, including perhaps the word *change* itself, are embedded with historical assumptions, new language, terminology and word imagery may be needed to help explain and support these new mindsets.

To help capture the imagery, if not the specifics of continuous whole-system change, I first suggested the computer animation term for transformation, *morphing*, several years ago in a keynote address at an international change conference in Singapore (Marshak, 1998). This term had already started to come into popular use in the press and media to describe rapid, seamless, and more or less total change. The term *morphing* has also very recently been introduced in an academic context to describe comprehensive, continuous organizational change. "Continuous morphing refers to the comprehensive, continuous changes in products, services, resources, capabilities, and modes of organizing through which firms seek to regenerate competitive advantage under conditions of hyper-competition" (Rindova & Kotha, 2001, p. 1276).

Whether or not morphing is the right term to adopt, it does have some advantages that are needed to help describe the emerging contexts and dynamics of organizational change. Those advantages include its lack of association with prior terms and concepts of change; its origins in the Information Age; its connotation of rapid, seamless transformational change – unlike, for example, metamorphosis that implies stages of transformation over longer time periods – and imagery that is both evocative and understandable. In short, morphing, or some term like it, may be needed as a generative metaphor or analogy to advance our thinking about continuous whole-system change (Schön, 1993).

In the meantime, what do we know now about how to go about organizational morphing? Based on recent research by Brown & Eisenhardt (1997) and Rindova & Kotha (2001), some of the principles of morphing are beginning to be defined.

Table 5.4
Principles of Morphing

- Create limited organizational structures and principles such that there is both enough form and fluidity for rapid, organized action
- Create resource flexibility in both availability and application
- Ensure organizational learning to quickly develop and deploy new competencies
- Bridge from the present to the future with clear transition processes while avoiding focusing on the future to the detriment of the present
- Have top management mindsets that fully embrace the concepts of continuous change and flexible organizational forms, i.e., develop "managers with morphing mindsets"

A list of several of the key emerging principles for how to go about organizational morphing is offered in Table 5.4. These principles place emphasis on the requirement to have managers with morphing mindsets who can create and maintain the flexible and fluid organizational forms and practices necessary for fast-paced, continuous, whole-system change. These principles of morphing, of course, apply to organizations facing high velocity, hyper-competitive, *hyperactive* business environments where rapid and nearly continuous whole-system change is a requirement for ongoing success. For example, operating in the hyperactive environment of the Internet, both Excite and Yahoo! underwent two transformations during the period of 1994 to 1998. They morphed from Internet search engines providing navigation tools to Internet destination sites providing content to Internet portals providing broad-based online services. These ongoing transformations required continuing shifts in strategy, organization form, key resources, and bases of competitive advantage (see Rindova & Kotha, 2001, p. 1268). Other organizations in less fast-moving and competitive environments might follow different change principles.

Implications for Organization Development

If continuous whole-system change, or morphing, is at the leading edge of organizational change in the twenty-first century, then there are a range of implications for organization development and its practitioners. These include review and expansion of existing change theories, augmentation of change practices, and searches for new change concepts.

A Contingency Theory of Organizational Change Is Needed

Because most existing change theories were developed with embedded assumptions in contexts different in varying degrees from some of today's conditions, new theories with different assumptions are needed to guide responsive practices. Some of the ideas presented here are suggestive of what may be needed. At the same time, we must also understand how and when to use the extensive range of existing theories and practices. One way would be to move more explicitly to a contingency theory of change, which would simply be a way of saying, "Use different change assumptions, theories and practices depending on the context and situation." This is not a new approach per se, and contingency theories of leadership and organization are familiar to most organization development practitioners, but applying a contingency approach to change theories in the way envisioned here might be somewhat new or novel. Just as Burns and Stalker (1961) in one of the first conceptualizations of open systems contingency theory during the late Industrial Age suggested that organizational forms should be contingent upon the nature of their environments, we might also consider that change concepts and approaches should be contingent upon organizational environments and contexts.

So, for example, building on the Burns and Stalker premise that mechanistic organizational forms are appropriate in stable environments and organic forms in more turbulent environments, we might add that *morphogenic* forms are needed in the *hyperactive* environments of the early Information Age. Similarly, we might also add that models and assumptions of change conceived in the Industrial Age might still be highly appropriate for organizations facing stable to moderately turbulent environments, but that Information Age models and assumptions of change, including perhaps morphing, may be more appropriate for highly turbulent to hyperactive environments. A summary of these initial ideas is shown in Table 5.5. In terms of whole-system change, it might also mean that many of our existing theories and practices for organization transformation would be applicable to *episodic* transformations, but that a theory of organization morphing would be more applicable for organizations facing *continuous* transformation.

Table 5.5
Organizational Change Contingencies

Environment	Stable	Turbulent	Hyperactive
Organizational Form	*Mechanistic*	*Organic*	*Morphogenic*
Change Approach	Periodic Operational Adjustments	Adaptations and Periodic Systemic (Re)Arrangements	Continuous Systemic Alignments

Modify and Augment Traditional Change Practices

Regarding change practices, morphing would require some shifts and/or augmentation in both the task(s) and methods of traditional organizational change. The primary task in organizational morphing would be to help foster a morphogenic organization, that is, an organization capable of continuous whole-system change. Note especially that the emphasis would be on creating and maintaining capability rather than arriving at some preferred or planned end state. The characteristics of a morphogenic organization, as previously noted, would include clear, but limited, organizational structures and principles to promote both form and fluidity, resource flexibility, organizational learning, clear transition processes, and managers with morphing mindsets. Since in continuous morphing there is no end state per se, a wide range of organization development theories and practices that are explicitly or implicitly based on the classic Lewinian model of unfreezing, movement, refreezing (Lewin, 1951) would need to be reexamined. Theories and practices related to the psychology of episodic change, where there is an expectation of an end to the movement or transition phase, would also need to be reexamined, modified and/or augmented with additional theory and practice explicitly based on continuous whole-system change.

Such shifts in the change task and practices of both managers and consultants will require preceding shifts in their mindsets. Minimally, there would need to be shifts from implicit assumptions about relative stability, certainty and episodic change to morphing mindsets based on fluidity, flexibility and continuous change. Reliance on mechanistic, engineering or planned movement concepts and imagery would need to be avoided. Such shifts in consciousness or mental models, of course, do not just happen and are not always amenable to the rational, databased change technologies of traditional organization development. Organization development consultants working with organizations facing continuous whole-system change will need to augment their traditional skills and competencies with new or extended social technologies focused on changing consciousness or mindsets in key individuals and organizations. This emerging area of theory and practice will need to become a core competency of organization development consultants who wish to help create morphogenic organizations (see for example, Ackerman-Anderson & Anderson, 2001; Anderson & Ackerman-Anderson, 2001).

Morphing and Concepts of Change from the New Sciences

To aid and augment shifts from episodic to continuous change mindsets, greater knowledge of and interventions based on the new sciences may be helpful. The new sciences, such as quantum physics, chaos theory, and complexity science, provide concepts for thinking about organizational dynamics in new ways (Wheatley, 1992). These concepts directly challenge assumptions of stability and episodic change that must be initiated, planned, and managed. Instead, it is assumed that change is continuous and that complex systems can be self-organizing. For example, in their analysis of four types of change (life-cycle, evolution, dialectic and teleology), Van de Ven and Poole (1995) come close to suggesting that chaos might be a fifth type of change. "Advances in dynamic systems theory provide mathematical tools for examining chaos as an alternative explanation of organizational change and development processes" (p. 535).

In particular, the concepts associated with complexity theory, strange as they may seem to some, may offer relevant ideas to help guide in part those interested in how to better understand and address continuous whole-system change. For example, Olson and Eoyang (2001) said, "We need a simple, coherent alternative to the old machine model before we can work responsibly in the complex environments of today and tomorrow" (p. 6). They advocated the concepts of complex adaptive systems to escape the limitations of the Newtonian and Industrial paradigms. "The emerging science of complex adaptive systems offers such a paradigm. It provides metaphors and models that articulate and make meaning out of the emerging adaptive nature of organizations" (p. 19). The concepts and imagery of complex adaptive systems invite thinking about continuous, self-organizing instead of episodic, engineered change.

Morphing and Concepts of Change from Other Cultures

The search for new concepts to help explain and address continuous whole-system change need not be limited to the Western tradition. Insights and ideas from other cultures and eras where cosmologies of continuous change are the established worldview might also prove helpful in developing new theories and practices to address continuous whole-system change. One such possibility comes from Eastern mysticism, which Capra (1976) equates with the ideas of the new sciences. In Taoist and Confucian philosophy the universe is composed of constantly changing interdependent manifestations of one entity and change is both spontaneous and cyclical. "According to Aristotle, it is normal for all things to be at rest, whereas for the Chinese, in contrast, universal dynamism is the primary assumption (Gernet, 1985, p. 210). Furthermore, chaos is a needed aspect of transformation. "... Daoism is based upon the affirmation rather than the negation of chaos. In the Anglo-European tradition, chaos as emptiness, separation, or confusion is to be overcome. In Daoism, the chaotic aspect of things is to be left alone to contribute spontaneity to the process of transformation" (Hall & Ames, 1995, p. 236).

An analysis of the Confucian and Taoist worldviews reveals an alternative set of assumptions and orientations about change that can help guide how to address continuous whole-system change or morphing (Marshak, 1993; 1994). Among other differences, there is a primary assumption that change is continuous and cyclical with a resulting orientation towards attending to the past-present-future, knowing how to let go and realign, maintaining balance and harmony, thinking of both/and, cultivating system self-renewal, thinking holistically, using artistry and composition, and being values or principles centered. This orientation represents a shift in mindsets from desires for the presumed certainty provided by planning and control to greater comfort with more spontaneous alignments based on maintaining harmony and equilibrium while adhering to a few core principles during the continuous cycles of organizational change. A more Confucian or Taoist orientation is also consistent with recent research characterizing the dynamic capabilities required for success in hyperactive environments. "Simple principles and limited routines enable firms to self-organize, which in turn enables them to respond to rapid change" (Eisenhardt & Martin, 2000, p. 1274). See Table 5.6 for a summary analysis of some of the differing East-West historical worldviews, assumptions and orientations about the dynamics of change.

Table 5.6
Summary Analysis of Some East-West Concepts of Change

Traditional Western European Worldview	Chinese Taoist and Confucian Worldview
The universe is composed of separate, independent entities normally in static or equilibrium states. Movement results when things act on each other. The universe had a beginning and will have an end. Progress or evolution is expected over time.	The universe is composed of constantly changing, interdependent manifestations of one entity. The universe is. Change is both spontaneous and cyclical.
Assumptions that change is:	**Assumption that change is:**
Linear	Cyclical
Progressive	Processional
Destination oriented	Journey oriented
Based on creating disequilibrium	Based on maintaining equilibrium
Planned and managed by people who are separate from and act on things to achieve their goals	Followed by people who are one with all and must act correctly to maintain harmony in the universe
Unusual, because everything is normally in a quasi-stationary or static state	Usual, because everything is normally in a continually changing dynamic state
Resulting change orientation:	**Resulting change orientation**
Focus on the future	Attend to the past-present-future
Assume satisfied people hold on	Wise people let go and realign
Overcome resistance	Maintain balance and harmony
Think in terms of either/or	Think in terms of both/and
Plan and manage change	Cultivate system self-renewal
Think analytically	Think holistically
Use reason and logic	Use artistry and composition
Measure progress	Be values centered

Source: Marshak, 1993 & 1994

Finally, some succinct advice on continuous change and morphing is provided by the Taoist sage Zhuangzi (399-295? BCE) and the Confucian sage Ch'eng Yi (1033-1107 CE):

The life of things passes by like a galloping horse. With no activity is it not changing, and at no time is it not moving. What shall we do? What shall we not do? The thing to do is to leave it to self transformation (Zhuangzi in Chan, 1963, p. 206)

Thus being long lasting does not mean being in a fixed and definite state. Being fixed and definite, a thing cannot last long. The way to be constant is to change according to circumstances. (Ch'eng Yi in Chan, 1963, p. 571)

Concluding Comments

As we move into the twenty-first century, organizational change is changing and so must the theories, concepts, practices and word imagery used by managers and organization development consultants in leading change efforts. This change will require a conscious shift from our implicit biases for stability and start-stop models of change to adopting alternative theories and assumptions that better support thinking and acting within the concept of continuous whole-system change. We will also need to be mindful that an episodic shift in our theories and mindsets, no matter how dramatic, may not remain effective for very long. Instead, it is likely that continuous and comprehensive changes to our concepts and practices will be needed to stay aligned with the rapidly changing organizational contexts and dynamics of the twenty-first century.

References

Ackerman-Anderson, L., & Anderson, D. (2001). Awake at the wheel: Moving beyond change management to conscious change leadership. *OD Practitioner, 33*(3), 4-10.

Anderson, D., & Ackerman-Anderson, L. (2001). *Beyond change management: Advanced strategies for today's transformational leaders*. San Francisco: Jossey-Bass/Pfeiffer.

Brown, S., & Eisenhardt, K. (1997). The art of continuous change: Linking complexity theory and time-paced evolution in relentlessly shifting organizations. *Administrative Science Quarterly, 42*, 1-34.

Bunker B. B., & Alban B. T. (1997). *Large group interventions: Engaging the whole system for rapid change.* San Francisco: Jossey-Bass

Burns, T., & Stalker, G. M. (1961). *The management of innovation*. Oxford: Oxford University Press.

Capra, F. (1976). *The tao of physics.* New York: Bantam Books.

Chan, W. T. (Trans.) (1963). *A source book in Chinese philosophy.* Princeton: Princeton University Press.

Davis, S., & Meyer, C. (1998). *Blur: The speed of change in the connected economy.* Addison-Wesley: Reading, MA.

Eisenhardt, K. M., & Martin, J. A. (2000). Dynamic capabilities: What are they? *Strategic Management Journal, 21*, 1105-1121.

Gernet, J. (1985). *China and Christian impact: A conflict of cultures.* Janet Lloyd (trans.) Cambridge: Cambridge University Press.

Gersick, C. J. G. (1991). Revolutionary change theories: A multi-level exploration of the punctuated equilibrium paradigm. *Academy of Management Review, 16*(1), 10-36.

Greiner, L. E. (1972). Evolution and revolution as organizations grow. *Harvard Business Review, 50*(4), 37-46.

Hall, D. L., & Ames, R. T. (1995). *Anticipating China: Thinking through the narratives of Chinese and Western culture.* Albany: State University of New York Press.

Huy, Q. N. (2001). Time, temporal capability and planned change. *Academy of Management Review, 26*(4), 601-623.

Ilinitch, A., D'Aveni, R., & Lewin, A. (1996). New organizational forms and strategies for managing in hyper-competitive environments. *Organization Science, 7*, 211-220.

Jacobs, R. W. (1994). *Real time strategic change: How to involve an entire organization in fast and far-reaching change.* San Francisco: Berrett-Koehler

Lee, D. (trans.) (1971). Plato, *Timaeus*, London: Penguin Books.

Lewin, K. (1951). *Field theory in social science.* New York: Harper and Row.

Macy, B. A., & Izumi, H. (1993). Organizational change, design, and work innovation: A meta-analysis of 131 North American field studies – 1961-1991. In R. W. Woodman & W. A. Pasmore (Eds.). *Research in organizational change and development,* vol. 7, 235-313. Greenwich, CT: JAI Press.

Marshak, R. J. (1993). Lewin meets Confucius: A review of the OD model of change. *The Journal of Applied Behavioral Science, 29*(4), 393-415.

Marshak, R. J. (1994). The Tao of change, *OD Practitioner, 26*(2), 18-26.

Marshak, R. J. (1998). Sustaining balance and harmony in a constantly changing world. Keynote address at the *Asia-Pacific conference and exhibition on change management '98,* Singapore, 20-21 August 1998.

Olson, E. E., & Eoyang, G. H. (2001). *Facilitating organization change: Lessons from complexity science.* San Francisco: Jossey-Bass.

Pettigrew, A. M., Woodman, R. W., & Camerron, K. S. (2001). Studying organizational change and development: Challenges for future research. *Academy of Management Journal, 44*(4), 697713.

Rindova, V., & Kotha, S. (2001). Continuous "morphing": Competing through dynamic capabilities, form, and function. *Academy of Management Journal, 44*(6), 1263-1280.

Romanelli, E., & Tushman, M. L. (1994). Organization transformation as punctuated equilibrium: An empirical test. *Academy of Management Journal, 37,* 1141-1186.

Schön, D. A. (1993). Generative metaphor: A perspective on problem-setting in social policy. In A. Ortony (Ed.) (1993). *Metaphor and thought, second edition.* Cambridge: Cambridge University Press.

Vaill, P. B. (1989). *Managing as a performing art: New ideas for a world of chaotic change.* San Francisco: Jossey-Bass.

Van de Ven, A. H., & Poole, M. S. (1995). Exploring development and change in organizations. *Academy of Management Review, 20,* 510-540.

Wagner, C. K. (1995). Managing change in business: Views from the ancient past. *Business Horizons, 38*(6), 8-12.

Weick, K. E., & Quinn, R. E. (1999). Organizational change and development. In J. T. Spence, J. M. Darley, & D. J. Foss (Eds.), *Annual Review of Psychology, 50,* 361-386. Palo Alto, CA: Annual Reviews.

Wheatley, M. J. (1992). *Leadership and the new science.* San Francisco: Berrett-Koehler Publishers.

Whittington, R., Pettigrew, A., Peck, S., Fenton, E., & Conyon, M. (1999). Change and complementarities in the new competitive landscape: A European panel study, 1992-1996. *Organization Science, 10,* 583-600.

6
Emerging Directions: Is There a New OD?

Background

There has been a great deal of commentary and controversy about the current state of organization development (OD). One ongoing concern is the underlying value system of OD and whether the traditional humanistic values espoused by the founders of the field are still relevant or whether they should be replaced by a set of more pragmatic business considerations as articulated by newer practitioners (Worley & Feyerherm, 2003). As I experienced in teaching a class titled "Values and Ethics in Organization Development," this set of issues reveals itself in stark terms. After reviewing several OD statements of values and ethics (for example, Gellermann, Frankel & Ladenson, 1990), I was asked if I really believed in "all that stuff?" I was then told that if anyone actually practiced that value system they would not get any work. The controversy over OD's values continues today and is part of a larger set of concerns about the field's future, relevance and continued viability (Bradford & Burke, 2004, 2005).

Overlooked in these discussions, however, is a larger and more basic issue: OD may be facing a challenge from within the field – an emerging "New OD," not necessarily different in values so much as in ontology and epistemology. This emerging set of OD beliefs and practices is based on philosophical assumptions and methodologies about social phenomena and social reality that are widely different from the key assumptions of the field's founders. This chapter explores the possibilities of an emergent new OD and outlines potential implications for the field and its practitioners.

Classical Organization Development

The original formulation of OD included a strong positivist orientation based in mid-twentieth-century social science research methodologies. The whole idea of data-based change, like action research and survey research methods, presumes the existence and validity of an objective, discernable reality that can be investigated to produce valid data and information to influence change. For example, one of Argyris's three core tasks of a change agent is the creation of valid data. "It has been accepted as axiomatic that valid and useful information is the foundation for effective intervention" (Argyris, 1973, p. 17). This theme is echoed by Chin and Benne (1976) in their classic discussion of general strategies for effecting change in human systems. "One element in all approaches to planned change is the conscious utilization and application of knowledge as an instrument or tool for modifying patterns and institutions of practice" (p. 22). Knowledge in this perspective is discovered through the scientific method, which historically assumed an objective, transcendent and knowable reality. Blake and Mouton (1976) also reflect this theme in their extended discussion of five basic types of interventions, including catalytic interventions which are closest to classic OD. "Catalytic interventions assist the client in collecting data and information to reintegrate his or her perceptions as to how things are" (p. 4).

Marshak, R. J. (2006). Emerging directions: Is there a new OD? In J. V. Gallos (Ed.) *Organization development: A Jossey-Bass reader* (p. 833-841). San Francisco: Jossey-Bass Publishers. Republished with permission.

In sum, classical OD is based explicitly or implicitly in an ontology and epistemology that assume an objective, transcendent, knowable world. The ideas are consistent with the central assumptions of most mainstream mid-twentieth-century social, biological, and physical sciences. Methodologies based on these assumptions, such as action research, are then employed to help discover or reveal this reality to client systems in order to help correct distortions and misperceptions. The use of objective data in a process of social discovery, therefore, is a central foundation in classical OD's approach to change.

The New Organization Development

In the 1980s, constructionist and postmodern approaches heavily influenced the social sciences with their ideas about multiple realities and the inherent subjectivity of experience (for example, Berger & Luckmann, 1966; Bergquist, 1993; Searle, 1995). Their notion of multiple realities implies that there can be no transcendent, objective truth to be discovered. Instead the issue is how immanent agreements about the reality of a situation are or could be most effectively negotiated among the contending points-of-view. This framing raises issues of power and how it is used to create or impose a socially agreed-on or "privileged" version of things. In addition, ideas from the new sciences, including chaos theory and self-organizing systems, influenced how people thought about change in organizations, especially assumptions about and approaches to planned change (Wheatley, 1992).

These ideas naturally made their way into the OD world. They have been incorporated into theory and practice in recent years, although perhaps without a conscious intent to create a new OD. At least six contemporary OD-related theories and practices are based on these newer assumptions and will be explored in this chapter: appreciative inquiry; large group interventions; approaches to transformational change through individual mind-sets and consciousness; practices that address diversity and multi-cultural realities; approaches based on the new sciences such as complex adaptive systems theory; and models of change that differ from the classical "unfreezing-movement-refreezing" paradigm.

Appreciative Inquiry

The development of appreciative inquiry is based on the social constructionist premise that reality is partially (if not completely) a result of one's mindset. Watkins and Mohr (2001) assert that appreciative inquiry is postmodern in orientation and is "grounded in the theory of social constructionism" (p. 26). They contrast it with practices based on a "modernist," objectivist, and scientific orientation and conclude: "Post-modernism, on the other hand, rejects the idea of an underlying structure and of an underlying truth. Post-modern thought embraces the idea of multiple and contextually determined realities. Social constructionism is a formative theory of the post-modern era" (p. 27).

The power of socially constructed mind-sets is also reflected in appreciative inquiry's concerns about the negative impact of the "deficit-focused thinking" of traditional action research. "Positive-focused thinking" is at the core of appreciative inquiry.

Common Ground and Social Agreements

Large group interventions seeking "common ground" – as opposed to objective common truth – are designed to achieve agreement among multiple constituencies, all of whose points-of-view are considered legitimate versions of reality (see, for example, Bunker & Alban, 2005). Although data are gathered and used in these approaches, data gathering is more for the purpose of presenting multiple possibilities and perspectives than for bringing "facts" to bear on the situation. Greater emphasis is on reaching social agreements and adopting new ways of seeing reality that will guide future actions. "Future Search is designed to help the group arrive at agreements about the future they want and actions to achieve it" (Lent, McCormick, & Pearce, 2005, p. 61). The underlying power and political dimensions involved in large group interventions are recognized by researchers, if not practitioners. In analyzing a case example of a Search Conference (SC), for example, Clarke (2005) comments that "it was found that the most important outcome from the SC was its predominately political effects" (p. 42). Tenkasi and Chesmore (2003) provide additional evidence for the impact of large group interventions on networks, connections, influence, politics, and power dynamics in organizations.

Changing Mind-Sets and Consciousness

In another stream of work related to multiple realities is the development of theories and models that promote changes in mind-sets and consciousness as the route to organizational transformation (for example, Anderson & Ackerman-Anderson, 2001). These have been developed by OD consultants and academics in direct reaction to the perceived limitations of the classical, Newtonian, Industrial Age views of change and are being used to think, talk about, and address contemporary and emerging change dynamics. For example, Ackerman-Anderson and Anderson (2001) assert, "We call the traditional leadership mindset, most prevalent today, the Industrial Mindset. This worldview contains the very blinders that prevent leaders from seeing the dynamics of transformation" (p. 7). Organizational transformation from this perspective requires shifts in individual consciousness, starting with the leadership and extending throughout the organization.

Diversity and Multcultural Realities

A third change in the field has been an increased interest in diversity and multicultural realities, and explorations of how power is used to establish or reinforce exclusionary standards, practices and paradigms. Miller & Katz (2002) capture the essence of the issues: "Most organizations are filled with barriers – rigid structures, poor training processes, outmoded equipment, misguided incentive programs, and discriminatory promotion and assignment practices that keep people from contributing the full breadth of their skills, ideas, and energies to the organization's success. Expressed in conscious and unconscious behaviors, as well as routine practices, procedures, and bylaws, these barriers are typically rooted in the very culture of an organization. They favor people who are most like the founders or senior leaders of the organization" (p. 7).

Most contemporary approaches to diversity and multicultural dynamics in organizations also include explicit recognition of the linkages between power dynamics and the version of reality that favors some groups and interests over others, and they have practices for addressing this kind of political asymmetry.

Applications of the New Sciences

Some OD practitioners have embraced ideas from the new sciences, such as complexity theory and self-organizing systems. Olson and Eoyang (2001), for example, see the need for a new OD change paradigm that incorporates these ideas. "The use of rational planned change approaches, driven by leaders with the help of change facilitators, has fallen short even when bolstered by formal (and expensive) programs such as TQM and re-engineering" (p.19). They believe that "the emerging science of complex adaptive systems offers such a paradigm" (p. 19) and "establishes a foundation for a new theory of change" (p. 19).

Different Models of Change

Finally, these trends and changes in the contexts, technologies, and requirements of twenty-first-century organizations have raised questions about the theories and practices needed to address contemporary change dynamics and have led to the development of new change models. These include interests in cyclical change that flow from the new sciences as well as from some cultural traditions, and stand in contrast to classical OD's linear unfreezing-movement-refreezing model (Marshak, 1993); continuous, as opposed to episodic approaches to change (Weick & Quinn, 1999); "spiral dynamics," which combines consciousness-changing with other nonlinear approaches to change (Beck & Cowan, 1996), and processes of continuous transformation (Marshak, 2004). For OD practitioners, these new models and approaches will require a conscious shift from the field's implicit bias for stability and "start-stop" models of change to alternative theories and assumptions that better support thinking and acting within the concept of continuous whole-system growth.

All these changes and factors – emphases on socially constructing reality, transforming mind-sets and consciousness, operating from multicultural realities, exploring different models and assumptions about change, and creating common social perceptions and agreements – contribute to a contemporary OD whose theories, assumptions, and practices are vastly different from OD's classical roots. Table 6.1 summarizes classical OD and what I call the new OD.

Table 6.1
Classical OD and the New OD

Classical OD	New OD
Approach is influenced by classical science and modern thought and philosophy	Approach is influenced by the new sciences and postmodern thought and philosophy
Reality is an objective fact	Reality is socially constructed
There is a single reality	There are multiple realities
Truth is transcendent and discoverable	Truth is immanent and emerges from the situation
Reality is discovered by using rational and analytic processes	Reality is negotiated and involves power and political processes
Change results from collecting and applying valid data using objective problem-solving methods	Change results from creating new social agreements through explicit or implicit negotiation
Change can be created, planned and managed	Change is inherent and can be self-organizing
Change is episodic and linear	Change is continuous, cyclical, or both
Emphasis is on changing behavior and what one does	Emphasis is on changing mind-sets and how one thinks

Implications

If a new OD is emerging (or has emerged), there are important implications for theory and practice.

1. *We will need to do something about definitions and terminology.* When practitioners, academics or managers talk about organization development, are they referring to classical OD, new OD or something else? We need better definitions and ways to know and to compare the variations of OD over time. In this chapter, two types of OD have been highlighted, but there may be more. Without additional philosophical and conceptual clarity, talking about the current state of the field is difficult. Witness the discussions in recent years about whether or not organization development (OD) and organization transformation (OT) are different. Add to that the ongoing discussion about whether appreciative inquiry is revolutionary, or simply another form of action research. Clarifying concepts, assumptions, and philosophy also brings benefits to clients and client systems. Now, practitioners of both classical OD and new OD claim they are doing "organization development" yet each offers different services and expertise often based on differing, but unarticulated, philosophical premises.

2. *We will need to explicitly identify philosophical differences when discussing and teaching OD and its practices.* Presently, OD practitioners and scholars discuss the theory and practice of organization development as if it is a single entity and based on the same set of values and premises. This chapter raises questions about whether that is true. Differing perspectives can easily lead to cross-communication and confusion. Worse, those entrenched in one set of assumptions may question or challenge the practices of those in another. The two parties may never fully recognize that they are not talking about the same things at all. Discussions about

organization development theory and practice are no longer univocal; they are plurivocal. The field must find ways to contend with its own multiple realities, philosophical differences, and competing discourses in order to advance theory and practice, as well as support all engaged in our shared efforts to enhance organizational effectiveness. By clarifying and differentiating premises and associated practices, we have the opportunity to develop new social technologies and approaches based on the field's well-established principles.

3. *We may need to purposefully articulate and legitimate the new OD.* A fully articulated and legitimated new OD needs a more self-conscious foundation in constructionist approaches in the social sciences and in the latest developments in the new sciences. The new OD might have an emphasis on affecting consciousness or mind-sets and on using social interaction in large and small groups to create or negotiate meaning and reality. Its core methods would be based more on practices in constructionist social and symbolic interaction, not on objectivist action research focused on problem-solving. It would explicitly recognize that reality is created and maintained through negotiations involving power. It would develop and advance values, theories, and methodologies for dealing effectively with these kinds of political dynamics.

Developing new premises and practices related to the role and uses of negotiation, for example, would be in order. So would new approaches to the power and political processes that establish and maintain socially constructed realities, agreements, and mind-sets that guide day-to-day behavior. All this may be challenging to the field given classical OD's seeming aversion to the positive possibilities of power and its preference for rational, objective and fact-based processes. Many OD consultants presently treat power and political processes as if they were evil forces operating in organizations. At best, many have a profound ambivalence towards power and its manifestations (Marshak, 1992, 2001). Exactly when, how, and what kinds of power can be used in the new OD to facilitate social agreements among contending realities will be a critical and complex question for the field to confront and explore.

The new OD does not necessarily negate other classical OD practices. It would, however, ultimately require those practices to be consistent with the philosophical premises of the new approach. All this might also stimulate academics and practitioners to pursue new approaches, innovative practices, and social technologies for addressing change in human systems.

A Concluding Comment

The jury is still out as to whether or not there is a distinctive new OD. Nevertheless, it is important to acknowledge that there have been ongoing developments and evolutions in the philosophy, values, theories, and practices of organization development since its origin. These need to be more clearly articulated, distinguished, and addressed by practitioners and scholars in the field. Absent clearer delineations and understandings, we continue to risk miscommunication, confusion, or worse.

References

Ackerman-Anderson, L., & Anderson, D. (2001). Awake at the wheel: Moving beyond change management to conscious change leadership. *OD Practitioner, 33*(3), 4-10.

Anderson, D., & Ackerman-Anderson, L. (2001). *Beyond change management: Advanced strategies for today's transformational leaders.* San Francisco: Jossey-Bass/Pfeiffer.

Argyris, C. (1973). Intervention theory and method: *A behavioral science view.* Reading, MA: Addison-Wesley.

Beck, D. E., & Cowan, C. C. (1996). *Spiral dynamics: Mastering values, leadership and change.* Malden, MA: Blackwell Publishers, Inc.

Berger, P., & Luckmann, T. L. (1966). *The social construction of reality.* London: Penguin.

Bergquist, W. (1993). *The postmodern organization: Mastering the art of irreversible change.* San Francisco: Jossey-Bass.

Blake, R. R., & Mouton, J. S. (1976). *Consultation.* Reading, MA: Addison-Wesley.

Bradford, D. L., & Burke, W. W. (2004). Introduction: Is OD in crisis? *The Journal of Applied Behavioral Science, 40*(4) 369-373.

Bradford, D. L., & Burke, W. W. (Eds.) (2005). *Reinventing OD.* San Francisco: Jossey-Bass Publishers.

Bunker, B. B., & Alban, B. T. (Eds.) (2005). Special issue on large group interventions, *Journal of Applied Behavioral Science, 41*(1).

Chin, R., & Benne, K. D. (1976). General strategies for effecting change in human systems. In W. G. Bennis, K. D. Benne, R. Chin, & K. E. Corey (Eds.). *The planning of change, third edition.* (pp. 22-45). New York: Holt, Rinehart and Winston.

Clarke, N. (2005). Transorganizational development for network building. *Journal of Applied Behavioral Science, 41*(1), 30-46.

Gellermann, W., Frankel, M. S., & Ladenson, R. F. (Eds.) (1990). *Values and ethics in organization and human systems development.* San Francisco: Jossey-Bass.

Lent, R. M., McCormick, M. T., & Pearce, D. S. (2005). Combining future search and open space to address special situations. *Journal of Applied Behavioral Science, 41*(1), 61-69.

Marshak, R. J. (1992). Politics, public organizations, and OD. *OD Practitioner, 24*(4), 5-8.

Marshak, R. J. (1993). Lewin meets Confucius: A re-view of the OD model of change. *The Journal of Applied Behavioral Science, 29*(4), 393-415.

Marshak, R. J. (2001). Claiming your power and leadership as an OD practitioner. *Organization Development Practitioner, 33*(4), 17-22.

Marshak, R. J. (2004). Morphing: The leading edge of organizational change in the twenty-first century, *Organization Development Journal, 22*(3), 8-21.

Miller, F. A., & Katz, J. H. (2002). *The inclusion breakthrough: Unleashing the real power of diversity.* San Francisco: Berrett- Koehler.

Olson, E. E., & Eoyang, G. H. (2001). *Facilitating organizational change: Lessons from complexity science.* San Francisco: Jossey-Bass.

Searle, J. R. (1995). *The construction of social reality.* London: Allen-Lane Publishers.

Tenkasi, R. V., & Chesmore, M. C. (2003). Social networks and planned organizational change: The impact of strong ties on effective change implementation and use. *Journal of Applied Behavioral Science, 39*(3), 281-300.

Watkins, J. M., & Mohr, B. J. (2001). *Appreciative inquiry: Change at the speed of imagination.* San Francisco: Jossey-Bass.

Wheatley, M. J. (1992). *Leadership and the new science.* San Francisco: Berrett-Koehler.

Weick, K. E., & Quinn, R. E. (1999). Organizational change and development. In J. T. Spence, J. M. Darley, & D. J. Foss (Eds.), *Annual Review of Psychology, 50,* 361-386. Palo Alto, CA: Annual Reviews.

Worley, C. G., & Feyerherm, A. E. (2003). Reflections on the future of organization development, *The Journal of Applied Behavioral Science, 39*(1) 97-115.

PART II
Cross Cultural Views on Organization Development

Introduction
Robert J. Marshak

    The articles and book chapter in this section marked a significant shift in my thinking and writing as well as a clear example of "views from the edge" presented via contrasting ideal types. The impetus for these writings came from a business trip to Seoul, Korea in 1991. I had been to Korea many times before, and had been taught Korean in the Army before being stationed there during the Vietnam War, so I was not a naïve visitor. Nonetheless, while I was facilitating a workshop on organizational change the responses from the Korean participants seemed slightly "off" to me. I figured it must have something to do with deep aspects of the Korean culture that I did not understand and that my Korean hosts and colleagues couldn't explain to me. I knew that Korean culture had been heavily influenced by Confucianism, so I figured I'd see if I could learn anything by reading about that and promptly went out and bought a copy of *The Analects of Confucius* (Confucius said…; The Master said…) when I returned home.

    Well, I spent the next few years reading all the Confucian classics, books about Confucian philosophy, Daoism, traditional Chinese philosophy, and so on. It all remained pretty opaque and mystical to me until one day I had the insight that they were writing about a different world than the one I had been acculturated into. I lived in a Western world of independent elements and forces that acted on each other (think Newton). These actions produced "movement" and also change (think Lewin's unfreeze-movement-refreeze theory of change). In contrast, the Confucian (and Daoist) worldview was based on a totally interdependent universe where change was inherent, cyclical (think yin-yang and the tide coming in and going out), and part of the natural order of all things. One observed, followed, and participated in those changes in order to be one with the natural harmony and equilibrium of the universe (follow the Way). Once I started reading the same writings from this cultural worldview everything suddenly made complete sense to me.

    I eventually decided to write up my ideas, and, furthermore, to try to get them published as an article in a refereed academic journal, something I had not previously considered. After the original version, *Lewin Meets Confucius: A Re-View of the OD Model of Change*, was accepted by *The Journal of Applied Behavioral Science*, I thought I should write something for a more practitioner audience. This led to the publication of *Training and Consulting in Korea* and later *The Tao of Change* in the *OD Practitioner*.

    More than ten years later, I was asked if I would prepare a slightly revised version of this work to be included as a chapter in a book about international OD. I used this as an opportunity to do something I had always wanted to do, but could not because of the space limitations of journal articles. In the book chapter, *Organization Development and Post-Confucian Societies,* I integrated the three previously published articles on learning and change, added some ideas about Confucian relationships, and provided some anecdotes from my training and consulting experiences in East Asia.

The significance of the original *Lewin Meets Confucius* article for me turned out to be profound. It was my first refereed journal publication and encouraged me to believe I could contribute in that mode of writing. It also grounded in me that there were different cultural views of change and that most of what I had learned and knew was based dominantly in one cultural worldview. It benefited me enormously to be able to at least briefly glimpse the world through my version of Confucian eyes. This brought my own tacit assumptions about change and other social phenomena to awareness and also helped me in my consulting work in Korea, China, Hong Kong, and Singapore. The experience also sensitized me to how other dimensions of my "natural" worldview might be influencing how I and others think about and experience change. This later led to further reflections and other articles, to be covered in the next section, focused on contrasting assumptions, mental models, and world views of change.

There were also two other important learnings or experiences connected to my work on contrasting traditional East Asian and OD models of change. One was that my ideas seemed to be better understood or accepted when published versus verbally presented. I vividly recall trying to explain my insights about cyclical change to some seasoned colleagues who immediately challenged my thinking before I had even laid it all out. These same colleagues later read the article and, apparently not remembering their earlier comments, remarked how insightful and helpful it was. This taught me the power of the written versus the spoken word, at least in terms of my thoughts and ideas. It also was a clear encouragement to write more than I had previously.

The second learning had to do with repeated experiences where people responded to the central thesis of this work – that different cultural assumptions about change exist and the dominant OD model is based on one set of assumptions – in one or both of two ways. One type of response was to angrily challenge me about raising an alternative cultural model of change. "Are you saying the Confucian model is better?" "Are you saying Chinese culture is better than Western culture?" The second type of response, sometimes following the first, was to assert that the OD model of change actually encompassed both sets of assumptions, for example, that it was both linear and cyclical, both destination and journey oriented, interested in both creating disequilibrium and maintaining equilibrium, and so forth. In those moments the possibility that there might be something outside of, and different from, the dominant OD model of change seemed to be an unacceptable proposition. These experiences taught me a great deal about being on the edge looking both inward and outward while drawing contrasts based on that vantage point. I have since had similar experiences connected to other of my ideas and writings that share the same "view from the edge" orientation. Plato may have had it right with his analogy of the cave story.

7

Lewin Meets Confucius: A Re-view of the OD Model of Change

Questions have been raised in recent years about the cultural limits and overall efficacy of organization development (OD) to address the current and emerging problems of contemporary organizations. This discussion attempts to speak to both issues by examining the OD model of change, that is, Lewin's three-stage change process of unfreezing, movement, and refreezing. When the OD model is compared to the model(s) of change based in East Asian and Confucian cultural traditions, different assumptions about change are revealed. The analysis suggests that different culturally based models of change exist and are likely to lead adherents to employ different change methods and approaches. Consideration of both models as valid points to a possible synthesis that would address developmental and transformational change processes. More research into the change models and assumptions inherent in different cultures and cosmologies is needed not only to inform current OD practice but to expand the range of change theories and methods available for dealing with contemporary organizational issues.

> When you know a thing, to recognize that you know it, and when you do not know a thing, to recognize that you do not know it. That is knowledge. (Confucius quoted in Waley, 1938, p. 91)

Organization development (OD) is facing at least two important challenges to its efficacy for addressing the current and emerging dilemmas of contemporary organizations. One challenge derives from the increasing application of OD in cross-cultural and/or multicultural settings. This has generated a wide variety of commentary on whether or not OD is culturally limited. The other challenge is less well defined but brings into question, implicitly at least, whether or not OD can address the scope, pace, and/or nature of the required changes facing postindustrial organizations. This article attempts to speak to both issues by critically examining the fundamental theory of change underlying OD. This is done via a comparison with an alternative "theory of change" derived from ancient Chinese cultural traditions. The resulting analysis suggests that different culturally based models of change exist, that differences in how change is conceptualized are likely to lead to different intervention approaches, and that consideration of alternative cultural paradigms can help in the development of OD theory and practice.

Cross-Cultural Questions

In recent years, a wide variety of authors have pointed out the cultural biases of American management theories in general (Adler, 1991; Boyacigiller & Adler, 1991; Hofstede, 1980a, 1993; Hofstede & Bond, 1988) and OD values and processes in particular (Golembiewski, 1987, 1991; Jaeger, 1984, 1986; Marshak, 1993a; Mirvis & Berg, 1977). For example, Jaeger (1986), using the OD values outlined by Tannenbaum and Davis (1969) and the cultural dimensions advanced by Hofstede (1980b), found OD values to be

Marshak, R. J. (1993). Lewin meets Confucius: A re-view of the OD model of change, *Journal of Applied Behavioral Science*, 29(4), 393-415. Republished with permission.

inconsistent with the values of most national cultures, and in some cases to be polar opposites. Others have echoed Jaeger's critique in a variety of cultural settings. Richards (1991) found the introduction of change and management development not possible in South-East Asia due to contrasting underlying cultural orientations. Reyes-Sagun (1988) notes that the value system of the Philippines is inconsistent with most OD values. Boss and Mariono (1987) report that various confrontation and team-building designs will not work in Italy due to cultural values related to personal pride and potential loss of face in a group setting. Johnson (1990) asserts that the cultural orientation of Venezuela is so far removed from OD values that there is no support for the application of any OD technique in that country. There are also reports by those who believe that OD or aspects of OD can be adapted to most any cultural setting by sensitive and alert practitioners (e.g., Golembiewski, 1991; Kiggundu, 1990; Rikuta, 1987;   Tainio & Santalainen, 1984). Nonetheless, the recent critique of organizational science by Boyacigiller and Adler (1991) is unequivocal: "One of our primary conclusions is that of parochialism. Americans have developed theories without being sufficiently aware of non-U.S. contexts, models, research, and values" (p. 263). Their critique suggests OD practitioners and researchers need to be more than simply sensitive and alert in the application of OD in a global context.

Change Technology Questions

The adequacy of OD change technology to address contemporary organizational problems is also a topic of discussion, especially in the practitioner community (see, e.g., Armstrong, 1993; McDonald, 1990; Thorne & Hogan, 1993; Van Eynde & Coruzzi, 1993; Zilber, 1993). One dominant theme that runs through a wide range of both practitioner and academic discussions is the nature of the changes required to deal effectively with the issues facing organizations today. Different authors have different ways of describing the types of change required, but most distinguish between developmental (evolutionary) and transformational (revolutionary) change. Thus Greiner (1972) distinguishes between evolutionary and revolutionary change; Ackerman (1986) between developmental, transitional, and transformational change; Gersick (1991) explores revolutionary change theories in depth; Land and Jarman (1992) advance the concept of breakpoint change; Hammer and Champy (1993) argue that transformational reengineering, not incremental change, is needed; and Marshak (1993b) explores the metaphors associated with fix and maintain, build and develop, move and relocate, and liberate and re-create types of change.

This is not just a question of classification but of theory and practice as well. Over the years, whether or not OD includes, or should include, transformational change technologies has been widely and hotly debated, especially among practitioners. Another aspect of the questions about the OD model of change is whether or not a change model that emphasizes creating change is as relevant to contemporary managers and organizations facing continual change, "permanent white water" (Vaill, 1989), as it was to their counterparts of past decades when organizational life was more stable and bureaucratic. Indeed, a model of change that addresses how to deal with continual change might be especially appealing in today's organizational world. Consequently, because the efficacy of OD for dealing with change in contemporary organizations has been questioned, it is appropriate and necessary to review its most fundamental assumptions (Argyris, 1990; Katz & Marshak, 1993; Weick, 1990). In this case, that means a re-view of the assumptions underlying the OD model of change.

Approach and Methodology

This article might best be described as an exploratory analysis of some of the fundamental assumptions about the phenomenon of change believed to exist in two different cultural settings. The primary thesis is that different assumptions about change are likely to lead to different theories and practices related to change methods. Because the discussion is cross-cultural in nature, a phenomenological and/or anthropological orientation is necessary; that is to say, assumptions must be interpreted from the frame of the originating culture. Evaluating the meaning of an assumption, or set of assumptions, from a viewpoint other than its own cultural context would be inherently specious and probably pernicious. The methodology was first to derive a set of candidate assumptions through induction from a review of pertinent literature within each of the subject cultures (see Hall & Ames, 1987, for a discussion of a similar approach). Candidate assumptions were then reviewed for logical consistency with the "theories" and practices related to change as reported in the relevant professional and/or philosophical literature of each culture. Candidate assumptions were also reviewed for consistency with attributes and assumptions associated with each culture as described by other commentators (see, e.g., Capra, 1982; Hall & Ames, 1987; Loewe, 1982; Nakamura, 1964; Tarnas, 1991). The final sets of assumptions were selected based on their apparent internal logic, consistency with culture specific theory and practice related to change, and attempts to be parsimonious. The comparisons and discussions of potential implications that follow the presentation of the assumption sets were then developed to test their utility and to stimulate the thinking of both theorists and practitioners of OD.

The discussion focuses first on the model of change advanced by the European-American social scientist Kurt Lewin (1890-1947). This model is in the Enlightenment tradition of European science and is consistent with that worldview (Tarnas, 1991). Lewin's model was selected because his theories of change are generally recognized as the "underlying and guiding frames of reference for any OD effort" (Burke, 1987, p. 53; also see Marrow, 1969). Next, the "model(s)" of change underlying Confucian, Neo-Confucian, and Taoist philosophies are examined. These philosophies offer another worldview with quite different assumptions about change. For the purposes of this discussion, these models are "attributed" to the Chinese philosopher-sage K'ung Fu-Tzu (Master K'ung), called Confucius (551-479 B.C.) in the West (Chai & Chai, 1973; DeBary, Chan, & Watson, 1960; Eno, 1990; Legge, 1893). However, it should be remembered throughout that these models could just as easily be considered Taoist models of change, as readers familiar with Taoist philosophy will quickly recognize. Confucius and Confucian/Neo-Confucian philosophy were selected in particular for several reasons: [1] First, because by attribution and legend Confucius studied, arranged, and then wrote the first philosophical commentaries to the I Ching (Book of Changes) (Cleary, 1992; Legge, 1882; Wilhelm & Baynes, 1950). The I Ching is one of the oldest (circa 1143 B.C.) and most influential East Asian paradigms of change and the universe. As such, it represents a cosmology and philosophy embraced by both the Confucian and Taoist traditions alike (Chan, 1963). [2]Confucius was also selected because he and his followers advocated action and intervention in the world, unlike the Taoists and Buddhists who sought withdrawal or escape from it (Munro, 1969). Partly as a consequence, Confucian and Neo-Confucian philosophy became state-endorsed doctrine in China and Korea and deeply influential in Japan and the rest of East Asia. As one of the primary cornerstones of East Asian civilization, the Confucian tradition is still influential, if no longer orthodox or endorsed, in modern-day China, Korea, Japan, Hong Kong, Taiwan, Vietnam, and Singapore (Rozman, 1991; Tu, Hejtmanek, & Wachman, 1992; also see Hofstede & Bond, 1988). As Chan (1963) observes, "Confucius ... can truly be said to have molded Chinese civilization in general" (p. 14).

What should become clear from the following analysis is that many of the almost taken-for-granted assumptions about change underlying OD may be different in kind or emphasis from deeply rooted cultural beliefs about change in most East Asian countries. Differences in assumptions could, of course, lead to difficulties in the application of OD in countries or cultures with alternative change concepts. Of equal or greater importance for OD theory and practice is the recognition of the potential bounds and limits to current OD theories of change and the awareness of new possibilities and options revealed by alternative paradigms (Kuhn, 1962). The presentation begins with a brief overview of the Lewinian and Confucian (and Taoist) models of change, compares and contrasts them, and concludes with a discussion of some of the implications for OD theory and practice.

The Lewinian / OD Model Of Change

The basic image representing the theory of change underlying OD is shown in Figure 7.1. The translation of this image is simple. There is a current state (A) and a desired future state (B). Through planned change interventions (→), one moves from State A to the more desirable State B.

Figure 7.1
OD Image of Change

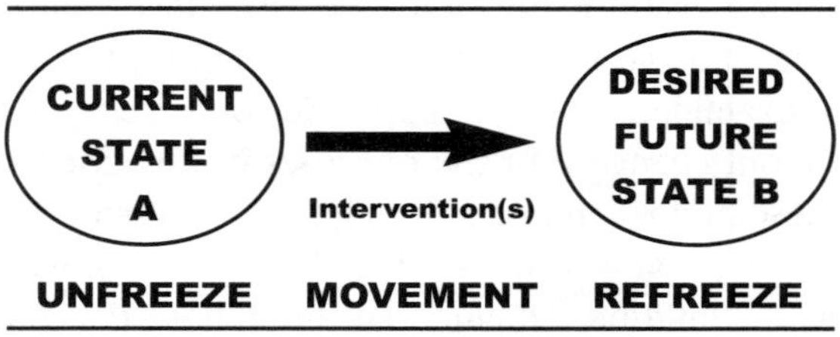

How to do this is informed by Lewin's three-stage change process, based on his field theory (Lewin, 1951). Current State A is maintained by a field of forces in equilibrium. By altering the field of forces through a planned and managed intervention, State A will unfreeze and there will be movement. When the desired State B is reached, an equilibrium of the field of forces is reestablished so as to refreeze the situation and maintain the desired State B. As Burke (1987) summarizes,

Thus, according to Lewin, bringing about lasting change means initially unlocking or unfreezing the present social system. This might require some kind of confrontation. ...Next, behavioral movement must occur in the direction of desired change. ...Finally, deliberate steps must be taken to ensure that the new state of behavior remains relatively permanent. (p. 56)

This particular image and underlying theory is so much a part of OD that most practitioners would be hard pressed to react other than "So what?" Indeed, it is only when it is contrasted with an alternative image of change that the underlying assumptions and limits of the model become clear.

The Confucian Model of Change

Although it would be inappropriate to say that there is a single Confucian/East Asian model of change, it is fair to assert that there is a dominant image and it is cyclical (see, e.g., Wilhelm, 1960; Wilhelm, 1979). The two representations of cyclical change underlying Confucian, Neo-Confucian, and Taoist philosophy, in addition to the *I Ching* system of hexagrams, are shown in Figures 7.2 and 7.3.

Figure 7.2
Yin-Yang Cyclical Change

YANG	YIN
Light Side of the Mountain	Dark Side of the Mountain
Heaven	Earth
Sun	Moon
Fire	Water
Hot	Cold
Dry	Wet
Active	Receptive
Outside	Inside
Expand	Contract
Ascend	Descend

In the image shown in Figure 7.2, there is inherent and continual alternation between the cosmic forces of yin and yang and they are understood to be the polar aspects of one unity, the *T'ai Chi*, the Great Ultimate. The concept of polarity is critical to an understanding of yin and yang. It denotes an existential interdependence wherein each defines the other, unlike the concepts of dualism and dialectic wherein each exists independent of the other. Furthermore, yin and yang are constantly in the process of becoming the other in an endless cycle. That is why yin and yang are represented as two intertwined aspects of one circle. The polarities represented by yin and yang are inherent in everything and reflect a cosmology that views everything in the universe to be in constant flux as the balance between them continually changes. According to Chou Tun-I (1017-1073 A.D.), a Sung, Neo-Confucian philosopher,

> The Great Ultimate through movement generates yang. When its activity reaches its limits, it becomes tranquil. Through tranquility the Great Ultimate generates yin. When tranquility reaches its limits, activity begins again. So movement and tranquility alternate and become the root of each other, giving rise to the distinction of yin and yang. (quoted in Chan, 1963, p. 463)

In the image shown in Figure 7.3, there is inherent and continual cyclical movement among the Five Forces or Agents that make up the universe (represented as Earth, Metal, Water, Wood, and Fire).

Figure 7.3
Five Agents of Cyclical Change

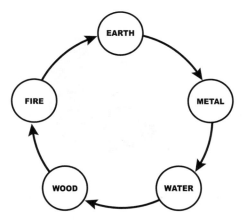

Movement from one to another is a natural process and occurs in a specific sequence when there is harmony and equilibrium in the universe (e.g., from wood to fire, not fire to wood). Thus the Five Agents image reflects cyclical change that is harmonious and in balance when it occurs in its natural, correct order. When it is out of balance (e.g., one agent overwhelms the other agents, as in too much fire) or out of order (e.g., fire consumes wood rather than being fed by wood), unfortunate consequences result, hence the emphasis in traditional Chinese medicine and geomancy (Feng Shui), which are based on this model, on maintaining and restoring natural harmony, balance, and equilibrium (Beinfield & Korngold, 1991; Porkert, 1974; Veith, 1972; Walters, 1991). Furthermore, the Five Agents are derived from the interplay of yin and yang and are, therefore, conceived of as being but five aspects of the same one unity. Chou Tun-I also wrote,

By the transformation of yang and its union with yin, the Five Agents of Water, Fire, Wood, Metal and Earth arise. When these five material forces are distributed in harmonious order, the four seasons run their course. The Five Agents constitute one system of yin and yang, and yin and yang constitute one Great Ultimate. (quoted in Chan, 1963, p. 463)

Thus in the Confucian model everything and everyone in the universe is interconnected and part of continuous cycles of change. When these cycles follow the natural order of the universe there is harmony and equilibrium, and when there is harmony and equilibrium the natural order of the universe will be manifest. In both the Confucian and Taoist traditions, the natural order and cycles of the universe are called the Tao, or Way (Graham, 1989). If one follows the Way, all will be right; if one loses the Way, misfortune will result.

We are now in a position to compare and contrast the assumptions underlying these two different images/models of change. Selected quotes from leading proponents associated with each model are used to help document the analysis.

Assumptions about Change

The Lewinian-based model underlying OD includes beliefs/assumptions that change is

- *Linear.* One moves from one state to another state in a forward direction through time (past-present-future). "Beckhard and Harris, based on the earlier thinking of Lewin, view the change process in three states: Present State (→) Transition State (→) Future State" (Burke, 1987, pp. 115-116).

- *Progressive.* One moves forward from a current, lesser state to a future, better state. According to Burke (1987), "Developing a new mission, a new vision, a fresh image of the future is the process of creating a desired state . . . that is more desirable than the present state" (p. 115).

- *Destination or goal oriented.* One moves toward a specific end state or goal that one sets out to achieve. "In their formulations of change objectives, most change agents reveal an implicit assumption that movement toward the final change goal is a sequential process" (Lippitt, Watson, & Westley, 1958, p. 100).

- *Based on creating disequilibrium.* To get movement from the current state, one intentionally creates disequilibrium to alter the field of forces. Then one moves to the desired state where equilibrium is reestablished. According to Lewin (1951), "The unfreezing of the present level may involve quite different problems in different cases. ... To break open the shell of complacency and self-righteousness it is sometimes necessary to bring about deliberately an emotional stir-up" (pp. 228-229).

- *Planned and managed by people who exist separate from and act on things to achieve their goals.* People learn and apply the principles about how to master and manipulate the forces in the world so as to achieve their intended ends. "(The) question of planned change or any 'social engineering' is identical with the question: what 'conditions' have to be changed to bring about a given result and how can one change these conditions with the means at hand?" (Lewin, 1951, p. 172). People also exist separate and apart from the objects of their planned change interventions. As Argyris (1970) notes,

  > To intervene is to enter into an ongoing system of relationship, to come between or among persons, groups, or objects for the purpose of helping them. There is an important implicit assumption in the definition that should be made more explicit: the system exists independently of the intervenor. (p. 15)

- *Unusual, because everything is normally in a quasi-stationary or static state.* Unless something is done proactively, things tend to stay in the same place or condition. In fact, extra force is often needed to overcome inertia. Furthermore, once you disrupt the steady state and move to a new state, it is then assumed that you can and will remain there if some stabilizing actions are taken. "A successful change includes, therefore, three aspects: *unfreezing* (if necessary) the present level, *moving* to the new level, and *freezing* group life on the new level" (Lewin, 1947, p. 34, emphasis in the original).

The Confucian (and Taoist) model(s) includes beliefs/assumptions that change is

- *Cyclical.* There is a constant ebb and flow to the universe and everything in it is cyclical. No matter what begins, it always ends. No matter what ends, it always begins. According to the Sung Neo-Confucian philosopher Chu Hsi (1130-1200 A.D.),

  > There is no other event in the universe except yin and yang succeeding each other in an unceasing cycle. This is called Change" (quoted in Chan, 1963, p. 641).

- *Processional.* One moves from one condition/form/state to the next condition/form/state in an orderly sequence. If not, disharmony, disequilibrium, and misfortune result. The Han Confucian philosopher Tung Chung-shu (c. 179-c. 104 B.C.) wrote,

  > Wood produces Fire, Fire produces Earth, Earth produces Metal, Metal produces Water, and Water produces Wood. ... Each of the Five Agents succeeds the others according to its order. Each of them performs its official function by fulfilling its capacity (quoted in Chan, 1963, p. 279).

- *Journey oriented.* Because there is continual cyclical change it makes no sense to aspire to reach an "end state." What matters is how well one follows the Way along the great wheel of life. Confucius said, "The Odes are three hundred in number. They can be summed up in one phrase: swerving not from the right Path" (quoted in Lau, 1979, p. 63).

- *Based on maintaining equilibrium.* The universe and everything in it is naturally harmonious, perfect, and in flux. Therefore, one intervenes/acts only as it is necessary to maintain or restore balance, harmony, and equilibrium. The Confucian classic, The Doctrine of the Mean (unknown, 500-200 B.C.?) states in part,

> Equilibrium is the great foundation of the world, and harmony its universal path. When equilibrium and harmony are realized to the highest degree, Heaven and Earth will attain their proper order and all things will flourish (quoted in Chan, 1963, p. 98).

- *Observed and followed by people who are one with everything and must act correctly to maintain harmony in the universe.* One constantly strives to be in harmony with the Way, the natural order of the universe. Because everything and everyone in the universe is interconnected, by bringing oneself into harmony one brings the universe into harmony. Yi Yulgok (1536-1584 A.D.), a Korean Neo-Confucian philosopher, wrote,

> The ruler, by correcting his mind, corrects all directions. When all directions are corrected the *ch'i* (vital energy) of Heaven and Earth is also corrected. ...Once the *ch'i* of Heaven and Earth is in correct order, how can the sun and moon invade each other, or the stars lose their correct places? Once the *ch'i* of Heaven and Earth is in harmony, how can storm and lightning threaten with their fearsome power, or wind, cloud, frost and snow lose their proper time? (quoted in Ro, 1989, p. 34)

- *Usual, because everything is normally in a continually changing dynamic state.* The continual process of everything in the universe is change. The Yin-Yang Law of Opposites says everything contains its own negation, so nothing remains the same forever (Munro, 1969). The Ming Neo-Confucian philosopher Wang Ji (1498-1583 A.D.) wrote,

> As human beings, we must take creation and transformation as our study. From nonbeing, creation manifests being. From being, transformation returns to nonbeing. Our pure awareness gives birth to heaven, earth, and the myriad things, and heaven, earth, and the myriad beings in turn go back to nonbeing. There is no time when creation and transformation are not operating; they never stop or pause. (quoted in Cleary, 1991, p. 49)

Implications for Action

Thus being long lasting does not mean being in a fixed and definite state. Being fixed and definite, a thing cannot last long. The way to be constant is to change according to circumstances. (Ch'eng I, quoted in Chan, 1963, p. 571)

The major contrasting characteristics of the OD and Confucian models of change are summarized in Table 7.1.

Table 7.1
Assumptions about Change

Lewinian / OD   **Confucian / East Asian**

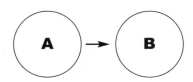   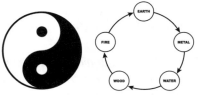

Change Is:	**Change Is:**
1. *Linear.* One moves from one state to another state in a forward direction.	1. *Cyclical.* There is a constant ebb and flow to the universe and everything in it is cyclical.
2. *Progressive.* One moves from a less to a more desired state.	2. *Processional.* One moves constantly from one condition/form/state to the next condition/form/state in an orderly sequence through a cycle.
3. *Destination Oriented.* One moves towards a specific end state.	3. *Journey Oriented.* Because there is constant cyclical change, what matters is how well one follows the Way.
4. *Based on Creating Disequilibrium.* In order to get movement from the current state, one must alter the equilibrium of the status quo.	4. *Based on Restoring/Maintaining Equilibrium.* Everything is naturally in harmony and perfect. One acts only as needed to restore balance and equilibrium.
5. *Planned and Managed by People Who Exist Separate From and Act on Things to Achieve their Goals.* One learns the principles about how to master and manipulate the forces in the world in order to achieve one's own ends.	5. *Observed and Followed by People Who are One With Everything and Must Act Correctly to Maintain Harmony in the Universe.* One constantly strives to be in harmony with the Way, the natural order of the universe.
6. *Unusual, Because Everything Is Normally in a Quasi-Stationary or Static State.* Unless something is done, things will stay the same because a body at rest stays at rest until force is applied.	6. *Usual, Because Everything Is Normally in a Continually Changing Dynamic State.* The continual process of everything in the universe is change. The Yin-Yang Law of Opposites says everything contains its own negation, so nothing stays forever.

What is most important to realize about this analysis is that the differences in underlying assumptions between the two models are likely to lead to quite different actions and orientations toward change and change methods. To illustrate this point more clearly, consider the following comparisons.

Linear-Progressive versus Cyclical-Processional

When change is viewed as linear and progressive, it is logically inappropriate and/or impossible to go back to something that came before (in the less effective past). The focus of attention and action(s) is on striving toward the (better) future. As a result, redoing something in the linear-progressive model is likely to be viewed as "going backward," "not making progress," or "going around in circles." To repeat something is almost synonymous with failure and is frequently avoided even when needed. Thus in a team-building intervention, the focus might be to move the team through various stages of group development until it becomes a "high performing team." Returning at that point to an earlier stage, such as group formation or norm setting, would be viewed negatively because the (implicit) objective is to achieve and maintain (permanently) the high performance stage. This contrasts with the Confucian model where cyclical and processional change is the natural Way and returning to some stage/phase/state, albeit in a different form perhaps, is normal and needed to maintain continuing harmony and equilibrium. In a cyclical model, after all, "going around in circles" is both normal and necessary. Returning to something is not only expected but, in fact, needed to "keep things moving."

Furthermore, in a cyclical-processional model no stage is presumed to be better than another. Each stage is just different and necessary to maintain the natural cycle. Consequently, in the cyclical-processional model, one would assume there is a stage after high performance (perhaps decline or deforming) that the team would naturally move into after achieving peak performance. Deforming or decline would then inherently lead to team re-forming, re-norming, and so on, back to high performance and decline in endless cycles. Thus the Confucian change agent would work to facilitate harmonious movement through all the natural stages of the cycle, whereas the OD change agent might be more likely to be called in to help move the team to a higher level of performance and then try to keep it there (see Figure 7.4).

Table 7.4
Two Views of Team Development

Linear – Progressive   **Cyclical – Processional**

As a result, each might respond differently to the situation of a mature team beginning to experience increased conflict, loss of purpose, challenges to established norms and/or leadership, and the like. The OD change agent might view this as a form of "backsliding" and pursue interventions to reestablish the team's purpose, norms, collaboration, and leadership. The Confucian change agent might see, instead, a team entering the deforming stage and pursue interventions to help the team first deform (de-establish itself) so as to begin forming new purposes, new norms, new ways of resolving conflict, and new leadership patterns.

Destination versus Journey Oriented

When change is viewed as goal or destination oriented, the primary emphasis is on setting and achieving objectives, targets, and end states. Indeed, many could scarcely conceive of starting a change effort without the clear goal of an end state that is better than the present situation. Thus most OD interventions begin with data collection to help establish the discrepancies between current and desired conditions or with a visioning or goal-setting session to establish what to achieve in the change effort. Milestones and targets are set and evaluations conducted to assess how well or to what degree the desired end state is really achieved. The reward is not in the journey but in reaching the pot of gold at the end of the rainbow. In a cyclical model, however, where there is no end state per se, one strives continuously to enhance in the present moment how well one conducts the journey, that is, follows the Way. The better one follows the Way, the more every aspect of one's being and doing is enhanced and, therefore, the more likely just rewards will naturally result. Consequently, improvements for the sake of improvements, without the need for a specific goal, or problem to fix, are more likely to be compatible with a cyclical journey model than with a linear destination one. The journey-oriented change agent therefore would be prepared to help a client system learn how to improve itself continuously, regardless of its current condition. This could be done, for example, by helping the system align itself with some set of universal principles to follow and emulate constantly (e.g., the Way). Thus at the beginning of a change effort, an OD-oriented change agent might seek first to initiate activities and interventions intended to set specific goals and/or objectives. The Confucian-oriented change agent might instead first pursue activities and interventions that emphasize the "proper" orientation, way of being, and/or behavioral values that would need to be continuously exhibited.

Create Disequilibrium versus Maintain Equilibrium

When change is viewed as something initiated by creating disequilibrium, it is both appropriate and necessary to disrupt current conditions so as to "break away" and move forward. Consequently, the OD model instructs change agents to focus on developing the means and methods for creating disruptions to the status quo to overcome resistance and get movement toward the change goal(s). In short, change must be consciously induced by a change agent acting on an otherwise fixed situation.

On the other hand, when change is seen to be initiated by the natural ebbs and flows of the universe, then unnatural disruptions should be avoided because they would interrupt and/or distort the natural change process. This, in turn, would threaten the inherent harmony and equilibrium of the universe. The Confucian model, therefore, instructs the change agent to find, follow, and/or restore the natural harmony and equilibrium inherent in all situations. Thus the focus would be on harmonizing disruptions and/or restoring balance to a client system. An organization experiencing rapid growth might require additional emphasis on systems and procedures to keep things in balance, or too great an emphasis on existing product lines might signal a need for more innovation.

The Confucian approach could also include seemingly nonsense or paradoxical interventions from the frame of the OD model. In the OD model, the way to move to the desired future state is to focus on breaking away from the present state. In a cyclical processional model, where each state succeeds the completion of the prior state, the way to move from one state to the next is to focus on fully realizing the present. Change toward the next state begins immediately after the present state reaches its zenith (e.g., the way to induce activity is to become fully tranquil). Thus the Confucian change agent might first help an organization become more completely centralized to facilitate movement toward decentralization. One follows the Way to the correct future by fully actualizing and harmonizing the present.

Another example might be the challenge of changing an "authoritarian" management system into a more open and participative one. The OD-oriented change agent might immediately pursue interventions to confront and/or expose the negative impacts of the authoritarian system so as to disrupt the status quo and facilitate movement to a more open and participative system. In contrast, a change agent oriented toward maintaining harmony might pursue one or another of the following approaches. First, by looking to harmonize with the natural, continuous changes inherent in all situations, the change agent might assume that the authoritarian system was a stage/phase that needed to be fully "played out" before the system would move, on its own, to another management stage/phase. Therefore the approach would be to wait to intervene until the time was ripe and then act to facilitate harmonizing with the new and/or emerging system. Alternatively, the authoritarian system might be viewed as "out of harmony" with the proper Way. If viewed in that manner, the approach would be to pursue more direct interventions to restore balance and harmony, even if fundamental and/or "revolutionary" change was required. After all, in Confucian China, revolution was considered a legitimate means to replace an emperor who had lost the "Mandate of Heaven" by ruling in a manner not in harmony with the Way.

Separate From versus One with the Client System

When people are understood to exist separate from, but capable of acting on, things in the rest of the universe, it is appropriate to begin a change effort by planning the desired end state and then working with the client system to bring it into alignment with the desired change goal(s). Alternatively, when people are seen as being one with everything and needing to behave correctly to maintain the Way, it would be appropriate to begin and continue a change effort by working to bring oneself into alignment with the Way, modeling the Way to the client system, and ensuring that one and all behave correctly, according to the Way, in all circumstances. Thus the fundamental relationship of change agent and system differs in the two models. In the one it is assumed that the change agent stands apart, as a neutral catalyst, from the change itself. In the other, the change agent is one with the system, and both are inexorably linked as interdependent aspects of the same Way. As a result, the OD change agent may be more preoccupied with planning what *to do* and how to do it in a client system, whereas the Confucian change agent might focus more on serving as a role model of how *to be* so as to bring the client system into harmony (with the Way). Thus in a contracting meeting, the OD change agent might focus more on what needs to be done, when, where, and how in such areas as diagnosis, feedback, intervention planning, and so forth. The Confucian change agent might instead emphasize and role-model the need for the change agent and client leader to behave consistent with the Way (or some set of principles), as the primary means to bring the client system into proper alignment. Although each might be concerned to some degree about what to do and how to be, the primary emphasis would be different.

Static versus Dynamic Universe

When the normal condition of most entities in the universe is thought to be primarily static, or reflecting quasi-stationary equilibrium, constant change would be experienced as dangerous, abnormal, or chaotic. People would likely seek to stop continuous changes so as to restore "order," that is, a more stable, stationary state. After all, the OD change model instructs change agents that their final task is to *refreeze* a situation. This is done precisely to stop the continuous movement of the unfrozen state. Alternatively, when the normal condition of all entities is viewed as undergoing continual, inherent change (i.e., being fluid), then stopping the ongoing changes would be experienced as dangerous, abnormal, and inviting chaos. Instead, people would likely seek to restore and/or harmonize with the natural change cycles. Thus the Confucian change agent would seek to discover and remove blockages so as to restore the natural ebb and flow of everything. In sum, the OD change agent plans how to start and stop movement to achieve a desired steady state, whereas the Confucian change agent seeks to release or remove blockages created by static, stagnant, and/or stuck conditions to restore the natural flow, harmony, and balance of the Way. For example, at the end of a change initiative, an OD change agent might focus on interventions intended to maintain the change (e.g., adding new norms, new reward systems, new values, new training, etc.). The Confucian change agent might focus less on maintaining anything and more on how to keep changing with grace and harmony (e.g., ways to enhance continuous learning and/or adaptation).

Summary

The above discussion suggests that change agents operating from the OD model will approach situations and take actions based on a different conception of change and change processes than will change agents operating from a Confucian model. The change agent guided by the OD model of change is likely to seek to help determine an end state that is better than the current state, to find ways to unfreeze the current situation so as to move directly to the desired state, and then help refreeze the situation so as to maintain it. This is all done from the stance of a neutral third party, that is, someone not an integral part of the system in question. In contrast, the change agent guided by a Confucian model of change is likely to seek to help the system find and follow the Way (the natural order and principles guiding the situation), to work to help restore balance and equilibrium to the system, and help enable the system to move continuously through the natural cycles inherent to its existence. This would all be done from the stance of a person who is one with the system and who has the responsibility to role-model or embody the Way in everything that is said or done (as a primary form of intervention).

Implications for Research and Theory

The ranks of stars revolve in procession, the sun and moon shine in turn, the seasons succeed one another, the forces of yin and yang (alternate) in great transformation. (Hsün Tzu, quoted in Eno, 1990, p. 198)

Based on the above analysis it is possible to conjecture about the relative robustness of each set of assumptions for addressing different change scenarios. An illustrative list of such hypotheses is shown in Table 7.2.

Table 7.2
Some Potential Impacts of Different Aspects of Change

Assumption	More Effective When	Less Effective When
Linear-progressive	The current situation can be contrasted unfavorably with some future condition	It is hard to prove there is something wrong with current conditions
Cyclical-processional	Required to move from a current satisfactory situation to a different one	Need to secure "gains" and/or maintain a specific plateau or condition
Destination oriented	A specific achievable goal can be clearly articulated	A specific goal is absent, unclear, and/or cannot be provided
Journey oriented	Continuous enhancements are needed without a given problem or goal	Need to focus more on the goal than the means
Create disequilibrium	Need to challenge the status quo or marshal forces to create change	Need to accept things as they are and harmonize with them
Maintain equilibrium	Need to harmonize while waiting for the appropriate moment of change	Challenging or disrupting the (natural) order of things
Planned and managed	Need analysis of what to do to modify or change existing factors and forces	Required to "go with the flow" against one's wishes and desires
Observed and followed	Observing natural "rhythm" of change and aligning oneself and other with it	Need to act in opposition to flow of events (e.g., "swim against the tide")
Change is unusual	Dealing with stuck or static situations	Facing continual change without the chance to stop and plan
Change is usual	Adapting to constantly changing conditions while maintaining equilibrium	Need to plan ways to defend and/or stabilize a particular situation

Taken individually, and especially as a set, the examples can be formulated into testable hypotheses about the relative effectiveness of the Lewinian model of change in different situations and the relative effectiveness of the Confucian model of change in the same or similar settings. For example, two hypotheses are suggested by Table 7.2:

Hypothesis 1:   OD will be more successful when called on to create change toward a specific goal and less successful in addressing continual change, especially absent clearly stated goals. This will be particularly true in cultural settings with similar assumptions about change.

Hypothesis 2:   A Confucian approach to change will be more successful when called on to pursue continuous enhancements without need of a specified problem and less successful in challenging the (natural) order of things. This will be particularly true in cultural settings with similar assumptions about change.

Anecdotal and testimonial data alone would suggest that these hypotheses cannot be rejected on their face. Therefore, this might be a fruitful line of inquiry for field research.

A second line of inquiry is also suggested by Table 7.2. Based on the alternative assumption sets about change presented in Table 7.2, it is possible to hypothesize about the nature of cross-cultural difficulties that could be experienced in the application of OD. For example, an OD consultant operating from the assumptions associated with the Lewinian model of change when dealing with a client system operating from the assumptions associated with the Confucian model of change would be predicted to encounter confusion and various forms of "resistance." Furthermore, based on a consideration of the specific assumptions involved, the nature of the "resistance" might also be predictable. For example, attempts to focus on setting and achieving clear-cut goals might be "resisted" if appropriate attention was not also being paid to observing the proper way of doing things. Requests for the client to take a stand and speak out against the system might be "resisted" because that would threaten the (natural) order of things. Alternatively, the client might perceive the OD consultant as unusually brash and/or reckless because of a failure to pay adequate attention to the rhythm of change and therefore the proper time for action.

The Confucian-oriented client might also wonder about the OD consultant's ability to maintain balance and equilibrium in the face of constantly changing conditions, especially if the consultant's first response is to challenge and/or confront the causes of the changes in an attempt to gain stability and control. Thus a range of hypotheses related to the outcomes of specific interactions in cross-cultural settings could be developed and tested.

A third line of inquiry might combine the first two approaches into a contingency model based on the nature of the change(s) and the assumption set. For example, if the OD model of change is an effective approach for dealing with a particular situation and it also matches the client system's assumptions and models about change, then success might be predicted. Similarly, a mismatch on both dimensions would be predictive of failure. Of more interest is what happens when the situation is mixed: OD fits the change situation but not the client system's assumptions about change; or OD fits the client system's assumptions about change but not the nature of the change situation. These possibilities are summarized in Table 7.3.

Table 7.3
OD Contingencies

		OD and Nature of Required Change	
		Match	Mismatch
	Match	Successful Approach and Outcomes	Support for Approach, but Potential for Poor Results
OD and Client Models of Change			
	Mismatch	Resistance to Approach, but Potential for Good Results	Failure in Approach and Outcomes

Research that controlled for differences in types of required change(s) as well as for the models of change held by the OD consultant and host system could be especially revealing. This line of research might be clearest in international settings but could also be conducted within a particular national culture, as assumptions vary across subcultures and organizations.

Finally, this analysis, along with the earlier discussion of different types of change, suggests at least one approach for developing a unified theory incorporating both models of change. As previously noted, many authors have commented on the differences between the change processes that occur during times of an established underlying paradigm (Kuhn, 1962), deep structure (Gersick, 1991), or "pattern" (Land & Jarman, 1992) and those that occur when the underlying pattern itself shifts. The former processes are usually described as developmental/evolutionary, whereas the latter are seen as revolutionary/transformational. When looked at together, however, the ongoing process of paradigm/pattern birth, development, maturity, decline, death, and birth of a new paradigm/pattern is best described using both models. Change is both linear within a particular pattern and cyclical as different patterns emerge, then dissolve, emerge, and then dissolve again (Land & Jarman, 1992). Change may be progressive within a pattern but is processional between patterns (Gersick, 1991). Changes within a pattern may be goal oriented, but it is the quality of the journey that matters when moving between patterns (Land & Jarman, 1992). Creating disequilibrium may be necessary for change to occur within a pattern, but harmonizing with a new pattern as it emerges is essential for successful change between patterns (Kuhn, 1962).

Table 7.4
Within and Between Pattern Change

Change Processes Within a Pattern Are:	Change Processes Between Patterns Are:
Linear	Cyclical
Progressive	Processional
Goal oriented	Journey oriented
Based on creating disequilibrium	Based on returning to equilibrium
Planned and managed	Observed and followed
Unusual, or temporary, because conditions are more stable	Usual, or continuous, because conditions are more dynamic

Change can be planned and managed within the context of an established pattern but must be observed and followed when an old pattern ends and a new pattern emerges (Land & Jarman, 1992). Finally, an established underlying pattern provides a more stable, or quasi-stationary, context within which (temporary) changes occur, whereas change between underlying patterns is inherently more fluid, dynamic, and chaotic (Gersick, 1991). These observations about within- and between-pattern-change processes are summarized in Table 7.4.

This embryonic unified theory of developmental-transformational change, incorporating aspects of both the Lewinian and Confucian models, may or may not prove viable. It does, however, offer a promising schema that includes yin and yang, the Five Forces, and present-to-future-state "models" and images. That is, patterns emerge, dissolve, emerge, dissolve; there is continuous cyclical movement from birth (Wood) to growth (Fire) to maturity (Earth) to decline (Metal) and then death (Water), leading again to birth (Wood); and there is movement from a present state to a future state both within and between patterns.

Conclusion

> To begin in an orderly fashion is the concern of the wise, while to end in an orderly fashion is the concern of a sage. (Mencius, quoted in Lau, 1970, p. 150)

The change model that one explicitly or implicitly operates from has a great deal to do with how one thinks about and goes about a change effort. To the degree that OD change agents follow the Lewinian model of change, their theories and methods may prove to be out of step with those operating, explicitly or implicitly, from other models of change. This is more likely to occur as OD moves from its North American roots into countries and cultures historically or presently based on different cosmologies. Thus more research into the change models and assumptions inherent in different cultures is needed not only to alert sensitive OD practitioners but to expand the range of change theories and methods. For example, this discussion focused on the dynamic cyclical model of change that is part of most East Asian cultural traditions. Beyond the scope of this article, but equally relevant, are the models of change inherent to other cultural traditions (e.g., different African cultures, Native American cultures, and so on). An example of this line of research is Srinivas (in press), who compares and contrasts different aspects of OD with traditional Indian religio-philosophical ideals and practices.

Furthermore, we may need to alter or amend our model(s) of change as we enter the 21st century and confront the revolutionary changes that lie ahead. Besides drawing on wisdom residing in other cultures, both ancient and modern, recent discoveries and theories in the "new sciences," especially physics, may prove helpful (Goldstein, 1993; Wheatley, 1992). Newton's mechanical universe has been challenged and is no longer preeminent in physics, yet the worldview he helped create lives on in many guises (Capra, 1982; Tarnas, 1991). One, perhaps, is OD, where the unfreeze-movement-refreeze change model is strikingly similar, both theoretically and metaphorically, to Newtonian physics where movement results from the application of a set of forces on an object (Capra, 1982; Lakoff & Johnson, 1980; Marshak, 1993b; Zukav, 1979). As a reminder, Newton's First Law of Motion (written in 1687) states, "Every body preserves in its state of being at rest or of moving uniformly straight forward, except insofar as it is compelled to change its state by forces impressed upon it" (quoted in Gregory, 1988, p. 23). Interestingly, "the new physics" that have challenged Newton's universe have been compared to the Eastern dynamic, cyclical, interconnected models of the universe presented here (Capra, 1982, 1984). Clearly, a new or greatly revised theory or theories of organizational change that reflects a synthesis of the linear and cyclical models needs to be born. That would surely please both Lewin and Confucius.

Notes

1. Confucian philosophy developed over a period of several thousands of years, beginning with Confucius (Master K'ung, 551-479 B.C.). Most notably, it was reinvigorated and further developed by Mencius (Meng K'e, 371-289 B.C.?) and then extended and organized into an orthodoxy by the Sung, Neo-Confucian Chu Hsi (1130-1200 A.D.), whose orthodoxy was challenged and modified by the Ming Neo-Confucian Wang Yang-ming (1472-1529 A.D.). In addition to further developing Confucian philosophy, Neo-Confucianism also incorporated various aspects of Taoism and Buddhism without abandoning the central tenets of the Confucian worldview. Hence there are both similarities and differences among the three great pillars of Eastern wisdom.

2. Indeed, the *I Ching* is one of the five Confucian classics of antiquity, along with the *Book of History, Book of Odes, Book of Ritual*, and *Spring* and *Autumn Annals*. Later, Chu Hsi (1130-1200 A.D.) grouped *The Great Learning* (500-200 B.C.?), *The Analects of Confucius* (551-479 B.C.), *The Book of Mencius* (371-289 B.C.?), and *The Doctrine of the Mean* (500-200 B.C.?) to form the classic canon of Confucian philosophy. In 1313, these "Four Books" became required texts of the Imperial Chinese education system and the basis for the prestigious civil service examinations. Korea followed in kind in 1392 with the founding of the Yi Dynasty as an official Confucian State. Confucianism remained the official doctrine in China and Korea until the end of the dynasties in both countries at the beginning of the 20th century.

References

Ackerman, L. S. (1986). Development, transition, or transformation: The question of change in organizations. *OD Practitioner*, 18(4), 1-5.

Adler, N. J. (1991). *International dimensions of organizational behavior* (2nd ed.). Boston: PWS-Kent.

Argyris, C. (1970). *Intervention theory and method: A behavioral science view*. Reading, MA: Addison-Wesley.

Argyris, C. (1990). Inappropriate defenses against the monitoring of organization development practice. *Journal of Applied Behavioral Science, 26*(3), 299-312.

Armstrong, T. R. (1993). Reflections on OD and its future. *Organization Development Journal, 11*(2), 33-38.

Beinfield, H., & Korngold, E. (1991). *Between heaven and earth: A guide to Chinese medicine.* New York: Ballantine.

Boss, W. R., & Mariono, M. V. (1987). Organization development in Italy. *Group & Organization Studies, 12*(3), 245-256.

Boyacigiller, N., & Adler, N. J. (1991). The parochial dinosaur: Organizational science in a global context. *Academy of Management Review, 16*(2), 262-290.

Burke, W. W. (1987). *Organization development: A normative view.* Reading, MA: Addison-Wesley.

Capra, F. (1982). *The turning point.* New York: Simon & Schuster.

Capra, F. (1984). *The tao of physics* (2nd ed.). New York: Bantam.

Chai, C., & Chai, W. (1973). *Confucianism.* New York: Barron's Educational Series.

Chan, W. T. (Trans. and Ed.). (1963). *A source book in Chinese philosophy.* Princeton, NJ: Princeton University Press.

Cleary, J. C. (Trans. and Ed.). (1991). *Worldly wisdom: Confucian teachings of the Ming dynasty.* Boston: Shambhala.

Cleary, T. (Trans.). (1992). *I ching.* Boston: Shambhala.

DeBary, W. T., Chan, W. T., & Watson, B. (1960). *Sources of Chinese tradition, Volume 1.* New York: Columbia University Press.

Eno, R. (1990). *The Confucian creation of heaven.* Albany: State University of New York Press.

Gersick, C. J. G. (1991). Revolutionary change theories: A multilevel exploration of the punctuated equilibrium paradigm. *Academy of Management Review, 16*(1), 10-36.

Goldstein, J. (1993). Revisioning the organization: Chaos, quantum physics, and OD - An interview with Margaret Wheatley, Ed.D. *Organization Development Journal, 11*(2), 85-91.

Golembiewski, R. T. (1987). Is OD narrowly culture bound? Prominent features of 100 Third World applications. *Organization Development Journal, 6*(Winter), 20-29.

Golembiewski, R. T. (1991). Organization Development in the Third World: Values, closeness of fit and culture-boundedness. *International Journal of Human Resource Management, 2*(1), 39-53.

Graham, A. C. (1989). *Disputers of the Tao.* LaSalle, IL: Open Court.

Gregory, B. (1988). *Inventing reality: Physics as language.* New York: Wiley.

Greiner, L. E. (1972). Evolution and revolution as organizations grow. *Harvard Business Review, 50*(4), 37-46.

Hall, D. L., & Ames, R. T. (1987). *Thinking through Confucius.* Albany: State University of New York Press.

Hammer, M., & Champy, J. (1993). *Reengineering the corporation.* New York: Harper Collins.

Hofstede, G. (1980a). Motivation, leadership, and organizations: Do American theories apply abroad? *Organizational Dynamics, 8*(Summer), 42-63.

Hofstede, G. (1980b). *Culture's consequences.* Beverly Hills, CA: Sage.

Hofstede, G. (1993). Cultural constraints in management theories. *The Executive,* 7 (1), 81-94.

Hofstede, G., & Bond, M. H. (1988). Confucius and economic growth: New trends in culture's consequences. *Organizational Dynamics, 16*(4), 4-21.

Jaeger, A. M. (1984). The appropriateness of organization development outside North America. *International Studies of Management and Organization, 14*(1), 23-25.

Jaeger, A. M. (1986). Organization development and national culture: Where's the fit? *Academy of Management Review, 11*(1), 178-190.

Johnson, K. R. (1990). Organization development in the context of opposed cultural values: The case of OD in Venezuela. *Organization Development Journal, 6*(3), 73-75.

Katz, J. H., & Marshak, R. J. (1993). Innovation: Reinventing our profession. In S. Zilber (Ed.), *Celebrating the spirit of renewal: Proceedings of the 1993 National OD Network Conference.* Portland, OR: National OD Network.

Kiggundu, M. N. (1990). Limitations to application of socio-technical systems in developing cultures. In A. M. Jaeger & R. N. Kanungo (Eds.), *Management in developing countries.* London: Routledge.

Kuhn, T. S. (1962). *The structure of scientific revolutions.* Chicago: University of Chicago Press.

Lakoff, G., & Johnson, M. (1980). *Metaphors we live by.* Chicago: University of Chicago Press.

Land, G., & Jarman, B. (1992). *Breakpoint change and beyond.* New York: Harper Collins.

Lau, D. C. (1970). *Mencius.* New York: Penguin Books.

Lau, D. C. (1979). *Confucius: The analects.* New York: Penguin Books.

Legge, J. (Trans.). (1882). *I ching: The sacred books of the East, Vol. 16.* Oxford: Clarendon.

Legge, J. (Trans.). (1893). *Confucian analects, the great learning and the doctrine of the mean: The Chinese classics, Volume 1* (2nd ed.). Oxford: Clarendon.

Lewin, K. (1947). Frontiers in group dynamics. *Human Relations,* 1(1), 5-41.

Lewin, K. (1951). *Field theory in social science.* New York: Harper & Row.

Lippitt, R., Watson, J., & Westley, B. (1958). *The dynamics of planned change.* New York: Harcourt, Brace & World.

Loewe, M. (1982). *Chinese ideas of life and death.* London: Allen & Unwin.

Marrow, A. J. (1969). *The practical theorist: The life and work of Kurt Lewin.* New York: Basic Books.

Marshak, R. J. (1993a). Training and consulting in Korea. *OD Practitioner, 25*(2), 16-21.

Marshak, R. J. (1993b). Managing the metaphors of change. *Organizational Dynamics, 22*(1), 44-56.

McDonald, M. (Ed.). (1990). Forging revolutionary partnerships: 1990 *OD Network Conference Proceedings.* Portland, OR: OD Network.

Mirvis, P. H., & Berg, D. N. (1977). *Failures in organization development and change: Cases and essays for learning.* New York: Wiley.

Munro, D. J. (1969). *The concept of man in early China.* Stanford, CA: Stanford University Press.

Nakamura, H. (1964). *Ways of thinking of Eastern peoples: India-China-Tibet-Japan.* Honolulu: University of Hawaii Press.

Porkert, M. (1974). *The theoretical foundations of Chinese medicine*. Cambridge: MIT Press.

Reyes-Sagun, L. (1988). Philippine value system: Its implications to a successful organization development effort. *Organization Development Journal, 6*(3), 73-75.

Richards, D. (1991). Flying against the wind: Culture and management development in South-East Asia. *Journal of Management Development, 10*(6), 7-21.

Rikuta, M. (1987). Organization development within Japanese industry: Facts and prospects. *Organization Development Journal, 5*(2), 21-32.

Ro, Y. C. (1989). *The Korean Neo-Confucianism of Yi Yulgok*. Albany: State University of New York Press.

Rozman, G. (Ed.). (1991). *The East Asian region: Confucian heritage and its modern adaptation*. Princeton, NJ: Princeton University Press.

Srinivas, K. M. (in press). Organization development: Maya or moksha. In R. N. Kanungo & M. Mendonca (Eds.), *Work motivation: Models for developing societies*. New Delhi: Sage.

Tainio, R., & Santalainen, T. (1984). Some evidence for the cultural relativity of organizational development programs. *Journal of Applied Behavioral Science, 20*(2), 93-111.

Tannenbaum, R., & Davis, S. A. (1969). Values, man and organizations. *Industrial Management Review, 10*(2), 67-83.

Tarnas, R. (1991). *The passion of the Western mind*. New York: Harmony Books.

Thorne, S., & Hogan, L. (1993). ODN future search: Listening to our membership. *OD Practitioner, 25*(1), 2-7.

Tu, W., Hejtmanek, M., & Wachman, A. (Eds.). (1992). *The Confucian world observed: A contemporary discussion of Confucian humanism in East Asia*. Honolulu, HI: East-West Center.

Vaill, P. B. (1989). *Managing as a performing art*. San Francisco: Jossey-Bass.

Van Eynde, D. E., & Coruzzi, C. (1993). ODN future search: A word from our senior practitioners. *OD Practitioner, 25*(1), 8-16.

Veith, I. (Trans.). (1972). *The Yellow Emperor's classic of internal medicine*. Berkeley: University of California Press.

Waley, A. (Trans.). (1938). *The analects of Confucius*. New York: Macmillan.

Walters, D. (1991). *The feng shui handbook*. London: Aquarian Press.

Weick, K. E. (1990). Fatigue of the spirit in organizational theory and organization development: Reconnaissance man as remedy. *Journal of Applied Behavioral Science, 26*(3), 313-328.

Wheatley, M. (1992). *Leadership and the new science*. San Francisco: Berrett-Koehler.

Wilhelm, H. (1960). *Change: Eight lectures on the i ching* (C. F Baynes, Trans). Princeton, NJ: Princeton University Press.

Wilhelm, R. (1979). *Lectures on the i ching: Constancy and change* (I. Eber, Trans.). Princeton, NJ: Princeton University Press.

Wilhelm, R., & Baynes, C. F (Trans.). (1950). *The i ching.* New York: Bollinger Foundation.

Zilber, S. (Ed.). (1993). *Celebrating the spirit of renewal: Proceedings of the 1993 National OD Network Conference*. Portland, OR: National OD Network.

Zukav, G. (1979). *The dancing wu li masters.* New York: William Morrow.

8
The Tao of Change

After more than 40 years of searching for the Promised Land of "desired end states," perhaps it is time OD as a profession started thinking about "going around in circles." This somewhat surprising conclusion came to me following a recently completed personal odyssey.

The focus of this article is on East-West assumptions about change, after previous speculation about culturally based differences in East-West learning styles (see Marshak, 1993a). The stimulus for both articles was the same: a series of training/consulting trips to South Korea during 1990-1991. Those trips came exactly 20 years after spending 47 weeks in intensive Korean language training before being stationed near the DMZ between North and South Korea. After leaving military service and Korea at the end of 1971 to resume graduate studies in OD, I thought I would never return and that my training and immersion into another language and culture had been mostly lost time.

When I eventually returned to Korea at the beginning of the 1990s, the changes were really remarkable, but none more so than my cross-cultural experiences related to change theory. I was scheduled to present a seminar on the "Strategic Management of Change," including developmental and transformational change. But just before leaving the United States, my Korean host called to tell me I was presenting on "management innovation," not "transformational change." When I inquired why, he explained: "Because there is really no word in the Korean language for transformational change the way you mean it." When I asked: "How do you say the caterpillar changed into the butterfly?" He replied: "In Korean, we say the caterpillar *becomes* the butterfly." He then went on to say that many of the Korean words/concepts associated with "transformational change" also carried negative connotations of violent revolution, loss of social order, dissolution, and the like. That telephone conversation, combined with later experiences discussing change and change concepts with Korean managers and trainers, convinced me I needed more than a good English-Korean dictionary to really understand the differences in how change can be viewed on each side of the Pacific Ocean.

Change: Perspectives from East and West

The clues to my questions regarding change somehow were located in the cultural roots of Korea and East Asia. Because Korea, like most of East Asia, is a post-Confucian society, my curiosity led me to the great Chinese sage, Confucius (K'ung Fu-Tzu, 551-479 BC) and Confucian/Neo-Confucian philosophy. Along the way I learned, among other things, that the *I Ching* (*Book of Changes*, circa 1143 BC) is one of the five classics of Confucian philosophy and that, by attribution and legend, Confucius himself wrote the first philosophical commentaries that are incorporated as part of the text. I also learned much more about *yin* and *yang*, and the five forces of wood, fire, earth, metal, and water as primary concepts in Neo-Confucian philosophy. Most important, I discovered an entirely

Marshak, R. J. (1994). The Tao of change. *OD Practitioner, 26*(2), 18-26. Republished with permission.

different world view about the universe and about change. Furthermore, the more I began to understand the Confucian world view the more clearly I came to understand, through contrast, my own world view based primarily in Judeo-Christian, Greco-Roman, and European Enlightenment (e.g., Descartes and Newton) beliefs, assumptions, and concepts.

My intention now is to provide a glimpse of these two views of change as I have come to understand them, and my thoughts about some of the potential implications for OD theory and practice. A more in-depth discussion and analysis of these two models is available elsewhere (Marshak, 1993b).

Change: The OD Perspective

The primary model of change underlying most OD theory and practice is Kurt Lewin's three-stage change process of unfreezing, movement, and refreezing (Lewin, 1947). This model is in the tradition of the Western, scientific world view that presumes linear time, progressive evolution, free will, and the preeminence of rationality (see, for example, Tarnas, 1991). This world view also contains an inherent dualism, including the belief that human beings exist independent of a mostly static phenomenal world that they plan, manage, and otherwise act on. In terms of conceptualizing a change effort, this world view and change model imply a managed process to move from a current state to a more desired future state through the use of planned interventions to overcome resistance, get movement, and thereby alter the status quo. This is shown in Figure 8.1.

Figure 8.1
The OD Model of Change

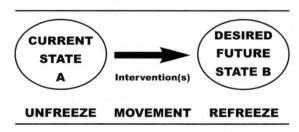

The assumptions inherent in this approach/model include beliefs that change is:

1. *Linear.* One moves from one state to another state in a forward direction.
2. *Progressive.* One moves from a less to a more desired state.
3. *Destination oriented.* One moves toward a specific goal or end state.
4. *Based on creating disequilibrium.* In order to get movement from the current state, one must alter the equilibrium of the status quo.
5. *Planned and managed by people who exist separate from and act on things to achieve their goals.* One learns the principles and practices about how to master and/or facilitate the forces in the world in order to achieve preferred outcomes.

6. *Unusual, because everything is normally in a quasi-stationary or static state.* Unless something is done proactively, things will tend to stay the same. After all, according to Newton's First Law of Motion, a body at rest stays at rest unless force is applied.

This way of thinking about change is so much a part of OD theory and practice, and the cultural milieu from which it was created, that I never thought twice about these underlying assumptions until I discovered a world view based on a different set of assumptions.

Change: The Confucian Perspective

Underlying both Confucian and Taoist philosophy is an alternative world view that presumes the inherent oneness, or interdependence, of everything and everyone in the universe. All are governed by the universal principles of the Way (the *Tao*), including the principle of continual cyclical alternation between the polarities inherent in everything (*yin* and *yang*). In terms of change, this world view is represented by the images of the *T'ai Chi* (the union of *yin* and *yang*) and the *Wu Hsing* (the ordered cyclical relationship among the five forces of the universe represented by wood, fire, earth, metal, and water). These are shown in Figure 8.2.

Figure 8.2
The T'ai Chi and Wu Hsing

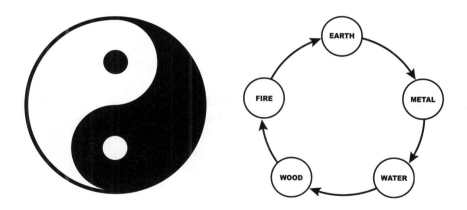

In brief, everyone and everything in the universe is part of ongoing processes of cyclical change. Therefore people, who are interdependent with everything else, must observe and align themselves with the on-going cyclical changes in order to maintain the natural harmony, equilibrium, and perfection of the universe. The assumptions inherent in this approach/model include beliefs that change is:

1. *Cyclical.* There is a constant ebb and flow to the universe and everything in it is cyclical.

2. *Processional.* Everyone and everything moves constantly from one condition/form/state to the next condition/form/state in an orderly sequence through a cycle.

3. *Journey oriented.* Because there is continual cyclical change, there can be no end state, per se. What matters is how well one conducts the journey, i.e., follows the Way.

4. *Based on restoring/maintaining equilibrium.* Everything is naturally in harmony and perfect. Therefore, one acts only when and how needed to restore balance and equilibrium.

5. *Observed and followed by people who are one with everything, and must act correctly to maintain harmony with the universe.* One must constantly strive to be in harmony with the Way, the natural order of the universe.

6. *Usual, because everything is normally in a continually changing dynamic state.* The continual process of everything in the universe is change. The Yin-Yang Law of Opposites says everything contains its own negation, so nothing stays the same forever.

This dynamic, interdependent, cyclical world view has formed Chinese and East Asian ways of thinking and acting for millennia. It is also the foundation for such practices as traditional Chinese medicine (e.g., acupuncture), martial arts (e.g., *T'ai Chi Chuan*), and geomancy (*Feng Shui*). Needless to say, in a dynamic, cyclical world, day becomes night, honor becomes shame, loss becomes gain, death becomes birth, and the "caterpillar becomes the butterfly" – naturally.

Reflections

The more I began to understand these two views of the world and of change, the more I realized not only the cross-cultural implications but the inherent limitations of the "pure" OD model. While I know OD practitioners are eclectic, inventive, and rarely bound by any model, still I had previously known of no alternative paradigm to guide dramatically different ways of acting and intervening. Besides, a model of change that specifically addressed a world of continual change seemed intriguing after dealing with the paradox of how to unfreeze and refreeze "permanent white water" (Vaill, 1989). When I then began to consider the implications of each model of change, several meta-themes emerged. These seemed to follow logically from the assumptions underlying each model and help to contrast the two differing world views.

Implications: The OD Change Model

I believe the assumptions underlying the Lewinian model of change are likely to lead to several tendencies in the theory and practice of OD. These include the following orientations:

Focusing on the Future. Emphasis is placed on the desired future state where the problems of the past and present will be resolved and/or transformed. This tends to produce a future bias wherein most of the attention and activities focus on creating a compelling image of the future and forgetting or getting away from the past and present.

(Clients) Holding on to a Satisfactory Present. Paradoxically, because one is supposed to move (change) only when there is a clearly better alternative, clients may want to hold on to the present state, particularly if it is satisfactory and/or better than all known options. After all, why should anyone want to move to a downsized, pressurized, highly competitive future? This is especially true when – as this view of change implies – you don't have to move unless "forced" to do so.

Focusing on Overcoming Resistance. In order to change, resistance to movement (inertia) must be overcome, usually by altering the field of forces. Holding on to the present tends to be viewed (by change agents) as resistance. The intervention approach, as a result, focuses on ways to overcome the resistant forces/persons. This, in essence, ends up casting the change effort as a win-lose conflict between the forces of movement and the forces of inertia.

Thinking in Terms of Either/Or. A tendency toward dichotomous either/or thinking is created and reinforced by several dynamics. By far the most important is the inherent dualism embedded in the change model and most Western thinking since at least Descartes. In dualism, entities are considered to be not only different but separate and independent of each other as well. For example, one may choose the current state or a future state, but not both. Finally, in an either/or dualistic world, when the future is presumed to be better and therefore good, the present must be unsatisfactory and therefore bad. Thus, in a blink of the eye a change effort can become a drama between the forces of good seeking to establish a more progressive, preferred future and the forces of evil seeking to maintain the flawed current state.

Planning and Managing. Because change (movement) results when something is acted on, it is possible to choose what to change and how to change it. To insure you get what you want, it is appropriate and necessary to plan and manage your actions. Planning and managing movement toward the desired future state also presumes both dualism and causality. A separate, independent entity (change agent) acts on/with (intervenes) another separate, independent entity (client system) and thereby causes (facilitates) movement (change).

Thinking Analytically. Good analysis is needed in order to anticipate, plan, manage, and/or deal correctly with the myriad factors and forces that must be considered in order to successfully move to the desired future state. Analytic thinking, i.e., the separation of a whole into parts, is the preferred way to plan and manage because entities are conceived to be separate and independent and to act on each other causally. Remember, even Lewin equated planned change with social engineering (Lewin, 1951, p. 172).

Intervening Based on Reason and Logic. Intervention choices are supposed to be made on the basis of reason and logic, i.e., rationally. Interventions should be data (fact) and theory (premises) based, using reasoned logic to infer conclusions about appropriate actions. Emotional and unconscious forces may be addressed, as long as they are surfaced, named, and then worked (in a rational manner). Interventions based on emotionality, spirituality, intuition, instinct, and/or feelings are suspect, because such factors are presumed to detract from "pure" reason and logic. It is no accident that action research is the name given to the core methodology of OD. Action research involves, in essence, an iterative, systematic, participatory process, using data-based reason and logic, to address and resolve systemic issues.

Measuring Progress. Because the implicit theme of most change efforts is to move toward a more desired future state, ways to measure "progress" become integral to the change process. Progress can be measured in many dimensions, the more the better. These include distance traveled (milestones and gaps), speed and time (how fast and how long), increases in things (e.g., more money, markets, productivity, quality, effectiveness, satisfaction, etc.), and decreases in things (e.g., less cost, time, defects, problems, turnover, etc.). Inability to measure "progress" on at least one dimension becomes, therefore, a valid reason to question whether or not a change is needed, possible, or has occurred.

These tendencies, if left to their own excesses, can conspire to create scenarios wherein change efforts become win-lose struggles between the forces of progress and the forces of stagnation. The forces of progress will try to use superior planning, management, analysis, and reason to overcome the resistance and defenses of the forces of stagnation who seek to hold on to the current flawed conditions by being emotional, irrational or demanding concrete, measurable proof before they will even consider movement.

Implications: The Cyclical Change Model

In contrast, the Confucian cyclical change model generates an alternative set of tendencies. These will be described and contrasted with aspects of the OD change model to help highlight salient differences. The cyclical change model is likely to lead to the following orientations:

Focusing on the Past-Present-Future. In a cyclical change model becoming and transformation are continual processes. To understand the present requires understanding the past from which it emerged and the future it is becoming. The future in turn will soon become the present and then the past. As a result, diagnosis and intervention must focus on the entire past-present-future cycle, rather than being primarily concerned with getting to the future. Origins and legacies, the pattern(s) and procession of change, and knowing where one is in a cycle of becoming and transformation are all as important as focusing on the future.

Letting Go and Aligning With the Emerging Future. In a cyclical-processional model of change, every condition/form/state is presumed to be both a beginning and an ending. Furthermore, no condition/form/state is considered to be better than another. They are just different, and all are needed to maintain the balance, harmony, and equilibrium necessary to keep things moving in a dynamic universe. As a result, the dominant orientation is less on "holding on" to a desired (end) state, and more toward "letting go" in order to "join up" (align) with a newly emerging state. In short, how to maintain balance and equilibrium while aligning with a newly emerging situation becomes the principal concern.

Focusing on the Relationships Needed to Maintain Balance and Harmony. Attention is focused on balance and harmony as necessary requirements to maintain the dynamic equilibrium of continuous, cyclical change. One does not "overcome resistance" so much as one looks to "release blockages" or "re-balance relationships" in order to maintain harmony and equilibrium among the constantly changing aspects of a system. In addition, the win-lose dynamics that often emerge from an "overcome resistance" orientation are replaced by the recognition that "coordination-collaboration" is essential for maintaining balance in a constantly changing universe.

Thinking in Terms of Both/And. Recognition of the need for continual coordination-collaboration helps contribute to syncretic both/and thinking. More important, however, is the concept of monism ("all is one") that is inherent to the cyclical change model and most East Asian traditional philosophies. In a monistic universe there may be different aspects/manifestations, but all are interdependent and essentially one. This is most strongly represented by the polarity of *yin* and *yang* wherein each creates and is created by the other, and both are aspects of the *T'ai Chi*, the Great Ultimate. Consequently, in a monistic universe one cannot "win out over" or negate another without negating oneself. Thus, for example, the orientation is not past vs. present vs. future, but rather the relative balance and emphasis of each. How much of our history and traditions will be part of our future, given where we are (in an on-going cycle)? What new traditions do we wish to create in the future so they will become part of our on-going legacies? What if our thinking and acting were guided by simultaneous consideration of our past, present and anticipated future? From this view, a change process is a continual dance among polarities where attention to balance, harmony, grace, and natural movement becomes the focus.

Self-Renewing Through Release and Augmentation. In a dynamic cyclical model of change, attention is focused on maintaining balance and harmony during the inherent changes so that the appropriate next condition/form/state in the cycle will be fully and properly realized. As a result, efforts related to release and augmentation (letting go and adding on) become critical. Also, because the universe is monistic and therefore interconnected and interdependent, no thing/person acts on another thing/person. All action and change is self-generated. The concept of causality is replaced by self-renewal or self-cultivation. In short, when interdependent aspects (clients and consultants) act to maintain on-going balance and harmony in a system (release and augmentation interventions) there will be natural self-renewal (change). For a related discussion, see Land & Jarman, 1992.

Thinking Holistically. A cycle is a circle, and circles are inherently holistic. All is part of, or contained within, the circle. One is immediately and constantly conscious of the whole and the parts. This differs from a linear orientation where the tendency is to focus on one end (aspect) or the other (aspect). When everything is interdependent and self-creating, the ability to maintain proper balance and harmony throughout the continual change processes is essential. This calls for holistic thinking, seeing the patterns and relationships as well as the parts. This means more than just seeing the forest and the trees; it also means seeing the natural ecosystem that is the forest and the interrelationships and balance among all aspects of the forest throughout the seasons and years. Consequently, diagnosis and intervention must constantly stress a holistic, systemic orientation. Emphasis is on linkages and putting more things together. After all, in a monistic universe to see and deal with any thing apart from the rest is to misread reality.

Intervening Based on Artistry and Composition. Because everything is self-evolving, holistic, and must be in balance and harmony for optimal conditions to prevail, interventions are based more on artistry and composition than on pure reason and logic. In essence, the logic of artistic composition, rather than the logic of scientific research, guides actions (see Hall and Ames, 1987). Factors, forces, values, thoughts, feelings, moods, etc., are all constituent elements that, in combination, compose any system and/or intervention. Thus the resulting total aesthetic, or "beauty," of a system becomes the legitimate objective for any intervention. This logic/approach is aided by the traditional Chinese concept that mental activities are located in the heart. The Chinese word *hsin* means the "heart-mind," i.e., thoughts and feelings are inseparable. This, of course, contrasts with the complete separation, and presumed opposition, of the mind (thoughts/reason) and the heart (feelings/emotions) postulated by Descartes and embedded in the scientific thinking of the West. To coin a new phrase: action composition is an iterative, participatory methodology, based on artistic sensibilities, used to compose and re-compose situations and systems to reflect harmony and balance in thoughts, feelings, and actions.

Being Values Centered. When change is self-generating, continual, and cyclical, the primary consideration is how to maintain balance, harmony, and equilibrium. In Confucianism, this was done by following the Way (*the Tao*) and adhering to the five constant virtues of benevolence or human-heartedness (*Jen*); righteousness or duty (*Yi*); propriety or following correct principles (*Li*); good faith or living up to one's word (*Hsin*); and wisdom or using knowledge to benefit the world (*Chih*). One might thereby become an exemplary person (*Chün Tzu*) or a sage (*Sheng Jen*) who could serve as a model for others to emulate. Consequently, respect ("face"), not fame or fortune, was most important (see Munro, 1969; and Hall & Ames, 1987).

Thus, how well one adheres to values or principles (e.g., is "centered" in virtue) replaces linear progress as the primary consideration. In OD, this would mean clarity about and adherence to a set of core values that should be exhibited constantly throughout any change process. This might include, for example, core values related to humanism, democratic processes, equality, respect, dignity, and so forth (for a more detailed discussion of OD values, see Gellerman, Frankel & Ladenson, 1990). In a cyclical process, being centered is paramount. Remember, a wheel doesn't roll very far if the hub is misaligned.

These tendencies, in combination, are likely to lead to change processes and interventions intended to help maintain harmony and balance while fully realizing the current condition/form/state, and also being prepared and able to let go and align with another condition/form/state as it begins to emerge. This is accomplished from an aesthetic, values centered, both/and, past-present-future, holistic orientation.

Commentary

The discussion so far has been primarily devoted to a presentation and analysis of the two different change models (see Table 8.1 for a summary of the meta-themes).

Table 8.1
Two Views of Change

OD/Western	Cyclical/Confucian
• Focus on the Future	• Attend to the Past-Present-Future
• Assume Satisfied People Hold On	• Assume Wise People Let Go & Realign
• Overcome Resistance	• Maintain Balance & Harmony
• Think in Terms of Either/Or	• Think in Terms of Both/And
• Plan and Manage Change	• Cultivate System Self-Renewal
• Think Analytically	• Think Holistically
• Use Reason & Logic	• Use Artistry & Composition
• Measure Progress	• Be Values Centered

Next, some of the "so whats" that are implied or raised by the presentation will be highlighted and briefly discussed.

OD Is Culturally Based. Much or all of OD is based in the cultural tradition of the Western European Enlightenment, i.e., the "modern era" in the West. Consequently any organizational change beliefs, assumptions, theories, practices, etc., that exist outside that cultural matrix are likely to seem strange, illogical, nonscientific, and/or mystical. This includes both premodern and postmodern (e.g., the "new sciences") assumptions and theories.

OD Is Culturally Biased. Over the years a wide range of theorists and practitioners have wondered whether or not some, or all, OD values are culturally biased (see, for example, Jaeger, 1986). What is suggested here is that the fundamental model of change underlying OD is culturally based and therefore inherently biased toward that culture. This does not necessarily mean OD cannot be successfully applied outside its originating culture; it does mean that a lack of awareness and appreciation for the underlying assumptions and values of OD and the host culture could be a recipe for failure.

Different Fundamental Models of Change Reveal Different Options and Approaches. Most or all OD practitioners face the same "chronic" issues in their work, e.g., getting people to focus on the future, dealing with resistance, measuring success, to name a few. We also are alert to any new and/or different interventions for addressing these issues. What we may not be doing, however, is searching for different paradigms of change that would suggest fundamentally different ways to think about, and therefore deal with, change and change issues. It may not be time to "start going around in circles," but it is certainly time to explore options in addition to "unfreezing-movement-refreezing."

Raising Questions About Fundamentals Will Feel Threatening and/or Disorienting. Much like change work that raises questions about an organization's deep culture, looking critically at some of OD's most basic assumptions will feel threatening and/or disorienting to some or many in the profession. Nevertheless, this is the avenue that offers the greatest potential for innovation in the field.

OD, as a Profession, Must Attend to Its Own Renewal. We, like the systems we serve, are at a turning point (Capra, 1982; Katz & Marshak, 1993). This is amply documented by the ODN's Future Search process, the themes and topics of recent ODN conferences, and our own experiences as practitioners. Therefore, in the spirit of this article, following are some brief Confucian cyclical change perspectives to consider.

- *Focus on our past-present-future.* We should honor our origins and legacies, consider what we are becoming, and help shape and be shaped by the future. We should continually conceive of the profession as "in process." Debates pitting our past against our future against our present are ultimately a waste of energy and should be avoided.
- *Let go and align ourselves with the emerging future.* We cannot afford to delude ourselves into believing we can hang on to our past practices and orthodoxies. Nothing stays the same forever. We should discern what will be needed to be successful in the emerging future, and then create, continue, and/or align with the required theories, methods, and techniques.
- *Focus on the relationships needed to maintain balance and harmony.* As conditions and contexts change, we should continually balance and rebalance the profession's range of theories, technologies, and work foci. This also includes addressing the relationships needed to maintain harmony and balance among the different aspects and components of OD, the members of the practitioner community, our relationships with client systems, and our own supporting systems such as the OD Network.
- *Think in terms of both/and.* It would be helpful if we could use a both/and orientation to explore innovative and established ideas and practices together. Too much of our professional energy seems, at times, to get caught up in discussions about whose approach/idea is "right" or "wrong." We need innovation, and the essence of creativity has always been to bring together what had previously been disjoined.
- *Think holistically.* It would also be helpful to expand our horizons and use more holistic thinking about who we are, what we do, and where and how we fit in the scheme of things. This also includes incorporating more holistic approaches and

methodologies into our work, and working more interdependently with a wider range of others.

- *Intervene based on artistry and composition.* In working to compose our emerging future, we must be mindful of our heads and hearts and use artistry as well as rationality in our efforts. Practitioners and clients are attracted to OD not only for what it can do as a tool, but by the moods, feelings, emotions, and sensibilities it helps engender. In short, we should be guided by our heart-minds as we compose and re-compose the heart-mind of the profession. OD in the future must continue to be both efficacious and emotionally evocative.

- *Be values centered.* We should continually, and especially now, reexamine and rededicate ourselves and the profession to a set of values. This not only centers and unites us as a profession, but also forms us as a professional community worthy of emulation.

- *Seek self-renewal through release and augmentation.* We should trust that renewal will emerge naturally as we follow the above precepts and thereby release what is no longer needed, while adding or augmenting that which becomes essential.

The individual items discussed above may not necessarily seem new or different. In some ways, what may be most different is their interrelationship as a whole, as well as what's not included. What I can unequivocally assert, however, is that before I studied the Confucian cyclical change model (1) I would not have conceived of the situation facing OD in the same way, (2) my list of proposed remedies would have been different, and (3) my overall "sense" or gestalt of this moment in the life of the OD profession would have been quite different.

Endings & Beginnings

This discussion has chronicled some of my wanderings and discoveries over the past 20 years and marks both endings and beginnings. I am reminded that the journey of the hero is also cyclical: an outward search followed by a return home, transformed (Campbell, 1968). I returned to Korea after 20 years, bringing my knowledge and experience related to organizations and change. I returned from Korea and my subsequent research with new insights about organizations and change. From the vantage point of the present I looked to the ancient past to discover new ideas to address the future. Endings and beginnings and endings. Cycles of cycles; one journey ends, another now begins.

References

Campbell, J. (1968). *The Hero With a Thousand Faces* (2nd ed.). Princeton, NJ: Princeton University Press.

Capra, F. (1982). *The Turning Point.* New York: Simon & Schuster.

Gellerman, W., Frankel, M. S., & Landenson, R. F. (1990). *Values and Ethics in Organization and Human Systems Development.* San Francisco: Jossey-Bass Publishers.

Hall, D. L., & Ames, R. T. (1987). *Thinking Through Confucius.* Albany, NY: State University of New York Press.

Jaeger, A. M. (1986). Organization Development and National Culture: Where's the Fit? *Academy of Management Review, 11*(1), 178-190.

Katz, J. H., & Marshak, R. J. (1993). Innovation: Reinventing Our Profession. In S. Zilber (Ed.) *Celebrating the Spirit of Renewal: Proceedings of the 1993 National OD Network Conference*, Portland, OR: National OD Network, pp. 303-307.

Land, G., & Jarman, B. (1992). *Breakpoint and Beyond.* New York: Harper Collins Publishers, Inc.

Lewin, K. (1947). Frontiers in Group Dynamics, *Human Relations, 1*(1), 5-41.

Lewin, K. (1951). *Field Theory in Social Science.* New York: Harper & Row Publishers.

Marshak, R. J. (1993a). Training and Consulting in Korea, *OD Practitioner, 25*(2), 16-21.

Marshak, R. J. (1993b). Lewin Meets Confucius: A Re-view of the OD Model of Change, *Journal of Applied Behavioral Science, 29*(4), 393-415.

Munro, D. J. (1969). *The Concept of Man in Early China.* Stanford, CA: Stanford University Press.

Tarnas, R. (1991). *The Passion of the Western Mind.* New York: Harmony Books.

Vaill, P. B. (1989). *Managing as a Performing Art.* San Francisco: Jossey-Bass Publishers.

9
Training and Consulting in Korea

With the emergence of South Korea as a newly industrialized country and, to some, the "next Japan," there has been an increasing flow of American training and consulting programs and methods to Korean companies. This is especially true for US headquartered multinationals with operations in Korea. This situation is ripe for cross-cultural difficulties pertaining not only to what is learned but how learning is accomplished. Despite the degree of westernization in Korea, widespread knowledge of English, and a highly educated workforce, important cultural differences still remain. These differences are more significant, but often less visible, than the issues of "cultural etiquette" that many Americans quickly learn; for example, rituals related to bowing, exchange of business cards, gift giving, and so forth. They include, at their core, nothing less than fundamental differences in how the American and Korean cultures socialize people about learning. These include different assumptions and beliefs as to the purpose of learning, proper ways to learn, and the role of the learner – all based on culturally derived differences in world view.

Surprises In Korea

My interest in sharing insights about cultural differences that impact training and consulting programs aimed at Koreans began with some recent trips to South Korea. I had gone there to train and consult with Korean managers and trainers on such topics as organizational change and conflict management. I had looked forward to these trips as an opportunity to bring my more than 15 years of consulting/training experience to a country I thought I knew fairly well. During military service in the early 1970s I had studied Korean history and culture extensively; learned to read, write, and speak Korean; and had lived for almost a year in South Korea. While it was almost 20 years later, and I had forgotten a lot, I still felt well prepared. In addition, I was working with a Korean colleague who had studied for several years in the United States. Our work was delivered in Korean and English. I was attuned to the Korean customs and etiquette appropriate to the situation. Indeed, I thought all the bases had been covered until the first event actually began and I discovered recurring situations that just didn't quite work out as intended.

What appeared self-evident to me wasn't quite self-evident to the Korean participants. Methods for learning and applying ideas that I took for granted didn't always seem to make sense to them. In fact, some of the basic ideas themselves didn't seem to make sense. The following are a few examples to help illustrate what happened:

- When presented with American management models that show multiple aspects of an organization in mutually interdependent relationships (e.g., the Six-Box and 7-S Models), a group of Korean managers insisted on knowing in what specific order each aspect should be considered. When told any one of them could be first, second, third, etc., depending on the situation, they at first appeared confused and then continued to try to figure out the correct order.

Marshak, R. J. (1993). Training and consulting in Korea. *OD Practitioner, 25*(2), 16-21. Republished with permission.

- When asked to participate in an experiential exercise and then discuss the principles they had learned, a group of Korean trainers were anxious to do as requested, but were uncertain about what was wanted or what they should do despite seemingly clear and repeated instructions.
- When asked to discuss and report their own feelings, thoughts, and reactions to a set of ideas, a group of Korean managers complied but appeared unclear about what that had to do with what they were learning.
- After having been presented with the main points of a management theory, a group of Korean managers began asking detailed questions about all aspects of the theory and its relationship to other theories. When told they only needed to know the main points in order to apply the ideas, they continued to ask detailed questions and were reluctant to move on.

Eventually, I became convinced that the difficulties were related to our different ways of understanding and organizing the world; that is, differences in learning patterns and preferences based on underlying cultural differences.

Becoming an Anthropologist

The combination of slightly "off" experiences and my (now doubtful) knowledge of Korea perplexed me enough to turn anthropologist in an attempt to figure out what was going on. After each day's session my Korean colleague and I would analyze and process the events late into the night. Various hypotheses were generated at night only to be discarded based on what happened the next day. The breakthrough came one day when I remarked to my Korean colleague that the participants were behaving "as if everything had a specific sequence that must be followed." At that point he turned to me and responded, in essence, "Of course, didn't you know that?" Other insights quickly followed and we devised a working set of assumptions about some of the potential differences between Korean and American beliefs about learning, especially American adult learning theory. Further research into the cultural roots of Korea helped to expand, refine, and confirm these working hypotheses, particularly where they seem to follow Chinese and Korean Confucian and Neo-Confucian traditions. For example, the following excerpt from the Confucian classic, *The Great Learning*, suggests the importance of following a specific sequence:

> Only after knowing what to abide in can one be calm. Only after having been calm can one be tranquil. Only after having achieved tranquility can one have peaceful repose. Only after having peaceful repose can one begin to deliberate. Only after deliberation can the end be attained. Things have their roots and branches. Affairs have their beginnings and their ends. To know what is first and what is last will lead one near the Way. (Chan, 1963, p. 86)

Comparing Korean and American Learning Beliefs

Needless to say, it would be presumptuous to claim that this article captures the learning patterns and underlying beliefs of one culture, let alone two. Suffice it to say that the beliefs about learning presented here may provide some helpful hints as to some fundamental differences that need to be considered in conducting training and consulting programs in Korea.

As one can see from the review of Korean and American assumptions about learning listed in Table 9.1, each set of beliefs is logical and consistent within its own context, but each is quite different from the other. The one, American and based in Western cultural traditions, envisions a universe governed by scientific laws with people as separate, independent actors. Through the exercise of free will, people choose their preferred ends and the means to those ends. People are considered to be (relatively) equal, even when there are significant role differences. There is also a very pragmatic, "what works" orientation, coupled with an emphasis on application and doing things.

The purpose of learning, therefore, is to acquire enough knowledge so that things can be managed, controlled, and/or planned in ways to achieve desired ends. Knowledge may be learned in a variety of ways with a primary focus on discovering solutions and applications to current problems. One's own personal reactions, thoughts, and feelings related to ideas and experiences are an integral part of learning and bear directly on whether or not something will be considered useful and applied. In adult learning situations, trainers, consultants, and participants are all frequently viewed as being learners, with everyone having some expertise to contribute. Trainers and consultants are often considered to be facilitators/guides, and participants are expected to help set the direction by asking for and seeking what they want.

The other set of beliefs, Korean and based in East Asian and Confucian cultural traditions, envisions an interdependent universe of patterned relationships that govern all entities, including human beings. People find and follow their proper place in the natural order of the universe in order to realize their destiny. Each place (or role) has different duties and obligations that should be followed. There is also an emphasis on discovering and being in harmony with the natural order of all things.

The purpose of learning, therefore, is to know how to be part of and follow the natural order, pattern(s), and sequence(s) of the universe; i.e., to know the correct Way. To learn correctly, one should follow specific methods and steps with the primary focus on becoming a knowledgeable person. Learners must be open to the universal principles revealed by wise persons (sages) of the past and present. Consequently, one's own personal reactions, thoughts, and feelings should be put aside as potential impediments to understanding true knowledge. In learning situations, trainers, consultants, and participants are usually viewed as having separate roles and responsibilities that each must honor and fulfill. Trainers and consultants are expected to present the right knowledge and participants are expected to show respect and learn what is presented to them. An old Korean saying is instructive, "You must not step on even the shadow of your teacher."

Implications

If these working hypotheses about some of the underlying culturally based beliefs related to learning in America and Korea are reasonably accurate, then it is clear that aspects of adult learning theory and OD practice won't quite fit naturally in Korea. This means that training and consulting based on certain American cultural beliefs may tend to rub against the culturally preferred learning style of many Koreans. This can create a learning environment that feels less natural and sometimes more confusing to them. If we revisit the examples introduced earlier we can now readily understand why things didn't seem to "quite fit." The taken-for-granted American belief underlying the situation and an alternative Korean belief follow each example.

- *Presentation of management models showing mutually interdependent relationships with no specific sequence or order of interaction (e.g., the Six-Box and 7-S models).*

  American Belief: All things have properties and laws that govern how they function. They may be combined in many ways to achieve different ends.
  Korean Belief: All things exist as part of a patterned order. There is a correct sequence to everything that must be followed to realize a proper end.

- *Holding a discussion after an experiential exercise in order to discover relevant principles.*

  American Belief: One may learn theory and then act, or act and then generate theory.
  Korean Belief: One should learn pattern(s) and principle(s) before acting.

- *Holding a discussion and reporting about one's own feelings, thoughts, and reactions to a set of ideas.*

  American Belief: One's own ideas, feelings, and reactions are important aspects of learning.
  Korean Belief: One's own ideas, feelings, and reactions should be put aside in order to be fully present and open to learning.

- *Presenting only the main points needed for application of a theory.*

  American Belief: One may focus only on those aspects of a theory that are most relevant to the problem(s) at hand.
  Korean Belief: One should thoroughly probe and understand all aspects of what is studied.

These and other similar instances attest to the difficulties one can encounter if unaware of the taken-for-granted beliefs we all have learned from our cultures about almost everything, including learning. Fortunately for me, the Korean participants in our program also followed some cultural beliefs about working diligently and not showing their frustrations overtly.

Some Tips for Training and Consulting In Korea

Based on these experiences and working hypotheses, here are some lessons learned that may enhance your effectiveness in working with Korean participants:

1. *Provide context – an overarching framework – to your program.* Participants will understand better if your topic is first set in an overall context, then shown what is the beginning and end, and then the sequence of steps one should follow.

2. *Design activities and present information in a logical sequence.* Participants will understand and follow a clearly delineated sequence better than they will topics/activities that are not clearly related in a logical way. This is especially true if the sequence can be shown to move participants to a particular set of stated learning goals/outcomes. Models that in the United States show mutual interdependence and/or no specific order might better be presented with a suggested sequence or order of importance.

3. *Present or demonstrate linkages and deductions.* Participants will tend to prefer programs, processes, theories, models, concepts, ideas, etc., that are well thought through, with clear and logical patterns, steps, and progressions.

4. *Use role models of respected individuals and/or organizations.* Case examples that specifically delineate how others have successfully dealt with a situation will be appreciated and followed. This is especially true if the exemplar is well know or respected.

5. *Present theories and principles before experiential activities.* Experiential exercises may well work better when used to demonstrate a previously presented principle in application rather than used to develop principles from "one's own experience."

6. *Be prepared to provide time for exploration of concepts before application.* Participants may prefer to spend more time learning the material in-depth than applying it. Ideas are valued in themselves as well as in application. Participants are also likely to want to probe and test every aspect of the presented material for logical consistency and to learn how and where it fits in with other ideas/materials.

7. *Expect little in the way of reactions/feelings.* Do not be surprised if there is reluctance to share feelings and relatively little confrontation or feedback on "how things are going." The Korean cultural tendency is to make it your job to present and expose participants to the best ideas in as clear, logical, and comprehensive a way as possible; their job is to learn it. The American concept of adult learning, where a trainer or consultant's job is to help facilitate learning, differs from traditional Korean concepts and beliefs.

Finally, remember that you will never be able to present in a "perfectly Korean way." Nor should you try, since one of the reasons you are there is to expose Koreans to American theories, models, and beliefs. What you can do is lessen the cultural clash by (1) modifying, adapting, and designing in ways that account for or acknowledge culturally based learning preferences, and (2) presenting and explaining the theories and beliefs underlying why you are doing what you are doing. For example, presenting adult learning theory or the theory behind experiential learning before doing certain activities adds to learning and addresses the Korean preference for understanding the context, pattern(s), and/or sequence(s) before acting.

Table 9.1
Assumptions about Learning

American/Andragogy	Korean/Confucian
World View	**World View**
All things have properties and laws that govern how they function. They may be combined in many ways to achieve different ends.	All things exist as part of a patterned order. There is a correct sequence to everything that must be followed to realize a proper end.
Purpose	**Purpose**
The purpose of learning is to know how to do things. Knowledge is valued as a tool.	The purpose of learning is to know the correct way. Knowledge is valued for self-cultivation.
Learning Methods	**Learning Methods**
1. One may learn theory and then act, or act and then generate theory.	1. One should learn patterns and principles (theory) before acting.
2. One may test and challenge ideas for their usefulness and application.	2. One should accept the wisdom and examples of sages without question.
3. One may focus only on those aspects of a theory that are most relevant to the problem(s) at hand.	3. One should thoroughly probe and understand all aspects of what is studied.
4. One may read, discuss, observe, reflect, and/or experiment with something until you know enough to apply it.	4. One should read, recite, and even memorize something until it becomes a part of you.
5. One's own ideas, feelings, and reactions are important aspects of learning.	5. One's own ideas, feelings, and reactions should be put aside in order to be fully present and open to learning.
Trainers, Consultants and Learners	**Trainers, Consultants and Learners**
1. Trainers and consultants are expected to be skillful in helping others learn.	1. Trainers and consultants are expected to be very knowledgeable, wise, experts and role models.
2. A trainer or consultant's responsibility is to present information and facilitate processes that enable learners to acquire and apply practical knowledge.	2. A trainer or consultant's responsibility is to select and present in a logical manner, and in the proper sequence, the most important ideas to learners.
3. Learners are expected to be active participants with trainers or consultants in the learning process. Their responsibility is to challenge and then confront the content and process of learning when it isn't working for them.	3. Learners are expected to honor, respect, and show deference to trainers and consultants. Their responsibility is to be diligent in learning the information that is presented to them.
4. The roles of trainer, consultant, and learner should overlap and any status differences minimized.	4. The roles of trainer or consultant and learner should be separated, with clear status differences.
5. Learners are expected to apply and use what they have learned.	5. Learners are expected to know and embody what they have learned.

Cultural Legacies and Learning in East Asia

Although I believe that there are culturally based learning preferences in Korea that are different from those in the United States, it is important to remember that South Korea is in the midst of rapid change. This means that ideas and practices about learning are also changing rapidly. Thus, it might be difficult to find anyone in Korea overtly teaching the learning beliefs presented here, especially since many of them appear rooted in a now abandoned Confucian philosophy. Nonetheless, it would also be unreasonable to believe that the legacy of over 500 years of rigid Confucian orthodoxy, ending less than a century ago, as well as other Korean cultural traditions, have no influence in modern-day Korea. After all, we in this country are still influenced in how we think and learn by cultural patterns rooted in the philosophies of ancient Greece.

In addition, the current system of education in South Korea stresses national competitive examinations for entrance into colleges and universities. This is both an echo of past Confucian merit examinations and a current molder of learning behavior. In today's classrooms most Korean students, in order to succeed on the examinations, are expected to know, understand, and remember things – period. There is little or no application, discussion, sharing, feedback, or other forms of interactive learning. Thus, if the beliefs described in this article are reasonable working hypotheses, then it is probably safe to assume they will continue to be generally valid into the near future even as Korea continues to change.

It is also worth noting that while each of the countries of East Asia has its own distinct culture and history, they also share with Korea many of the same cultural roots, including Confucianism. Thus it is possible that the learning preferences in China, Taiwan, Hong Kong, Vietnam, Singapore, and Japan may share important similarities with Korea. Even if they are not similar, however, the safest bet is that they are not the same as American or British learning preferences. Trainers and consultants, therefore, should carefully review their underlying assumptions and beliefs about learning for cultural bias before delivering programs in Korea and East Asia. Hopefully, this presentation will provide some ideas, insights, and assistance toward that end.

References

Chan, W. T. (Translator and Editor). (1963). *A source book in Chinese philosophy*. Princeton, New Jersey: Princeton University Press.

Gardner, D. K. (Translator). (1990). *Learning to be a sage: Selections from the conversations of Master Chu, arranged topically*. Berkeley: University of California Press.

Korean Overseas Information Service (1987). *A handbook of Korea*. Seoul, Korea: Seoul International Publishing House.

Marshak, R. J. (1992). Lewin meets Confucius: East-west models of learning and change. In M. McDonald (Ed.), *Learning Together: Organization Development Network Conference Proceedings* (pp. 23-28). Portland, Oregon: Organization Development Network.

Ro, Y. C. (1989). *The Korean neo-Confucianism of Yi Yulgok*. Albany, New York: State University of New York Press.

10
Organization Development and Post-Confucian Societies

For some time now, various commentators have pointed out the cultural biases of American management theories in general (Adler, 1991; Boyacigiller and Adler, 1991; Hofstede, 1980a; Hofstede and Bond, 1988) and Organization Development (OD) values and processes in particular (Golembiewski, 1987, 1991; Jaeger, 1984, 1986; Marshak, 1993a, 1993b, 1994). For example, Jaeger (1986), using the OD values outlined by Tannenbaum and Davis (1969) and the cultural dimensions advanced by Hofstede (1980b), found OD values to be inconsistent with the values of most national cultures, and in some cases to be polar opposites. Others have echoed Jaeger's critique in a variety of settings (e.g. Boss and Mariono, 1987; Johnson, 1990; Richards, 1991).

This chapter contributes to this discussion by comparing OD assumptions, theories and orientations to traditional Confucian philosophy. For hundreds of years Confucian philosophy was state endorsed doctrine in China and Korea and deeply influential in Japan and the rest of East Asia. It was originally advanced by Master K'ung Fu-Tzu (551-479 BCE), called Confucius in the West, and further extended and then developed into an orthodoxy by his followers (Chai and Chai, 1973). As one of the primary cornerstones of East Asian civilization, the Confucian worldview is still influential, if no longer orthodox or officially taught, in modern-day China, Korea, Japan, Hong Kong, Taiwan, Vietnam, and Singapore. Thus this discussion is not about a specific country or national culture, but about an important and influential historical worldview that subtly, and in some cases overtly, influences the ways people think and behave throughout the post-Confucian countries of East Asia.

The presentation begins by comparing and contrasting the worldviews, assumptions and orientations of Organization Development and Confucianism with respect to learning and change. The importance of hierarchy and harmony as both the context and purpose for learning and change within the Confucian worldview is also presented. Hierarchy, harmony, learning and change are all involved in any type of OD activity and the comparison is intended to highlight how fundamentally different worldviews can lead to quite different emphases and practices. Finally, the discussion addresses the impacts that different organizational contexts and societal considerations may have on present day applications of Organization Development in post-Confucian countries.

Marshak, R. J. (2004). Organization development and post-Confucian societies. In P. F. Sorensen, T. C. Head, T. Yaeger, and D. Cooperrider (Eds). *Global and International Development, 4ᵗʰ Edition*, pp. 295-311, Champaign, IL: Stipes Publishing Co. Republished with permission.

OD and Confucian Learning

As one can see from a review of the assumptions listed in Table 10.1, both the OD and Confucian sets of beliefs about learning and relationships are logical and consistent within their own context, but each is quite different from the other.

Table 10.1
Assumptions about Learning and Relationships

Traditional OD World View:	Traditional Confucian World View:
• All things are separate entities governed by causal laws. They may be combined in many different ways to achieve different ends.	• All things exist as interdependent parts of a patterned order. There is a correct way that must be followed to realize a proper end.
Purpose of Learning:	**Purpose of Learning:**
• The purpose of learning is to know how to do things. Knowledge is valued as a tool.	• The purpose of learning is to know the correct way. Knowledge is valued for self-cultivation.
Learning Methods:	**Learning Methods:**
• One may learn theory and then act, or act and then generate theory.	• One should learn patterns and principles before acting.
• One may test and challenge ideas for their usefulness and application.	• One should accept the wisdom and example of sages without question.
• One may focus on those aspects of a theory that are most relevant to the problem(s) at hand.	• One should thoroughly probe and understand all aspects of what is studied.
• One may read, discuss, observe, reflect, and/or experiment with something until you know enough to apply it.	• One should read, recite, and memorize something until it becomes part of you.
• One's own ideas, feelings and reactions are important aspects of learning.	• One's own ideas, feelings and reactions should be put aside in order to be fully present and open to learning.
Consultants and Clients:	**Consultants and Clients:**
• Consultants are expected to be skillful in helping clients to learn.	• Teachers/sages are expected to be very knowledgeable, wise, experts and role models.
• Consultants are responsible for presenting and facilitating processes that enable learners to acquire and apply practical knowledge.	• Teachers/sages are responsible for presenting, in a logical manner and in the proper sequence, the most appropriate ideas to learners.
• Clients are expected to be active participants in learning. Their responsibility is to challenge and confront the content and process of learning when it isn't working for them.	• Learners are expected to honor, respect and show deference to teachers/sages. Learners are responsible for being diligent in learning the information presented to them.
• The roles of consultant and client should overlap and status differences minimized.	• The roles of teacher/sage and learner should be separated with clear status differences.
• Clients are expected to apply and use what they have learned.	• Learners are expected to know and embody what they have learned.

Organization Development Assumptions about Learning and Relationships

Organization Development, which is based in North American and Western cultural traditions, presumes a universe governed by scientific laws and inhabited by people who are separate, independent actors. Through the exercise of free will, people choose their preferred ends and the means to those ends. People are considered to be relatively equal, even when there are significant role differences. There is also a very pragmatic orientation, coupled with an emphasis on application and doing things (Stewart, 1972). Finally, learning is expected to be learner-centered as in the educational concept of andragogy, or adult learning (Knowles, 1978).

The purpose of learning during an OD intervention, therefore, is for clients to acquire enough knowledge to enable them to plan and manage things in ways to achieve their desired ends. Knowledge may be acquired in a variety of ways and with a primary emphasis on discovering solutions and applications to current problems or opportunities. A client's personal reactions, thoughts and feelings related to the situation are an integral part of the learning process and bear directly on whether or not something will be considered useful and relevant. During an intervention, both consultant and client are viewed as learners with each one having some expertise to contribute. Consultants are considered to be facilitators, coaches and/or guides, and clients are expected to set the direction and ask for and seek what they want or need.

Confucian Assumptions about Learning and Relationships

The other set of beliefs is based in traditional Confucian philosophy and presumes an interdependent universe of patterned relationships that govern all entities, including human beings. People find and follow their proper place in the natural order of the universe in order to realize their destiny. Each place or role exists within a hierarchical order that has different duties and obligations that must be followed to maintain harmony. There is also an emphasis on discovering and being in harmony and balance with the Way, the natural order of all things. Thus hierarchy and harmony in the universe go together. This may require some additional explanation. Unlike in Taoism, the Confucian perspective is that the world is inherently hierarchical, and that when hierarchical relationships are properly fulfilled there will be harmony. For example, harmony in music requires a hierarchy of pitches or notes to be played in their proper relationships. Contrast how your favorite melody might sound with hearing the same note played over and over again; or notes played out of relationship with each other, in dissonance.

In Confucianism there are five primary human relationships. Each presumes that there are mutual obligations and responsibilities between the superior and the subordinate parties in the relationship that must be performed. This is, in fact, what leads to harmony in the relationship and the sets of relationships in the broader society. The five primary relationships are ruler and subject, father and son, older brother and younger brother, husband and wife, and friend and friend. In general, the superior or senior person in each of these relationships has responsibilities to look after the welfare and advancement of the subordinate or more junior person. At the same time the more junior party also has responsibilities towards the more senior party; for example, the subject owes the ruler loyalty, the son owes the father filial piety, the younger brother owes the elder brother respect, the wife owes the husband obedience, and friends owe each other trust (Ryu, 1980, p. 207). When these reciprocal relationships are properly carried out harmony results and there will be a just, productive and peaceful society. For example, the Confucian classic, the *Doctrine of the Mean* states:

> Equilibrium is the great foundation of the world, and harmony its universal path. When equilibrium and harmony are realized to the highest degree, Heaven and earth will attain their proper order and all things will flourish. (Chan, 1963, p. 98)

Ultimately, then, the purpose of learning is to know how to be part of and follow the natural order, pattern(s) and sequence(s) of the universe, i.e., to know the correct Way. For example, the following excerpt from the Confucian classic, *The Great Learning*, suggests the importance of following a correct pattern or sequence:

> Only after knowing what to abide in can one be calm. Only after having been calm can one be tranquil. Only after achieving tranquility can one have peaceful repose. Only after having peaceful repose can one begin to deliberate. Only after deliberation can the end be obtained. Things have their roots and branches. Affairs have their beginnings and their ends. To know what is first and what is last will lead one near the Way. (Chan, 1963, p. 86)

This is further reinforced by a cosmology that conceives of everything as composed of the cyclical, interdependent, and balanced relationships between *yin* and *yang* and among the Five Forces or Agents of the universe (symbolized as wood, fire, earth, metal and water). According to the Confucian sage Tung Chung-shu (c. 179-104 BCE):

> Wood produces Fire, Fire produces Earth, Earth produces Metal, Metal produces Water, and Water produces Wood. ... Each of the Five Agents succeeds the others according to its order. Each of them performs its official function by fulfilling its capacity. (Chan, 1963, p. 279)

When this does not happen, disharmony, disequilibrium and misfortune result.

Consequently, to learn correctly one should follow specific methods and steps with the primary emphasis on becoming an exemplary and ethical person. Learners must be open to the universal principles revealed by sages and wise persons of the past and present. One's own personal reactions, thoughts and feelings should be put aside as potential impediments to understanding true knowledge (Gardner, 1990). In learning situations, sages/teachers and learners have separate roles and responsibilities that each must honor and fulfill. Sages/teachers are expected to present the right knowledge and learners are expected to show respect and learn what is presented to them. An old Korean saying illustrates the point: "You must not step on even the shadow of your teacher."

Some Implications

There are a great many implications that follow from this worldview and the resulting orientations towards hierarchy, harmony and learning. A few areas of particular interest include:

OD consultants are likely to be seen as part of a hierarchy. Unlike more egalitarian North American assumptions, the Confucian perspective places everyone somewhere in a hierarchy. One of the reasons for the exchange and study of business cards in East Asia is to help people figure out where they are in relationship to the other party. Organizational position (for example, title, job, size and importance of the organization, etc.) is one factor that helps determine one's position. Age and/or seniority is almost always another. Thus, people may try subtle and not so subtle ways to assess another's age in order to know how to behave towards that person. For example, I was involved in a NTL Institute workshop conducted in Korea. The trainers included the President of NTL (in his late 30s), a very experienced NTL trainer (in her 60s) and me (at that time in my late 40s). During the workshop and the events surrounding it the other trainer and myself kept trying to position situations to show respect to the President of NTL, but the Korean participants seemed to see it another way. The other trainer and I, in that order, received the most attention and deference. When we urged our Korean contact to focus more on the President of NTL, the response was, "He is too young for his position." Thus an important consideration when working in East Asia is always one's relative age for the nature of the assignment and in comparison to the people one will be working with.

Is the OD consultant superior or subordinate to the client? Establishing the roles and responsibilities of the client and OD consultant is also influenced by the expectation of reciprocal, hierarchical relationships. During another workshop I conducted on organizational consulting, I was trying to explain the role of an OD consultant as an equal partner with the client; and one who facilitates and does not direct or prescribe. This was met with the response "We understand that in expert consulting the consultant tells the client what to do. We also understand that in 'pair-of-hands' consulting, the client tells the consultant what to do. The idea that the consultant and client can be equals is new to us." Of course, it is also true that in North America people can have difficulty understanding the relatively equal partnership role and relationship advocated in OD consulting. In post-Confucian countries, however, there is the additional difficulty of a historical worldview that tends to place and understand people in superior-subordinate, junior-senior relationships. This tendency is further accentuated by the OD consultant functioning in a role that can seem similar to that of a sage (especially if the consultant is older, has advanced degrees, might be associated with a prestigious organization, etc.). This would then invite and invoke attempts to establish a sage-learner reciprocal relationship between the client and the consultant.

Harmony is central to everything. A pre-eminent value in Confucianism is maintaining equilibrium and harmony. One way of maintaining harmony is to observe the expected hierarchical, reciprocal relationships. In that context, subordinates or more junior persons will tend to defer to superior or more senior parties as a matter of course. In other situations, actions or behaviors that could disrupt harmony are avoided or worked around, if possible. When something must be addressed that could threaten harmony, it is often dealt with indirectly or sometimes through a third party. This contrasts with a number of OD practices wherein direct and public confrontation and/or feedback about issues and people, even superiors, are invited. Such invitations are almost universally declined in post-Confucian societies for reasons including the risk of possible loss of face and disharmony. In my experience, attempts at large group confrontational type discussions and direct feedback are typically met with silence. On the other hand, asking people to discuss issues in small groups will often work, although general public sharing afterwards will tend to leave out anything that might be confrontational or controversial. If superiors are interested in feedback, it is more likely to be forthcoming in interactions that are one-on-one, in private, sometimes indirectly and sometimes outside of the workplace.

Finally, it is important to keep in mind that different worldviews, assumptions and orientations about hierarchy and harmony will lead people to read and label situations differently. For example, what a Western OD worldview might describe as autocratic or paternalistic might be experienced from a traditional Confucian perspective as harmony and order. Likewise, what may be considered freedom or independent thought and expression by the one, may be described as anarchy by the other. Thus Western OD consultants working in post-Confucian societies must be especially alert to their own assumptions and perspectives about learning, hierarchical relationships, and maintaining harmony.

OD and Confucian Change Models

Next we turn to a consideration of the assumptions and models underlying how change is presumed to occur in OD theory and practice and how it occurs in Confucian and Taoist philosophy. A review of Table 10.2 provides a summary of the dramatically different worldviews, assumptions and orientations between traditional OD and Confucian change models.

Table 10.2
Assumptions about Change

Modern Western Worldview:	Traditional Confucian and Taoist Worldview:
The universe is composed of separate, independent entities normally in static or equilibrium states. Movement results when things act on each other. Progress or evolution is expected over time.	The universe is composed of constantly changing, interdependent manifestations of one entity. The universe is. Change is both spontaneous and cyclical.

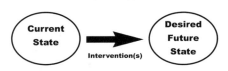

Unfreeze   Movement   Refreeze

T'ai Chi (The Great Ultimate)

Change is:	Change is:
• Linear	• Cyclical
• Progressive	• Processional
• Destination oriented	• Journey oriented
• Based on creating disequilibrium	• Based on restoring/maintaining equilibrium
• Planned and managed by people who exist separate from and act on things to achieve their goals	• Observed and followed by people who are interdependent with everything and must act correctly to maintain harmony in the universe
• Unusual, because everything is normally in a quasi-stationary or static state	• Usual, because everything is normally in a continually changing dynamic state

Resulting Tendencies:	**Resulting Tendencies:**
• Focus on the future	• Attend to the past-present-future
• Hold on	• Let go & realign
• Overcome resistance	• Maintain balance & harmony
• Think in terms of either/or	• Think in terms of both/and
• Plan and manage change	• Cultivate system self-renewal
• Think analytically	• Think holistically
• Use reason & logic	• Use artistry & composition
• Measure progress	• Be values centered

Traditional OD Change Model

The primary model of change underlying most traditional OD theory and practice is Kurt Lewin's three-stage change process of unfreezing, movement and refreezing (Lewin, 1947). This model is in the tradition of the Western scientific worldview that presumes, among other things, progressive evolution, free will and the preeminence of rationality (see, for example, Tarnas, 1991). This worldview also includes an inherent dualism, including the belief that human beings exist independent of a mostly static phenomenal world that they plan, manage and otherwise act upon. In terms of conceptualizing a change effort, this worldview and change model imply a managed process to move from a current state to a more desired future state through the use of planned interventions to overcome resistance, get movement and thereby alter the status quo.

Specifically, the Lewinian OD model of change includes assumptions that change is:

- *Linear.* One moves from one state to another state in a forward direction.
- *Progressive.* One moves from a less to a more desired state.
- *Destination oriented.* One moves towards a specific goal or end state.
- *Based on creating disequilibrium.* In order to get movement one must alter the equilibrium of the status quo.
- *Planned and managed* by people who exist separate from and act on things to achieve their goals. One learns the principles and practices about how to manage the forces in the world in order to achieve preferred outcomes.
- *Unusual, because everything is normally in a quasi-stationary or static state.* Unless something is done proactively, things will tend to stay the same.

These assumptions and change model are likely to lead to several tendencies in the theory and practice of OD, including the following orientations:

Focusing on the future. Emphasis is placed on the desired future state where the problems of the past and present will be resolved or transformed. This tends to produce a future bias wherein most of the attention and activities focus on creating a compelling image of the future and forgetting or getting away from the past and present.

Holding on. Paradoxically, because one is supposed to move (change) only when there is a clearly better alternative, clients may want to hold on to the present state, particularly if it is satisfactory or better than all known options. This is especially true when – as this model of change implies – you don't have to move unless "forced" to do so.

Focusing on overcoming resistance. In order to change, resistance to movement (inertia) must be overcome, usually by altering the field of forces. Holding on to the present tends to be viewed as resistance. Intervention approaches as a result tend to focus on ways to overcome the resistant forces or persons. This, in essence, ends up casting the change effort as a win-lose conflict between the forces of movement and the forces of inertia.

Thinking in terms of either/or. Western thinking since at least Descartes and the "mind-body split" has been frequently characterized as dualistic. In dualism entities are considered to be not only different, but separate and independent of each other as well. In a dualistic world if the future is presumed to be better and therefore good, the present must be unsatisfactory and therefore bad. Thus, in a blink of the eye a change effort can become a drama between the forces of good seeking to establish a more progressive, preferred future and the forces of evil seeking to maintain the flawed current state.

Planning and managing. Because change results when something is acted upon, it is possible to select what to change and how to change it. To insure you get what you want, it is appropriate and necessary to plan and manage your actions. Thus a change agent plans and manages interventions on/with a client system and thereby causes change.

Thinking analytically. Good analysis is needed in order to anticipate, plan, manage, and/or deal correctly with the myriad factors and forces that must be considered in order to successfully move to the desired future state. Analytic thinking, that is the separation of a whole into parts, is the preferred way to plan and manage because entities are conceived to be separate and independent and to act on each other causally.

Intervening based on reason and logic. Intervention choices are supposed to be made on the basis of reason and logic; in other words, rationally. Interventions should be data and theory based, using reasoned logic to determine conclusions about appropriate actions. Emotional and unconscious forces may be addressed as long as they are surfaced, named, and then worked on in a rational manner. Interventions based on emotionality, spirituality, intuition, instinct, feelings and the like are suspect because such factors are presumed to detract from "pure" reason and logic.

Measuring progress. Because the implicit theme of most change efforts is to move towards a more desired future state, ways to measure progress become integral to the change process. Progress can be measured in many dimensions, the more the better. Inability to measure progress on at least one dimension becomes, therefore, a valid reason to question the effectiveness of the change initiative.

Traditional Confucian and Taoist Change Model

Underlying both Confucian and Taoist philosophy is an alternative worldview that presumes the inherent oneness, or interdependence, of everything and everyone in the universe. All are governed by the universal principles of the Way (the Tao), including the principle of continual cyclical alternation between the polarities inherent in everything, the *yin* and the *yang*. The Confucian sage Zhu Xi (1130-1200 CE) observed:

> There is no other event in the universe except yin and yang succeeding each other in an unceasing cycle. This is called Change. (Chan, 1963, p. 641)

The assumptions inherent in this model of change include beliefs that change is:

- *Cyclical.* There is a constant ebb and flow to the universe and everything in it is cyclical.
- *Processional.* Everything and everyone moves constantly from one state to the next state in an orderly sequence through a cycle.
- *Journey oriented.* Because there is continual cyclical change, there can be no end state per se. What matters is how well one conducts the journey, i.e., follows the Way.

- *Based on restoring/maintaining equilibrium.* Everything is naturally in harmony and perfect. Therefore, one acts only when and how needed to maintain or restore balance and equilibrium.
- *Observed and followed by people who are interdependent with everything and must act correctly to maintain harmony in the universe.* One must constantly strive to be in harmony with the Way, the natural order of the universe.
- *Usual, because everything is normally in a continually changing dynamic state.* The continual process of everything in the universe is change. The yin-yang law of opposites says everything contains its own negation so nothing stays the same forever.

The orientations that follow from this set of assumptions about change include:

Focusing on the past-present-future. In a cyclical change model becoming and transformation are continual processes. To understand the present requires understanding the past from which it emerged and the future it is anticipating. The future in turn will soon become the present and then the past. As a result, diagnosis and intervention must focus on the entire past-present-future cycle, rather than being primarily concerned with getting to the future. Honoring the past and correctly being in the present will inherently lead to the proper future.

Letting go and realigning with the emerging future. In a cyclical-processional model of change, every state is presumed to be both a beginning and an ending, and no state is considered to be better than another. They are just different, and all are needed to maintain the balance, harmony and equilibrium necessary to keep things flowing in a dynamic universe. How to maintain balance and equilibrium while aligning with a newly emerging situation becomes the principal concern.

Focusing on the relationships needed to maintain balance and harmony. Consistent with the Doctrine of the Mean, attention is focused on balance and harmony as necessary requirements to maintain the dynamic equilibrium of a universe undergoing continuous, cyclical change. One does not "overcome resistance" so much as one looks to release blockages or re-balance relationships in order to maintain harmony and equilibrium among the constantly changing aspects of a system. In addition, the win-lose dynamics that often emerge from an "overcome resistance" orientation are replaced by the recognition that mutuality and reciprocity are essential for maintaining balance in a constantly changing interdependent universe.

Thinking in terms of both/and. Recognition of the interdependence of everything and the need for mutuality and reciprocity helps contribute to syncretic both/and thinking. More important, however, is the concept of monism (everything is a manifestation of a single interdependent entity) that is an inherent part of most East Asian traditional philosophies. This is most strongly represented by the polarity of yin and yang wherein each creates and is created by the other, and both are aspects of the *T'ai Chi*, the Great Ultimate. In a monistic universe one cannot "win out over" or negate another without negating oneself. From this point of view a change process is a continual dance among polarities where attention to balance, harmony, grace, and natural movement become the focus.

Self-renewing. In a dynamic cyclical model of change, attention is focused on maintaining balance and harmony during the inherent changes so that the appropriate next state in the cycle will be fully and properly realized. Also, because the universe is monistic, and therefore interconnected and interdependent, no thing or person acts on another thing or person. All action and change is self-generated. The concept of causality is replaced by that of self-renewal or self-cultivation.

Thinking holistically. A cycle is a circle and circles are inherently holistic. One is immediately and constantly conscious of the whole and the parts. This differs from a linear orientation where the tendency is to focus on one end (aspect) or the other (aspect). When everything is interdependent and self-creating, the ability to exercise holistic thinking, that is, seeing the patterns and relationships simultaneously with the parts, is essential. This means more than just seeing the forest and the trees; it also means seeing the natural ecosystem that is the forest and the interrelationships and balance among all aspects of the forest throughout the seasons and the years, as well as one's own connection to the system. Emphasis is on seeing linkages and putting more things together. In a monistic universe to deal with any thing separate from the rest is to misread reality.

Intervening based on artistry and composition. Because everything is self-evolving, holistic and must be in balance and harmony for optimal conditions to prevail, actions are based more on artistry and composition than on pure reason and logic. In essence, the logic of artistic composition, rather than the logic of scientific research, guides actions (see Hall and Ames, 1987). The total aesthetic, or "beauty," of a system becomes the legitimate objective of any action or initiative. In contrast to the scientific logic of action research in OD, the Confucian approach might be more akin to aesthetic composition.

Being values centered. When change is self-generating, continual and cyclical, the primary consideration is how to maintain balance, harmony and equilibrium. In Confucianism, this was done by following the Way (the *Tao*) and adhering to the five constant virtues of benevolence (*Jen*), righteousness (*Yi*), propriety (*Li*), good faith (*Hsin*), and wisdom (*Chih*). One studied and learned in order to become an exemplary person (*Chün Tzu*) or a sage (*Sheng Jen*) who could serve as a role model for others to emulate. Thus how well one adheres to values and principles (e.g., is "centered" in virtue) replaces linear progress as the primary consideration. In a cyclical process, being centered is paramount. A wheel doesn't roll very far if the hub is misaligned.

Some Implications

The orientation of the traditional OD model of change is likely to lead to conceptualizing change efforts, in essence, as win-lose struggles between the forces of progress and the forces of stagnation. The forces of progress will try to use superior

planning, management, analysis, and reason to overcome the resistance and defenses of the forces of stagnation who seek to hold on to the flawed conditions of the current state by being emotional, irrational or demanding concrete, measurable proof before they will even consider movement.

On the other hand, a more Confucian or Taoist worldview may lead to conceptualizing change in terms of processes and actions that help maintain balance and harmony while attempting to fully realize the current state, and also being prepared and able to let go and align with a new state as it begins to emerge naturally. This is accomplished from an aesthetic, values centered, both/and, past-present-future, holistic orientation. It is also worth noting that the episodic, start-stop nature of the Lewinian model of change may not be as helpful as the dynamic, Confucian/Taoist model of change for understanding and dealing with the continuous change challenges of contemporary organizations.

Contexts and Considerations

An important remaining question is to what degree does Confucian thinking still influence organizational behavior in post-Confucian countries of the twenty-first century? Another important question is just how sensitive should a consultant try to be when working in post-Confucian contexts? Unfortunately the answers to these questions are not simple and straightforward. The following are some thoughts based on recent experiences working in East Asia.

Family, Country and Transnational Contexts

How directly traditional Confucian values, assumptions and orientations influence management and organizational mindsets may depend to some degree on the specific East Asian country in question. All post-Confucian societies retain vestiges of their Confucian past, and therefore also in their managerial practices (e.g. Chen, 1995), but some may manifest it more clearly or to a greater degree than others. For example, Korea which embraced a very conservative and State endorsed Confucian orthodoxy for over 500 years, might retain stronger strains of Confucian principles then some other countries in East Asia, even though all of them, including Korea, have moved away from or renounced their Confucian pasts (Chung and Lee, 1989).

Another contextual factor is the specific type of organization one is dealing with. In East Asia as in other parts of the world, there are family-run organizations, national companies that may also trade overseas, and global, transnational corporations with significant operations throughout East Asia and the rest of the world. The potential impact of Confucian values and mindsets may vary depending on which one of these organizational settings one is dealing with. In my experience, in many parts of East Asia, Confucian influences are more noticeable in family-run and also national companies, more so than in transnational corporations. Especially in some family-run businesses, the traditional Confucian family and filial piety values can be quite prominent, and norms around hierarchy and harmony are still typical in most national companies. In transnational corporations where the day-to-day language of business might not even be the local national language, the expectations and the norms of behavior can be different and the Confucian influences less noticeable or tempered by more Western orientations. In transnational corporate settings how one behaves at work may be different than how one might normally behave back home with one's family. East Asians who succeed in these settings tend to have both multi-lingual as well as multicultural skills and competencies. For example, a colleague of mine who works for a transnational corporation was recently facilitating a workshop in English for their Tokyo office. During the workshop several participants commented that the more direct and somewhat confrontational style of conversation and feedback was more or less acceptable because it was a Western transnational corporation. They also said that it would not be possible to behave that way if it were a completely Japanese company. As a Japanese colleague once told me, "If you want to understand the Japanese, you must understand that harmony is more important than anything else."

When Being Sensitive Could Be Insensitive

As a Westerner, trying to be sensitive to cultural differences, including possible Confucian-influenced differences, like many other things in East Asia, is not always a very straightforward matter. Part of the difficulty, of course, is simply trying to understand the cultural differences and nuances and how they may be influencing a particular situation. Another difficulty I have encountered relates to the status of many of the post-Confucian countries as formerly colonized (mostly by Western countries), developing economies. This impacts attitudes about the motives of Westerners, especially where the transfer of management and organizational knowledge to advance economic development is concerned. The issue is two-fold. First, there may be suspicion that the Westerner might not think the local person or people are competent enough to understand or learn the latest knowledge, and second, that the Westerner might be purposefully withholding knowledge as a way to keep the locals less competent and therefore less competitive. It is in this context that trying to be sensitive to local culture by not fully advancing Western practices can sometimes be considered to be insensitive. I have run into variations on this theme in China, Korea and Singapore over the past ten years or so. An anecdote from a luncheon discussion in Beijing a number of years ago best illustrates the phenomenon.

I was at a table having a conversation with some Chinese managers and remarked, in essence, that "I want to be sensitive to traditional Chinese culture and am concerned about suggesting that Western ways are the only or best ways to do things. There is a great deal of wisdom about management and organization in traditional Chinese thought." This was met first with the remark/question: "Which traditional culture do you mean? Do you mean pre-Mao? Pre-Cultural Revolution …?" Of course at the time I was thinking traditional Confucian culture and silently felt like an idiot. This moment of quiet embarrassment was interrupted by an angry question, "Do you think we are not capable of learning Western management and organization practices?" Before I could respond, another angry question was directed at me, "Don't you think we are smart enough to figure out what to use and how to adapt it to our circumstances?" This was then followed by the accusation/question, "Are you withholding information so we won't be able to catch up to you?" At this point it was clear that the situation was much more complex than I had thought and that my attempt at trying to be culturally sensitive had ended up coming across as being insensitive or worse to people who were trying to rapidly advance themselves and their society. In that situation what they wanted from me was the most advanced Western ideas and practices about management and organization I could provide them. It would be up to them to decide whether or not or how to use the information in a Chinese context.

Concluding Comments

Although I believe that there are Confucian based influences in the social, management and organizational practices of most East Asian societies, it is important to remember that the entire region is undergoing rapid change along with the advent of new generations who have been more exposed to Western ideas and values. Thus it might be difficult to find much overt or explicit teaching of what is now an abandoned Confucian philosophy. At the same time, it would also be unreasonable to believe that the legacy of hundreds and even thousands of years of Confucian principles and ideas, ending less than a century ago, would have no continuing influence in these countries.

It should also be noted that while each of the countries of East Asia has its own distinct history and culture, all also share many of the same cultural roots, including Confucianism. Thus the ideas presented here may prove useful to some degree throughout the region. Finally, it is hoped that this presentation will prove helpful to Western and East Asian managers and OD consultants alike as we all work together to improve the effectiveness of our organizations, communities and institutions.

References

Adler, N. J. (1991). *International dimensions of organizational behavior* (2nd ed.). Boston: PWS-Kent.

Boss, W. R., & Mariono, M. V. (1987). Organization development in Italy. *Group & Organizational Studies,* 12(3), 245-256.

Boyacigiller, N., & Adler, N. J. (1991). The parochial dinosaur: Organizational science in a global context. *Academy of Management Review,* 16(2), 262-290.

Chai, C., & Chai, W. (1973). *Confucianism.* New York: Barron's Educational series.

Chan, W. T. (Trans. and Ed.). (1963). *A source book in Chinese philosophy.* Princeton, NJ: Princeton University Press.

Chen, M. (1995). *Asian management systems: Chinese, Japanese, and Korean styles of business.* New York: Routledge.

Chung, K. H., & Lee, H. K. (1989). *Korean managerial dynamics.* New York: Praeger.

Gardner, D. K. (Trans.). (1990). *Learning to be a sage: Selections from the conversations of master Chu, arranged topically.* Berkeley: University of California Press.

Golembiewski, R. T. (1987). Is OD narrowly culture bound? Prominent features of 100 Third World applications. *Organization Development Journal,* 6(Winter), 20-29.

Golembiewski, R. T. (1991). Organization Development in the Third World: Values, closeness of fit and culture-boundedness. *International Journal of Human Resource Management, 2*(1), 39-53.

Hall, D. L., & Ames, R. T. (1987). *Thinking through Confucius.* Albany: State University of New York Press.

Hofstede, G. (1980a). Motivation, leadership, and organizations: Do American theories apply abroad? *Organizational Dynamics, 8*(Summer), 42-63.

Hofstede, G. (1980b). *Culture's consequences.* Beverly Hills, CA: Sage.

Hofstede, G., & Bond, M. H. (1988). Confucius and economic growth: New trends in culture's consequences. *Organizational Dynamics, 16*(4), 4-21.

Jaeger, A. M. (1984). The appropriateness of organization development outside North America. *International Studies of Management and Organization, 14*(1), 23-25.

Jaeger, A. M. (1986). Organization development and national culture: Where's the fit? *Academy of Management Review, 11*(1), 178-190.

Johnson, K. R. (1990). Organization development in the context of opposed cultural values: The case of OD in Venezuela. *Organization Development Journal, 6*(3), 73-75.

Knowles, M. (1978). *The adult learner: A neglected species* (2nd ed.). Houston, TX: Gulf Publishing Company.

Lewin, K. (1947). Frontiers in group dynamics. *Human Relations, 1*(1), 5-41.

Marshak, R. J. (1993a). Lewin meets Confucius: A re-view of the OD model of change, *Journal of Applied Behavioral Science, 29*(4), 393-415.

Marshak, R. J. (1993b). Training and consulting in Korea, *OD Practitioner, 25*(2), 16-21.

Marshak, R. J. (1994). The Tao of change, *OD Practitioner, 26*(2), 18-26.

Richards, D. (1991). Flying against the wind: Culture and management development in South-East Asia. *Journal of Management Development, 10*(6), 7-21.

Ryu, S. G. (1980). *Confucianism in Korea.* Seoul: King Sejong Foundation.

Stewart, E. C. (1972). *American cultural patterns: A cross-cultural perspective.* Yarmouth, ME: Intercultural Press.

Tannenbaum, R., & Davis, S. A. (1969). Values, man and organizations. *Industrial Management Review, 10*(2), 67-83.

Tarnas, R. (1991). *The passion of the Western mind.* New York: Harmony Books.

PART III
Metaphors, Language, and Change

Introduction
Robert J. Marshak

For as long as I can remember I have always listened carefully to the exact words, language, and phrases of the people and situations around me. I still frequently ask people to recount to me exactly what was said by someone and not give me their version of the message in their own words. I will also wonder if something has been written by someone else because the purported author would never use the kind of language or phrases contained in a particular missive. Behind this curiosity originally was an untrained belief that specific words and phrases might also reveal unspoken or even unconscious beliefs and understandings. This early predilection has over the years grown into a more educated and practice-proven orientation about how metaphors and language reflect inner cognitive schemata.

The first article, *Managing the Metaphors of Change,* is special for a number of reasons. It was the first serious articulation of my thinking about the connection between words and inner beliefs about change. It was also well received and created opportunities for me to continue my thinking and writing on this topic, as will be noted below. Interestingly, I wrote it as a type of "time out" from my work on another article. I had been working between consulting assignments for several years on what became Lewin Meets Confucius and needed a break from the intense study and concentration needed for that project. As a break in my thinking, I decided to write up a short article based on some ideas I had been talking about and verbally presenting for six or seven years about the connection between different types of change and the word images associated with them. In short order I produced a draft of the article, decided it had turned out better than I had originally intended, polished it and sent it off for review. As things turned out it was accepted and published the same year as Lewin Meets Confucius. It is probably one of if not the best known of all my publications.

Metaphors, Metaphoric Fields and Organizational Change became an opportunity to more thoroughly document my thinking about metaphors and organizational change and also add some thoughts about metaphorical diagnosis and intervention coming from my consulting practice. It resulted from a telephone call from two people I had never met or heard about before, David Grant and Cliff Oswick who were then at King's College London. They had read the Metaphors of Change article, were editing a book on Metaphor and Organization and called out of the blue to ask me to contribute a chapter to the book. After originally declining because I was "a consultant and not an academic who wrote things," I sent along the book chapter and was invited by them to attend an academic conference they were hosting in 1996 on an emerging field called "Organizational Discourse."

That invitation turned into a request that I give a plenary session addressing the subject of "talk and action," which was one of the themes of the conference. It was my first presentation of any kind at an academic conference, but went over well despite my private concerns. I later wrote it up and it was published as *A Discourse on Discourse: Redeeming the Meaning of Talk*. It was and still is one of my more "philosophical" works – as I was concerned about being academic enough in my remarks – and centrally addresses the marginalization of "talk" (discourse) in favor of "action." It is also an argument for the importance of paying attention to "talk" and the embedded assumptions behind or beneath the talk surrounding change and especially transformational change efforts.

The connections made at that conference led to my being invited by David Grant, who had moved to the University of Sydney, to give a presentation at an academic conference in Australia in 2001. That presentation became *Changing the Language of Change: How New Contexts and Concepts are Challenging the Ways We Think and Talk about Organizational Change*. It became the vehicle for me to argue that our language of change, indeed the word "change" itself, was embedded with concepts and assumptions that limit our ability to address continuous change in organizations. For example, we tend to think about change, especially transformational change, as something that is accomplished and then we are supposed to return to a more or less "steady state." Despite the current talk about "constant or continuous change," the notion of "continuous transformational change" didn't seem to me to be supported by our mainstream theories and ideas, or even the language we use to talk about change. Instead I thought then and still think that most of our thinking about change is embedded in "start-stop" ideas, models, and language/metaphors of change.

The connections made during my first organizational discourse conference also introduced me to Tom Keenoy, who was a collaborator with David Grant and Cliff Oswick at King's College. The three of them were kind enough to invite me onto the editorial team for what became a special issue of the Journal of Applied Behavioral Science devoted to organizational discourse. Together we wrote a concluding discussion to the issue called *From Outer Words to Inner Worlds*. In addition to commenting on the potential contributions of organizational discourse to the study of organizational change, it also outlined how outer words may sometimes be clues to unspoken and sometimes unconscious inner worlds. This perspective was a departure from most of the organizational discourse literature that tended to treat the analysis of organizational discourse from a consciously intended language perspective. The short note on *Metaphor and Analogical Reasoning in Organization Theory: Further Extensions* was another opportunity to briefly articulate the perspective that word images and metaphors might reflect unconscious phenomena.

The next article in this section called *A Discursive Approach to Organization Development* also reflects the theme of serendipitous collaboration in my writings about language and change. My co-author, Loizos Heracleous, was invited to present at the same conference as I was in Australia. We were the two out of country participants (at the time he was at the University of Singapore) and ended up sightseeing together and getting to know each other. That led to a desire to see if we could collaborate on a project that brought together some of his more theoretical thinking about discourse with my consulting experiences. This led to a consideration of how discourse could be conceived of as "situated symbolic action" and how that might shape the way one might interpret and intervene in a "real world" discussion of organizational change.

The final article in the section, *Organizational Discourse and New Organization Development Practices*, recently co-authored with David Grant, continues my thinking about discourse, language and change by attempting to bridge ideas from the organizational discourse literature with some of the newer emerging practices in organizational development. It was a good opportunity to collaborate with a longtime colleague who is more conversant in the organizational discourse literature than I and also to try to encourage more linkage of theory and practice pertaining to organizational discourse and change.

11
Managing the Metaphors of Change

For most leaders and change agents, one seven-word expression has become synonymous with resistance to change: "If it ain't broke, don't fix it!" On the surface, it's a straightforward, rather blunt statement of fact and advice: "Don't mess with what's already working." As usually interpreted, however, it's a slogan of resistance, defiantly asserting: "No change is wanted or needed here; go tinker somewhere else!" Considered symbolically, it may also reveal an unarticulated set of assumptions about change and the organization in question. Every individual, and for that matter, cultural system, views and interprets empirical events through a set of beliefs and assumptions. Often these beliefs and assumptions are subconscious and rarely examined or questioned. They just are. Yet they exert a profound influence over how a person sees a situation, and what actions will or will not be taken. If, for example, someone implicitly assumes that interpersonal communication is like calling another person on the telephone, then any miscommunication might be attributed to a "bad connection" or "static on the line." Viewed as a computer-to-computer interface, the difficulties might be alternatively defined as "incompatible software or hardware." Depending on the implicit view, different remedies are likely to be suggested: "Let's hang up and try again," or "Let's make sure we are both using the same (computer) language."

This discussion advances the proposition that these underlying, usually unarticulated understandings about a situation are often shaped and revealed metaphorically. Furthermore, because these understandings are critical to how people assess the need for change–and indeed, their conception of change itself–paying attention to managing the metaphors of change becomes a critical competency for leaders and change agents.

Metaphors and Metaphoric Analysis

A metaphor is a form of symbolic, rather than literal, expression. The Webster's New World Dictionary defines a metaphor as: "A figure of speech containing an implied comparison, in which a word or phrase ordinarily and primarily used for one thing is applied to another, e.g., the curtain of night." Beyond their usefulness to poets and politicians, some psychologists assert that metaphors serve as the essential bridge between the literal and the symbolic, between cognition and affect, and between the conscious and the unconscious.

As such, metaphors are often the medium for understanding and presenting ideas, insights, and intuitions not always available to analytic reasoning and discourse. Others, including linguists and philosophers, go further to suggest that metaphors serve as a primary method for understanding and expressing abstract, affective, and/or intuitive experience.

From these points of view, the statement "If it ain't broke, don't fix it!" is more than a phrase signifying resistance to change. It is the manifest expression of a deeper, sometimes preconscious, symbolic construct that informs and maintains "reality" for the speaker. It is, therefore, a key to what a person may really be thinking, even when the person "hasn't really

Marshak, R.J. (1993). Managing the metaphors of change. *Organizational Dynamics*, 22(1), 44-56. Add Republished with permission.

thought about it." Consequently, for diagnostic purposes, the way to approach and listen to metaphorical expressions is "as if" they were literally true. A closer look at our example slogan will reveal the potential power of this form of analysis.

First, consider what "it" in the slogan stands for. Clearly, "it" refers to the organization, system, policy, etc., in question. Thus the phrase is really saying: "If the organization ain't broke, don't fix it!" Now let's consider the rest of the phrase. Things that literally break and require fixing in the "real world" are typically machines – toasters, washing machines, lawn mowers, automobiles, etc. The phrase is essentially equating the organization to a machine that requires fixing only when there is a breakdown or malfunction. Thus, it would not be unreasonable to assume that at the moment of invoking the slogan the speaker conceives of the organization, at a conscious or preconscious level, as if it were a machine and is inviting others to do the same. This is not a trivial association when we consider the implications of the extended metaphor of an organization as a machine. If it is a machine, then things should be smooth running, well-oiled, predictable, efficient, and designed such that all the parts fit together to fulfill a single, unambiguous function or purpose. This bears more than a passing similarity to the Scientific Management theory of organizations and reminds one that the Father of Scientific Management, Frederick Winslow Taylor (1856-1915), was a trained mechanical engineer and machinist.

This leads to another important aspect of the extended metaphor. If an organization is a machine, then who are the managers and leaders of the organization/machine? Typically, machines are run by operators and engineers who determine output standards, maintain the equipment, and set commands and controls that dictate what the machine will do. Furthermore, when a machine breaks down or needs servicing, a repair person, maintenance worker, or mechanic is called in, asked to bring a tool kit, and told to "fix it."

The concept of change itself is also part of this extended metaphor system. Thinking in terms of a machine metaphor invites thinking about organizational change in terms of something "breaking down" and therefore "needing repairs." Ideally, this should be done with "minimal downtime," doing just enough to "get things up and running again." Consequently, in the machine metaphor system of thought, change is often equated to something being poorly maintained or broken. Accordingly, from this mind set, the arrival of a change agent (repair person) at your place of work implies psychologically that you've done something wrong, or worse, broken something. This helps explain the sometimes emotionally-charged reaction: "There's nothing wrong... nothing's broken!" Thus, one way people understand the abstract phenomena of organizational change is as if a broken-down machine is being returned to smooth-running performance through the assistance of a repair person who was called in and who works under the direction of the machine's operator or engineer.

An Example of Being Stuck In Machine Metaphor Thinking

A large high-tech company was faced in the 1990s with a host of dilemmas: Its traditional market base was eroding, new competitors had entered the field, costs and overhead had to be drastically cut to increase competitiveness, structural re-alignment was needed to promote greater synergy and quicker response, long-time customers were demanding more responsiveness and less arrogance, and the "everyone can do their own thing as long as you are successful" culture was getting in the way of the teamwork and collective focus needed to respond to the new challenges.

Unfortunately, the top executives of this corporation were caught in an implicit machine metaphor model of change. The CEO called meetings of all the VPs, and ordered them to "fix things quickly in order to maintain our market position." The VPs dutifully went looking for "what was broken" so they could "fix it," but came back perplexed. Everything was working the way it always had been – "nothing was broken"– so they couldn't find anything to "fix." Because they had always been successful, they rationalized that there was nothing wrong with them; it was just a temporary thing and soon everything would be back to normal. Conditions, however, continued to get worse.

Next, they decided to hold a series of retreats to find the problems in how they were producing their traditional products and services. They identified a number of problems that surely had to be "what was broken." These were "fixed" with great fanfare and everyone was convinced that "things would soon be up and running again" the way they always had been. Instead, conditions continued to worsen. Employees began to get worried and angry at the top leaders because they were failing to "fix the problem." Leaders and managers, in turn, were blaming supervisors and employees for not working harder to "fine-tune operations and/or operate at full throttle." This led to a series of all-employee meetings where the top leadership assured everyone that the situation would soon be "under control and smooth running again." Employees were further assured that a series of task forces was going to "take apart the operation from top to bottom to find out what was wrong." Everyone just needed to have some patience. When conditions didn't get better, the CEO held a week-long special retreat with all the key managers of the corporation. In concurrent sessions, different aspects of the corporation were "broken down and put back together again." The reports all came back with minimal or marginal ideas for improvements. Everyone kept saying: "Things are working correctly – the way they were designed to work." Furthermore, the existing "set-up" was the most effective and efficient way to "run the organization."

As conditions continued to decline, and in desperation, the CEO called in a group of management consultants. Their backgrounds varied, but their advice was the same: "You have to re-think your whole business; up until now you have only been tinkering." Somewhat taken aback, the CEO assured each of the consultants that every conceivable way to "fix or improve operations" had been tried, and that perhaps the consultants didn't really understand how the business worked. All of the consultants were steadfast and assured the CEO that nothing less than a "new conception" of the business and how it operated would save the corporation. At this point the CEO, somewhat defensively, challenged the consultants: "You are the experts, find something in your tool kits to fix the problem." The consultants all replied it was not a question of "fixing" anything, rather a need to "re-invent" the corporation. This just further annoyed the CEO, who couldn't figure out how business results could be so poor, if "nothing needed fixing."

Recently, the CEO was replaced by the board of directors. In taking this action, the board explained that they needed "a new leader who was not a captive of the past, had some vision, and was capable of giving birth to a new era."

The story of this corporation is a familiar one in the 1990s. CEOs who try to "fix" or "repair" their organizations are being replaced in favor of new leaders who promise "a new way of thinking." One need only look at GM, IBM, American Express, and even the U.S. presidential election of 1992, to see leaders who thought they knew how to "keep the machine running" being replaced by new leaders with "the vision thing." The following discussion may shed some new light on this phenomenon and raise questions about whether or not a change in implicit metaphor could make a difference.

Metaphors of Change

The "Fix and Maintain" imagery described above, while frequently encountered, is hardly the only metaphor of organizational change. We can consider three additional types of organizational change processes: Developmental, Transitional, and Transformational. Each has its own characteristics and associated change technologies:

- **Developmental** change builds on the past and leads to better performance over time, e.g., better teamwork.
- **Transitional** change involves a move from one state or condition to another, e.g., from manual to automated operations.
- **Transformational** change implies the transfiguration from one state of being to a fundamentally different state of being, e.g., from a regulated monopoly to a market-driven competitive business.

Clearly what is happening is different in each case. Significantly, the metaphors and imagery used to understand and describe each type of change are also different.

In **developmental** change, one builds on a foundation to achieve higher levels of performance. The metaphors and imagery are analogous to construction and/or developmental growth. The organization is described as if it were a building under construction or a developing person. This kind of change is often perceived as positive (getting bigger, getting better, etc.), especially when the developmental plan and/or goals are agreed upon in advance. Developmental change agents are often referred to as **trainers**, **coaches**, and/or **developers**. They may be asked to do organization "development" or team "building" to help "lay a better foundation" in order to "improve" performance, "increase" capabilities, "build" additional competencies, and/or "stimulate" and "nurture" growth.

An example of a developmental change effort was a series of strategy sessions conducted by the editors of a national travel magazine. They saw their task as figuring out ways to "build and develop" the magazine. Consequently, they focused on strategies to "build" circulation, "develop" new features, and "increase" advertising based on the "strong foundation" of their traditional audience "base." The possibility that changing trends and demographics might call for more radical changes was consistently ignored because "our job is to develop what we've got."

In **transitional** change, an organization goes from one state to another state, such as moving from a centralized to a decentralized operational system. The metaphors and imagery are analogous to relocating and/or moving from one place to another place. Expressions such as "moving forward," "knowing the right path," "taking the best route," "keeping to the timetable," "avoiding obstacles and dead ends," "leaving the old behind," and so forth, are common. The lack of "a clear destination," disagreement over the need or desirability of "the move," conflict over "the best route to take," debates over who has "to move," "how fast to go," and whether or not this is the best time "to pack up and leave" are all ways to describe common difficulties encountered in transitional change efforts. Transitional change agents are called upon to be **planners**, **guides**, and/or **explorers** because they are supposedly more familiar with "the journey" and with what to expect "along the way." Consequently, they are usually asked to help make plans for the "duration of the journey," or at least to make sure everyone is "headed in the right direction." They are also supposed to help facilitate "movement," insure things "stay on track," and that no one is "left behind." Once the organization "arrives" at its desired "destination," it is assumed their guidance will no longer be needed.

An example of a transitional change was the planning process carried out by a leading daily newspaper to introduce a new printing technology in its publishing plant. The process included specifications of the "desired end state" and the exact time the plant would "get there." Meetings were held with the union to insure that everyone was "on board", that "things stayed on track," and that "the road ahead stayed clear." A major sticking point in the discussions with the union was "how fast to make the changeover." After following a very detailed "schedule and timetable," everyone in the plant celebrated "the arrival" of the new equipment and had a moment of silence for the old presses that were being "abandoned and left behind." Indeed, many of the workers talked about how hard it would be to get used to the sounds and rhythms of the "new place." Despite all the detailed planning and work with the union, no one ever considered working on other changes such as re-designing jobs or the pay system because "our job was to move to a new way of printing, not create a whole new plant."

In **transformational** change, there is also language about change from one state to another state. However, the metaphors and imagery are not about geographic movement so much as they are about an alteration in the state of being, as in becoming a fundamentally different kind of organization. The imagery of "becoming" in transformational change is also more radical and extreme than in developmental change, where the organization becomes better at something, but doesn't abandon its foundation, roots, or essential being. In transformational change, the metaphors and imagery are about a fundamental alteration in who or what the organization is – its very identity and way of being, e.g., "abandoning the past in order to become a completely different kind of company."

A range of metaphors is often used to describe organizational transformation. These include images and metaphors associated with awakening, uncovering, escaping, purifying/purging, enlightening, becoming whole, returning to the core, unfolding, and dying and being reborn. Thus, in organizational transformation, we might hear expressions or a need "to wake up," "remove the blinders," "get out of the box," " "get rid of excess baggage," "see the light," "become more holistic," "return to the basics," and "recreate ourselves anew." Organizations experiencing transformational change may ask change agents to help them "remove their blinders" in order to develop new visions and values, assist in "breaking out of the box," help people "to see" or "to get it," and/or help the organization "re-invent" itself or "give birth" to a whole new way of doing things. At such times, the change agent is likened to a **liberator, visionary**, or **creator** who possesses the ability to help "unlock the situation," "see new possibilities," and "give birth" to the new organization. One of the clearest examples of (forced) transformational change was the break-up of the Bell system into the new AT&T and the regional "Baby Bells." In addressing this change, the leadership and employees of the new organizations were initially stymied in their efforts to "build and develop" their businesses based on past practices. It was only after they struggled with "letting go" of time-honored values, traditions, and ways of thinking in order to create new structures and systems, all in the context of new visions and missions, that they began to experience success.

Table 11.1
Metaphors of Change and Change Agents

Image of Change	Image of Change Agent
Fix & Maintain	Repair Person, Maintenance Worker, Mechanic
Build & Develop	Trainer, Coach, Developer
Move & Relocate	Planner, Guide, Explorer
Liberate & Recreate	Liberator, Visionary, Creator

Mixing and Matching Metaphors

The four dominant types of metaphors about organizational change and change agents are summarized in Table 11.1. Knowing how to understand, use, and align these metaphors can be a powerful tool in any change effort. Consider Table 11.2, where an organizational situation is presented and then described through each of the four different change metaphor systems.

Table 11.2
The Impact of Metaphors on Assessment and Action

Objective Situation: Processing of customer orders is being delayed as paperwork moves back and forth among four different departments. Invoices are late and sometimes inaccurate. Inventory control is described as "out of control."

Metaphor	Internal Assessment	External Action
Fix & Maintain	*The "processing machine" is broken somewhere. We may need to fix the machine and/or fix (re-train) the operators.*	"Things just aren't in sync. A lot of things are fouled up. I don't know if anything's broken or not, but we've got to fix things fast. We can't afford a lot of downtime. Find someone with a good set of tools fast!"
Build & Develop	*The basic set-up is fine. We need to learn how to work faster with better hand-offs and teamwork between the departments.*	"We can do better than we have been doing. We have a strong foundation to build on, we just need to improve our performance. I'd like to set some stretch goals to shoot for, construct a winning team, and then develop the business. Find someone who can help build us into a better team!"
Move & Relocate	*We need to move from our old, familiar manual processing system to a new, automated one. It will be hard to leave the old ways behind, but we need to move on.*	"We've got to keep moving. We've stayed with our old system too long. It's time to leave that behind and go on to a more modern operation. We've a long way to go, so we better start out now. Find someone who's been down this road before to help us plan how to get there!"
Liberate & Recreate	*We need to open our eyes and rethink the business. Our hierarchical, sequential operation must end. We need to become a whole new kind of organization.*	"It's time we woke up to reality. We need to get rid of a lot of things and get down to the essence. We need to break away from our habitual ways of thinking. We need a new beginning and an end to our past practices. Find someone who can help us create a new vision of the future, re-invent the organization, and get us out of the box we're in!"

These metaphors help to first define and then address the situation. Consequently, knowing which metaphor(s) a person is using, whether they are aware of it or not, helps enormously in understanding how they see the situation. Paying attention to how someone talks or writes about the change is a key to the underlying metaphor. For example, if someone says in response to the situation described in Table 11.2, "We have a strong foundation to build on, we just need to improve our performance," it would be a good guess to assume they are operating from some form of an underlying "Build and Develop" metaphor system. With this understanding, one can then choose to get "in sync" with the person by communicating using the same metaphor or image system, or invite an alternative way of conceiving things by purposefully using a different metaphor or image system. This is illustrated in Table 11.3.

Table 11.3
Aligning the Metaphors of Change

Example 1:	Out of Sync
Leader A:	So what do you think about the task force's recommendation?
Manager B:	It's going to be quite a haul to get from where we are now to where they want us to go. (Move & Relocate)
Leader A:	You're not kidding. It will be quite a job to wake up this organization. How about you? Have you seen the light? What do you think we need to do to make sure we successfully break free from past practices and create the new organization? (Liberate & Recreate)
Manager B:	Well, as long as everyone is perfectly clear where we're headed, why we're going there, and the milestones along the way, it shouldn't impact on current operations too badly. When will we get our marching orders? (Move & Relocate)
Example 2:	In Sync
Manager X:	So what do you think about the task force's recommendation?
Manager Y:	It's going to be quite a haul to get from where we are now to where they want us to go. (Move & Relocate)
Manager X:	Are you up for the trip? What do you think we need to do to make sure we get to where we are headed? (Move & Relocate)
Manager Y:	Yes, I'm on board. Let's be clear about where we're going and then map out the best way to get there. (Move & Relocate)
Example 3:	Re-Sync
Leader Q:	So what do you think about the task force's recommendation?
Executive P:	It's going to be quite a haul to get from where we are now to where they want us to go. (Move & Relocate)
Leader Q:	I think we need to first realize the box we're stuck in before we can go anywhere. (Move & Relocate)
Executive P:	Yeah, I know what you mean. It's hard to get anyone to think about going anywhere – you know, change – around here. We're all stuck. (Move & Liberate)
Leader Q:	What do you think might help get us unstuck – get out of the box we're in – so we can see some new possibilities? (Liberate & Recreate)
Executive P:	It's funny. I've never thought of it that way. I guess you can't go anywhere as long as you're trapped in a box. Maybe we need an escape hatch! (Liberate & Recreate)
Leader Q:	That's a great idea! Do you have any ideas where the escape hatch is located or how we could create one? (Liberate & Recreate)
Executive P:	Well, now that you mention it, we could try…

In fact, because of the relationship between the underlying metaphor and how someone conceives of and then acts in a situation, it is possible to:

- **Diagnose** unarticulated assumptions and beliefs by paying attention to the metaphors and images used to describe any particular change.
- **Prepare** and **align** people with the true nature and requirements of the change by using congruent and appropriate metaphors and images.
- **Confuse** or **mislead** people by using inappropriate or incongruent metaphors and images.

With the examples in Tables 11.2 and 11.3 in mind, let's look at these assertions in more detail. First, it's important to remember that the same situation can be viewed and assessed in many different ways. Everyone sizes up a situation based on their own set of assumptions, beliefs, and metaphors for dealing with and describing reality. It is possible to view and interpret the same situation as if one were dealing with a machine, a construction project, a cross-country move, and/or breaking free from some limitation. Test this yourself. Think of a recent change in your organization. Was this done because "something was broken," because "it would make things bigger, better, faster," because "it made sense to move from one place (or way of doing things) to another place," and/or because "it was time to let go of the past and (re)create a new way of working"?

Second, how a situation is assessed – the metaphor(s) one uses to help define what is happening – will lead to differing courses of action. Depending on the metaphorical perspective, a wide variety of change initiatives could be recommended, from "tinkering" to "re-creating" the business. If a "well-oiled machine" metaphor is used explicitly or implicitly to assess the problem, it is likely the remedy will be some form of "repair and maintenance," perhaps a "tune-up." It is unlikely, however, that a machine metaphor assessment would lead to a values or inspirational vision-driven intervention. It just wouldn't make sense to say: "We need a tune-up, so let's break free of the past and envision the future in order to breathe new life into the business." Nor would it make sense to say: "We need to move from where we are now to a new state, so let's keep what we've got, build on it, and strengthen it." Our actions tend to follow our assessments.

The previous example of the Bell system is a case in point. During the first few months (some would say years) after the break-up of the Bell system, managers and employees had a hard time adjusting to the changes. In a series of workshops convened to help people talk about what was happening and what they needed to do, the same sentiments came up over and over again: "Nothing was broken to begin with; we don't know what to fix." "They've taken away everything we were based on. How can they expect us to improve our performance now?" "We've been reorganized before, but this isn't like other moves; we've abandoned everything we stood for and we don't know where we're going." It was only after the concept and imagery of transformational change was introduced that people found the words to express what they had been feeling: "Yes, that's it. It's like we died and are waiting to be reborn." "No wonder I felt so lost. Now I understand that we have to create a whole new organization." "No wonder I felt so confused trying to build on what I had done in the past."

Third, the metaphors and images used by people in publicly describing a situation are usually a strong indicator of the private, underlying assessments and premises from which they are operating. For example, hearing someone say: "We've got to **move from** a hierarchical organization **to** a flatter structure" is a reasonable signal to assume that they are looking at the situation through a "Move and Relocate" metaphor system. When different people in the organization share the same underlying metaphor(s) there is usually agreement and focus on what to do. A common metaphor provides a shared understanding for everyone. When the underlying metaphors are different, conflict over what to do and how to do it is common. Thus one person may be trying to "fix the machine," while another wants to "move the organization," and still another doesn't want to "tear down what we've spent so much time building up." In such situations, people may fight over the causes and cures to the problem without ever realizing that their differing, unexpressed, metaphorical reasoning may be preventing them from really understanding one another.

This is illustrated by a planning session involving managers of a major government agency addressing what to do about workforce diversity. During the session, there was strongly divided opinion about how much needed to be done. Some felt a major effort involving retraining managers and redesigning the organization would be needed. Others were equally adamant that not much more than a few directives would handle the situation. It was when they were asked to complete the sentence: "Dealing with workforce diversity issues is like doing _____ to an automobile," that they realized what their conflicts really were. About half of the managers responded: a "tune-up," a "new paint job," or a "good cleaning and washing." Meanwhile, the other half said: "a complete overhaul," "installing a new engine and frame," or "a complete re-design and re-engineering." It was only after the implicit imagery that had been guiding their thinking was revealed that they were able to have a substantive discussion about what needed to be done.

Fourth, people will be confused and misled when a manager or leader uses metaphors and imagery in public discussions about a change effort that do not match the actual intended change. For example, if the leader privately believes there is a need to "rethink the business," "break free from the past," "wake up to the new realities," and "create anew," then some form of transformational change is probably intended. Such changes can be traumatic, lengthy, and require a fundamental alteration in thinking and doing by organizational members. If, however, in public presentations the leader tells the organization that: "We've entered a new phase where we need to build on our past successes, strengthen ourselves further, and insure a smooth running operation," then it is likely that "Fix and Maintain" and/or "Build and Develop" metaphors and images will be evoked in the minds of the audience. Thus, they will be ill prepared, psychologically and emotionally, if they are then sent to workshops to learn how to "think outside of the box." If they then act confused or slow to get it, they may be labeled as resisters, rather than people who have been confused and/or misled by inappropriate imagery. Sometimes such mixed messages are unintended or derive from some confusion or lack of clarity by the leader. In other cases, they may be intended, but in the hopes of helping versus hurting the situation.

For example, in a large corporation heavily dependent on Defense Department spending, its president realized that world events, shifting priorities, and declining governmental budgets would seriously impact the company's future unless the organization fundamentally repositioned itself, changed its product/service mix, and altered its traditional culture. Nonetheless, when addressing middle managers about the need for these changes, the president kept (inappropriately) describing the changes called for as "based on our long history and traditional values" and "building on our past successes." The president ended the session by exhorting the managers to go out and "develop their operations for the future." Unfortunately, the president became increasingly dismayed as manager after manager began developing plans to expand on what they were already doing, rather than rethinking the business. When later asked why imagery related to "building on the past" was used, the president responded: "I thought it would help reduce resistance if they thought the changes weren't really that drastic. I just couldn't imagine telling them the 'past was dead' and that we had to 'wake up' to the new realities and 'invent' a new organization."

Finally, one way to help people align themselves with an intended change effort is to insure first that everyone is operating from the same metaphor/image system, and then that the metaphors and images are congruent with the intended change. If people seem confused about what to do, changing or altering the implicit and explicit metaphors may either free up their thinking, or cast the situation in a new light. When Total Quality Management (TQM) is talked about as a way to "provide more tools to fix more problems," it is unlikely that people will understand the aspects of TQM that call for a new management philosophy because a "Fix and Maintain" image is being evoked. Alternatively, if TQM is described using a "Liberate and Recreate" metaphor system as "a whole new way of being that breaks from past practices and calls for new ways of working together," then it is more likely that it will be understood as intended to change existing management practices. People may still resist, but at least they and you know what they are resisting.

A good example of this was a large accounting firm where the introduction of TQM was met with fierce resistance from all levels of employees and managers. They objected to the idea that something might be wrong with the professional quality of their work and "needed fixing." The change strategy that emphasized training managers in TQM problem-solving tools and techniques ("because it was more hands-on") had been a serious miscalculation. Everyone was angry that top management thought something "was broken" in the quality of their work and therefore they were being given "tool kits to fix things." When the change strategy was shifted to also explain the underlying logic, rationale, and factors and forces driving the change, tempers finally abated.

Table 11.4
Some Keys for Managing the Metaphors of Change

1. Listen to the word images you and others use to describe the change effort in order to assess clarity, consistency, and comprehension.

2. Make sure what you tell yourself and others metaphorically is what you mean literally.

3. Describe the change situation using all four (or more) change metaphor systems as an exercise to gain new insights and guard against blind spots.

4. Work to align the symbolic language system to help get people fixing, building, moving, or recreating in unison.

5. Seek to intentionally shape how people conceive and think about the change through the creative and constructive use of metaphors, images, and symbols.

6. When stuck, deliberately change the prevailing metaphor(s) and image(s) as a way to get out of the box and induce new ways of thinking.

Managing the Metaphors Of Change

Based on the above discussion, the following ideas (summarized in Table 11.4) offer some specifics to consider when dealing with organizational change:

1. Pay careful attention to how you and others describe, verbally and in writing, the change in question. Are you describing the change as if what is needed is to:
   - Fix & Maintain: repair, tinker, adjust, fine-tune, deal with what's broken, get the right tools, etc.?
   - Build & Develop: add to, grow, lay a good foundation, nurture, train, get bigger, get smarter, get faster, etc.?
   - Move & Relocate: move forward, go from ____to____, leave something behind, watch for obstacles, timetables, clear steps, milestones, etc.?
   - Liberate & Recreate: wake up, think out of the box, create a new paradigm, see the light, break free from the past, end _____ and give birth to _____, reinvent, recreate, etc.?

   Listen to yourself and others as an act of diagnosis to test clarity, intent, and understanding regarding the change.

2. Make sure what you say is what you mean. Insure that how you think about and describe the change metaphorically is consistent with the intended change. Otherwise, you may be confusing others and/or yourself. Don't talk about "building on the past" if what you really want to do is "escape the past and create a new future." Note that any recurring inconsistencies in how you and others describe the change could be a possible indicator of continuing doubt, confusion, or lack of clarity as to what is really intended and why.

3. Describe the intended change using all four, or more, metaphor systems as a planning exercise. Pay attention to the ways in which you see the situation the same or differently through each metaphor. Note the implications for intervention and action. For example, imagine a meeting of Kremlin leaders in 1990 going through such an exercise:
   - We need to **fix and maintain** communism because _____. In order to do that, we need to _____.
   - We need to **build and develop** communism because _____. In order to do that, we need to _____.
   - We need to **move from** the old form of communism **to** a new and different communism because _____. In order to do that, we need to _____.
   - We need **to end** communism and **begin anew** because _____. In order to do that, we need to _____.

   While there is no guarantee how such an exercise will turn out, it does assure that multiple views will be examined. It might also turn up some blind spots created by unspoken beliefs associated with unexpressed metaphorical reasoning.

4. Work to align the symbolic language system of everyone involved to match the desired change. It does no good for the CEO to be talking about "moving and relocating" if lower-level managers are talking exclusively in terms of "fixing and/or building." It's hard to imagine a successful organizational change effort where the CEO sends a message about a "faster, more responsive, more effective organization" to middle managers who tell supervisors to "go fix your operation," but are greeted by angry workers who say: "What's the problem? Nothing's broken!" This also means that a change agent should not unintentionally reinforce inappropriate metaphors, and, in turn, the underlying ways of conceiving the situation. If a manager worries that a change effort may "require too much downtime" and that "a good set of tools is needed," then the response "Don't worry, I'll get my tool kit and keep downtime limited" is reinforcing. That's appropriate if the intended change is a "Fix and Maintain" type of change. If it isn't, then a more appropriate response might be:"I'm not sure we're fixing anything, so much as we are moving from an old system to a new system. The move may take some time, so we need to plan it carefully. The first step will be to map out the direction we're headed in and where we want to be by next year."

5. Lead by helping to shape how people conceive and think about things. The creative and constructive use of symbolic language systems is a critical leadership competency, especially during organizational change. Leaders simply cannot afford to let their change initiatives be recast and/or misunderstood as a result of implicit or unexamined metaphors. Leaders must be clear in what they want and help shape and inform change through congruent use of literal and symbolic reasoning. They must also be sensitive to their own blind spots created by unthinking use of favored metaphors or images that may be limiting their own reasoning processes.

6. Intentionally change prevailing metaphors and images as a way to induce new ways of conceiving of a situation. "In the box" thinking is created by habitual use of thought patterns that inevitably lead to the same conclusion. New patterns are needed to "get out of the box." Because most people naturally use metaphors for abstract reasoning, one way to "get out of the box" is to deliberately change the underlying metaphors and images being applied to the situation. Any organizational change that requires people to reconceive the situation they face will require a change in the underlying and usually unexamined metaphors. To ignore this aspect of managing change is to jeopardize the whole change effort.

Concluding Remarks

In sum, how one conceives of something is often based on the implicit or explicit metaphorical system(s) used to comprehend and engage reality. Therefore, how an organizational change is described metaphorically is both:

- an indicator of the speaker's internal understanding and assessment of the situation, and

- a way to cue and influence how listeners should understand and respond.

Change may be change, but the symbolic languages associated with Maintenance, Development, Transition, and Transformation are all quite different. The next time someone in your organization says: "But if it ain't broke, why fix it?," recall this discussion and seize the opportunity to paint a word picture of what you really want to communicate.

Selected Bibliography

The pervasive use and influence of metaphors in how people talk and think about their everyday experience is thoughtfully presented by George Lakoff and Mark Johnson in *Metaphors We Live By*, Chicago: The University of Chicago Press, 1980. The extensive use and validity of metaphorical language and reasoning in the sciences as well as religion is addressed by Earl R. MacCormac in *Metaphor and Myth in Science and Religion*, Durham, N.C.: Duke University Press, 1976.

A wide range of authors have applied metaphors and metaphorical analysis to the study of organizations. Among the very best is Gareth Morgan's book, *Images of Organization*, Beverly Hills, CA: Sage Publications, Inc., 1986. The case for the inclusion of metaphorical analysis in the management of organizations is presented in Louis R. Pondy's article, "The Role of Metaphors and Myths in Organization and in the Facilitation of Change," in L.R. Pondy, P. J. Frost, G. Morgan, and T.C. Dandridge, eds., *Organizational Symbolism*, Greenwich, CT: JAI Press, 1983 and by Haridimos Tsoukas, "The Missing Link: A Transformational View of Metaphors in Organizational Science," *Academy of Management Review*, Vol. 16, No.3, 1991, pp. 566-585.

How metaphors can be used for diagnosis and intervention in counseling or therapeutic settings is discussed by Ellen Y. Siegelman in her book, *Metaphor and Meaning in Psychotherapy*, New York: The Guilford Press, 1990. The use of symbolic data, including metaphors, in organizational diagnosis and intervention is addressed by Robert J. Marshak and Judith H. Katz in "The Symbolic Side of OD," *OD Practitioner*, Vol. 24, No.2, 1992, pp. 1-5.

The differences among developmental, transitional and transformational change, and associated types of change interventions, are addressed by Linda S. Ackerman in her article, "Development, Transition, or Transformation: The Question of Change in Organizations," *OD Practitioner*, Vol. 18, No.4, 1986, pp. 1-5. An extended discussion and review of the literature on how revolutionary (transformational) change differs from evolutionary (developmental/transitional) change is presented by Connie J. G. Gersick in her article, "Revolutionary Change Theories: A Multilevel Exploration of the Punctuated Equilibrium Paradigm," *Academy of Management Review*, Vol. 16, No.1, 1991, pp. 10-36.

The power of metaphors to help explain and create the experience of human transformation is discussed in depth by Ralph Metzner in his book, *Opening to Inner Light*, Los Angeles: Jeremy P. Tarcher, Inc., 1986.

One of the first and best discussions on the paramount role of the leader in shaping organizational reality through conscious management of value and symbol systems is presented by Edgar H. Schein in *Organizational Culture and Leadership*, San Francisco: Jossey Bass Publishers, 1985. The classic discussion of socially-defined reality remains P. L. Berger and T. Luckmann, *The Social Construction of Reality,* Garden City, N.Y.: Doubleday, 1966. Per-Olof Berg addresses the role that symbols and metaphors play in creating and shaping organizational change in "Organizational Change as a Symbolic Transformation Process," in P. J. Frost, L. F. Moore, M. R. Louis, C. C. Lundberg, and J. Martin, Eds., *Organizational Culture*, Beverly Hills, CA: Sage Publications, 1985.

12
Metaphors, Metaphoric Fields, and Organizational Change

While this chapter intends to increase awareness about metaphors and organizations, its real purpose is to suggest the instrumental power of metaphors and metaphorical analysis in organizational change. The chapter is in three parts. The first part reviews recent trends in organization theory in order to then propose a meta-theory of organizational change that can be used to address an organization's symbolic meaning system. The second part explores the dimensions of such systems and introduces the more specific concept of an organizational "metaphoric field." The final part addresses the use of metaphors in organizational diagnosis and intervention.

Cognition, Culture, and the Unconscious in Organizational Change

Beginning in the 1980s the literature related to organization theory and organizational change began to pay increasing attention to three newer approaches, or "schools," for thinking about organizational behavior. For our purposes we will name these the cognitive, cultural and unconscious or psychoanalytic schools. While they are quite distinct from one another, theoretically, each emphasizes the importance of subjective social meaning in determining perception and response. It is for this reason that they all help form the theoretical foundation for our discussion of metaphors and organizational change.

The Cognitive School

The cognitive school advances the premise that problem-solving and/or adaptive behavior in individuals and organizations is guided by sets of conscious, but usually implicit, governing beliefs. Governing beliefs are technically referred to as schemata (DeRubeis and Beck, 1988; Lau and Woodman, 1995; Markus and Zajonc, 1985), but also include such terms as "paradigm" (Kuhn, 1970), "frame" (Goffman, 1974), "theory-in-use" (Argyris and Schön, 1978), "cognitive map" (Bougon et al., 1977), "template" (Bartunek and Moch, 1987) and "prism" (Marshak and Katz, 1991). To avoid routine, repetitive and/or self-defeating behavior requires "getting out of the box" created by these governing schemata. Questioning and then changing governing beliefs will achieve this since such processes are presumed to lead to creativity and innovation, and the possibility of fundamental rather than marginal change. Argyris (1985) has noted how an absence of reflection about these implicit beliefs can leave an organization's focal system "trapped" in a cycle of familiar, but useless or even dysfunctional, routines. Drawing on cybernetic theory (e.g., Ashby, 1952, 1960; Beer, 1959, 1972; Morgan, 1982), the "cognitive revolution" in psychology (e.g., Beck, 1967, 1970; Dobson, 1988; Ellis, 1962, 1970; Guidano and Liotti, 1983; Mahoney, 1974, 1977; Mahoney and Thoreson, 1974; Markus, 1977; Meichenbaum, 1973, 1977) and their own research and thinking, a range of organization theorists have advanced versions of this model (e.g. Argyris, 1990, 1992; Daft and Weick, 1984; Gray et al., 1985; Mitroff, 1983; Morgan and Ramirez, 1984; Senge, 1990).

Slightly edited from Marshak, R. J. (1996). Metaphors, metaphoric fields and organizational change. In D. Grant & C. Oswick (Eds.), *Metaphor and Organizations*, 147-165. London: Sage. Republished with permission.

Perhaps because new behavior is presumed to result from rational change of beliefs, the favored metaphor of this school, especially among writers about organizational change, appears to be "organizations as learning systems" (e.g., Argyris, 1990, 1992; Senge, 1990). This metaphor includes action learning and single-loop, double-loop and even triple-loop learning (Argyris et al., 1985; Nielsen, 1993). The distinction between single-loop and double-loop learning is particularly important in organizational change. In single-loop learning organizational problem-solving or change initiatives are carried out within the framework of existing assumptions, beliefs, theories-in-use, paradigms, etc. Double-loop learning, on the other hand, requires first understanding and then altering the existing framework in order to generate new thought and behavior patterns. This distinction has also been used to separate what some have called first-order change from second-order change (e.g., Bateson, 1972, 1979; Goldfried and Robins, 1983). According to Bartunek and Moch: "First-order changes are incremental modifications that make sense within an established framework or method of operating. Second-order changes are modifications in the frameworks themselves" (1987, p. 484). The various theoretical approaches that make up the cognitive school are classified by Morgan (1986) under the metaphor of "organizations as brains."

The Cultural School

Following the lead of cultural anthropologists, organization theorists began to posit that behavior in organizations was influenced or governed by multi-layered systems of collective beliefs called "cultures" (Davis, 1984; Deal and Kennedy, 1982; Frost et al., 1985; Kilmann et al., 1985; Schein, 1985). Even though they may be visible and manifest themselves in many ways, the most influential of these beliefs, or basic assumptions, tend to be "forgotten," preconscious, or what has otherwise been termed as out-of-awareness (see, for example, Schein, 1985). Unlike the cognitive school, where governing beliefs are assumed to be expressed literally, cultural beliefs are assumed to be most powerfully expressed through symbolic modalities such as myths, stories, rituals and, of course, metaphors (Martin, 1982; Pondy et al., 1983). An organization's multi-layered system of beliefs, and therefore its culture, is considered to be a primary determinant of organizational behavior and success by providing implicit control over individual and organizational choice (Peters and Waterman, 1982).

In terms of organizational change, any significant change in the environment or business situation facing an organization might bring into question the continued applicability of its traditional assumptions and beliefs, and therefore its culture. While different theorists have argued whether or not organizational cultures can be changed (Kilmann, 1985; Kilmann et al., 1985; Schein, 1985), most agree that significant organizational change in response to new conditions, such as new technologies, markets, competitors, business paradigms, etc., requires changing the controlling organizational culture. In essence, second-order organizational change is required, or, in terms of Kuhn's (1970) paradigm theory of scientific revolutions, there has to be a "cultural revolution." The various concepts and theories that make up this approach to organization theory and change are classified by Morgan (1986), not surprisingly, under the metaphor of "organizations as cultures."

The Unconscious or Psychoanalytic School

Interest in the influence of unconscious dynamics in organizations began to gather momentum in the 1980s and 1990s as psychoanalytically trained writers turned their attention to corporate life (Baum, 1987, 1989; De Board, 1978; Diamond, 1986; Gabriel, 1991; Hirschorn, 1988; Katz, 1983; Kets de Vries and Miller, 1984; Levison and Rosenthal, 1984; Schwartz, 1987). Drawing on the seminal ideas of both Freud and Jung, a major premise of this school is that unconscious dynamics influence perception, meaning and action in organizations. This may result from unconscious dynamics within the psyche of a key individual such as the organization's leader (Kets de Vries, 1990; Mazlish, 1990), or from the collective unconscious of the group (Bion, 1959) and/or organization (Mitroff, 1983). Unconscious forces are presumed to control individual, group and organizational behavior to varying degrees and significant change may not be possible without addressing controlling unconscious elements. In most psychoanalytic traditions, and especially in the work of Jung, symbols are considered the primary medium for communication with the unconscious (Campbell, 1971; Fontana, 1993; Jung, 1964). According to Jung (1968), symbols are expressions of underlying psychic patterns, called archetypes, that give form and meaning to "reality." For purposes of this discussion, archetypal patterns are, in essence, unconscious schemata that are revealed symbolically, including metaphorically (Siegelman, 1990).

From the perspective of the psychoanalytic school, individual and organizational change result from addressing the schemata of the unconscious and/or ameliorating its consequences or expression. Addressing the unconscious is considered necessary for second-order change in organizations by Olson, who argues that "to reach the deep levels of second-and third-order change, organizational change agents should understand and address the unconscious" (1990, p. 70). While comparatively under-represented, interest in addressing organizational change issues using an orientation that deals with unconscious dynamics is on the rise (Barry, 1994; Katz and Marshak, 1995; Kets de Vries, 1991; Marshak and Katz, 1992; Merry and Brown, 1987; Mitroff, 1983; Olson, 1990). Morgan (1986) classifies this set of theories and approaches under the metaphor of "organizations as psychic prisons."

Common Elements

These three schools or approaches are normally thought of separately, probably because they are based on different theoretical traditions and social units of analysis. Those differences notwithstanding, they also all suggest a singular meta-theory of organizational change that incorporates the following features:

1. Organizational behavior is influenced by out-of-awareness schemata. These schemata may be underlying theories-in-use, cultural assumptions and beliefs, and/or unconscious material or archetypes.
2. Organizational schemata may be accessed and modified. Different methods are suggested depending on whether or not the schemata are considered to be conscious, pre-conscious or unconscious.

3. Second-order organizational change requires modification of controlling schemata in order to create innovative behavior that is different from "automatic" or "habitual" patterns.

What also unites the cognitive, cultural and unconscious/psychoanalytic schools are metaphors. Metaphors are unifying in two ways. First, metaphors are themselves schemata that structure or mediate meaning and response (Lakoff & Johnson, 1980). Consequently, the ability to diagnose and then modify the metaphors that may be controlling how an organizational situation is perceived and understood becomes a primary instrument of organizational change (Marshak, 1993). In short, metaphors are schemata that play a crucial role in structuring organizational reality and response. To significantly change organizational behavior may well require accessing and modifying controlling metaphorical constructs.

The second way metaphors are unifying is through their ability to serve as the communications bridge between the literal and the symbolic as well as the conscious and the unconscious (Marshak, 1993; Siegelman, 1990). Consequently, metaphors can serve as the common medium for diagnosing and addressing theories-in-use, cultural assumptions and beliefs, and unconscious dynamics. The ability to use metaphors for diagnosis and intervention is therefore critical for successful second-order change in organizations. When we consider that the most important changes facing postmodern organizations all require second-order change (e.g., from industrial to postindustrial paradigms), the instrumental role for metaphors should be clear. Organizations are not just "brains" or "cultures" or "psychic prisons." They are multi-layered systems of symbolic meaning operating at individual, group and organizational levels simultaneously.

Organizational Change and Symbolic Meaning Systems

It is appropriate at this point to expand on what is meant by a "multi-layered symbolic meaning system" and the function of metaphors in it. Broadly conceived it implies a whole or system that has depth, breadth, interrelationships and coherence among its various symbolic components.

- *Depth* implies that aspects of symbolic meaning are at relatively deep and/or tacit levels providing the foundation or "root" for symbolic meanings and manifestations at more surface and/or explicit levels (Guidano, 1988).
- *Breadth* implies there is a range of symbols and symbolic meanings covering the extent of the organization's domain. There will be symbols and symbolic manifestations for the organization as a whole as well as for different organizational functions, components and dynamics.
- *Inter-relationship* means that the various symbolic components do not exist independently in isolation from each other. Instead, they are linked from "top to bottom" (surface to root), and also from "side to side" through entailments and overlaps in extended meaning (Lakoff and Johnson, 1980). Increasing aggregates of symbols and symbolic manifestations organized around a core theme may be considered to form symbolic sets, clusters and constellations within the total system.

• *Coherence* is said to exist when there is overall thematic integrity and/or consistency among most, or all, of the various components that make up the symbolic meaning system (Lakoff & Johnson, 1980). Even though there may be more than one primary symbol or set of symbols involved, all will be informed by one or a related set of core symbolic themes. If multiple core themes exist in isolation or opposition to each other, the organization could be considered to be "unintegrated" or even "schizophrenic."

Metaphoric Fields

Metaphors are, of course, a principal component of an organization's symbolic meaning system. In fact, if other manifestations of a symbolic meaning system, such as art, spatial arrangements, myths, etc., were ignored, one might substitute the phrase "metaphoric field" without much loss of meaning. The metaphor of "field" is particularly apt since it conveys depth, breadth, inter-relationship, coherence and, of course, domain. It also conveys in its scientific sense an invisible "force" that can powerfully influence or determine behavior, as in the gravitational field (Gregory, 1988). An organization's metaphoric field is considered to be an inter-related set of conscious to unconscious, explicit to tacit, core to peripheral, organizing themes that are expressed metaphorically and which structure perception and behavior. These themes inform conscious, pre-conscious and unconscious assumptions, beliefs and patterns. They are therefore analogous to Jungian archetypes.

The image of an organizational metaphoric field is also intended to imply that organizational dynamics are influenced by "internal programming" (organizations as brains) and are mediated by "layers of inter-related symbolic meaning" (organizations as cultures), including "invisible, unconscious" dimensions that, in toto, "bound" or "restrict" perception and behavior (organizations as psychic prisons). The metaphoric field may be said to define reality and response for the organization, and thereby both enable and block innovation and action. Organizational change and change strategies that are consistent with the operative theme(s) of the metaphoric field will be readily engaged because they will be coherent and easily understood, even if not fully accepted. Organizational changes and change strategies that are fundamentally inconsistent with the core theme(s) of the organization's metaphoric field will appear incoherent, be easily misunderstood, and will be quickly discarded (Marshak, 1993). Members of the organization "just won't get it." Whereas the metaphoric field helps define and enable first-order change, in second-order change the field itself is the restricting element that must be addressed. If an organization's metaphoric field contains a strong symbolic theme that "business is like war," perhaps including "all's fair in love and war," it will be difficult to introduce changes related to emphasizing fairness, integrity and spiritual values. The typical response might be something like: "What does that have to do with business?" Unless or until the metaphoric field is modified to include or accentuate a different core theme(s), the organization's reality and response will be driven by a "wartime mentality."

Metaphoric Fields and Organizational Change

To further illustrate the concept of metaphoric fields in relation to organizational change let us examine a potential organizational change in terms of the questions: What will be changed, why, how and by whom? While these questions do not necessarily invoke all aspects of an organization's metaphoric field, they do invite consideration of multiple inter-related factors pertaining to the question of change in organizations.

To begin our analysis, and borrowing from Morgan (1986), let us consider that an organization's metaphoric field might contain the image that the organization is like a *machine, living organism, brain,* or *pattern of political alliances.* Next, let us consider some metaphors that might be used to understand organizational change. Changes intended to maintain current operations or to develop, transition or transform an organization are frequently distinguished in the professional literature (e.g. Ackerman, 1986). In the metaphoric field these "technical terms" might be understood as requests to *fix and maintain, build and develop, move and relocate* or *liberate and recreate* (Marshak, 1993). Very different actions and responses would be evoked depending on which metaphor was shaping perception. Yes, we need to change but should we "build and develop" sales, "move from" a centralized sales force "to" a decentralized sales force, "free-up" our thinking and "invent" a new sales strategy, or perhaps just "fine tune" the sales operation?

Thematic Coherence

Table 12.1 shows that when the four metaphorical types of organizations are related thematically to the four types of organizational change, they assume an underlying thematic coherence. In short, a picture of what might be included in a metaphoric field begins to emerge. Reviewing Table 12.1 makes it clear that, depending on the operative core theme(s) and its associated metaphors and symbols, quite different perceptions and actions related to organizational change will occur. In the examples that follow consider how different themes and metaphors shape the experience of organizational change and what is highlighted or overlooked. Consider also the implications if only one of the themes existed or was the dominant theme providing coherence to the organization's metaphoric field.

Table 12.1
Examples of Thematic Coherence in the Metaphoric Field

	Core Theme			
	Mechanical	**Biological**	**Cognitive**	**Relational**
Organization as:	Machine	Organism	Brain	Pattern
Leader as:	Engineer or operator	Survival needs and instincts	Reason and logic	Fashioner and maker
Assisted by:	Mechanics and repair workers	Healing agents	Teachers and experts	Cutters and tiers
Fix and Maintain:	Repair breakdowns	Cure sickness	Correct errors	Mend tears
Build and Develop:	Enhance output	Grow in ability	Learn knowledge	Strengthen bonds
Move and Relocate:	Replace with better model	Adjust to new life stage	Switch methods	Reconfigure interests
Liberate and Re-create:	Re-engineer capacity	Metamorphosis	Rethink premises	Re-compose design

Mechanical. If the metaphoric field is rooted in mechanistic themes and symbols, then the organization will be perceived to be some type of machine made up of independent parts, put together by design. It will therefore be run by engineers or operators who set commands and controls and who will be assisted by mechanics and repair workers who use their tool kits to fix anything that is broken. Sometimes enhancements will be made to the machine to increase productivity or ease of use. Other times machine operators and workers will have to learn how to use a new machine that replaced the previous one because it is faster, cheaper or more productive. On rare occasions the machine may need to be totally re-engineered in order to incorporate new technologies. This may also require operators to work in completely new ways.

Biological. If the thematic coherence of the metaphoric field is based on biological symbols, then it is likely that the organization will be understood to be some type of organism living in an environment. It will have to rely on its instincts and natural abilities to adapt and respond to the opportunities and threats in its environmental niche. When sick it will seek out a healing agent to be cured. When healthy it will grow and develop into something that is bigger, faster, quicker and more powerful. It will transition from one stage in its life-cycle to another and each transition may be awkward and/or traumatic, requiring an adjustment period. Certain organisms may even be able to radically alter their form and essential being through a transformational process called metamorphosis.

Cognitive. If the metaphoric field is organized around the implicit theme of cognition, then mediating symbols and metaphors related to thinking, knowing, reasoning, calculating, learning, awareness and so on, will shape organizational reality and response. Strategies will need to be calculated based on solid intelligence and careful reasoning in order to avoid any errors in judgment. If an error does occur it should be corrected quickly in order not to compound the mistake. The organization may engage trainers to help develop abilities to think more clearly and creatively, while also avoiding the misperceptions and mental blocks associated with group-think. For certain problems, where things just don't add up, there may be a need to switch methods and use a different calculus or equation. If mistakes or miscalculations are consistent and persistent, it may become necessary to reexamine fundamental premises and assumptions in the hopes of arriving at a more satisfactory solution. This may require rethinking based on heightened awareness of the real facts and figures.

Relational. If the organizing theme of the metaphoric field is based on the imagery of a pattern of political alliances, then organizational experience may well be mediated through symbols and metaphors emphasizing relationships, bonds, ties and connections. These are often rooted in textile imagery, including weaving, sewing, pattern making, fabric cutting, knitting, knotting and linking. Within the organization a pattern of alliances may need to be fashioned in order to create the common bonds necessary to hold together the different components. This may require sewing up support, possibly by cutting a deal that ties down loose ends. Being clear about the fundamental organizational pattern will help bind together the different lines of work and ensure everyone stays in the loop. Work in different components should be carefully interwoven to avoid any gaps or holes while ensuring a seamless appearance to customers. If important relationships become frayed or torn it is important to mend or patch them quickly so things don't unravel. Sometimes weak ties or weak links will need to be more securely fastened. Other times it may be necessary to reconfigure the existing relationships in order to bring together new interests that better cover the issues. At certain times it may even be necessary to take things apart or loosen and unwrap everything in order to start over and compose a new mosaic or tapestry.

As is readily apparent, the organizational answer to "what is going on here?" will be quite different depending on which metaphors of organization and change are operative. Are we "fixing" the situation by "repairing," "curing," "correcting" and/or "mending" the problem? How dramatic do the required changes need to be? Do we need to "repair," "enhance," "replace" and/or "re-engineer" the production system? When people say: "If it ain't broke, don't fix it," they are undoubtedly speaking from a metaphoric field that implies the organization is a machine that should be repaired only when broken. Consequently, requests to "get out of the box" (rethink premises) might be ignored simply because they are incoherent within the metaphoric framework of "fixing a machine."

Metaphoric Diagnosis and Intervention in Organizational Change

From an instrumental point of view there are primarily three questions worth answering with respect to organizational change: (1) what is going on presently; (2) what should be going on; and (3) what needs to be done to make things the way they should be? The answers to these questions are mediated by the metaphoric fields of the involved individuals, groups and/or organization. Furthermore, both the questions and their answers are frequently expressed, explicitly and implicitly, through metaphors (Keidel, 1994; Morgan, 1993). The first two questions are basically diagnostic, while the last pertains to intervention. The following discussion, therefore, will address key considerations in the use of metaphors in organizational diagnosis and intervention. The principal thesis is that symbolic expressions and especially metaphors are an integral part of second-order organizational change efforts (Barry, 1994; Katz and Marshak, 1995; Marshak and Katz, 1992; Olson, 1990).

Metaphors and Diagnosis

Working with metaphors as an integral part of organizational diagnosis requires the ability to track literal and symbolic communication simultaneously. This process is guided by four basic premises and an overriding principle (Marshak and Katz, 1992). The four basic premises are as follows:

1. Communication is complex and expressed through multiple modalities. All messages contain literal, conscious components, as well as symbolic dimensions which may be out-of-awareness.
2. Messages conveyed through symbolic expression, such as metaphors, communicate real and legitimate issues, just as do those conveyed through literal language.
3. Symbolic, metaphorical communication provides people with a way in which to express aspects both of themselves and of situations about which they may not be consciously aware, nor be able to express analytically and/or literally.
4. More is known than what is in a person's conscious mind and is often communicated symbolically through metaphors regardless of what they consciously say or think.

With these premises serving as a reminder to constantly pay attention to the symbolic aspects of communications, a paradoxical principle informs the diagnostic process: *Explore literal messages symbolically, and symbolic messages literally*. This principle requires the diagnostic process to remain open to the potential multiple meanings that may be conveyed by a seemingly single communication.

Explore the symbolic literally. When metaphors are listened to for their literal as well as symbolic meaning a wider range of diagnostic speculation and/or inquiry is revealed. For example, if someone in an off-handed comment uses the metaphor "This office is like a prison", it can be heard as a symbolic way of expressing the range of feelings and thoughts they have about their workplace. In this instance they may be conveying a sense of little or no freedom, confinement, isolation, punishment and the like. Pursued literally, however, would mean following up on the metaphorical comment as if it were actually true. Therefore, appropriate diagnostic follow-up could include inquiry as to: How exactly is this place like a prison? Who are the inmates, guards, and the warden? Why are you here? All of these, and other inquiries, serve to expand understanding of the original metaphor by treating it as if the person were literally telling you: "I am in prison." Expanding the inquiry to include closely related images in the metaphoric field, or to explore root images, are also aspects of metaphoric diagnosis. For example, images related to law enforcement, justice, freedom, escape and so on, might also be explored. Deeper images related to being wrong and/or being unfairly punished might also be operative and worth inquiry.

Explore the literal symbolically. Conversely, seemingly literal statements should also be read or listened to symbolically. For example, if people say: "You can't tell the truth around here because too many people would get hurt," or "You can tell the boss the truth, but only if you are willing to take your lumps," or "We need to be brutally honest," it is appropriate to hear that telling the truth can be difficult and painful. It is also appropriate to speculate about what is being communicated symbolically. What implicit and/or unconscious metaphoric image would lead people to talk about telling the truth in such a way? In other words, at a symbolic level these people are talking as if telling the truth is like a _____? In this instance it could be reasonable to hypothesize that people in this organization symbolically experience truth as a weapon, or that honesty brutalizes people. If so, what are the implications of such a message? Needless to say, it would be difficult to imagine much honesty in an organization that consistently evokes such strong images and feelings. In sum, to receive the full range of data and messages available for organizational diagnosis it is important to be able to pay attention to both the literal and symbolic levels of communication.

Metaphors and Interventions

There are six major types of interventions that can be used in working with metaphors and organizational change, especially second-order organizational change (Marshak and Katz, 1990). Within each major type of intervention there are a wide variety of specific methods and techniques that can be used when working with individuals, groups and/or organizations. The following discussion includes vignettes drawn from the author's experiences as an organization change consultant, and is intended to briefly present and then illustrate each of the major types of interventions. They are: (1) recognizing, (2) repudiating, (3) reframing, (4) replacing, (5) releasing and (6) reintegrating. Three of these interventions – repudiating, reframing and replacing – might also be considered subsets of a single broader category of intervention called *rethinking*. Each of the interventions may be used separately in organizational work, but more frequently they are employed in some combination. While in any particular organizational change situation the exact order may not matter, often a rough sequence of moving from recognizing to rethinking followed by releasing and reintegration is a natural progression.

Recognizing. The first step towards second-order change is to be able to identify the metaphor and/or theme(s) in the metaphoric field (the schemata) that is influencing perception and action. Just identifying or naming the metaphor is often all that is required for the focal system to realize how reaction and response have been limited, and to then select another mental model, image or set of beliefs to guide future actions. Recognition alone is more likely to be all that is necessary when the controlling metaphor is more surface and/or more peripheral to the core theme(s) in the system's metaphoric field.

An example of a recognizing intervention occurred during a strategic planning session with the training department of a governmental agency responsible for watching over the operations of other agencies for various forms of malfeasance or inefficiencies. The team of top training managers was stuck trying to decide the proper balance among technical-, managerial-, and people skills-oriented courses. Although there were no specific comments during the discussions, the participants were clearly concerned about the degree of emphasis on people skills in the training curriculum. Being familiar with the agency's culture, the consultant working with them played a hunch and asked: "What's the dominant image or phrase people use to describe this agency?" The quick response was, "We're the government's watchdog!" The consultant then suggested, "You must therefore be planning the curriculum for an obedience school for watchdogs. How is that impacting your discussions?" Several of the participants were quick to realize that the unspoken organizational fear of being seen as a "lapdog" might be influencing perceptions of courses designed to increase trust, caring, and collaboration. Recognizing a metaphor that may have been implicitly shaping their discussions, the team re-engaged the curriculum question by explicitly asking: "What should be the proper mix of courses to best prepare individuals to lead or be members of project teams doing professional analytic work?"

Repudiating. Recognizing that an implicit or explicit metaphor in the metaphoric field may be guiding how a situation is perceived may not be enough to change the situation. Instead, interventions intended to challenge or raise questions about the appropriateness of the metaphor, in whole or in part, are often necessary. The ways in which the metaphor has prevented the system from resolving some situation of importance may need to be highlighted or exposed in order for the controlling metaphor or theme to be abandoned, even temporarily. The more central or core the metaphor in the metaphoric field, the more difficult, but ultimately impactful, the task of repudiation.

The following situation demonstrates the value and impact of a repudiating intervention. Repudiation arose during a planning meeting with an executive task force that had been charged with developing strategies to support a major change initiative in a high tech corporation. The intended change was to become less "bureaucratic" and to encourage operating across organizational boundaries in ad hoc, cross-departmental teams. The effort was bogged down with middle managers who either "couldn't get it" or were reluctant to give up direct authority or control over their people and projects. The executive task force had been talking about the idea of a two-hour slide presentation as the way to explain to middle managers what to do. When the consultant working with them suggested a range of other more involved or involving options, the uniform reaction was negative. "Our people are too smart for that." "That would be like playing kiddie games." "They don't need that much time, they're quick students." "Only really smart people work here, so we don't want to insult their intelligence." Finally the consultant observed: "You often describe this company as like a college campus or an elite graduate school. What I can't figure out is why so many really smart people just can't get it? Maybe they need remedial management. Maybe they are a group of engineers having a hard time in a poetry course. Maybe they haven't had any of the prerequisites for this course. All I know is that acting as if they are really bright, quick students just doesn't seem to fit the facts of this situation." After a short pause, the meeting resumed with different members of the task force offering new perspectives. "Maybe we need to bring them along more slowly." "I'll bet none of them have had any management training – what can you expect." "We could put them through a series of workshops, sorta like in building block fashion."

Reframing.   Sometimes a metaphor and its associations need only be looked at differently, rather than abandoned entirely. This may include considering alternative ways to apply the metaphor and/or bring into focus an overlooked component or aspect of the broader metaphor set, cluster, or constellation.

An example is the reframing of an organizational change effort from that of "fixing" to "re-engineering" a machine. During a meeting with a task force that had been given the task of designing and implementing a whole new way of doing business, certain phrases kept coming up throughout the discussion. "Look, if it ain't broke, let's not fix it." "Remember, we have to minimize down time and get this up and running quickly." "Maybe we only need to tinker with what we're doing." "That's been running well for twenty years. I don't see why we need to fix it now." Such statements made it appear that the task force was operating from an implicit shared metaphor – that the organization was a machine that was somehow broken. This was consistent with their discussions, which invariably seemed more focused on making small incremental changes (tinkering), rather than the more fundamental shifts that appeared to be called for in the situation. Hypothesizing that the group might be constrained by an unexpressed limiting belief ("We're here to fix the machine"), the consultant working with the task force intervened directly, but implicitly, by reframing the suspected underlying metaphor. "You know, maybe what you are doing is designing a fundamentally new model of the organization that incorporates the latest technology and achieves higher performance standards." The invitation to think in terms of designing a higher performance machine (re-engineering) rather than trying to repair an old outdated one (fixing) worked as different members of the task force began to see their assignment in a new way. Soon they were talking about making fundamental changes that they had earlier not addressed because those aspects of the organization were "still working OK and therefore did not need fixing."

In part, the effectiveness of reframing interventions such as that illustrated by the last vignette rests on their ability to alter the way things are perceived without having to directly challenge a deeply held core metaphor or theme itself. This, of course, is also one of its limitations. One might reframe what needs to be done to the machine, but it is still a machine that does not need emotional or spiritual attention.

Replacing.   When the controlling metaphor or part of the metaphoric field cannot be repudiated or reframed in a way that invites new perceptions and behaviors, it may be necessary to replace the metaphor or theme with another. This is done by attempting to substitute a metaphor or metaphor set, cluster or constellation from a less central or less potent part of the metaphoric field. Another approach would be to import a new metaphor/theme into the focal system's metaphoric field. Sometimes new themes or metaphors that have recently become part of the field can serve as effective substitutes. However, and as the following example shows, it is important that the metaphor or theme selected as a replacement is appropriate to the circumstances in which it is applied.

The example of a replacement intervention occurred at a large manufacturing-based corporation. The organization found itself having to cope with the need to shift from industrial to post-industrial business paradigms and practices, for example global strategies, mass customization, horizontal work processes, self managed teams. Although this invited re-examining and possibly changing fundamental values and premises, a key divisional vice-president none the less tended to use mechanical "fix and maintain" or "build and enhance" metaphors in meetings devoted to working the changes. "We need to take apart and clean up our operation." "We need to reduce tolerances and achieve a zero-defect way of doing business." "Everything has to be tightened up and made to run more efficiently." The consultant working with the vice-president considered reframing the situation from "fixing" or "enhancing" to "re-engineering." This was not pursued, however, because "re-engineering" might tend to emphasize an exclusive focus on operating differently when there was also the need to "think" differently.

Given this need to think differently, metaphors related to religious or ideological "conversion" were briefly considered as replacements because they connote a re-examination and eventual change in fundamental thinking patterns. These too were not pursued. They were deemed as inappropriate and too controversial, despite the fact that aspects of the religion metaphor cluster such as "vision," "creed," "faith,", "ten commandments" or "our bible" are routinely used in most organizations. Instead the metaphor of computer "reprogramming" was tried as a replacement for the "fix and maintain" mechanical imagery. "We need to change not only what we do, but the programming that tells us how to think about what we do." "Our old program is hopelessly out-of-date; we need to develop a cutting edge program to guide our operations into the future." The reprogramming metaphor was tried because it was related through computer imagery to mechanistic metaphors and themes, and might therefore be more readily accepted as a substitute. It was also selected because it placed emphasis on cognitive processes ("software") rather than structural components ("hardware") which is often the case with the "re-engineering" metaphor (e.g. Hammer and Champy, 1993).

In this instance, then, attempting to replace a mechanistic fix or maintain metaphor with a cognitive reprogramming one appeared the appropriate course of action. Further, it would undoubtedly have been much harder, and inappropriate, to try to apply the metaphor of "religious conversion." Asking someone to metaphorically "change their religious faith" as opposed to asking them to "use a different calculus or program to solve a problem" may well have turned out to be the difference between a successful and unsuccessful replacing intervention.

Releasing. Following repudiating, reframing and especially replacing, interventions intended to assist or support the focal system in letting go of previously held perceptions, interpretations and feelings about a situation are often necessary. This is especially true when the metaphor represents a core or defining theme in the organization's metaphoric field. Interventions to help the organization learn how to better use the new, less familiar image system, that reinforce any new perceptions and interpretations that reveal new options, and that monitor attempts to return to using the previous metaphor(s) are all forms of releasing interventions. Additionally, because metaphors evoke affect as well as analysis, attention to emotional release may also be needed.

Take, for example, a chief executive's sense of self-worth. As a "captain of industry" issuing commands that control complex operations, they might feel threatened, consciously or unconsciously, by an invitation to become a "master weaver" responsible for pulling together many different organizational strands into a harmonious pattern that is both functional and aesthetically pleasing. Analytically, shifting to a metaphor cluster that emphasizes patterns over parts, interdependence over independence, and pleasing the customer over productive capacity may all be quite appropriate and needed. Nevertheless, unless the emotional affect such metaphors evoke is also addressed, it is unlikely there would be a change from a more to a less emotionally attractive metaphorical image.

Reintegrating. Repudiating, reframing, replacing and releasing impact the structure and relationships of the symbolic themes and metaphors contained within the metaphoric field. This will necessitate some modification of the existing system of thematic coherence, or, in the extreme, require reorientation around a new system of coherence. The more dramatic the changes in the metaphoric field, the greater the need for thematic reintegration to restore systemic coherence. Emotional as well as cognitive realignment must occur for reintegration to be successful. The structure of meaning provided by the "re-cohered" metaphoric field must "make sense" and "feel right" before it can be said that the organization is fully reintegrated, that is, has fully achieved second-order change.

For instance, a large corporation was engaged in a change effort to develop long-term dedicated relationships with key suppliers. This involved work on a new vision, design of new work processes, and a variety of training programs. Implementation was slow, however, as managers reported difficulty "feeling safe" with the proposed new relationships. During interviews, imagery related to being vulnerable to thieves came up repeatedly. "We've got to be careful or they will steal us blind." "It's in their interest to take whatever they can get." "Rule number one is to remember they are out for themselves." This prompted an explicit effort to replace the metaphor of "suppliers as thieves" with that of "suppliers as strategic allies." Suppliers became "allies in our efforts to win new customers" and part of a "strategic partnership" needed to keep costs down. The new imagery also led to the development of "strategic alliance" workshops between managers of the organization and various supplier organizations. The president of the organization felt a major corner had been turned when a purchasing manager remarked after one of the workshops, "That's the first meeting I've had with them when I didn't feel like I needed to check to see if I still had my watch and wallet."

Conclusions

Second-order change in organizations requires addressing and modifying controlling organizational schemata. These include conscious, pre-conscious and unconscious assumptions, beliefs and patterns held by individuals, groups and the organization. Symbols, especially metaphors, are the common building blocks and forms of expression for conscious, pre-conscious and unconscious elements of an organization's schemata. The organization's system of symbolic meaning, or more specifically its metaphoric field, is therefore a principal, but implicit, framework that structures organizational reality and response. In order to diagnose an organization's metaphoric field it is necessary to explore literal communications symbolically, and symbolic communications literally. Only then is it possible to address and/or alter the metaphoric field for purposes of second-order organizational change. This can be accomplished using some combination of recognizing, rethinking, releasing and reintegrating interventions.

References

Ackerman, L. (1986). Development, transition, or transformation: The question of change in organizations. *OD Practitioner, 18*(4), 1-8.

Argyris, C. (1985). *Strategy, change, and defensive routines*. Marshfield, MA: Pitman Publishing.

Argyris, C. (1990). *Overcoming organizational defenses*: Facilitating organizational learning. Boston: Allyn and Bacon.

Argyris, C. (1992). *On organizational learning*. Cambridge, MA: Blackwell.

Argyris, C., & Schön, D. (1978). *Organizational learning*. Reading, MA: Addison-Wesley.

Argyris, C., Putnam, R., & Smith, D.M. (Eds.) (1985). *Action Science*. San Francisco: Jossey-Bass.

Ashby, W. R. (1952). *Design for a brain*. New York: John Wiley and Sons.

Ashby, W. R. (1960). *An introduction to cybernetics*. London: Chapman and Hall.

Barry, D. (1994). Making the invisible visible: Using analogically-based methods to surface unconscious organizational processes. *Organization development journal, 12*(4), 37-48.

Bartunek J. M., & Moch, M.K (1987). First-order, second-order, and third-order change, and organization development intervention: A cognitive approach. *Journal of Applied Behavioral Science, 23*(4), 483-500.

Bateson, G. (1972). *Steps to an ecology of mind*. New York: Ballantine.

Bateson, G. (1979). *Mind and nature: A necessary unity*. New York: Bantam.

Baum, H. S. (1987). *The invisible bureaucracy*. Oxford: Oxford University Press.

Baum, H. S. (1989). Organizational politics against organizational culture: A psychoanalytic perspective. *Human resource management, 28*, 191-207.

Beck, A.T. (1967). *Depression: Causes and treatment*. Philadelphia: University of Pennsylvania Press.

Beck, A. T. (1970). Cognitive therapy: Nature and relation to behavior therapy. *Behavior therapy, 1*, 184-200.

Beer, S. (1959). *Cybernetics and management*. New York: John Wiley and Sons.

Beer, S. (1972). *Brain of the firm*. New York: Herder and Herder.

Bion, W. R. (1959). *Experiences in groups*. London: Tavistock.

Bougon, M. G., Weick, K. E., & Brinkhorst, D. (1977). Cognition in organizations: An analysis of the Utrecht Jazz Orchestra. *Administrative Science Quarterly, 22*(4), 609-639.

Campbell, J. (Ed.) (1971). *The portable Jung*. New York: Penguin.

Daft, R. L., & Weick, K. E. (1984). Toward a model of organizations as interpretation systems. *Academy of Management Review, 9*, 284-295.

Davis, S. M. (1984). *Managing corporate culture*. Cambridge, MA: Ballinger.

Deal, T. E., & Kennedy, A. A. (1982). *Corporate cultures: The rites and rituals of corporate life*. Reading, MA: Addison-Wesley.

De Board, R. (1978). *The Psychoanalysis of organizations*. London: Tavistock.

DeRubeis, R. I., & Beck, A. T. (1988). Cognitive therapy. In K. S. Dobson (Ed.), *Handbook of cognitive-behavioral therapies*. New York: Guilford Press, pp. 273-306.

Diamond, M. A. (1986). Resistance to change: A psychoanalytic critique of Argyris and Schön's contributions to organization theory and intervention. *Journal of Management Studies, 23*(5), 543-562.

Dobson, K. S. (Ed.) (1988). *Handbook of cognitive-behavioral therapies*. New York: Guilford Press.

Ellis, A. (1962). *Reason and emotion in psychotherapy*. New York: Stuart.

Ellis, A. (1970). *The essence of rational psychotherapy: A comprehensive approach to treatment*. New York: Institute for Rational Living.

Fontana, D. (1993). *The secret language of symbols: A visual key to symbols and their meaning*. San Francisco: Chronicle Books.

Frost, P. J., Moore, L. F., Louis, M. R., Lundberg, C. C., & Martin, J. (1985). *Organizational culture*. Beverly Hills, CA: Sage Publications.

Gabriel, Y. (1991). Organizations and their discontents: A psychoanalytic contribution to the study of organizational culture. *Journal of Applied Behavioral Science, 27*(3), 318-336.

Goffman, E. (1974). *Frame analysis*. New York: Harper.

Goldfried, M. R., & Robins, C. (1983). Self-schemas, cognitive bias, and the processing of learning experiences, In P. C. Kendall (Ed.), *Advances in cognitive-behavioral research and therapy*, Vol. 2. New York: Academic Press.

Gray, B., Bougon, M. G., & Donnellon, A. (1985). Organizations as constructions and destructions of meaning. *Journal of Management, 11*, 83-95.

Gregory, B. (1988). *Inventing reality: Physics as language*. New York: John Wiley and Sons.

Guidano, V. F. (1988). A systems, process-oriented approach to cognitive therapy. In K. S. Dobson (Ed.), *Handbook of cognitive-behavioral therapies*. New York: Guilford Press, pp. 307-356.

Guidano, V. F., & Liotti, G. (1983). *Cognitive processes and emotional disorders: A structural approach to psychotherapy*. New York: Guilford Press.

Hammer, M., & Champy, J. (1993). *Re-engineering the corporation*. New York: Harper Collins Publishers.

Hirschorn, L. (1988). *The workplace within*. Cambridge, MA: MIT Press.

Jung, C. G. (Ed.) (1964). *Man and his symbols*. New York: Dell Publishing.

Jung, C. G. (1968). *Analytical Psychology: Its Theory and Practice*. New York: Vintage Books.

Katz, G. A. (1983). The noninterpretation of metaphors in psychiatric hospital groups. *International Journal of Group Management Review, 31*(1), 53-67.

Katz, J. H., & Marshak, R. I. (1995). Re-inventing OD theory and practice. *Organization Development Journal, 13*(1), 63-70.

Keidel, R. W. (1994). Rethinking organizational design. *The Academy of Management Executive, 8*(4), 12-30.

Kets de Vries, M. F. R. (1990). Leaders on the couch. *Journal of Applied Behavioral Science, 26*(4), 423-431.

Kets de Vries, M. F. R. (Ed.) (1991). *Organizations on the couch: Clinical perspectives on organizational behavior and change*. San Francisco: Jossey-Bass.

Kets de Vries, M. F. R., & Miller, D. (1984). *The neurotic organization.* San Francisco: Jossey-Bass.

Kilmann, R. H. (1985). *Beyond the quick Fix.* San Francisco: Jossey-Bass.

Kilmann, R. H., Saxton, M. J., Serpa, R., & Associates (1985). *Gaining control of the corporate culture.* San Francisco: Jossey-Bass.

Kuhn, T. S. (1970). *The structure of scientific revolutions* (2nd ed.). Chicago: University of Chicago Press.

Lakoff, G., & Johnson, M. (1980). *Metaphors we live By.* Chicago: University of Chicago Press.

Lau, C. M., & Woodman, R. W. (1995). Understanding organizational change: A schematic perspective. *The Academy of Management Journal, 38*(2), 537-554.

Levison, H., & Rosenthal, S. (1984). *CEO: Corporate leadership in action.* New York: Basic Books.

Mahoney, M. J. (1974). *Cognition and behavior modification.* Cambridge, MA: Ballinger.

Mahoney, M. J. (1977). Personal science: A cognitive learning therapy. In A. Ellison and R.Grieger (Eds.), *Handbook of rational psychotherapy.* New York: Springer, pp. 280-302.

Mahoney, M. J., & Thoreson, C. E. (1974). *Self-control: Power to the person.* Monterey, CA: Brooks/Cole.

Markus, H. (1977). Self-schemata and processing information about the self. *Journal of Personality and Social Psychology, 35*, 63-78.

Markus, H., & Zajonc, R. B. (1985). The cognitive perspective in social psychology. In G. Lindzey and E. Aronson (Eds.), *The handbook of social psychology*, Vol. I. New York: Random House, pp. 137-230.

Marshak, R. J. (1993). Managing the metaphors of change. *Organizational Dynamics, 22*(1), 44-56.

Marshak, R. J., & Katz, J. H. (1990). Covert processes and revolutionary change. In M. McDonald (Ed.), *Forging Revolutionary Partnerships: Proceedings of the 1990 National OD Network Conference.* Portland, OR: National OD Network, pp. 58-65.

Marshak, R. J., & Katz, J. H. (1991). Covert processes at work. *Chesapeake Bay Organizational Development Network Newsletter, 6*(2), 1-5.

Marshak, R. J., & Katz, J. H. (1992). The symbolic side of OD. *OD Practitioner, 24*(2), 1-5.

Martin, J. (1982). Stories and scripts in organizational settings. In A. Hastorf and A. Isen (Eds.), *Cognitive social psychology.* New York: North Holland, pp. 255-305.

Mazlish, B. (1990). *The leader, the led and the psyche.* Middletown, CT: Wesleyan University Press.

Meichenbaum, D. H. (1973). Cognitive factors in behavior modification: Modifying what clients say to themselves. In C. M. Franks and G. T. Wilson (Eds.), *Annual review of behavior therapy, theory, and practice.* New York: Brunner/Mazel, pp. 218-230.

Meichenbaum, D. H. (1977). *Cognitive behavior modification.* New York: Plenum.

Merry, U., & Brown, G. I. (1987). *The neurotic behavior of organizations.* Cleveland, OH: Gestalt Institute of Cleveland Press.

Mitroff, I. I. (1983). *Stakeholders of the organization mind.* San Francisco: Jossey-Bass.

Morgan, G. (1982). Cybernetics and organization theory: Epistemology or technique? *Human Relations, 35*, 521-538.

Morgan, G. (1986). *Images of organization*. Beverly Hills, CA: Sage Publications.

Morgan, G. (1993). *Imaginization: The art of creative management*. Newbury Park, CA: Sage Publications.

Morgan, G., & Ramirez, R. (1984). Action learning: A holographic metaphor for guiding social change. *Human Relations, 37,* 1-28.

Nielsen, R. P. (1993). Woolman's "I am we" triple loop action-learning: Origin and application in organization ethics. *Journal of Applied Behavioral Science, 29*(1), 117-138.

Olson, E. E. (1990). The transcendent function in organizational change. *Journal of Applied Behavioral Science, 26*(1), 69-81.

Peters, T. J., & Waterman, R. H. (1982). *In search of excellence: Lessons from America's best run companies*. New York: Harper and Row.

Pondy, L. R., Frost, P. I., Morgan, G., & Dandridge, T. C. (Eds.) (1983). *Organizational symbolism*. Greenwich, CT: JAI Press.

Schein, E. H. (1985). *Organizational culture and leadership: A dynamic view.* San Francisco: Jossey-Bass.

Schwartz, H. S. (1987). Anti-social actions of committed organizational participants: An existential psychoanalytic perspective. *Organization Studies, 8*(3), 327-340.

Senge, P. M. (1990). *The fifth discipline: The art and practice of the learning organization*. New York: Doubleday/Currency.

Siegelman, E. (1990). *Metaphor and meaning in psychotherapy*. New York: Guilford Press.

13
A Discourse on Discourse: Redeeming the Meaning of Talk

What happens when we think about thought and talk about talk?
Bruner and Feldman (1990), p. 237

The end of the twentieth century is witnessing a rapidly growing movement of ideas away from the traditional, objectivist conception of reality towards a still not fully defined, but more subjective, constructionist ontology. Although the objectivist view has been a central part of the privileged dogma of Western philosophy and science since Plato (Finocchario, 1990; Soyland, 1994), in the last few decades there has been an impressive outpouring of alternative and ultimately constructionist views. As Laughlin et al. observe:

There have emerged at least two principal themes from this revolutionary readjustment of view: (1) a shift away from a fragmented, mechanical, nonpurposive conception of the world toward a holistic, organic, and purposive conception ...; and (2) a shift away from a concern with objectivity toward a concern with subjectivity - that is, with the role of perception and cognition in the process of scientific inquiry.... (1992, p. 5)

A central aspect of this shift has been increased inquiry into the role of language in the ongoing creation of "reality." For example, according to Hall and Ames:

The transition from modem to postmodern perspectives is not merely a theoretical shift. It entails a vast network which has drawn together in a single mix movements as seemingly diverse as deconstruction, the new historicism, cultural studies, and feminist criticism - all of which at one level or another are rooted in the critique of the rationality of language. (1995, p. 145-146)

The growing interest in, and indeed legitimacy conferred upon, metaphor in recent years is another clear and specific indicator of this shift (Johnson, 1987; Lakoff, 1987; Lakoff and Johnson, 1980; Leary, 1990; Ortony, 1993). In the administrative sciences, despite attempts to uphold the objectivist view (Bourgeois & Pinder, 1983; Pinder & Bourgeois, 1982; Tsoukas, 1992), metaphor has become an area of legitimate and serious inquiry (Grant & Oswick, 1996; Marshak, 1996; Morgan, 1980, 1983, 1997; Oswick & Grant, 1996; Palmer & Dunford, 1996). The emerging outlines of a field or school of inquiry more broadly focused on "organizational discourse," marked in part by the publication of this book, is another indicator of this trend. There is now a growing, if still quite eclectic, group of scholars actively asking questions, doing research and communicating their ideas about the impacts of linguistically mediated experience in management and organizational settings (Combes et al, 1996). For this group of people talk is more than simply a means to communicate, report or, through sophistry, manipulate information. Instead, talk is one, if not the primary, means of socially constructing reality; privileging some stories, narratives or accounts of that reality over others; and generating alternative conceptions of both proper questions and their

Marshak, R. J. (1998). A discourse on discourse: Redeeming the meaning of talk. In D. Grant & C. Oswick (Eds.) *Discourse and Organization*, (pp. 5-30). London: Sage. Republished with permission answers (Berger & Luckmann, 1967; Bergquist, 1993; Schön, 1993). Put simply, the real action is in the talk.

This perspective, however, runs counter to not only the objectivist views of other social scientists, but the embedded "folk models" or "folk theories" of many managers in organizations in the United States, and possibly many other countries as well. According to Lakoff:

> Ordinary people without any technical expertise have theories, either implicit or explicit, about every important aspect of their lives. Cognitive anthropologists refer to such theories as *folk theories or folk models*. (1987, p. 118)

If one listens with an ethnographer's ear to day-to-day management discussions, notes the terminology of popular management terms and theories, and reflects on broader cultural themes, a very different assessment of talk and its relationship to action is revealed. Implicit in most discourses, and the broader culture, are assumptions that signal the paramount importance of action over talk. There is, in short, a strong "bias for action" (for example, Peters & Waterman, 1982). Characteristics of "action," such as being observable, measurable, concrete, practical and specific, are routinely lauded over those associated with "talk," which is considered to be more contextual, interpretative, elusive, abstract and emotional. The traditional American cultural icon is the "strong, silent type," exemplified in popular culture by the action-adventure hero (for example, Eastwood, Schwarzenegger, Stallone) who says little, but gets things done by letting his "fists do the talking." This contrasts with another icon, "the loquacious type," best exemplified in popular culture by the talk show host/hostess whose role is to amuse, empathize and/or entertain. That the bias for action over talk may also extend to a bias for the masculine over the feminine should be obvious.

The remainder of this chapter will explore in more detail the everyday discourse and implicit folk model(s) about "talk" and "action," articulate a broader conception of talk to include three types of talk and an alternative folk model, and conclude with a discussion of some of the implications for organizations and the emerging field of organizational discourse.

The Rhetoric about Talk and Action

As implied by the opening discussion, developing and legitimating a field of inquiry based on the importance of organizational discourse ("talk") may have more than a few difficulties to surmount. These include the weight of a Western philosophical tradition that cautions against the illusion of sophist rhetoric, as well as an objectivist scientific tradition that prefers literal or mathematical statements to anything that might reflect subjective, mediated experience. Talk is the province of the poet not the philosopher-scientist. Talk is more about rhyme than reason, emotion not fact.

The legitimacy and importance of organizational discourse as a field of inquiry is also challenged by the embedded folk model(s) about "talk" and "action" expressed in the daily rhetoric of most (American) organizations. In these implicit models talk is routinely demeaned and devalued, with potentially serious, but unacknowledged consequences. Action, on the other hand, is highly lauded and valued. Not only is action valued over talk, but talk is implicitly considered as an impediment to action, something that must be "gotten over," "gone through" or "finished with" before there can be any action. It is instructive to take a closer look at some of this rhetoric and the model(s) it implies.

First, *talk is worthless*. Expressions conveying a sense that talk has no real value are commonplace. How often have we heard: "talk is cheap"; "it's just empty words"; "idle talk, idle chatter"; or that "talk is a waste of time?" And because everyone knows that "time is money," if talk is a waste of time, it must also be a waste of money. Remember, "Silence is golden."

On the other hand, *action counts; action is valued*. We are routinely reminded that "it's deeds that count, not words," or that one should "watch what we do, not what we say." People in organizations are admonished to "walk the talk," guard against "too much talk and not enough action," engage in "less talk and more action," and to avoid being seen as "all talk and no action."

Not only is action valued over talk, but *talk must stop for action to start*. We are frequently told in meetings and discussions that we need to "stop talking and start doing something" or that "it's time to stop all the talk and get down to business." Finally, we all know that "if everyone would just stop talking, maybe we could get something done."

The bias for action is also demonstrated by such commonplace terms in the workplace as: "action lists," "actionable issues" and "to do lists." The professional literature is not exempt from a bias for action either, at least in nomenclature, for example "action science," "action research" and "action learning." Consequently it would not be unusual to attend a management meeting where after the participants engaged in some "action research" or "action learning" they proved the event was not a waste of time by developing a detailed "to do list" with specific "action items" assigned to accountable persons so that everyone would know "who was to do what by when." Meetings that fail to generate any or enough specific action items are routinely dismissed as having been "all talk and a waste of time."

Underlying Folk Model(s) About Talk and Action

Underlying these common expressions would appear to be implicit conceptions about the nature and interrelationship of talk and action. These implicit constructs, or folk themes/folk model(s), have powerful influences over everyday experience. The critical question, then, becomes: what conceptions or folk model(s) related to talk and action would lead to the conclusions that talk is worthless, action counts, talk must stop for action to start, and, consequently, to a strong bias for action over talk?

First: we note that talk and action are conceived of as disjoint entities. There is something called talk and something else called action with no apparent overlap between them. Either one talks, which is worthless, or acts, which really matters. In no cases do the everyday expressions imply that talk and action occur simultaneously in the same time and place, for example "if everyone would stop talking maybe we could start doing something." At any point in time the expressions imply you either have the one or the other. Furthermore, not only are talk and action disjoint entities, but they are separated in time as well as space. Talk precedes action; action follows talk. They also occur in a linear sequence: from talk to action. Finally, the sequence is uni-directional, with talk always preceding and sometimes leading to action. The reverse direction is mostly or totally absent in everyday workplace conversations. We simply do not hear people being told to "stop getting things done so we can start talking," or that "we should stop all the action so we can have a good discussion." On the few occasions when people are asked to "stop working so we can talk things over," the purpose of the talk is to (again) lead to *doing* things better. In sum, the constructs underlying many of our everyday expressions imply a folk theory where talk and action are separate entities, disjoint in time, space and value. Furthermore, the preferred sequence of events over time is to quickly move from, or through, talk in order to get on to the more valuable action. Talk can also be an implicit impediment or barrier preventing action, for example: "getting stuck in too much talk," "spinning our wheels in endless debate" or "getting sidetracked in long-winded discussions."

The Path-Goal Image Schematic

At this point it is hard not to notice the similarities between these constructs and the path-goal image schematic extensively discussed in the research of the cognitive linguists Lakoff and Johnson (see, for example, Johnson, 1987; Lakoff, 1987; Lakoff & Johnson, 1980). An "image schematic" is essentially a pre-conscious, cognitive analogue that functions as a "template" to order experience. According to Johnson:

> Image schemata exist at a level of generality and abstraction that allows them to serve repeatedly as identifying patterns in an indefinitely large number of experiences, perceptions, and image formations for objects or events that are similarly structured in relevant ways. Their most important feature is that they have a few basic elements or components that are related by definite structures, and yet they have a certain flexibility. As a result of this simple structure, they are a chief means for achieving order in our experience so that we can comprehend and reason about it. (1987, p. 28)

The path-goal image schematic always has the same pattern or structure: there is (i) a source or starting point, (ii) a destination or goal, and (iii) a path of contiguous locations connecting the starting point to the destination. Moreover, the further along the path you go, the more time has passed since starting (see Johnson, 1987, p. 113-117). This particular image schematic is ubiquitous, especially in the analogy *life is a journey* which helps explain why such terms as *forks* in the road (choice), getting *over* traumatic events (obstacles on the path), *mapping* out one's life (setting the course), and so on, can make analogical if not logical sense.

Reviewing how talk and action are described in everyday expressions against the path-goal image schematic reveals a great deal of correspondence and coherence. While inaction may be the source or starting point, talk is certainly at an early point on the path towards the destination or goal of action. After all, isn't talk supposed to lead to action? As a location(s) along the path to action, talk can take on several analogical or metaphorical characteristics. For example, talk can be a necessary stage or state that one must pass through in order to get to action; or an impediment or obstacle that can bog things down or get you stuck; or where you can get side-tracked or lost. Because the goal, or what is valued, is the destination of action, one should not waste too much time along the way "in talk." Thus many of our most common expressions and implicit valuations of talk and action seem rooted in an underlying folk model based on the path-goal image schematic. This folk model implicitly structures talk and action as: (i) separate states, disjoint in time and space, (ii) where talk is an initial or earlier location(s) on a path or journey (iii) to the goal or destination of action, and (iv) where talk must be gone through, gotten over or finished before one is able to move on to the goal of action. In this folk model talk at best helps lead to action and at worse can block or prevent one from getting to action.

Expanding the Folk Model

Once revealed, it is easy to see how this folk model or image schematic may structure the rhetoric about talk and action as well as the implicit and explicit language and metaphors used in that rhetoric. This becomes even clearer as we add in some other aspects of the folk model. One is the role of "conclusion" as the transition "point," "state" or "bridge" between talk and action. Conventionally, conclusions are where the talking stops and action begins. First we talk, then we "reach" a conclusion, and after that we begin action. Reaching a conclusion is usually considered to be the last "step" before starting to act. When all the talk has ended and a conclusion has been reached, it is then time to "get on" to action. Thus a conclusion must be reached as a key milestone along the way to achieving the action destination. This is shown in Figure 13.1 (A and B).

Figure 13.1
Linear Paths of Talk and Action

A. Talk → Action

B. Talk → Conclusion → Action

C. Discuss → Decide → Do → Deed

When only talk, conclusions and action are considered, talk tends to be located as an early or beginning point leading to a conclusion, followed immediately by action. This linear sequencing places action at the end of the path as the final destination or goal of the journey. The end result we want is action, not a return to more talk. So strong is this orientation that action can literally become an end unto itself. "We don't care what you do, just stop talking about it and do something!" "Just get on with it!" This tends to obscure some other everyday injunctions about not making action the goal of the journey. We are also reminded to avoid aimless or meaningless action. When these injunctions are added to the folk model of talk and action they imply that action, too, is a point or location along a path leading to a desired goal or outcome. Thus our actions lead to our outcomes.

The expanded folk model suggests a linear sequence moving from talk to a conclusion, followed by action(s) that leads to an outcome. Modifying our descriptors for purposes of alliteration we now have the implicit folk model of Discuss-Decide-Do-Deed. This is shown in Figure 13.1 (C).

This sequence occurs in time and space with each step along the way bringing us closer to our goal. Because the outcome or goal is what is valued, the steps along the way also connote gradations of worth. Action(s) that leads directly to our desired outcomes is most valuable; aimless action(s) is not. Talk, which is at the beginning or an earlier point of the journey, farthest away from the desired outcome, is hardly worth anything at all.

Based on this analysis it appears clear that many of our everyday discussions at work reflect an implicit theory about talk and action wherein action is exalted and prized, while talk is routinely demeaned as worthless or an impediment to action. The rhetoric reveals not only the strong bias for action, but a powerful folk model implicitly at work in many organizations. This has implications in the work setting, as will be discussed later, but also for the emerging field of organizational discourse.

Redeeming the Meaning of Talk

As long as the rhetoric about talk and action, as well as conclusions and outcomes, is implicitly ordered by an underlying path-goal image schematic, or folk model, talk will continue to be demeaned. Unless, or until, an alternative model comes into use, talk in most organizations may continue to be, implicitly at least, not much more than idle chatter. This, of course, impacts on the nascent field of organizational discourse. Put simply, given the folk model described so far, can a field devoted to organizational talk ever be taken seriously? It seems hard to escape the conclusion that without another folk or formal model it will be difficult to legitimate organizational discourse as an important field of inquiry, especially as compared to anything related to addressing organizational action(s). Maybe the field will need to be marketed as "action discourse" or "discursive action" to imply it is part of the "real" action and therefore worthwhile.

Towards Another Model

As we have seen, in an implicit path-goal folk model where action is considered to be the goal or leading directly to the goal, talk will be devalued and demeaned. We have also noted that although action in general is highly valued, aimless or meaningless action can also be disparaged. This suggests a two-part approach to redeeming the value of talk. The first part is to reassert the function of talk in providing meaning, and specifically imbuing action with meaning. The second is to link such a theory of meaningful action with an image schematic different from the path-goal one.

In the first part, we will need to side with the constructionists and assert that actions are behaviors devoid of meaning until redeemed by talk. Talk, in the form of narratives, stories, accounts, and so on, interprets what actions mean and thereby performs an evaluative function. To be meaningful an action(s) must be evaluated as producing a "significant outcome." Such interpretative evaluations are created and applied through "talk." In essence talk makes action meaningful by turning behaviors and outcomes into "deeds" worthy of recognition and commentary (Starbuck, 1985; Weick, 1995). Actions may or may not be purely objective, empirical events. What those actions mean and how worthwhile they are, however, is inherently subjective and based on what we say about them.

Types of Talk

To advance this proposition further requires the development of a way of talking about "talk." We must be able to distinguish several types of talk, including talk that leads to action, and talk that makes action(s) meaningful. Three types of talk are proposed with labels intended to convey their primary function.

The first type is *tool-talk*. Tool-talk includes all instrumental communications required to discuss, conclude, act and evaluate outcomes. It is utilitarian, that is, used to accomplish some purpose. Tool-talk is usually literal, conscious and intentionally objective.

The second type is *frame-talk*. Frame-talk provides the interpretative frameworks and symbols that generate and evaluate the meaning of discussions, conclusions, actions and outcomes (for example, Donnellon, 1996; Fairhurst & Sarr, 1996; Goffman, 1974; Schön, 1993). By providing context, frame-talk enables implicit and explicit assessments while also conveying subjective meaning and accomplishment. Frame-talk usually includes symbolic, conscious, pre-conscious and contextually subjective dimensions.

The third type is *mythopoetic-talk*. Mythopoetic-talk conveys the ideogenic ideas and images (for example, myths, cosmologies, *logos*) that create and communicate the nature of reality within which frameworks and symbols are applied. It creates and communicates the privileged narratives that guide frame-talk and tool-talk within a particular culture or society. Mythopoetic-talk is usually mythic and metaphorical; conscious, pre/conscious, and unconscious; and intuitive and mystical.

This three-part typology is not intended to imply rigid categorization of types of talk. Rather it is more a fuzzy delineation or gradation intended to distinguish the different functional contributions of what would otherwise be the undifferentiated term "talk" (Lakoff, 1987, p. 21-22; Zadeh, 1965). Talk, of course, in this context implies both oral and written forms of communication, discourse, narrative, account, and so on. It should also be noted that two-part delineations between talk and "meta-talk" have been made by others concerned with the practical aspects of discourse (for example, Nierenberg & Calero, 1973; Tannen, 1986, 1990). In their usage, meta-talk is the hidden meaning beyond or behind the literal words. Meta-talk involves paying attention to or listening for unarticulated assumptions, contextual relationships, symbolism, and so forth. While by no means equivalent to the formulation presented here, meta-talk is more like frame-talk, with some possible overlap with mythopoetic-talk. What is clearly consistent in both typologies, however, is the desire to invent a special form of the word "talk" that conveys the power to create and convey meaning beyond literal, instrumental language.

Cycles and Containers of Meaning

As somewhat implied by their names, tool-talk is contained or framed by frame-talk, and frame-talk is contained or informed by mythopoetic-talk. This is shown in Figure 13.2.

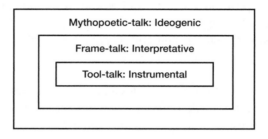

Figure 13.2
Types of Talk

Furthermore, not only are the three types of talk related to each other through containment, but they also re-create and reinforce each other in ongoing cycles of meaning, interpretation and events. This is shown in Figure 13.3. Mythopoetic-talk creates the fundamental ground of ideas which are then selectively used through frame-talk to set the context or interpretation within which tool-talk occurs. The outcomes or deeds resulting from tool-talk are then interpreted or evaluated through further frame-talk in terms of how well they do or do not meet the fundamental premises established by mythopoetic-talk.

Figure 13.3
Containers of talk and cycles of meaning

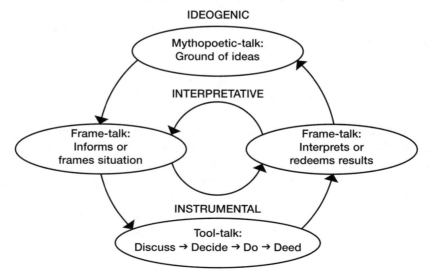

To the degree that frame-talk can successfully interpret or provide meaning to the outcomes or deeds, it will also reinforce and uphold the legitimacy and validity of the ideogenic ideas conveyed by mythopoetic-talk. Thus we have a system of talk that has self-referencing cycles and containers of meaning:

> Cosmological understanding is depicted in symbolic dramas that in turn lead to individual experiences, which are then interpreted within the framework of the cosmology that first produced the experience – thus completing a "cycle of meaning" (Laughlin, et al., 1992, p. 335)

There are two aspects of this model of talk and action that importantly, for our purposes, distinguish it from the previously discussed path-goal folk model of talk and action.

First, talk and action are not conceived of as separate, independent entities. Instead talk *contains* action. Following the container metaphor (Johnson, 1987; Lakoff, 1987), the action is *in* the talk. Frame-talk and mythopoetic-talk form containers of meaning within which action occurs and takes on significance. Actions themselves are meaningless until interpreted in the context of the frame and foundations provided by frame-talk and mythopoetic-talk. In that sense all action is bound, contained and embedded within the "cage" of language (Wittgenstein, 1968). Because, metaphorically, buildings are a form of container (Lakoff & Johnson, 1980), frame-talk about social *constructionism* (Foucault, 1972) or *deconstructionism* (Derrida, 1978, 1982) is coherent within the mythopoetic-talk of constructionist philosophy and science. Thus a shift to a containment image-schematic regarding talk and action seems also to be a prerequisite for most postmodern perspectives.

Second, talk and action do not form a linear sequence ending in action or some outcome(s). Rather they are linked in self-referencing cycles of meaning and experience. Mythopoetic-talk establishes the fundamental set of ideas that frame-talk applies selectively to form the interpretative context within which tool-talk addresses a particular issue. Any resulting actions and outcomes are then evaluated through further frame-talk in terms of how well the actions and outcomes fit/support a prevailing set of fundamental ideas. When actions and outcomes are interpreted by frame-talk as fitting or supporting the fundamental ideas, the cycle of meaning is reinforced, thereby continuing the cycle of self-referencing talk, meaning and action. A cyclical image schematic, wherein linked entities or events form circular relationships, is also clearly part of most postmodern perspectives in all the sciences (Capra, 1982, 1996; Maturana & Varela, 1980, 1987).

The proposition of this argument, then, is that a shift from an implicit path-goal, linear folk model of talk and action to a formal and/or folk model(s) based on cyclical and container image schematics will be a necessary condition for the redemption of talk in comparison to action. Such a shift will also be required to help establish and support the appropriate formal and informal theoretical constructs upon which to build a meaningful field of organizational discourse (for example, see Munro, 1988, for a discussion of the crucial importance of metaphorical or structural images in Chinese philosophy). Talk would thereby be re-located from a position implicitly distant, removed and secondary to action to a more immediate, encompassing and meaningful relationship with action.

An Illustration: The Great Chain of Being

At this point it is perhaps appropriate to attempt to provide greater elucidation to the discussion of types of talk and containers and cycles of meaning. This will be done through a brief exposition of a set of mythopoetic concepts that are collectively known as "the Great Chain of Being."

> We shall first discriminate not, indeed, a single and simple idea, but three ideas which have, throughout the greater part of the history of the West, been so closely and constantly associated that they have often operated as a unit, and have, when thus taken together, produced a conception – one of the major conceptions of Occidental thought – which came to be expressed by a single term: "the Great Chain of Being." (Lovejoy, 1936, p. 20-21)

According to Lovejoy and others, "the Great Chain of Being is rooted in Platonic and Neoplatonic thinking, though adopted by Christians for most of their history in order to relate perfect spirit to imperfect matter" (Hardy, 1987, p. 112). The image of the concept is simple, powerful and implicitly familiar to almost any Western reader. There is a transcendent perfect good or perfect God, at the apex of the universe and the most imperfect, most mutable, primitive matter (or devil) at the bottom. In between, arranged in descending order of perfection, is everything in the universe: angels, humans, animals, plants, slugs, and so on. From saints to sinners, "higher" to "lower" forms of life, the ideal to the gross and base, everything has its place in the Great Chain of Being.

This image is created and supported by three principal ideas set in the context of the assumption of a transcendent, perfect, ideal good or God. Those three ideas are: (i) plenitude, (ii) continuity and (iii) unilinear gradation. As Lovejoy explains, plenitude is the concept that everything that is possible exists; continuity, that everything is contiguous without gaps, empty spaces or vacuums; unilinear gradation, that everything is ordered in a hierarchy from most to least perfect, ideal, spiritual, good. Taken together, these concepts easily engage and evoke such ascent-descent image schematics and metaphors as great chains, ladders, levels and staircases.

Thus the ideogenic conception of the Great Chain of Being provides us with a universe ordered in levels from top to bottom, where one's place denotes degrees of goodness, perfection and/or accomplishment. As Lovejoy richly documents, this set of ideas permeates the mythopoetic-talk of the Western tradition. Examples include the perfect creator who filled the universe with everything possible in Plato's *Timaeus* and *Critias*, and Dante's precise demarcation of the rings and levels between the lowest and highest parts of the universe, from the depths of Hell to the pinnacle of the Godhead in the *Divine Comedy*.

The mythopoetic-talk that creates and re-creates the primal image of the Great Chain of Being also provides the context or ground for how frame-talk positions problems and possibilities. This will be demonstrated through two examples: one biological, the other organizational. First, for the biological example:

> No history of the biological sciences in the eighteenth century can be adequate which fails to keep in view the fact that, for most men of science throughout that period, the theorems implicit in the concept of the Chain of Being continued to constitute essential presuppositions in the *framing* of scientific hypotheses. (Lovejoy, 1936, p. 227; emphasis added)

Hence, the mythopoetic-talk that first creates a chain of being provides implicit legitimacy and coherence to frame-talk that might "set naturalists to looking for forms which would fill up the apparently 'missing links' in the chain" (Lovejoy, 1936, p. 231). This would then be followed by the appropriate tool-talk required to instrumentally search for new and/or missing species. The act of discovering a previously unknown life form might then be interpreted through frame-talk as finding *a missing link*, thereby reinforcing the original conception that there is a Great Chain of Being encompassing all possible beings. As Lovejoy points out,

> Every discovery of a new form could be regarded, not as the disclosure of an additional fact in nature, but as a step towards the completion of a systemic structure of which the general plan was known in advance, an additional bit of empirical evidence of the truth of the generally accepted and cherished scheme of things. (1936, p. 232)

Support for the primal conception would then provide encouragement for the continued framing of situations, experiences and hypotheses in terms of hierarchical forms, missing links and the like. Furthermore, little or none of this would occur explicitly; instead the concepts would be implicitly embedded in how people talked, literally and figuratively, about the universe. A schematic showing the pattern of containers and cycles of meaning for this and the next example is provided in Figure 13.4.

Figure 13.4
The Great Chain of Being: Missing Links and Ladder Levels

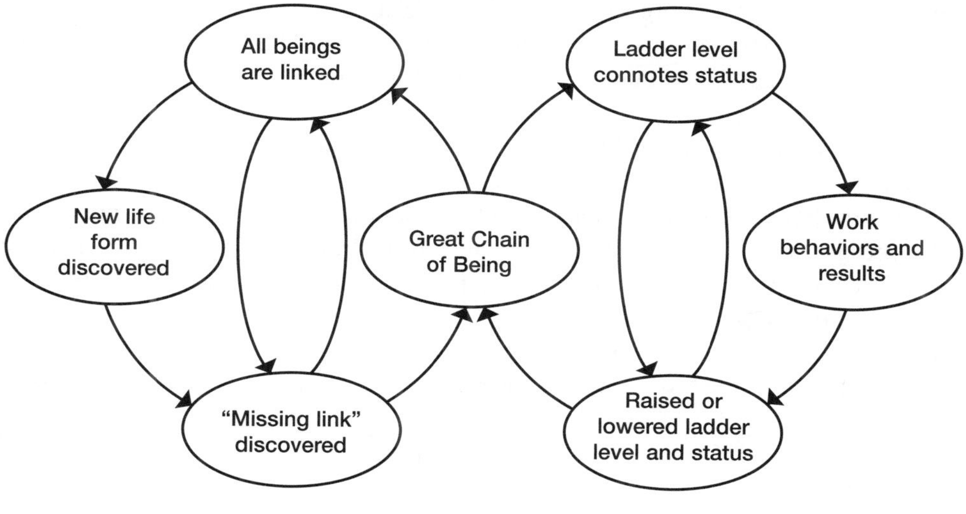

Staying within the container provided by the mythopoetic image of the Great Chain of Being, but switching focus from biology to organizational behavior, reveals similar types of talk and containers and cycles of meaning. Take, for example, the metaphorical framing of personal organizational success in terms of "climbing a ladder." There are job ladders, career ladders and corporate ladders of success. One attempts to avoid getting stuck at too low a level, or otherwise plateaued or topped-out. Instead, success is measured by how fast and how far you climb the ladder. The fast track is not horizontal, it's vertical. Those at the top are presumed to be somehow wiser, smarter, better and/or more talented than those at successively lower levels.

An exception is when you didn't advance on your own but were "kicked upstairs." Where one is stationed in the organizational hierarchy matters, therefore, as an indicator not only of role and responsibility, but of existential and status levels as well. Tool-talk about how to succeed – what actions to pursue to achieve desired outcomes – is implicitly formulated within this framework. The resulting actions and outcomes are then interpreted by frame-talk within the context of movement up or down the ladder.

For example, a negative evaluation might lead to a person being characterized as having been knocked down a peg or two, having fallen off the fast track, or having his or her position lowered in the overall scheme of things. Alternatively, a favorable evaluation might be described in terms of someone being elevated, raised up, moved up, advanced a few rungs, or otherwise headed to the top. All of these evaluative framings serve to confer varying degrees of power and status on individuals, thereby reinforcing and reminding people of the importance of location on the Great Ladder of Corporate Success.

The Bias for Action: Some Organizational Implications

The discussion so far has argued that the conventional path-goal folk model of talk and action supports an implicit, but pervasive, bias for action, at least in the United States. A shift to a "containers and cycles of meaning" folk or formal model(s) would reveal another relationship between action and different types of talk. This relationship would help demonstrate the critical importance of talk in creating meaningful action. It would also be consistent with a paradigmatic shift from an objectivist, linear, reductionist philosophy to one that is more constructionist, cyclical and relationship-oriented. A viable field of organizational discourse could well depend on such a shift. This would require a change in the mythopoetic- and frame-talk used in the discourses of the administrative sciences.

The bias for action over talk, however, has more than mere philosophical and academic consequences. It also has real consequences for what happens in real organizations. In today's organizations the foci of attention, what's valued, what's rewarded and, therefore, what's done are all biased towards action and away from talk. At first this may seem appropriate, even necessary. After all, aren't organizations created to foster collective action, to do things? The answer, of course, is yes, ... but. The "but" serves as a marker to note that there may be some unintended implications, some consequences to privileging action at the expense of talk. One, which we have already noted, is the potential to value and pursue any action, even meaningless or aimless action, to "spinning our wheels in endless talk *that goes nowhere.*" Another is the potential gender bias created by a folk discourse that implicitly favors strong, silent, linearly oriented action to reciprocal, relationship, and emotionally oriented conversation. When talk is demeaned as relatively worthless, and, if as it is for some, "talk is women's work," then the consequences are obvious for women in the workplace. Even the most cursory review of feminist or gender-oriented literature reveals the central importance of how language is constructed and framed for how women (and men) are treated in the workplace (for example, Acker, 1992; Cameron, 1990; Gherardi, 1995; Tannen, 1994b). Other gender and cross-cultural implications should also be considered, including the possibility that the path-goal image schematic is more a preference of Western men than women or people raised in the context of alternative mythopoetic ideas and images (see, for example, Hall & Ames, 1995; Marshak, 1993b, 1994).

The last area of potential consequence to be addressed here has to do with change in contemporary organizations. The transition from the Industrial Age to the Information Age is compelling organizations to pursue new management and organization paradigms and possibilities (Marshak, 1995). The nature of the required changes to established patterns and practices is more transformational or revolutionary in nature than simply maintaining or developing existing capabilities and competencies (Marshak, 1993a). This is forcing organizations and their leaders to rethink fundamental assumptions, theories and practices in the pursuit of competitive success in a global economy. Rethinking, however, demands time in reflection and contemplation, in *talking* to oneself and others to discover the implicit frameworks that may be constraining innovation and adaptation. Rethinking, reflection and contemplation are therefore analogically and metaphorically related to "talk," at least first-cousins if not siblings. The same or similar folk stigmas also seem to apply, whether the talk is with others or oneself through "talk-in-the-mind." For example, psychology is nothing more than "mind games"; theorizing is "fine in the abstract, but not in practice"; thinking and rethinking run the risk of "analyzing too much"; reflection is "navel gazing"; and contemplation is just "staring at the ceiling." None are described as doing anything worthwhile, and most as valueless, *inactive*, wastes of time and therefore money.

At the same time, the professional and popular literatures related to organizations and organizational change have reflected an increasing interest in theories and techniques related to rethinking, reflection, contemplation and learning in organizations. These include theories and concepts related to single-loop, double-loop and triple-loop learning (Argyris, 1982, 1990, 1993; Argyris & Schön, 1974, 1978; Nielsen, 1993); reflective practice (Schön, 1983); sense-making (Weick, 1995); learning organizations (Senge, 1990); and dialogue as "a process for transforming the quality of conversation and, in particular, the thinking that lies beneath it" (Isaacs, 1993a, p. 25; also see Bohm, 1989; Isaacs, 1993b; Schein, 1993). All of these approaches are more consistent with a containers and cycles of meaning model of talk and action rather than a linear, path-goal model. All must also deal with the countervailing managerial folk wisdom that such concepts are perhaps interesting or entertaining in theory, but in reality only action counts. Thus, in the United States at least, while having their adherents and places of application, few or none of these approaches have acquired the same status of centrality as the theories and methods that promise or promote tangible actions in pursuit of a goal. Interestingly, and possibly as a result of competing with the "only action counts" folk wisdom, many of the promoters of these concepts have packaged or framed them with action, not talk, as the central reference point. Presumably, talk, by itself, doesn't sell. For example, there is action-learning, knowledge-in-action, action-reflection-learning, reflection-in-action, and the promise that "dialogue ... is at the root of *all* effective group action" (Schein, 1993, p. 42).

The paradox facing many leaders and organizations, then, is that there is a clear and compelling need to talk about, think about and confront the prevailing assumptions and taken-for-granted practices that are constraining organizational success in the Information Age. This requires reflection about the containers and cycles of meaning that restrict current thinking and action, including the frame-talk and mythopoetic-talk that are keeping management thinking "in-the-box." At the same time, there has been a profusion of formal theories and techniques to help leaders and managers address fundamental ways of thinking and knowing. Nonetheless, such approaches are still not considered mainstream, and it is difficult to get most managers to spend much time in reflective discourse. Instead, they are usually anxious and agitated to "get on with it," to "stop talking and move into action," because "there is no time to waste." They are, after all, responsible, "action-oriented" managers.

The analysis here suggests that one culprit behind this apparent paradox may be the folk model that talk is worthless, action counts, and talk must stop for action to start. In short, the power of this culturally based folk model may covertly undermine the overt logic of the formal theories and competitive challenges (Marshak & Katz, 1997). Your formal theory may claim that talk is critical, but my folk model keeps telling me that "talk is cheap and only action counts."

Closing Comments

The primary purpose of this discussion has been to highlight the dimensions and impacts of the implicit folk models about talk and action. Moreover, the chapter has argued that a viable field of organizational discourse is timely, needed and not open to serious debate. When all is said and done, however, the viability of organizational discourse may well rest on whether or not we are able to leave the action trail and redeem the meaning of talk – for as we have seen, the everyday talk about talk is not favorable, leaving it with a tarnished and questionable reputation. All of this presents a major challenge for the nascent field of organizational discourse. Clearly there are many folk prejudices that will need to be overcome in order to establish discourse as a serious and central part of contemporary management and organizational narratives.

Bibliography

Acker, J. (1992). *Gendering organizational analysis*. Thousand Oaks, CA: Sage.
Argyris, C. (1982). *Reasoning, learning and action*. San Francisco: Jossey-Bass.
Argyris, C. (1990). *Overcoming organizational defenses*. Boston: Allyn & Bacon.

Argyris, C. (1993). *Knowledge for action*. San Francisco: Jossey-Bass.

Argyris, C., & Schön, D.A. (1974). *Theory in practice*. San Francisco: Jossey-Bass.

Argyris, C., & Schön, D.A. (1978). *Organizational learning: A theory of action perspective*. Reading, MA: Addison-Wesley.

Berger, P., & Luckman, T. L. (1967). *The social construction of reality*. London: Penguin.

Bergquist, W. (1993). *The postmodern organization: Mastering the art of irreversible change*. San Francisco: Jossey-Bass.

Bohm, D. (1989). *On dialogue*. Ojai, CA: Ojai Institute.

Bourgeois, V. W., & Pinder, C. C. (1983). Contrasting philosophical perspectives in administrative science: A reply to Morgan. *Administrative Science Quarterly, 28*, 608-613.

Bruner, J., & Feldman, C. F. (1990). Metaphors of consciousness and cognition in the history of psychology. In D. E. Leary (Ed.), *Metaphors in the history of psychology*. Cambridge: Cambridge University Press.

Cameron, D. (Ed.) (1990). *The feminist critique of language: A reader*. London: Routledge.

Capra, F. (1982). *The turning point*. New York: Simon & Schuster.

Capra, F. (1996). *The web of life*. New York: Anchor Books.

Combes, C., Grant, D., Keenoy, T., & Oswick, C. (Eds.). (1996). *Organizational discourse: Talk, text, and tropes*. London: KMCP.

Derrida, J. (1978). *Writing and difference*. Chicago: Chicago University Press.

Derrida, J. (1982). *Margins of philosophy*. Chicago: Chicago University Press.

Donnellon, A. (1996). *Team talk: The power of language in team dynamics*. Boston, MA: Harvard Business School Press.

Fairhurst, G. T., & Sarr, R. A. (1996). *The art of framing: Managing the language of leadership*. San Francisco: Jossey-Bass.

Finocchario, M.A. (1990). Varieties of rhetoric in science. *History of the Human Sciences, 3*, 177-193.

Foucault, M. (1972). *The archeology of knowledge*. London: Tavistock.

Gherardi, S. (1995). *Gender, symbolism, and organizational cultures*. Thousand Oaks, CA: Sage.

Goffman, E. (1974). *Frame analysis*. Cambridge, MA: Harvard University Press.

Grant, D., & Oswick, C. (Eds.). (1996). *Metaphor and organizations*. London: Sage.

Hall, D. L., & Ames, R. T. (1995). *Anticipating China: Thinking through the narratives of Chinese and western culture*. Albany, NY: State University of New York Press.

Hardy, J. (1987). *A psychology with a soul*. London: Routledge and Kegan Paul.

Isaacs, W. N. (1993a). Taking flight: Dialogue, collective thinking and organizational learning. *Organizational Dynamics, 2*(3), 24-39.

Isaacs, W. N. (1993b). Dialogue: The power of collective thinking. *The Systems Thinker, 4*(3), 1-4.

Johnson, M. (1987). *The body in the mind: The bodily basis of meaning, imagination, and reason*. Chicago: Chicago University Press.

Lakoff, G. (1987). *Women, fire, and dangerous things: What categories reveal about the mind*. Chicago: Chicago University Press.

Lakoff, G., & Johnson, M. (1980). *Metaphors we live by*. Chicago: Chicago University Press.

Laughlin, C. D., McManus, J., & d'Aguili, E. G. (1992). *Brain, symbol and experience: Toward a neurophenomenology of human consciousness*. New York: Columbia University Press.

Leary, D. E. (Ed.). (1990). *Metaphors in the history of psychology*. Cambridge: Cambridge University Press.

Lovejoy, A. O. (1936). *The great chain of being*. Cambridge, MA: Harvard University Press.

Marshak, R. J. (1993a). Managing the metaphors of change, *Organizational Dynamics, 22*(1), 44-56.

Marshak, R. J. (1993b). Lewin meets Confucius: A re-view of the OD model of change. *Journal of Applied Behavioral Science, 29*(4), 393-415.

Marshak, R. J. (1994). The tao of change, *OD Practitioner, 26*(2), 18-26.

Marshak, R. J. (1995). Managing in chaotic times. In R. A. Ritvo, A. H. Litwin & L. Butler (Eds.), *Managing in the Age of Change*. Alexandria, VA: Irwin Professional Publishing.

Marshak, R. J. (1996). Metaphors, metaphoric fields, and organizational change. In D. Grant & C. Oswick (Eds.), *Metaphor and organizations*. London: Sage.

Marshak, R. J., & Katz, J. H. (1997). Diagnosing covert processes in groups and organizations, *OD Practitioner, 29*(1), 33-42.

Maturana, H., & Varela, F. (1980). *Autopoeisis and cognition: The realization of the living*. London: Reidel.

Maturana, H., & Vareala, F. (1987). *The tree of knowledge*. Boston: Shambhala.

Morgan, G. (1980). Paradigms, metaphors and puzzle-solving in administrative science, *Administrative Science Quarterly*, 25, 605-22.

Morgan, G. (1983). More on metaphor: Why we cannot control tropes in administrative science, *Administrative Science Quarterly*, 28(4), 601-07.

Morgan, G. (1997). *Images of organization*, 2nd edn. London: Sage.

Munro, D. J. (1988). *Images of human nature: A Sung portrait*. Princeton, NJ: Princeton University Press.

Nielsen, R. P. (1993). Woolman's "I am we" triple loop action-learning: origin and application in organization ethics, *Journal of Applied Behavioral Science, 29*(1), 117-38.

Nierenberg, G. I., & Calero, H. H. (1973). *Meta-talk: The guide to hidden meanings in conversation*. New York: Cornerstone Library.

Ortony, A. (Ed.). (1993). *Metaphor and thought*, 2nd ed. Cambridge: Cambridge University Press.

Oswick, C., & Grant, D. (Eds.). (1996). *Organization development: Metaphorical explorations*. London: Pitman.

Palmer, I., & Dunford, R. (1996). Conflicting use of metaphors: Reconceptualizing their use in the field of organizational change, *Academy of Management Review, 21*(3), 691-717.

Peters, T. J., & Waterman, R. H. (1982). *In search of excellence: Lessons from America's best-run companies*. New York: Harper and Row.

Pinder, C. C., & Bourgeois, V. W. (1982). Controlling tropes in administrative science, *Administrative Science Quarterly*, 27, 641-52.

Schein, E. H. (1993). On dialogue, culture, and organizational learning, *Organizational Dynamics, 2*(3), 40-51.

Schön, D. A. (1993). Generative metaphor: A perspective on problem-solving in social policy, in A. Ortony (Ed.), *Metaphor and Thought*, 2nd ed. Cambridge: Cambridge University Press.

Senge, P. M. (1990). *The fifth discipline: The art and practice of the learning organization.* New York: Doubleday.

Soyland, A. J. (1994). *Psychology as metaphor.* London: Sage.

Tannen, D. (1986). *That's not what I meant.* New York: Ballantine Books.

Tannen, D. (1990). *You just don't understand.* New York: William Morrow.

Tannen, D. (1994). *Talking from 9-5.* New York: William Morrow.

Tsoukas, H. (1992). The missing link: A transformational view of metaphors in organizational science, *Academy of Management Review, 16*(3), 566-85.

Weick, K. E. (1995). *Sensemaking in organizations.* Thousand Oaks, CA: Sage.

Wittgenstein, L. (1968). *Philosophical investigations.* 3rd ed. New York: McMillan.

Zadeh, L. (1965). Fuzzy sets, *Informational Control, 8,* 338-53.

14
Changing the Language of Change: How New Contexts and Concepts are Challenging the Ways We Think and Talk about Organizational Change

Introduction

There is no question that change is a dominant aspect of contemporary organizations. Faced with the forces of globalization and information technology, change initiatives such as downsizing, re-engineering, mergers and acquisitions, restructuring and drives to get "better–faster–cheaper" by "doing more with less" have all become ubiquitous components of most executives' jobs as well as consultants' services. Moreover, and as Pettigrew *et al*. (2001, p. 704) note: "The ideas and techniques of change management are now a global industry led by international consulting firms, gurus, a few high-profile chief executive officers, mass media business publications, and business schools." Thus, given the scope of organizational change, and the change industry of consultants, trainers and academics that has grown up to define and support it, examining organizational change from many perspectives is both timely and appropriate. Valid points of inquiry include discerning the ingredients distinguishing successful from unsuccessful change efforts, consideration of alternative change processes or methods, determination of causal models of key variables influencing or leading to change, isolating what triggers, accelerates or retards organizational change, and so forth.

From a discursive perspective, however, there is an important question that should precede such inquiries because "(t)he language of change can be a liberating force or an analytical prison" (Pettigrew *et al*., 2001, p. 700). The preliminary question, therefore, is: "Do we have the words and conceptual language to address the current and emerging change dynamics of contemporary organizations?" The position of this article is: "No, we do not." There are at least three principal difficulties with the current inventory of words and conceptual language for addressing contemporary organizational change. First, our current language of change is ambiguous and imprecise, especially considering the multifaceted nature of organizational change. Second, the context of organizational change is changing, leaving us with language and concepts that may have been highly appropriate in a different context, but are less applicable now. Third, the current dominant language of change reflects embedded concepts and assumptions that make it difficult to address certain types of emerging change dynamics and possibilities.

As a result of these difficulties, executives, employees and consultants no longer have effective ways to talk about the range of organizational change dynamics they are currently confronting. Put another way, "(t)he dominant change language then seems to uphold 'preferred' ways of designing and implementing change that suppresses alternative, and possibly more appropriate, courses of action" (Morgan, 2001, p. 85). Even the word "change"

Marshak, R. J. (2002). Changing the language of change: How new contexts and concepts are challenging the ways we think and talk about organizational change. *Strategic Change*, *11*, 279-286. Published online in Wiley InterScience. Republished with permission.

may be embedded in and encumbered by the very contexts and concepts that are being challenged by current and emerging change dynamics.

Our Current Language of Change Is Ambiguous and Imprecise

The word "change" has a variety of dictionary definitions connoting varying processes including: *to substitute, replace, switch, alter, become different, convert and transform.* The word, and its range of meanings, is then applied generically to all aspects of the change experience, implying that "changing" an organization's structure is the same as "changing" its culture in terms of reasons, methods, outcomes, time, cost, etc. Furthermore, the generic term "change" does not differentiate among different sources, types or magnitudes of change. For example, "fine tuning" and "re-engineering" are both organizational changes, as are changes "to seize the initiative" or "respond to competitor or market-place innovations."

Partially in response to the ambiguous and imprecise meanings for the word change, as well as to account for new insights and ideas, consultants and academics alike have been busy developing new typologies and terminology to try to clarify one or more dimension of change. The full range of attempts to classify different types or aspects of change is extensive and beyond the scope of this discussion. Table 14.1, however, summarizes some of these efforts to help illustrate the point.

A review of Table 14.1 makes clear that clarifying the nature or magnitude of change has been a central concern of academics and consultants for over thirty years. If anything, trying to be clear about "What kind of change are we talking about?" has become even more difficult in recent years. The change from single- to multi-variable typologies is probably a reflection of both our greater understanding of change dynamics as well as increased difficulty in communicating unambiguously what we mean when using the term "change" by itself.

Despite the attempts to clarify our understandings by classifying different aspects of change, we are still left with ambiguity and confusion when we try to talk about it. There is simply no agreed upon terminology or typology to guide us in our thinking and acting with respect to "change." The use of different words and phrases referring to the same change dynamic, and/or the same words and phrases referring to different dynamics, also impedes communications among and between executives, employees, consultants and academics. Each community also seems to have some preferences for different terminology, adding to the difficulties in communicating across researchers and practitioners. For example, academics may use the term "punctuated equilibrium" (e.g. Gersick, 1991) to refer to the same change dynamic that executives and consultants may call "radical," "revolutionary," "fundamental," or, increasingly, "transformational" change.

Table 14.1
Some Typologies and Terms of Change

Single variable: nature of change	
Greiner (1972)	Evolutionary or revolutionary
Bartunek & Moch (1987)	First-order, second-order or third-order
Ackerman (1996)	Development, transition or transformation
Weick & Quinn (1999)	Episodic or continuous
Multivariable: nature of change and ways of managing or focus	
Nadler (1998)	Nature of change combined with ways of managing leads to *tuning, adapting, redirecting* or *overhauling.*
Huy (2001)	Nature of change combined with focus of change leads to *commanding, engineering, teaching* or *socializing.*
Palmer & Dunford (2002)	Nature of change combined with ways of managing leads to *directing, navigating, caretaking, coaching, interpreting* or *nurturing.*

It is clear that efforts to clarify and further define change dynamics, leading to more agreed-upon typologies and terms, would greatly assist our ability to study, compare, and guide organizational change efforts. In the meantime, however, we are left with a cacophony of terms and compound words to try to communicate the whats, whys, and hows of organizational change. As a result, it remains hard to know what we are really talking about when we talk about organizational change, except perhaps that something, at some level, due to some set of circumstances or processes will be different to some degree.

The Context of Organizational Change is Changing

As we enter the Information Age, the scope, speed, and even nature of change seems to be changing. The new information technologies of the past 50-60 years (TV, satellite communications, PCs, the Internet, mobile phones, etc.) are creating a new era, marked by the ability of people to access and share information with virtually anyone, anywhere, anytime about anything on a continuous, interactive and unrestricted basis. These new capabilities have altered both the organizational game and the rules of the game. "Connectivity, Speed, and Intangibles – the derivatives of time, space, and mass – are blurring the rules and redefining our businesses and our lives" (Davis and Meyer, 1998, p. 6). The result of these shifting conditions and capabilities is the emergence of a new context that invites different organization and change principles from those most applicable in the Industrial Age. For example, some of the keys to success in the context of the Industrial Age, such as productive and/or technological capacity, certainty and stability, and independence and autonomy, are being replaced by market and/or customer orientation, speed, flexibility and innovation, and interdependence and partnership.

Because of this change in contexts, contemporary organizational change also appears to be changing. Two major indicators that this may be true are the beginning shifts in organizational change emphasis, first, from addressing parts/segments of an organization to addressing more encompassing patterns/wholes, and second, from episodic change to virtually continuous change (e.g., Weick & Quinn, 1999). For example, since the 1990s both practitioners and researchers have suggested that whole-system, rather than part-system, change is more likely to lead to successful organizational performance (e.g. Bunker & Alban, 1997; Macy & Izumi, 1993). Similarly, Brown and Eisenhardt (1997) argue that continual, not episodic, change is required to deal with the increased speeds of the new business context. "Moreover, in high-velocity industries with short product cycles and rapidly shifting competitive landscapes, the ability to engage in rapid and relentless continual change is a crucial capability for survival" (1997, p. 1).

When we combine the dimensions of parts-wholes and episodic-continuous change into a matrix, the emerging nature of contemporary organizational change is suggested. The four change scenarios created by this matrix are shown in Table 14.2.

Table 14.2
Four Change Scenarios

Dimensions	Focus on parts/segments	Focus on patterns/wholes
Episodic Change	Periodic Operational Adjustments	Periodic Systemic (Re) Arrangements
	• Gap analyses	• Re-engineering
	• Fix its	• Systemic Redesign
Continuous Change	Continuous Operational Adaptations	Continuous Systemic Alignments
	• On-going improvements	• On-going organization
	• *Kaizen*, TQM	• "Morphing"

Periodic Operational Adjustments are episodic changes to parts or segments of an organization, for example gap analyses and "fix its" to some aspect of strategy, structure, processes, etc., but not to all at the same time. This was, implicitly, one of the dominant approaches to organizational change in past years, memorably captured in the phrase, "If it's not broke don't fix it." Continuous Operational Adaptations also focus on parts or segments, but do so on an on-going basis. Continuous improvements, *Kaizen*, or TQM reflect this approach to organizational change. Periodic Systemic Re-Arrangements address organizational patterns or wholes, but on an episodic basis. Re-engineering and systemic redesign efforts are examples of this approach to organizational change. Finally, Continuous Systemic Alignments call for on-going changes to the whole organization, for example virtually simultaneous changes to an organization's strategies, structure, processes, boundaries, culture, and so on.

Although we have some experience, language and concepts to help us talk about the first three scenarios, we have little to adequately describe the last one. Yet the need for virtually continuous change of whole systems is now the context confronting many organizations, or at least those in "high velocity" industries such as electronics and the Internet. The difficulty extends beyond a lack of experience with new capabilities and contexts. The difficulty also includes the absence of language and terms to appropriately describe and explain this emerging type of organizational change. For example, the term "transformational change" typically presumes the punctuated equilibrium paradigm where a radical shift is preceded and then followed by a more "normal" and stable period of development. Within the context of the Industrial Age and the punctuated equilibrium paradigm, a suggestion that there could be continuous transformational change of whole systems might sound like science fiction. Nonetheless, at least some contemporary organizations are confronting new contexts and must be able to think and talk about organizational change in new ways. Because so much of our existing language of change is encumbered with concepts developed in a different context, we may need to develop new words to help express new understandings and possibilities.

To help capture the imagery, if not the specifics of continuous whole-system change, I first suggested the computer animation term for transformation, "morphing," in a keynote address at a change conference in Singapore in 1998. Morphing had already started to come into popular use in the press and media to describe rapid, seamless, and more or less total change. The term morphing has also very recently been introduced in an academic context to describe comprehensive, continuous, dynamic organizational change. "Continuous morphing refers to the comprehensive, continuous changes in products, services, resources, capabilities, and modes of organizing through which firms seek to regenerate competitive advantage under conditions of hyper-competition" (Rindova & Kotha, 2001, p. 1276). Drawing on recent research (Brown and Eisenhardt, 1997; Rindova & Kotha, 2001) some of the "principles of morphing" include:

- Creating limited organizational structures and principles such that there is both enough form and fluidity for rapid, organized action.
- Creating resource flexibility in terms of both availability and application.
- Insuring organizational learning to quickly develop and deploy new competencies.
- Bridging from the present to the future with clear transition processes while avoiding focusing on the future to the detriment of the present.
- Having top management mindsets that fully embrace the concepts of continuous change and flexible organizational forms, i.e., "managers with morphing mindsets."

Whether or not morphing is the right term to adopt, it does have some advantages that are needed to help describe the emerging context(s) of organizational change. Those advantages include its lack of association with prior terms and concepts of change, its origins in the Information Age, its connotation of rapid, seamless transformational change, unlike, for example, metamorphosis which implies stages of transformation over longer time periods, and an imagery that is both evocative and understandable. In short, morphing, or some term like it, may be needed as a generative metaphor or analogy to advance our thinking about continuous whole-system change.

Our Current Language of Change is Limited by Implicit Fundamental Assumptions

Our language and concepts of change are not only challenged by contemporary change dynamics, they are also limited by powerful implicit assumptions about the fundamental nature of change. These implicit assumptions are rooted in the dominant philosophical worldviews of the Industrial Age and are supported in day-to-day conversation by related, but mostly unconscious, metaphors and word images. What, then, are some of these assumptions and why are they so limiting?

We begin first with the Greek philosophers who helped to shape the Western worldview. From Plato and Aristotle we inherit the assumptions that permanence and stability are in all cases preferred over chaos and change. Plato and Aristotle also equated change with motion and asserted that motion/change must have a cause. In both cases their ideas prevailed over the earlier views of Heraclitus who claimed that the world is an "everlasting fire" in a state of continual change (Wagner, 1995). The metaphorical equation of change with motion also coincides with the recent work of the cognitive linguists Lakoff and Johnson (1999) who claim that the dominant conceptual metaphor (a cognitively unconscious image that structures reality) used to express change is "Change is Motion." The metaphorical linking of change with motion also links assumptions about change to the Newtonian worldview that helped create and shape the Industrial Age. Thus the movement of objects, including the laws of motion, causal forces, inertia, resistance, mass, momentum, and so on, as well as a mechanistic universe, are all likely to be implicitly invoked in any discussion of organizational change. Unfortunately, however, a language of change embedded with implicit assumptions of a mechanical universe where permanence and stability are preferred, chaos is feared, and change results from forced movement may limit our ability to talk and think about continuous whole-system change in contemporary organizations.

In explicit reaction to the limitations of the Newtonian and/or Industrial Age worldview of change, some consultants and academics have recently been searching for alternative concepts, assumptions, language and metaphors to help think and talk about contemporary and emerging change dynamics. "We call the traditional leadership mindset, most prevalent today, the Industrial Mindset. This worldview contains the very blinders that prevent leaders from seeing the dynamics of transformation" (Ackerman-Anderson & Anderson, 2001, p. 7). To illustrate, we will briefly review two alternative conceptions of change along with their associated language and metaphors. One tends to equate transformational change with altered consciousness rather than movement. The other draws upon the post-Newtonian "new sciences" for concepts, language and images to help facilitate and guide organizational change.

For some, the kind of radical whole-system change called "organization transformation" requires a change in consciousness, often starting with the leadership and extending throughout the organization. This orientation "… understands transformation as being primarily driven by shifts in human consciousness" (Ackerman-Anderson & Anderson, 2001, p. 7). Here we have not only an alternative conception of change, but a different language and set of metaphors used to describe and explain the phenomenon of transformation. Consider that with movement metaphors change occurs in physical space, "Despite resistance, the organization moved from a national to a global strategy." This evokes images and ideas of inertia, forces, resistance, end-states, paths, and so on. This is the language of planning, managing and engineering change. Unlike physical movement, however, altered consciousness occurs in psychological space and evokes a different set of metaphors and images. Frequently the imagery is not about going somewhere, but about *enlightenment* or seeing more clearly. Note that in the earlier quote from Ackerman-Anderson and Anderson, they write about *blinders* that prevent leaders from seeing.

In a summary of spiritual and traditional ways of describing the transformation of consciousness, Metzler (1986) identifies eleven major metaphors or images that are used to help describe and evoke that experience. Many relate directly or indirectly to seeing more clearly, some suggest organic processes, a few imply a transformational journey, and none invoke mechanistic or engineering imagery. See Table 14.3 for the complete list.

Table 14.3
Metaphors for the Transformation of Consciousness

From caterpillar to butterfly
Awakening from the dream of "reality"
Uncovering the veils of illusion
From captivity to liberation
Purification by inner fire
From darkness to light
From fragmentation to wholeness
Journey to the place of vision and power
Returning to the source
Dying and being reborn
Unfolding the tree of life

Source: Metzler (1986).

This implies organization transformation requires that executives release their existing worldviews and acquire new mindsets in order to "see," think and act differently. For example, abandon assumptions about organizational stability and adopt "morphing mindsets" in order to create an organization capable of continuous change. In sum, this point of view urges managers to think and talk about transformational change more in terms of "helping people to see new realities or possibilities" than "how to move the organization to a new strategy, structure, and/or product offering." The imagery invites thinking and talking in terms of psychological processes versus physical movement.

The "new sciences," for example quantum physics, chaos theory, and complexity science, provide another set of concepts, language and metaphors for talking and thinking about organizational dynamics (Wheatley, 1992). They also directly challenge assumptions of stability and episodic change that must be initiated, planned and managed. Instead, it is assumed that change is continuous, and that complex systems can be self-organizing. These concepts, strange as they may seem to some, offer relevant ideas and images to help guide those interested in how to better understand and address continuous whole-system change.

Currently, the term and metaphor "complex adaptive system" seems to be a favored way to describe organizational change dynamics from a new sciences perspective. "Continuously changing organizations are likely to be complex adaptive systems with semi-structures that poise the organization on the edge of order and chaos..." (Brown & Eisenhardt, 1997, p. 32). Olson and Eoyang (2001) also advocate the concepts and language of complex adaptive systems to escape the limitations of the Newtonian and Industrial paradigms. "We need a simple, coherent alternative to the old machine model before we can work responsibly in the complex environments of today and tomorrow" (2001, p. 6). "The emerging science of complex adaptive systems offers such a paradigm. It provides metaphors and models that articulate and make meaning out of the emerging adaptive nature of organizations" (2001, p. 19). The language and images associated with complex adaptive systems include *self-organization, cyclical change, patterns, containers, significant differences* and *transforming exchanges*. The image or metaphor of a "complex adaptive system" is intended to invite managers to think and talk in terms of "cultivating or enabling continuous self-organization" rather than "how to plan, create and then stabilize change." The preferred imagery is continuous, self-organizing instead of episodic, engineered change.

Concluding Comments

Talk is never "just talk." Language is not a neutral medium. Language both enables and limits what and how we think and therefore what we do. The new organizational challenges presented by our increasingly hyperactive business environments may require new language to help managers, employees and consultants think through and appropriately talk about what needs to be done. We must also be mindful that our traditional terminology, metaphors and word imagery for organizational change, useful in certain contexts and situations, may elicit or encourage ideas and associations less applicable to current and emerging change dynamics (Marshak, 1993). Given the powerful, but usually hidden, role that our language of organizational change plays in creating mindsets and resulting actions, here are a few things to keep in mind:

- Be specific. Don't assume the term "organizational change" means the same thing to everyone. Specify exactly what you mean. Ask specific questions of others. Check assumptions.
- Be self-reflective. Ask yourself what are your assumptions, mental models, metaphors and terminology for organizational change? How might these be limiting how you think and act with respect to organizational change dynamics?
- Rethink the use of, or reliance on, mechanistic, engineering or planned movement concepts, metaphors and imagery in transformational change initiatives.
- Consider a "morphing mindset" or some other novel mental and word imagery to help address continuous whole-system change in hyperactive business environments.

Remember, as we enter the Information Age you may need to put aside the organizational change scripts inherited from the past and author your own future.

References

Ackerman L. S. (1996). Development, transition or transformation: Bringing change leadership into the 21st century. *OD Practitioner 28*(4): 5-16.

Ackerman-Anderson L., & Anderson, D. (2001). Awake at the wheel: Moving beyond change management to conscious change leadership. *OD Practitioner 33*(3): 4-10.

Bartunek, J. M., & Moch, M. K. (1987). First-order, second-order, and third-order change, and organization development intervention: A cognitive approach. *Journal of Applied Behavioral Science 23*(4), 483-500.

Brown, S., & Eisenhardt, K. (1997). The art of continuous change: Linking complexity theory and time-paced evolution in relentlessly shifting organizations. *Administrative Science Quarterly, 42*, 1-34.

Bunker, B. B., & Alban, B.T. (1997). *Large group interventions: Engaging the whole system for rapid change.* Jossey-Bass: San Francisco, CA.

Davis, S., & Meyer, C. (1998). *Blur: The speed of change in the connected economy.* Addison-Wesley: Reading, MA.

Gersick, C. J. G. (1991). Revolutionary change theories: A multi-level exploration of the punctuated equilibrium paradigm. *Academy of Management Review, 16*(1), 10-36.

Greiner, L.E. (1972). Evolution and revolution as organizations grow. *Harvard Business Review, 50*(4), 37-46.

Huy, O.N. (2001). Time, temporal capability and planned change. *Academy of Management Review, 26*(4), 601-623.

Lakoff, G, & Johnson, M. (1999). *Philosophy in the flesh: The embodied mind and its challenge to western thought.* Basic Books: New York.

Macy, B. A., & Izumi, H. (1993). Organizational change, design, and work innovation: A metaanalysis of 131 North American field studies – 1961-1991. In R.W. Woodman and W. A. Pasmore (Eds), *Research in organizational change and development,* Vol. 7, (pp. 235-313). JAI Press: Greenwich, CT.

Marshak, R. J. (1993). Managing the metaphors of change. *Organizational Dynamics 22*(1), 44-56.

Metzler, R. (1986). *Opening to inner light: Symbols and metaphors of human transformation.* Jeremy Tarcher: Los Angeles, CA.

Morgan, J. M. (2001). Are we 'out of the box' yet? A case study and critique of managerial metaphors of change. *Communication studies 52*(1), 85-102.

Nadler, D. (1998). *Champions of change: How CEO's and their companies are mastering the skills of radical change.* Jossey-Bass: San Francisco, CA.

Olson, E. E., & Eoyang, G. H. (2001). *Facilitating organization change: Lessons from complexity science.* Jossey-Bass: San Francisco, CA.

Palmer, I., & Dunford, R. (2002). Who says change can be managed? Positions, perspectives and problematics. *Strategic Change 11*(5).

Pettigrew, A. M., Woodman, R. W., & Cameron, K.S. (2001). Studying organizational change and development: Challenges for future research. *Academy of Management Journal 44*(4), 697-713.

Rindova, V., & Kotha, S. (2001). Continuous "morphing": Competing through dynamic capabilities, form, and function. *Academy of Management Journal 44*(6), 1263-1280.

Wagner, C. K. (1995). Managing change in business: Views from the ancient past. *Business Horizons 38*(6), 8-12.

Weick, K. E., & Quinn, R. E. (1999). Organizational change and development. *Annual Review of Psychology, 50,* 361-386.

Wheatley, M. J. (1992). *Leadership and the new science*. Berrett-Koehler Publishers: San Francisco.

15
From Outer Words to Inner Worlds

A principal aim of this discussion is to introduce and further demarcate the emerging field of organizational discourse, especially in terms of its prevailing theoretical orientations and methodological approaches. In particular, we wish to comment on the significance of discourse analysis for organizational intervention strategies and, furthermore, to suggest that thus far discourse analysis has largely failed to address the sociopsychological underpinnings of discourse itself. In short, although discourse analysis has focused on the outer words deployed to re-present social and organizational realities, it has had relatively little to say about the inner worlds from which such re-presentations have emerged as characterizations of reality.

Applications and Implications of Organizational Discourse

The ideas covered in this issue raise a range of theoretical and methodological considerations. They also address or comment on a variety of dynamics and issues at work in contemporary organizations and, as the foregoing articles in this issue illustrate, provide alternative and provocative accounts of the complex nature of organizational life. But, as some of our more action-oriented colleagues may ask, "So what? How are such accounts of relevance and use to organizational consultants or researchers?" In our view, there is a great deal of relevance revealed, in the form of three principal challenges to conventional practice. First, organizational discourse challenges existing applied theory and methods; second, there is the challenge to incorporate the insights of discourse analysis into diagnostic and intervention strategies; and third, there is the challenge to develop more innovative applications of a discourse-sensitive nature.

Applied theory and method. Organizational discourse directly questions the mirror-image theory of social reality, and this is its most profound challenge to prevailing positivist theory and practice. Consider for a moment the applied field of organizational development (OD). In many ways, the field is based on the bedrock positivist premise that valid, objective data can be collected, published (shared with the sources of the data), and acted upon through action research to bring about organizational change (Cummings & Worley, 1997; French & Bell, 1999; Marshak & Katz, 1992; Nadler, 1977). Similarly, in a related formulation by Chris Argyris (1970), the only role of the organization consultant is to facilitate the generation of valid data, informed choice, and commitment.

From a discourse-sensitive perspective, these key premises are challenged in this issue. Schneider's research (2000) demonstrates that interview data are co-created social constructions and that it is not possible to avoid interviewer participation in both the production of answers and the reinterpretation of interviewee meanings. Beech (2000) asserts that monological and/or objective realities may be questionable assumptions to hold and might better be replaced by presuming organizational actors will use contrasting and

Slightly edited from Marshak, R. J., Keenoy, T., Oswick, C., & Grant, D. (2000). From outer words to inner worlds. *The Journal of Applied Behavioral Science, 36*(2), 245-258. Republished with permission.

potentially contending narrative styles to account for reality. Furthermore, as Alvesson and Kärreman (2000) point out, any organizational reality is but a privileged story – one that may be created and enforced by those with power. From these points of view, the conventional assumptions of OD about neutral consultants using objective data to facilitate shared understandings and commitments may seem a bit naive. Certainly, the entire discourse about the role of the OD consultant as an objective, neutral facilitator seems open to serious revision or deconstruction (see, e.g., Clark & Salaman, 1997; Micklethwait & Wooldridge, 1996).

Diagnostic and intervention strategies. In addition to challenging positivist assumptions and practices, the articles in this issue posit several different frames that merit consideration for further field testing and possible application or incorporation by organizational change agents or researchers. For example, O'Connor's discussion (2000) of the embedded narratives about change that she identified at Horizon raises some important questions for organizational diagnosis and intervention. In terms of diagnosis, her analysis implies that it is not only the focal situation that needs to be considered but how this may be a reflection of, or thematically interwoven within, a complex of related narratives about the past, present, and emerging future of the organization. In addition, she alerts us to the potential significance of temporal and spatial meaning in the systemic consideration of organizational phenomenon.

Furthermore, if organizational change situations are embedded thematically, *matryoshka-like*, within broader temporal frames of action – at the corporate, industry, community, and societal levels – then where and how to intervene become critical questions. If, for example, a local reorganization merging two units is also, thematically, embedded in a larger organizational or industry narrative about mergers, then any change intervention might necessarily need to address past as well as present meanings of merger dynamics at multiple levels of the system. Regardless of the apparent objective facts of the local situation, such embedded narratives will tend to create and reinforce meanings among system participants that are associated with the overall themes. Consequently, any effective change strategy would require the ability to discern resonant embedded themes that need to be addressed, as well as ways to mitigate, modify, or link to alternative themes. This also highlights the much more troublesome and interesting question of where the most effective location or level of intervention is likely to be. Can one successfully intervene in a local manifestation of an embedded theme by altering its more global context, or could one attempt to alter a more global theme by changing one or a series of more locally embedded narratives? Although it is impossible to be confidently prescriptive on these issues, clearly, any choice will be better informed by an accurate diagnosis of the significance and organizational impacts of the embedded narratives.

Beech's discussion of the potential impact of multiple narrative styles on the creation of social meaning in organizations adds an additional layer of complexity to O'Connor's formulation. According to Beech, not only is organizational behavior influenced and, perhaps, determined by controlling narratives, but there is also likely to be no single, monolithic organizational narrative held by all organizational members. Instead, different actors and departments are likely to have their own narrative styles. Such a situation holds considerable potential for misconceptions and misperceptions across narrative boundaries; what is routinely referred to as a communication problem might, on inspection, turn out to be an alternative social reality. Thus, an O'Connor-inspired consultant might attempt to diagnose an organizational situation or problem in terms of a thematically related, or consistent, embedded narrative manifesting itself at different times and levels within the system, whereas a Beech-inspired consultant might be more likely to attempt to diagnose the situation in terms of the multiple and conflicting narrative styles held by different actors in the same time and place.

Clearly, such differences in diagnostic orientations also suggest alternative intervention strategies. Following the O'Connor orientation would likely lead to an intervention strategy focused on finding and then modifying or leveraging a single more or less monological narrative that provides the primary source of social meaning for the situation at issue. Beech, on the other hand, views organizational reality as being comprised of multiple narrative styles among different actors and organizational units, which suggests interventions directed toward developing good cross-cultural communication skills and an appreciation of plurivocality.

Discourse-sensitive applications. Although the articles in this issue are deliberately theoretical in nature, there are glimpses of some possible discourse-sensitive applications suggested by the reported findings.

In Mauws's research (2000), we learn not only about gatekeeping narratives in the culture industries but, by extension, some possible ways to positively or negatively influence decision makers involved in organizational changes. Mauws (quoting Bielby & Bielby, 1994) notes that "all hits are flukes" and then goes on to demonstrate how, as a consequence of this unpredictability and intrinsic ambiguity, decisions about which cultural products will be commissioned and manufactured are influenced by narratives of genre, imitation, and reputation. If, for purposes of analogy, we posit that all (successful) organizational changes are also flukes, then it would be fair to assume that leaders who make decisions about proposed organizational changes might be similarly influenced by genre, imitation, and reputation. Thus, rhetorically, if one wanted to get past the organizational change gatekeepers in a particular organization, one might be well advised to link a change proposal to the following:

- *Successful change genres.* Re-presenting a proposed change in terms of successful organizational changes that are known to decision makers and have been effective in the past could make or break an initiative. This may help explain why in many settings novel organizational change approaches are often couched in language associated with more familiar types of change. For example, although organizational transformation initiatives may fall on deaf ears, a proposed organizational transition strategy might be fully accepted (Marshak, 1993). Or, a cultural change initiative may be cast as a training intervention or even as a structural realignment. The oft-noted consultant complaint that change terminology in organizations is misused or even abused may not be a consequence of confusion or ignorance but a rhetorical ploy to position a change initiative to reflect a particular change genre. Someone opposed to the proposed change would, of course, follow this advice in reverse, that is, attempt to link a proposal to an unsuccessful change genre and thereby block the initiative from getting past the gatekeepers.

- *Imitating successful programs.* For television producers, the rule is, "If they have a successful cops-and-robbers show, we'll have one too." In business, it might be, "If they have a successful strategy for reengineering, culture change, or a merger or a new global strategy, then we should have one too." Thus, to gain agreement on a proposed change initiative may require the ability to validate its probable success by rhetorically linking it to what other leading-edge organizations are doing. Those opposed presumably would seek to do the opposite or attempt to link it to a well-known failure.

- *Reputation as legitimation.* Here, the rhetorical strategy is to link the proposed change initiative to someone perceived to be highly credible. Organizational executives and managers with track records of organizational change success would seem to be the logical choices, even if it means hiring someone from elsewhere or employing well-known consultants or management gurus. As before, those opposed might seek to point out any prior failures of those associated with the initiative.

All three tactics share the same objective, which is to induce an affirmative decision in an inherently uncertain, ambiguous context by rhetorically framing the situation in ways that reduce the perceived risk, uncertainty, and potential confusion of the organizational change gatekeepers. Thus, sensitivity to the range and impact of different rhetorical devices seems likely to enhance the potential success of any change proposal.

Similarly, Jackson's (2000) fantasy theme analysis of the learning organization suggests not only why Senge's vision was more successful than others but also the potential requirements for any successful and sustainable (organizational) vision. An alternative reading of Jackson's research might be to see it as a cogent analysis of how to create and sustain a compelling vision based on a case study of one of the most successful and enduring visions in recent management literature. Thus, an organizational leader seeking to induce change by articulating a new vision might be well advised to create and dramatize some or all of the following:

- a rhetorical vision that catches up members of the organization into a common symbolic reality;
- setting themes that depict where the action is taking place or the place where the members of the organization act out their roles;
- character themes that describe the different roles of members of the organization, ascribe qualities to them, and portray them as having certain characteristics;
- action themes that portray behavior in various situations;
- symbolic cues such as code words, phrases, slogans, or gestures that trigger previously shared fantasies and emotions;

- a sanctioning agent, or agents, who legitimize the symbolic reality portrayed by the rhetorical vision;
- a rhetorical community of organizational members who share a common symbolic ground and respond in ways that are in tune with the rhetorical vision; and
- a master analogue that is based on one of three deep structures: the righteous, the social, or the pragmatic.

These brief comments should serve to make the case that organizational discourse is an emerging field in organizational studies that offers new and, in some respects, radical ways of thinking about social and organizational phenomena. In addition, it offers an ontology and an epistemology that can generate alternative approaches to diagnosis and intervention in organizations. In brief, words and the meanings they create and convey matter. They matter a great deal.

Words, Meanings, and Their Origins

Researching words and the meanings they create and convey, however, is not sufficient. More is needed. What is missing, as many of this journal's readers may already have noted, is an account of the choice of the words deployed and their various meanings. Where do the discourses, narratives, texts, and words that are analyzed in organizational discourse come from?

Equally compelling, and analytically more challenging, is the question of the meanings attributed to the words. What is the relationship between the meanings presumably intended by the authors of the words and the meanings attributed to the same words by various analysts? This is a relatively underdeveloped aspect of organizational discourse, reflected not only in the selections in this issue but in the field in general (Fairclough, 1992, 1995; Grant, Keenoy, & Oswick, 1998; Potter & Wetherell, 1987).

Furthermore, although not usually explicitly addressed, much work in the field seems to imply that the words articulated by organizational actors can be taken as evidence of those actors' purposeful intentions and as indicators of their preferred outcomes. More radical versions of this implicit discourse would also assert or imply that the persuasion and/or power of elites intentionally privilege some words and narratives over others, raising issues of class or group consciousness and conflict (Foucault, 1972, 1980). These orientations, however, tend to ignore the possible contribution of arational, subliminal, or unconscious dimensions to the origin of words and their meanings in organizations (Egan, 1994). There are a number of reasons why most versions of organizational discourse tend to neglect the possibility that the origin of organizational texts, narratives, and their meanings may lie below the subtext of social interaction in the human unconscious.

First, organizational discourse is still in its early stages of development and has been led by scholars with backgrounds primarily oriented toward disciplines such as organizational sociology rather than psychology. In fact, one of the reasons for this special issue of *The Journal of Applied Behavioral Science* is to introduce organizational discourse to those who may be more psychologically oriented and thereby invite their contributions to the field.

Second, we might also note that despite the pioneering contribution of Lacan (Bracher, 1993; Lacan, 1998), the radical psychoanalyst who explored the relationship between language and the unconscious while introducing structural linguistics to Freudianism, organizational discourse has emerged primarily from more conventional sources such as speech act theory (Austin, 1962). In particular, advances made in literary analysis influenced by postmodernism have shaped the field (Keenoy, Oswick, & Grant, 1997). Given this background, it is perhaps unsurprising that the primary metaphors and analogues employed conceptualize organizational phenomena as narratives, texts, conversations, or discourses. Consequently, many of the methodological approaches are drawn from literary analysis in which discerning the social meanings of the text is emphasized over individual motivation or the possible psychological origins of the words and their interpretations.

Finally, the emergence of organizational discourse has taken place in the context of the decline of more structurally based radical perspectives on organization and organizing. In this respect, the field has provided a new forum where it has been possible for those with a radical orientation to maintain a critical perspective on management activity (Fairclough, 1995; Watson, 1994). This may also contribute to the reluctance of some organizational discourse researchers to speculate on the application of their work. At a recent organizational discourse conference, one presenter with a radical perspective not only declined to consider the possible applications of his research but suggested no one should, because "it might give too much insight and power to management." Nevertheless, whatever the cause or causes, the human unconscious seems mostly absent from early research in the field. Four examples from the articles in this issue serve to illustrate the marginalization of psychosocial and psychoanalytic explanations.

The Unconscious in the Margin

Alvesson and Kärreman's contribution carefully stresses the importance of studying meaning, not simply talk by itself. "The level of talk constitutes an important area of research, but any study remains incomplete without the incorporation and consideration of the level of meaning" (p. 149). However, meaning seems implicitly confined to the intended meanings of the authors or analysts of the narrative, text, or discourse. For example, commenting on the contributions researchers potentially make to the construction of meaning, they list more than 15 possible researcher biases and influences, but the potential effects of the researcher's subconscious or unconscious is not among them. Similarly, in their summary of the five linguistic turns, they conclude, "They are all consistent with an understanding of language users as socially situated, discursively constituted, sensitive, and responsive to dominant cultural norms, social rules, and available scripts for talk, oriented toward the effects of language use" (p. 154). The possibility that motivation and meaning may also be influenced by subliminal cues or situated in the unconscious is not mentioned.

O'Connor comes close to explicitly raising unconscious dynamics as the source for the fall-from-order themes she found recurring in her case study of the embedded narratives at Horizon. However, she opts for a more spiritual or religious explanation of the origins. "More figuratively, then, or even allegorically, this narrative addresses what Eliade . . . calls a fundamental, universal problem of human existence: the fall from order and the recovery of it through a return to origins, thus the hope of rebirth" (pp. 179-180). The possibility of Jungian archetypal origins for the allegories, myths, and themes is not considered.

The absence of deeper inquiry into the origin of the words is also evident in Beech's discussion. His analysis of the variation in narrative styles seems grounded in an implicit assumption that multiple narrative styles are predictable phenomena in all organizations. Although his identification of discreet narrative styles is convincing, there is no attempt to explain why particular individuals embrace particular styles.

Furthermore, the origins of the narrative styles are attributed to the dynamics of intergroup cultural and political boundary setting in organizations rather than personality or unconscious processes. Thus, even though Beech references the Jungian-influenced Joseph Campbell's (1968) analysis of the journey of the hero, he classifies it as a cultural narrative rather than an archetype in the collective unconscious. Nor does he consider that the four narrative styles that he discovered – heroic, romantic, tragic, and ironic – could also have archetypal origins.

Finally, Mauws (2000) explicitly advocates discourse analysis as a way to deal with the social science researcher's presumed inability to inquire more directly into the subliminal origins of words and their meanings. In his research on gatekeeping in the cultural industries, accessing the internal mental states of decision makers is assumed to be impossible:

> Because we have not yet found a way to access these internal thoughts, research such as that reported here may in fact be our best means of gaining a window into the minds of decision makers. More to the point, until such time that we have unmediated access to the things of which the world is thought to be comprised, the analysis of that to which we do have access, such as discourse, is likely to prove a more productive strategy for those who are engaged in social science research. (p. 243)

This formulation acknowledges that there may be internal thoughts, subliminal influences, and possibly even unconscious dynamics that influence the discourse of gatekeeping, but he seems to rule out inquiry or speculation into the origins of that discourse in the human psyche.

These examples highlight three salient points. First, most organizational discourse researchers appear to be primarily interested in an analysis of the meanings and impacts of organizational texts, narratives, and the like, taken in and of themselves. Second, there appears to be considerably less interest in speculating about the source or origins of the words, images, and ideas that compose those texts and narratives. Third, if a source is posited or implied, it is more likely to be located in the conscious, or semiconscious, rather than the unconscious mind.

Raising the Unconscious to the Level of Discourse

In fairness to the authors in this and other discursively oriented publications, speculating about the contributions of the unconscious to linguistic phenomena is not necessarily their area of expertise or focus of interest. Nonetheless, it is an aspect of inquiry that could add an important and missing element to the existing perspectives of this emerging field.

To begin thinking about adding an unconscious program to the field of organizational discourse, we must first consider what we mean by the unconscious. Here, two formulations are of particular interest for our purposes. The first broadly invokes the seminal works of Freud, Jung, and their followers (Bennet, 1983; Hall, 1954; Segal, 1997). These orientations imply that behavioral actions, including speech acts and written acts, are based not on objective or even present reality but on inner, nonrational dynamics that are neither conscious nor directly accessible. As previously noted, there is also some precedence in this tradition for considering discursive implications, for example, Lacan (Bracher, 1993). Similarly, Fromm (1978), in a more critical vein, employed a discourse-sensitive approach in his evaluation of the sociopsychological impact of materialism on human well-being.

The second perspective is a conception of the unconscious based in the cognitive sciences and most recently referred to as the cognitive unconscious by the cognitive linguists Lakoff and Johnson (1999). They assert, "Most of our thought is unconscious, not in the Freudian sense of being repressed, but in the sense that it operates beneath the level of cognitive awareness, inaccessible to consciousness and operating too quickly to be focused on" (p. 10). Examples they cite that are particularly relevant to organizational discourse include:

> picking out words and giving them meanings appropriate to context, making semantic and pragmatic sense of the sentences as a whole, framing what is said in terms relevant to the discussion, performing inferences relevant to what is being discussed, constructing mental images where relevant and inspecting them, filling in gaps in the discourse, noticing and interpreting your interlocutor's body language, anticipating where the conversation is going, planning what to say in response. ... It is not merely that we occasionally do not notice these processes; rather, they are inaccessible to conscious awareness and control. (pp. 10-11)

In their formulation, thought is based in human somatics, is mostly out of awareness, and carries out abstract reasoning through the use of prototypes, framings, and metaphors. Although not directly accessible to conscious inquiry, the cognitive unconscious can be studied empirically through the analysis of secondary evidence such as discourse, image schematics, metaphors, and the like (Johnson, 1987; Lakoff, 1987; Lakoff & Johnson, 1999).

Although clearly different, both formulations assert the existence of processes that influence thought, behavior, and action that are unconscious but accessible to study and influence through secondary means such as the analysis of dreams, archetypes, image schematics, and metaphors. Either or both formulations of the unconscious would seem, therefore, to have much to contribute to speculation about the potential deeper origins of any particular narrative, text, or discourse.

The Inner Worlds of Discourse

It may be useful to summarize briefly some basic psychological processes to help illustrate the potential impacts of the unconscious on discursive events. More sophisticated concepts undoubtedly would add to a deeper analysis, but here, we simply wish to demonstrate the possibilities.

In Freudian psychoanalysis, there are a number of unconscious processes, commonly known as defense mechanisms, that are related to the reduction of anxiety (Marshak & Katz, 1999; Segal, 1997). These include, but are not limited to, projection, where undesirable or unacceptable aspects of a person or group are attributed to another person or group; repression or denial, where some feeling, need, or thought is strongly negated or denied even as it gets expressed through some alternative means; regression and fixation, where a person or group that cannot deal with a present situation moves back to an earlier psychological stage (classically, there are four Freudian stages: oral, anal, phallic, and genital); and finally, transference, where a current situation or individual is perceived and responded to in ways that are based not on the present reality but on unresolved issues from someone's past history.

The potential impact of these defense mechanisms on both an author's narrative and/or an analyst's interpretation of that narrative is open to speculation and research. For example, through regression and fixation, a person can become stuck in a particular psychological stage. This could have a dramatic impact on that person's mental models and the words and narratives created to convey ideas and meanings. Drawing on this insight about the potential influence of the unconscious on discourse, Gareth Morgan (1997) has speculated about the underlying origins of Frederick W. Taylor's concern with the minutiae of work organization:

> Taylor's life provides a splendid illustration of how unconscious concerns and preoccupations can have an effect on organization, for it is clear that his whole theory of scientific management was the product of the inner struggles of a disturbed and neurotic personality. His attempt to organize and control the world, whether in childhood games or in systems of scientific management, was really an attempt to organize and control himself. (p. 222)

Morgan then goes on to conclude that "from a Freudian perspective, Taylor's case presents a classic illustration of the anal-compulsive type of personality" (p. 222). Thus, Taylor's narrative of scientific management may have been rooted more in anal fixation than in a desire to promulgate a master discourse to guide early-20th-century industrial organization.

Logically, it would also be appropriate to speculate on the potential impacts or biases of a researcher's unconscious processes in the interpretation of a particular narrative or text. If it is legitimate for Morgan or any other researcher to speculate about the impact of Taylor's personality on the creation of the scientific management narrative, it is equally fair to speculate on the potential impact of Morgan's personality on his re-presentation of Taylor's work. Thus, it would be legitimate to wonder if there is any form of projection, transference, regression, or repression on the researcher's part that may influence his or her analytic interpretation. In passing, we should also note that this example highlights the tenuous link between cause and effect that is routinely emphasized by many discourse analysts.

Turning to Jungian analytic psychology, which because of its emphasis on symbols, myths, and motifs may be easier to incorporate into organizational discourse, we find two concepts that may be of additional help in explaining the possible origins of discourse. Jung employed the term *collective unconscious* to refer to our common psychological and symbolic experiences as human beings (Campbell, 1971; Jacobi, 1973; Jung, 1964). His thesis was that the unconscious of human beings contains common psychic patterns, called archetypes, that provide form and meaning to external experience.

Archetypes are assumed to be universal and all encompassing in nature. Such patterns may be recognized as images, symbols, metaphors, and myths that recur throughout history in all cultures and societies. For example, Campbell's (1968) account of the universal nature of "the hero's journey" was subsequently generalized to a much wider range of myths that, throughout recorded history, appear to have been continually reconstituted and reconstructed to resonate with the times (Campbell, 1972). It could be instructive to investigate the extent to which such archetypes may influence discourse in organizations.

As previously noted, O'Connor chose to cite Eliade rather than Jung or a Jungian as a source to help explain the fall-from-order theme she found recurring at Horizon. A Jungian might interpret the same theme as a recurring archetype that could be shaping discourse, meaning, and experience at the individual and collective levels in Horizon and possibly within the psyche of the researcher as well.

In addition, because there is a collective unconscious and common archetypes, the existence of shared meanings may occur based on similar psychodynamic reactions to common situations or dilemmas. This provides an alternative explanation for how common narratives may be created and endorsed across individual, organizational, spatial, and temporal boundaries. Whereas a radical analyst might wonder about the power of elites to create and enforce privileged narratives, a Jungian might wonder about the power of archetypes to form common myths and meanings.

Finally, we wish to highlight Lakoff and Johnson's (1999) theory of conceptual metaphor that gives metaphor a role somewhat similar to Jung's archetypes in the ordering of abstract or subjective experience (for an alternative view of how to use metaphors from a more Freudian orientation, see Siegelman, 1990). According to this theory, metaphors are based in sensorimotor experiences that through conflation come to be associated with other types of subjective experience. "For example, for an infant, the subjective experience of affection is typically correlated with the sensory experience of warmth, the warmth of being held" (Lakoff & Johnson, 1999, p. 46). These associations are ubiquitous and, when formed in early childhood, "result in permanent neural connections being made across the neural networks that define conceptual domains" (p. 46). In short, we are literally "wired" metaphorically. More complex metaphors result from conceptual blending and combinations of simpler or primary metaphors. For example, the complex metaphor "a purposeful life is a journey" includes two primary metaphors: purposes are destinations and actions are motions (pp. 60-61). Because our sensorimotor experiences as human beings are for the most part universal, we organize experience and communicate with each other through metaphorical reasoning as if there were an objective reality. Finally, the operations of primary and complex metaphors, conflation, neural connections, conceptual blending, and so on all occur outside of direct awareness or access in the cognitive unconscious.

The influence of metaphors to shape meanings is currently an accepted part of organizational discourse, although typically not in terms of their unconscious influences or origins (Grant & Oswick, 1996). In particular, the influence of the journey metaphor on various discourses has been noted by a number of analysts. Inns (1996), for example, analyzed how the journey metaphor "seems to have underpinned and shaped the field of OD" (p. 20), although she refers to it more as a cultural belief than a conceptual metaphor in the (cognitive) unconscious. Marshak (1998) analyzed how the journey metaphor may influence the valuations of talk and action, including contributing to a bias for action over talk in organizations. Dunn (1990) and Keenoy (1991) have used the journey metaphor to analyze both the appeals of human resources management as a contemporary managerial discourse and its spread as a set of management practices.

Despite the acceptance of metaphorical analysis in organizational discourse, there is seemingly less interest in considering the origins of metaphors, especially the implications of their potential origin in the cognitive unconscious. For example, the power of generative metaphors to create and shape meaning is widely acknowledged in the literature (e.g., Schön, 1993). Yet they are usually described as if they were cross-domain references consciously created to generate new ideas or insights (e.g., Barrett & Cooperrider, 1990; Morgan, 1993). The possibility that those metaphors may have originated in personality factors or the (cognitive) unconscious is not usually considered or explored.

In contrast, and to help make our point about interest and emphasis, we turn to a metaphorical analysis of psychological theories conducted by a historian of psychology. Leary (1990) and his colleagues analyze how metaphors may have created and shaped most psychological narratives. "One example is Freud's reliance on the archaeological metaphor – or family of metaphors – according to which the mind is like an archaeological dig, with various layers or historical sediments being buried at different levels" (p. 44, note 41). Freud's well-known and long-term interest in archaeology, including possibly wanting to become an archaeologist, as well as his naming his new science "depth psychology," suggest that unconscious metaphors may have influenced the original formulation of the psychoanalytic narrative. Speculation of this type about how personality factors and/or the (cognitive) unconscious may influence the formulation of organizational narratives, texts, conversations, and so forth seems an area of neglected, but fruitful, inquiry.

Concluding Comments

It is important to also note the methodological complexities involved in any attempt to explore the potential role of the unconscious in organizational discourse. There are several strata of possible meanings that are mutually implicated in each other. The surface level of linguistic mirror images and the discourse analyst's interpretation of such linguistic usage (which may marginalize or ignore subliminal influences on the actor's choice of words) are, perhaps, the most obvious levels. There is also the case for exploring subliminal influences on the analyst's choice of interpretative scheme in the construction of the consultant's or researcher's report. Alvesson and Kärreman (2000) stress the value preferences implicit in such constructions, but such preferences may also be influenced by unconscious motivations. Elsewhere, Alvesson (1999) has argued that we must acknowledge not only the constructed nature of (discursive) data but also the intrinsic narcissism of "the author" in "framing the story-line" (p. 25). To ensure that the author alerts the reader to potential (author) misreadings, he even suggests "rewriting the account from a (self-) ironic position." Although such reflexivity has yet to become the rule among discourse analysts, it is indicative of possible future directions. And, when considering the unconscious, we should allow the possibility that either or both the analyst's and author's unconscious may be the origin of the narrative's meaning.

In closing, we hope this brief discussion suffices to make the point that a focus on the unconscious might be a useful supplement to existing approaches to the study of organizational discourse. Most important, it highlights three areas of concern that ought to be more directly addressed in future discursive research:

- explicit consideration of the origin of the themes, patterns, and meanings ascribed to different organizational narratives, texts, and discourses;
- augmentation of current theory and method with approaches that encourage exploration of the potential contribution of the unconscious to discourse analysis; and
- greater consideration of the potential influences of a researcher's unconscious on the creation of a narrative's meaning.

We trust those readers who are more psychologically or cognitively inclined will take this as an invitation to add their thoughts to this exciting and still emerging field.

References

Alvesson, M. (1999). *Methodology for close up studies: Struggling with closeness and closure*. Institute of Economic Research Working Paper Series, Department of Business Administration, Lund University, Sweden.

Alvesson, M., & Kärreman, D. (2000). Taking the linguistic turn in organizational research: Challenges, responses, consequences. *The Journal of Applied Behavioral Science, 36*(2), 136-158.

Argyris, C. (1970). *Intervention theory and method*. Reading, MA: Addison-Wesley.

Austin, J. (1962). *How to do things with words*. London: Oxford University Press.

Barrett, F. J., & Cooperrider, D. L. (1990) Generative metaphor intervention: A new approach for working with systems divided by conflict and caught in defensive perception. *Journal of Applied Behavioral Science, 26*(2), 219-239.

Bennet, E. A. (1983). *What Jung really said*. New York: Schocken.

Bielby, W. T., & Bielby, D. D. (1994). "All hits are flukes": Institutionalized decision making and the rhetoric of network prime-time program development. *American Journal of Sociology, 99*(5), 1287-1313.

Beech, N. (2000). Narrative styles of managers and workers: A tale of star-crossed lovers. *The Journal of Applied Behavioral Science, 36*(2), 210-228.

Bracher, M. (1993). *Lacan, discourse and social change: A psychoanalytic cultural criticism*. New York: Cornell University Press.

Campbell, J. (1968). *The hero with a thousand faces* (2nd ed.). Princeton, NJ: Princeton University Press.

Campbell, J. (1971). *The portable Jung*. New York: Penguin.

Campbell, J. (1972). *Myths to live by*. New York: Viking.

Clark, T., & Salaman, G. (1997). Telling tales: Management gurus' narratives and the construction of managerial identity. *Journal of Management Studies, 32*(2), 137-161.

Cummings, T. G., & Worley, C. G. (1997). *Organization development and change* (6th ed.). Cincinnati, OH: South-Western College Publishing.

Dunn, S. (1990). Root metaphor in the old and the new industrial relations. *British Journal of Industrial Relations, 28*(1), 1-31.

Egan, G. (1994). *Working the shadow side*. San Francisco: Jossey-Bass.

Fairclough, N. (1992). *Discourses and social change*. Cambridge, MA: Polity.

Fairclough, N. (1995). *Critical discourse analysis*. London: Longman.

Foucault, M. (1972). *The archaeology of knowledge*. London: Tavistock.

Foucault, M. (1980). *Power/knowledge*. New York: Pantheon.

French, W. L., & Bell, C. H., Jr. (1999). *Organization development: Behavioral science interventions for organizational improvement* (6th ed.). Englewood Cliffs, NJ: Prentice Hall.

Fromm, E. (1978). *To have or to be?* London: Jonathan Cape.

Grant, D., Keenoy, T., & Oswick, C. (Eds.). (1998). *Discourse and organization*. London: Sage.

Grant, D., & Oswick, C. (Eds.) (1996). *Metaphor and organizations*. London: Sage.

Hall, C. S. (1954). *A primer of Freudian psychology*. New York: New American Library.

Inns, D. (1996). Organization development as a journey. In C. Oswick & D. Grant (Eds.), *Organization development: Metaphorical explorations* (pp. 110-126). London: Pitman.

Jacobi, J. (1973). *The psychology of C. G. Jung.* New Haven, CT: Yale University Press.

Jackson, B. G. (2000). A fantasy theme analysis of Peter Senge's learning organization. *The Journal of Applied Behavioral Science, 36*(2), 193-209.

Johnson, M. (1987). *The body in the mind: The bodily basis of meaning, imagination, and reason.* Chicago: University of Chicago Press.

Jung, C. G. (1964). *Man and his symbols.* New York: Doubleday.

Keenoy, T. (1991). The roots of metaphor in the old and the new industrial relations. *British Journal of Industrial Relations, 29*(2), 313-328.

Keenoy, T., Oswick, C., & Grant, D. (1997). Organisational discourse: Text and context. *Organisation, 4*(2), 147-157.

Lacan, J. (1998). The seminar of Jaques Lacan: Book 11. *The four fundamental concepts of psychoanalysis.* New York: Norton.

Lakoff, G. (1987). *Women, fire and dangerous things: What categories reveal about the mind.* Chicago: University of Chicago Press.

Lakoff, G., & Johnson, M. (1999). *Philosophy in the flesh: The embodied mind and its challenge to Western thought.* New York: Basic Books.

Leary, D. E. (Ed.) (1990). *Metaphors in the history of psychology.* Cambridge, UK: Cambridge University Press.

Marshak, R. J. (1993). Managing the metaphors of change. *Organizational Dynamics, 22*(1), 44-56.

Marshak, R. J. (1998). A discourse on discourse: Redeeming the meaning of talk. In D. Grant, T. Keenoy, & C. Oswick (Eds.), *Discourse and organization.* London: Sage.

Marshak, R. J., & Katz, J. H. (1992). The symbolic side of OD. *OD Practitioner, 24*(2), 1-5.

Marshak, R. J., & Katz, J. H. (1999). Covert processes: A look at the hidden dimensions of group dynamics. In *Reading book for human relations training* (8th ed., pp. 251-258). Alexandria, VA: NTL Institute for Applied Behavioral Science.

Mauws, M. K. (2000). But is it art? Decision making and discursive resources in the field of cultural production. *The Journal of Applied Behavioral Science, 36*(2), 229-244.

Micklethwait, J., & Wooldridge, A. (1996). *The witch doctors.* London: Heinemann.

Morgan, G. (1993). *Imaginization.* Newbury Park, CA: Sage.

Morgan, G. (1997). *Images of organization* (2nd ed.). Thousand Oaks, CA: Sage.

Nadler, D. (1977). *Feedback and organization development: Using data-based methods.* Reading, MA: Addison-Wesley.

O'Conner, E. S. (2000). The embedded narrative as a construct for studying change. *The Journal of Applied Behavioral Science, 36*(2), 174-192.

Potter, J., & Wetherell, M. (1987). *Discourse and social psychology.* London: Sage.

Schön, D. A. (1993). Generative metaphor: A perspective on problem-solving in social policy. In A. Ortony (Ed.), *Metaphor and thought* (2nd ed., pp. 137-163). Cambridge, UK: Cambridge University Press.

Schneider, B. (2000). Managers as evaluators: Invoking objectivity to achieve objectives. *The Journal of Applied Behavioral Science, 36*(2), 159-173.

Segal, M. (1997). *Points of influence: A guide to personality theory at work.* San Francisco: Jossey-Bass.

Siegelman, E. Y. (1990). *Metaphor and meaning in psychotherapy.* New York: Guilford.

Watson, T. (1994). *In search of management.* London: Routledge.

16
Metaphor And Analogical Reasoning In Organization Theory: Further Extensions

Recently, Oswick, Keenoy and Grant (2002) provided an insightful discussion of the current use of metaphor and other tropes in organization theory. They review the influence of different types of tropes and conclude that the emphasis on metaphor versus, for example, irony may result in privileging similarity over dissimilarity in theory generation. They urge going beyond the orthodox use of metaphor to a greater application of the tropes of dissimilarity – anomaly, irony and paradox – in organization theory.

My comments here are not to dispute or debate their analysis and conclusions. Rather, I wish to extend their discussion by going beyond their contribution in two dimensions. First, I wish to extend awareness of the influence of metaphor and other word imagery to include unconscious framings or conceptualizations. While Oswick, Keenoy and Grant go beyond orthodoxy in one dimension, they remain mostly orthodox with regards to treating metaphor and other tropes as conscious, deliberate reasoning devices. Metaphor is knowingly used as a comparison method to help generate theory; for example, an organization is a "machine," "organism," etc. This follows and supports what may now be considered the "conventional," literal, literary approach to the use, impact and analysis of metaphor and other tropes in the administrative sciences.

Beyond Reason: Conceptual Metaphor

Another view of metaphor is based in the cognitive sciences, especially the research of the cognitive linguists Lakoff and Johnson. Following their earlier seminal work (1980), they have extended their view of metaphor and its role in cognition. Their most recent formulation is that abstract reasoning occurs through out-of-awareness application of *conceptual metaphors* that are located in the cognitive unconscious and help "frame" reality (1999). In simple terms, conceptual metaphors are part of the unconscious cognitive processes we use to reason about and analyze the world. For example, if a manager remarks, "We are on a sinking ship," it is likely to be a conscious, deliberate comparison. If, on the other hand, the manager talks about "being dead in the water" and "it's everyone for themselves," it is quite possible a situation is being described through an out-of-awareness conceptual metaphor of a sinking ship or some similar imagery. This invites us to pay attention to clearly specified metaphors ("this place is a prison"), and also listen for implicit conceptual metaphors that may be framing how a situation is experienced ("I feel like I am being confined, restricted, punished, watched"). It also raises the possibility that metaphor-based theory generation is not always a conscious, deliberate endeavor.

In a discussion of the role of metaphor in theory development, Leary (1990) suggests that most psychological theories are based on subconscious metaphors. Freud's early interest in archeology and later development of the theory of Depth Psychology, complete

Marshak, R. J. (2003). Metaphor and analogical reasoning in organization theory: Further extensions. *Academy of Management Review, 28*(1), 9-10. Republished with permission.

with formative experiences *buried in the past*, is a prime example. If we focus primarily on a literal, literary analysis of metaphor and other tropes, we miss the potential influence of conceptual metaphors and other unconscious symbolic processes on theory generation in the administrative sciences.

Beyond Theory: Tropes In Practice

Building on the mediating role of conceptual metaphors in reasoning, choice and action, I next would like to extend the impact of tropes beyond theory generation to include their impact on day-to-day organizational behavior. Given that managers and employees may be reasoning and acting, to some degree, based on out-of-awareness framings, then as a practical matter it makes sense to listen to the tropes they are using as clues or indicators of their preconscious, implicit conceptualizations. For example, if a manager is talking about a marketing campaign as if it were a war, "we have to strike hard and fast," "we have to destroy our competitors," then it is reasonable to conjecture that the manager is operating from a conceptual metaphor that "marketing is war." In many cases such framings may be helpful ways to recognize and address situations. In other cases, however, the implicit framing may be inappropriate or dysfunctional; for example, the same manager then being asked to collaborate with a rival company on a joint venture.

How might a fellow manager, coach or consultant use tropes to address such a situation? First, by recognizing the implicit framing(s) of the situation by listening to the way the manager talks about events. This includes listening to the use of explicit tropes, as well as descriptions that may be consistent with an underlying conceptual metaphor. Here the tropes of similarity – metaphor, metonymy, and synecdoche – provide clues to what may be the underlying conceptual framing of the situation.

Recognizing a potential framing is one step; doing something about it is another. To change the implicit framing requires raising its existence to awareness and also creating doubt as to its appropriateness in the particular instance. Here the tropes of dissimilarity – anomaly, irony and paradox – can be used as ways to intentionally invite consideration of new realities. A paradoxical or ironic comment may be all that is needed to invite a search for new possibilities. For example, commenting that "Yes, it's too bad we have so many customers getting in the way of operations" might suffice to help an executive realize that a machine-like conceptual metaphor is framing his or her responses to a work situation. If effective, the comment could create enough dissonance to trigger a search for another framing. The search might result in an alternative image, say an organic or open-systems image, or the creation of a paradoxical synthesis such as an organic-machine or cyborg. The point is that the use of dissonance tropes invites a creative search for alternative framings without specifying what those frames should be.

In sum, we might say that, in practice, tropes of similarity are indicators of conscious or unconscious framings, while tropes of dissimilarity can be used to bend or break existing frames. Consequently, artful attention to the use of frame making and frame breaking tropes can influence how managers and theorists conceptualize and address the world.

References

Lakoff, G., & Johnson, M. (1980). *Metaphors we live by*. Chicago: University of Chicago Press.

Lakoff, G., & Johnson, M. (1999). *Philosophy in the flesh: The embodied mind and its challenge to Western thought*. New York: Basic Books.

Leary, D. E. (Ed.) (1990). *Metaphors in the history of psychology*. Cambridge, UK: Cambridge University Press.

Oswick, C., Keenoy, T., & Grant, D. (2002). Metaphor and analogical reasoning in organization theory: Beyond orthodoxy. *Academy of Management Review, 27*, 294-303.

17
A Discursive Approach to Organization Development

Abstract

This article presents a conceptualization of organizational discourse as *situated symbolic action* that is then illustrated through an analysis of a meeting of senior managers during an organization development intervention. This perspective encourages a more holistic understanding of organizational contexts and offers an actionable framework to help make sense of workplace episodes and choose appropriate interventions. The ways in which action research was conceptualized and applied are also discussed.

Introduction

This discussion draws on ideas from the emerging field of organizational discourse to suggest a novel perspective that can be used to assess organizational situations and guide action choices. The specific context for the discussion is a meeting of the top management of a high-tech organization to decide on a new business model. One of the authors participated in the meeting in the role of an organization development consultant. An action research orientation, wherein the consultant is both an active participant and reflective observer, was used to reflect on and analyze the data and events. Some of the issues associated with an action research orientation in this instance are also identified and discussed.

We begin with a brief discussion of organizational discourse and how conceptualizing discourse as situated symbolic action helps to address important challenges and advances thinking in the field. This is followed by a discussion of the action research orientation used in the study. An extended discussion and analysis of the meeting based on a layered consideration of what the participants said in terms of "discourse as action," "discourse as situated action," and "discourse as situated symbolic action," is then presented. Finally, the implications of augmenting organizational discourse and organization development frameworks with a discourse as situated symbolic action orientation are presented.

Conceptualizing Discourse As Situated Symbolic Action

The term *organizational discourse* has come into use in the past decade to broadly define an emerging orientation in the organizational and social sciences. In organization theory the term connotes an eclectic variety of approaches based on a range of disciplines where the central focus is the role of language and linguistically mediated experience in organizational settings (Marshak, 1998). Whether focused on discourse, text or other abstract media, discourse analytic approaches are now used to study many aspects of managerial and organizational phenomena (Grant, Hardy, Oswick & Putnam, 2004). With these developments have also come scholarly questions about the theoretical,

Marshak, R. J. & Heracleous, L. (2005). A discursive approach to organization development. *Action Research, 3*(1), 69-88. Republished with permission.

methodological and empirical limits of the current approaches used in organizational discourse (e.g., Grant & Hardy, 2003).

Specifically, several scholars have called for the development of discourse analysis approaches that not only consider discourse and text as data sources, but that are more sensitive and holistic, paying attention to how nested levels of context interrelate and interpenetrate with the discourse (Hardy, 2001; Keenoy, Oswick & Grant, 1997). In this context, and with the organizational level of analysis in mind, we propose an approach for addressing the integration of text, context and symbolic meaning through conceptualizing organizational discourse as situated symbolic action. This conceptualization draws primarily on speech act theory, rhetoric, ethnography of communication and social constructionism.

Discourse As Action

Austin's (1962) speech act theory offers an influential statement of *discourse as action*. Austin's work challenged the traditional assumption of the philosophy of language, that "to say something . . . is always and simply to *state* something," that is either true or false, and developed the influential thesis that "to say something is to *do* something" (Austin, 1962, p. 12, emphases in original). Extending Austin's speech act theory, Searle (1975) introduced the notion of indirect speech acts where the connection between the intended meaning and the utterance is not clear and direct. In addition to being highly influential in the philosophy of language, the insights of speech act theory formed the theoretical foundation for discourse pragmatics, the study of language-in-use (Blum-Kulka, 1997).

Even though speech act theory has laid the groundwork for understanding discourse as action, it essentially remains at the micro level of single utterances without extending to the broader level of discourses as bodies of texts pervaded or patterned by structural features (Heracleous & Barrett, 2001). Nor does it explicitly address context. So, for example, speech act theory does not readily apply to what van Dijk (1977) has termed "macro" speech acts, or Alvesson and Kärreman (2000) term "grand" or "mega" discourses.

Discourse As Situated Action

Rhetorical analysis provides a contextually sensitive approach that can contribute significantly to viewing *discourse as situated action*. Rhetoric can explore holistically the situation, the audience, the rhetor, and textual features such as structure, temporality, and metaphor, not for their own sake, but to discover how rhetorical discourse can influence actors' perceptions and interpretations by eloquently and persuasively espousing particular views of the world (Aristotle, 1991; Gill & Whedbee, 1997). Rhetoric aims to explore the "dynamic interaction of a rhetorical text with its context (Gill & Whedbee, 1997, p. 159). The important influence of the context or situation on what should and could be said was highlighted by Aristotle's definition of rhetoric as "an ability, in each particular case, to see the available means of persuasion" (Aristotle, 1991, p. 36).

Ethnographies of communication (Hymes, 1964) offer further support for a view of discourse as situated action, emphasizing that discourse cannot be adequately understood or appropriately produced in separation from its context of use. In an organizational context, Samra-Fredericks (2003) has employed an ethnographic approach combined with conversation analysis to study how everyday discourse links to the accomplishment of strategy. Hymes (1964) has proposed several useful contextual elements for understanding communicative events: the participants, channels, shared codes, setting, messages, and topics. Furthermore, the embeddedness of discourse in its context is not limited to the immediate situation, but is nested in wider social and cultural systems (Gumperz & Levinson, 1991).

Discourse As Symbolic Action

Constructionist approaches present *discourse as symbolic action*, viewing reality as a social construction and individuals as symbol creators and consumers (Morgan & Smircich, 1980). Berger and Luckmann suggested that social reality is known to individuals in terms of symbolic universes constructed through social interaction. They viewed language as the "most important sign system of human society" (1966, p. 51), the primary means through which "objectivation," the manifestation of subjective meanings through actions, proceeds. Language makes subjective meanings "real," and at the same time typifies these meanings through creating "semantic fields or zones of meaning" (1966, p. 55) within which daily routines proceed. Searle (1995) more recently provided a further landmark rendition of social constructionism in his view of institutional facts as language-dependent. Discourse, in addition, creates mental frames that are "metacommunicative" (Bateson, 1972, p. 188), simultaneously highlighting certain meanings and excluding others. Discourse is thus not simply symbolic, but at a broader level of framing evokes particular associations through connotation (Phillips & Brown, 1993) and invites others to view the world in these terms.

Discursive construction takes place through social interaction; in the organizational context it occurs when organizational members "author" their experiences in the process of interacting with others, simultaneously constructing a shared sense of their identities, their organization, and of appropriate ways to discourse and act (Cunliffe, 2001). Language, in this perspective, does not simply mirror social reality but constitutes it, creating conditioned rationalities as widespread ways of thinking within particular social systems (Gergen & Thatchenkery, 1996).

The Emergent Process of Action Research at Systech

Background

In the spring of 2002 one of the authors met with the President and Vice President, Human Resources (HR) of one of the major divisions of Systech (all names have been disguised) to discuss possible organization development interventions to address a number of issues. These included pressures from the President's boss (the Group President) to change the organization's operating structure and culture, integrate a recent acquisition, and create alignment on business strategy within the top team of executives. At that time, detailed information about the situation and the actors involved was provided and recorded in notes taken during and immediately after the interview discussion. Shortly thereafter, however, the budding project was "indefinitely delayed," according to the VP, HR, "because the President was too consumed with the operational issues of a new work program."

No further contact occurred until almost six months later when the VP, HR called to request help for a critical meeting that would take place in a few days. The VP explained that "the President decided at the last minute that a good facilitator was needed, otherwise the meeting could be a real disaster; and you know the background and seem to have the skills." After agreeing to help out on extremely short notice, additional information was provided by an Assistant to the President and the President himself in a further telephone conversation. The main objective of the meeting, according to the President, was to "get everyone aligned around a new business model being advanced by my boss." The President went on to say that "the meeting could be very difficult because most of the top team will be opposed to the proposed new arrangement and I'm not so sure about it myself."

For the meeting the requested form of organization development was process consultation, or, in other words, to facilitate and make process interventions so as to help the group of executives reach the stated objective of achieving alignment around a new business model (Schein, 1969). This type of consulting work requires more than good meeting management skills, and depends on the facilitator's competencies to quickly "read" individual, group and organizational dynamics while making choices in real time about how to intervene. Running notes as to the events, impressions, quotes of participants, and "hunches" were kept during the meeting by the facilitator as a way of tracking developments as they emerged. More detailed notes and reflections as to emergent themes and patterns were recorded after the session in preparation for further interventions; and as a means of reflecting on and interpreting what took place in the meeting.

An Action Research Orientation

This consulting episode at Systech presented us with an opportunity to test and illustrate our conceptualization of discourse as situated symbolic action. Our approach is consistent with viewing *action research* as a process of both helping organizations as well as gathering data for further scholarly reflection and potential contribution to knowledge, wherein the researcher is an active, reflective participant in whatever effort is underway (e.g. Checkland & Holwell, 1998; Dash, 1999; Dickens & Watkins, 1999).

Although the organization development consultation was not originally conceived as a formal action research project, upon reflection we realized that the data collected would be valuable in illustrating how the perspective of discourse as situated symbolic action could prove useful for organizational discourse analysis. In addition, it could help us illustrate how this perspective can aid both managers and organization development practitioners in gaining a more informed, contextual understanding of organizational situations, thereby better informing their actions and interventions. As Eden and Huxham note in their discussion of the process of action research:

... this is not intended to imply that the researcher should have a precise idea of the nature of the research outcome of any intervention at the start. Indeed, since action research will almost always be inductive theory building research, the really valuable insights are those that *emerge* from the consulting process in ways that cannot be foreseen. Whilst it is legitimate for an action researcher to enter a consultancy interaction with no expectation about what the research output will be, it is crucial that an appropriate degree of reflection by the consultant is built into the process, and that the process includes a means of holding on to that reflection. (1996, p. 81)

Ethical Dilemmas in Action Research

There can be a number of ethical dilemmas associated with action research, relating to such issues as participant selection, divergences in the needs and interests of organizational actors and researchers, or anonymity and confidentiality of information provided (e.g., Walker & Haslett, 2002). The dual purposes in action research of combining interventions with research, and whether participants are fully aware of the research aspects of the process, however, are not generally considered to be key dilemmas. According to Huxman and Vangen, "... the approach does not imply inherently that the practitioners in the researched organization should be concerned with - or even conscious of - the research aspect of the intervention" (2003, p. 385).

Similarly, in our case, meeting participants were not aware that the facilitator's working observations and notes might later serve as field notes for an academic article. This was not possible as, at the time, the data were not intended to be utilized as such. However, we believed that the organization should be informed of any research relevance arising from the consultation. Consequently, a draft of this article was reviewed by the Vice President, Human Resources on behalf of Systech who both validated the description and analysis of the episode as well as approved publication as long as the names of the organization and participants were disguised for confidentiality reasons.

Action Research as a Methodological Approach

Some concerns about the action research approach include the low reproducibility of setting and findings, limitations on the means of collection and documentation of data, and the manner in which the personal interests, knowledge and competencies of the researcher influence the research (Huxham & Vangen, 2003). These apply to some extent in any research effort. Within the context of the action research approach, it would be impossible to replicate the setting given that it is a live, actual organizational situation with all its inherent complexity. What matters therefore is to document as much relevant data as possible, as accurately as possible given the circumstances, be reflective on what the data mean, apply a thoughtful analytical framework to the data, and arrive at some valid insights that contribute to knowledge in some significant way. In our case, the perspective of discourse as situated symbolic action was applied to arrive at a nested, additive interpretation of the episode.

Some of the important advantages of action research that were applicable in this case include being taken "behind the scenes," being afforded access to sensitive information and to the participants' real experience as it was happening. It also provided access to contextualized and live organizational settings which afforded rich data not obtainable through isolated and segmentalized laboratory experiments or surveys (Huxham & Vangen, 2003; Schein, 1987).

Role and Orientation of the Facilitator

An additional dimension of this particular project was the role and orientation of the facilitator. As previously noted, this role required making real-time process observations, interpretations and interventions as events unfolded. The diagnostic and intervention actions of the facilitator, which are usually based on knowledge of group and organizational dynamics, were in this case also augmented by a discursive orientation to organizational phenomena. The facilitation was therefore also guided by in-the-moment interpretations and hypotheses about the meaning and impact of the emerging group narratives. In that sense, the action research question constantly being asked during the episode was "How can I best understand the dynamics of this situation based on the actors' talk, in order to best facilitate the desired outcome?" This orientation was to an extent naturally occurring, given that the facilitator is also a scholar with an interest in organizational discourse. As will be discussed later, one of the ways to best understand what was happening overtly and covertly was to consider the discourse surrounding the episode as situated symbolic action.

The Systech New Business Model Meeting

The Context

Systech is a large, global computer systems and information technology (IT) corporation. Historically it was a primary provider of computer hardware and support services. In more recent years it expanded its system engineering, IT, and systems consulting services to become a major provider of information systems hardware, software and consulting services.

In 2002, the Advanced Services Division (ASD) of Systech expanded its consulting capabilities by acquiring an operating unit consisting of some 180 people from Consultco, a large management consulting company. These people were added to the existing ASD workforce of about 1500 people. The acquisition was spearheaded by Group President John Duke, a former partner at one of the "Big 5" accounting/consulting companies, who was hired in 2001 to head up the consulting services area for Systech. Duke's vision was to transform the more hardware and systems engineering "products" strategy of ASD into a high end "consulting services" business model.

Following the traditional "Big 5" model, he envisioned a business operating model wherein highly compensated Principals were responsible for P&L and all products, services and ASD employees associated with a particular client organization. In this model most of the actual client work is done by lower paid and more junior consultants, thereby achieving significant leverage and profitability for the services provided under the auspices of a Senior Principal. This was different from the traditional Systech operating model wherein Business Development (BD) and Sales Managers were responsible for bidding on and selling contracts which were then fulfilled through different functionally organized, operational Business Units (BU). There were also Customer Relationship Executives (CRE) to help coordinate different interfaces, while ensuring service and delivery to the client organization. Duke's principal-led business model would dramatically alter the relatively balanced power of the BD, CRE and BU managers in favor of Principals (most of whom would come from the ranks of the newly acquired Consultco employees), change the delivery operations of ASD, and impact the traditional culture(s) of ASD and Systech by placing greater emphasis on leveraging and profitability over technical depth and product/service development. It would also tend to alter the traditional distribution of power, status and rewards within ASD that was based on technical expertise and distributed across multiple functional areas, towards a much steeper and narrower distribution in favor of principals.

The Actors Involved

To initiate the new principal-led business model, a meeting of the top executives of ASD was set up so that "issues could be worked through and agreements reached." The meeting would be chaired by Sam Klein, the President of ASD, who reported to Group President Duke. Attending the meeting would be President Klein's direct reports and key staff. These included Lance Collins, Senior Vice President of Business Development and Sales; Steve Grant, Senior Vice President and Managing Principal; John Marshall, Vice President of Operations; Ron Hogan, Vice President of Sales; Cal Ramsey, Vice President of Business Development; and Mark Flowers, Vice President of Human Resources. All the participants except Steve Grant, who was the former Managing Partner of the newly acquired Consultco unit, had between 12 to 30 years' tenure with Systech.

An external consultant was asked to facilitate the meeting to help ensure it was as productive as possible since the general expectation of everyone was that it would be a highly contentious and unproductive session. In preparation for the session, Mark Flowers provided the consultant with further background information about the situation and also commented that "It had been decided that John Duke would not attend the meeting for two reasons. First, because of his domineering personal style and second to insure that President Klein and his team would accept and implement the new model on their own." In addition, it was thought that the new member of the ASD team, Steve Grant, who had recently headed up the acquired Consultco unit, would be able to fully describe the principal-led business model. Flowers went on to say that ASD President Klein was expected by Duke to implement the new principal-led business model even though Klein and the other members of the team were openly skeptical about it. Flowers concluded by observing, "Didn't we just buy Consultco? If the consulting model is so good and our model so bad, how come we bought them? We should be calling the shots."

The Showdown and Implicit Negotiation

President Klein opened the meeting by introducing the facilitator and stating that "the purpose of the meeting is to discuss how to take ASD forward" and that "first and foremost we have to remember that the customer's first!" There was no mention of the new principal-led business model. Different participants then offered comments about what had to be addressed with most agreeing that "motivation and morale are so low we could start losing people." After about 30 minutes the facilitator interjected that he thought morale was an important topic, "but wasn't the purpose of the meeting to address the new business model?" President Klein said nothing, but Steve Grant began to explain the proposed principal-led business model. Almost simultaneously, Lance Collins said that Systech "couldn't have a principal-led model because it is a publicly held company not a partnership." Both Grant and Collins continued to give virtually simultaneous "speeches" for a few minutes before the facilitator stopped the interaction and summarized the points each was making as a way to document the different considerations as well as to invite more listening and understanding.

The pattern of virtually simultaneous speeches, for and against aspects of the principal-led model, given by Grant and Collins and then summarized by the facilitator, continued for another 30 minutes or so with the other participants, including President Klein, mostly quiet or asking a few clarifying questions. The breakthrough in the meeting came when Steve Grant in a conciliatory voice acknowledged to Lance Collins that, "Yes, things are different in Systech than in Consultco and maybe some responsibilities should be shared." Lance Collins quickly remarked, "You're right," and began to discuss how things could be shared. Everyone then joined in with a burst of team productivity and quickly developed a new option where a matrixed "Integrated Strategy Team" for a client organization would be convened by a Principal and include the relevant Business Development, Customer Relations, and Business Unit managers, who would continue to report within their own organizational units. This integrative business model, as several of the team members remarked, "seemed to capture the best of both the new and the old ways of operating."

Naming the New Business Model: Should It Be "Principal-Led?"

The participants were pleased and surprised at their agreement and ability to work together on fleshing out the Integrated Strategy Team model. At this point Mark Flowers wondered if the model could just be called "the Business Model" and to drop the term "principal-led" entirely "because it would be unnecessarily provocative." This sparked some discussion that came to a halt when President Klein said "John Duke expects it to be called principal-led and he would not be happy if it was called something else." This generated considerable push-back from all the other participants, including Steve Grant, who said "the model we just agreed on was one of shared responsibility and saying it was principal-led would be misleading." The meeting adjourned with general agreement that the new way of working should be called "The ASD Business Model." It was proposed by Lance Collins and agreed to by all that Steve Grant should be the one responsible for writing up a summary of the ideas, concepts and agreements from the meeting, coordinating with Lance Collins as needed.

A week later, when President Klein's office distributed the summary report after clearing it with John Duke, the title read "The ASD Business Model (Principal-Led)." Naturally, this caused uncertainty whether or not Duke indeed accepted the substance of the proposed integrative model. A summary of the flow of events is provided in Table 17.1.

Table 17.1
Sequence of Events

Contest	Group President Duke, a newcomer from a "Big 5" consulting company, directs ASD President Klein to implement a new "principal-led" business model. Debate ensues between Grant, a newcomer from Consultco, and Collins, a 30-year Systech veteran, over existing and new models. Other meeting participants remain mostly quiet.
Transition	Grant acknowledges to Collins that: "Yes, things are different in Systech than in Consultco and maybe some responsibilities should be shared." Collins agrees and offers some ideas, which leads to a burst of productive energy by everyone.
Collaboration	Everyone participates in developing a new integrative business model combining features from the current and proposed "principal-led" business models.
	Grant, the newcomer, is invited to summarize the meeting.
	The name "principal-led" is intentionally dropped as too controversial and no longer accurately representing the adopted model.
Coda	Group President Duke via ASD President Klein reintroduces the label "(Principal-Led)" in the name of the ASD business model.
	Re-introduction of "(Principal-Led)" leads to uncertainty as to whether the Group President accepts the substance of the integrative model.

Analysis and Discussion

When we examine the Systech episode from the three key frames of analysis – discourse as action, discourse as situated action, and discourse as symbolic action – we discover that each adds a further layer of meaning to create a more holistic understanding of what went on in the meeting. Although these layers are presented sequentially, they are intended to provide a nested, complementary, and additive analysis. The raw material for this analysis comes from the consultant's field notes taken before, during and after the episode. The analysis is also informed by knowledge of the interactional and organizational contexts acquired through the intervention experience.

Discourse As Action

At the level of discourse as action, we might note the indirect introduction of the meeting by President Klein, not mentioning its purpose, and posing "customers first" as a superordinate goal. President Klein in this case may have been intending to start off the meeting by seeking to encourage unity, bearing in mind the divergent positions and political stakes that were involved. The relative silence by President Klein for the remainder of the meeting is also open to a range of interpretations, ranging from pre-existing intentions to give others a chance to own the issues, a desire to avoid conflict or confrontation, or even passive resistance to the new business model initiated by Group President Duke. The engagement by all participants in a discussion of declining motivation and morale could again be seen as an attempt at group unity and/or avoidance of the underlying conflict in the group. Both the style and substance of Grant's and Collins' remarks, in addition, could be seen as argumentative attempts to demonstrate that their positions were the right thing for the organization. This level of analysis of discourse as action focuses primarily on who said what and what they seemed to be overtly intending to achieve.

Discourse As Situated Action

In viewing discourse as situated action we must add several frames of context to more fully understand the actors' intentions and their effects. In addition to the interactional context of the meeting, we have to add the organizational context and the broader industry context. The meeting was mandated by Group President Duke to initiate a principal-led business model. Duke came from one of the "Big 5" accounting/consulting companies and had joined Systech less than two years earlier. Duke had initiated the acquisition of the Consultco unit where Steve Grant had been the Managing Partner. Duke intended to change the Systech Advanced Services Division's operating model and culture in line with his previous experience in a major accounting/consulting firm.

President Klein was a 23-year Systech employee charged with implementing this new business model. It might be inferred from his silence and introduction to the meeting that he was perhaps maneuvering to not get caught in the crossfire between his new boss and his old colleagues. Lance Collins had 30 years experience at Systech and as head of Business Development and Sales had the most to lose in power, status and rewards with a change to a principal-led model. It was hard to ignore in this context the irony that the relatively small, newly acquired, Consultco unit (represented by Grant) was now positioned by Duke to tell the much larger acquiring Systech ASD how to do business. Ultimately, then, the meeting was about power, change and adaptation; that is, a power struggle between old-timers and newcomers over the appropriate operating structure and culture of Systech. Would a new, principal-led business model advocated by newcomers win out over the interests of the old-timers? Was this model indeed superior to Systech's pre-existing model?

Discourse As Situated Symbolic Action

Finally, in viewing discourse as situated symbolic action, we go beyond the specific words and view the discursive exchanges at the meeting as a symbolic "showdown" between the proposed new culture and power arrangements and the established culture and power arrangements of Systech ASD. The initial discussion in the ASD team about low motivation and morale could be interpreted as an unconscious projection or an indirect means of expressing their own skeptical feelings about Group President Duke's intentions.

From a symbolic perspective, Grant and Collins can be seen as champions of each camp engaged in combat over power, prestige, respect and validation, in addition to the business future of ASD. After initial tests of strength, Grant's concession that "Yes, things are different in Systech than in Consultco and maybe some responsibilities should be shared" was a pivotal moment. That comment may have simultaneously signaled willingness to compromise and an acknowledgement of the legitimacy of the established ASD culture and its managers. In the context it is important to note that it was the newly acquired Grant representing the new business model who made the initial conciliatory remark. This was reciprocated by Collins and an understanding of how to share power in an integrated model containing aspects of both the old and the new models was quickly reached by everyone.

Thus, at a symbolic level, the participants worked out their relative power positions in ASD and the framework for how to integrate or blend the old and the new. Group President Duke, however, who was not part of the symbolic negotiation, would not necessarily agree with the negotiated outcome. Duke's absence may have allowed the agreement to be reached, but not necessarily carried out, at least in name.

At the level of the symbolism of words, the label "principal-led" was a focus of debate, not only because it would influence existing power arrangements by symbolizing who would have the power to control the sales and delivery process, but because it summed up and evoked in a single word the entire contest between old-timers and newcomers over the future business model and culture of ASD, including all the associated thoughts and feelings of the involved participants. The later re-introduction of "(Principal-Led)" into the title of the meeting report suggests that further negotiations with Duke may be needed to see if the substance of the new integrated model is, indeed, acceptable. Table 17.2 presents an outline of the above discussion.

Table 17.2
Discursive Outline of Systech Episode

Discursive context	Discursive action	Discursive symbolism
Group President Duke hired from a Big 5 consulting firm.	ASD President Klein introduces meeting without mentioning the new business model and posing customer satisfaction as primary goal.	Attempt by ASD President to encourage group unity and avoid conflict.
Group president aims to impose a new, "principal-led" business model based on professional services consulting model.	Participants begin to discuss low motivation and morale in ASD.	Archetypal struggle between old-timers and newcomers over future of Systech-ASD.
Systech acquires an operating unit from Consultco.	Debate between Grant and Collins over "principal-led" versus existing business model.	Contest between Grant and Collins, two leading representatives or heroes of each camp, to see which business model will win.
Advanced Services Division (ASD) meets without Group President to discuss new business model.	Grant acknowledges that the current model has value and the principal-led model may need to be modified.	Grant, hero of the newcomers, "yields" by acknowledging legitimacy of the old-timers and their ways of doing business.
ASD President Klein and top team are skeptical about the new model.	The entire team works to create a new, integrated model that is then labeled "The ASD Business Model."	With the contest over status, legitimacy and future directions settled, the entire team works on integrating the old and the new in a collaborative business model.
President Klein pressured by Group President Duke to change the Division's business model and by his team to resist this change.	Grant is invited to summarize the meeting.	Newcomer Grant is invited to write up a summary of the new integrative model as a sign of trust and acceptance.
	Announcement one week later by the President's Office of "The ASD Business Model (Principal-Led)."	Despite team agreements within ASD, the Group President's power and determination are asserted when the label "(Principal-Led)" is re-inserted in the name of the new business model.

Conclusions and Implications

Conceptualizing and analyzing discourse as situated symbolic action has a number of significant, interrelated implications. First, it can help to respond to some of the key challenges facing the field of organizational discourse. Second, it encourages a more holistic and discourse-sensitive understanding of empirical contexts by organizational researchers, in line with the tenets of methodological approaches such as action research. Finally, viewing discourse as situated symbolic action offers an actionable framework to organizational actors and organization development practitioners for making sense of workplace episodes and selecting appropriate interventions.

Responding To Organizational Discourse Challenges

In terms of organizational discourse, our analysis confirms the well-accepted insights that "discourse" cannot be adequately understood and interpreted in the absence of contextual knowledge; and that linguistic labels are more than just names, having the power, through their symbolic connotations, to influence interpretations and actions and thus social reality. Beyond that, however, the view of discourse presented here can potentially help to address some key challenges in the field of organizational discourse.

One key criticism of organizational discourse has been its lack of clarity with regard to the parameters of the field and in the specification or definition of the concept of discourse itself (Grant, Keenoy & Oswick, 2001; Keenoy et al., 1997). Alvesson and Kärreman, for example, suggest that "we cannot help sometimes feeling that the word discourse is used to cover up muddled thinking ... Discourse sometimes comes close to standing for everything, and thus nothing" (2000, p. 1128). Conceptualizing discourse as situated symbolic action can potentially contribute to addressing this challenge by providing a structured perspective that draws from well-established theoretical domains in philosophy (speech act theory, rhetorical analysis), anthropology (ethnography of communication) and social science (social constructionism). This perspective can potentially supply researchers in organizational discourse with an additional framework with which to theoretically ground the concept of discourse and with a contextually sensitive approach for conducting empirical discourse analyses.

A further main criticism of organizational discourse is that it is too abstract, an "intellectual self-indulgence with no practical payoff" (Grant et al., 2001, p. 10). On the contrary, our analysis helps to illustrate that organizational discourse can be compatible and complementary with more applied approaches to social science such as action research. Furthermore, this approach to discourse can help managers and organization development practitioners interpret both the literal and the symbolic aspects of discourse and interaction in particular organizational contexts in order to make more appropriate interventions.

More Holistic Understandings

In terms of empirical research in organizational settings, adopting a situated symbolic action perspective has a number of potential advantages. First and foremost it supports an integrative and practically oriented approach to research consistent with the purposes of action research as originally conceived by Kurt Lewin (1947). Lewin intended action research to help address the inherent limitations of studying complex social events in a laboratory as well as the artificiality of separating out single behavioral elements from an integrated system (Foster, 1972). Lewin advocated the study of social dynamics "not by transforming them into quantifiable units of physical actions and reactions, but by studying the inter-subjectively valid sets of meanings, norms and values that are the immediate determinates of behavior" (Peters & Robinson, 1984, p. 115). Action research is intended to describe holistically what happens in naturally occurring settings, and to derive from these observations more broadly applicable principles or actionable knowledge (Argyris, 1996; Perry & Zuber-Skerritt, 1994).

By postulating that discursive events have integrated and contextualized literal and symbolic components, a discourse as situated symbolic action perspective is supportive of the action research orientation by inviting a more holistic consideration of social phenomena. Additionally, it provides the action researcher, who is also a participant, with a dual applied and theoretical orientation to support a more reflexive stance as to the context and meaning of unfolding events. This helps to address a lacuna in the field of organizational discourse, the "challenge to incorporate the insights of discourse analysis into diagnostic and intervention strategies" (Marshak, Keenoy, Oswick & Grant, 2000, p. 246).

Actionable Framework

Lastly, a discourse as situated symbolic action perspective is potentially useful not only from a scholarly perspective but also from an action-oriented perspective. This is achieved by providing a holistic framework for making sense of the meaning of discourse and action in workplace contexts and thereby offering clues for appropriate interventions given the situation and context at hand. Incorporating this perspective into ways of interpreting both individual discourse and group dynamics could be especially useful when working in complex and emotionally loaded situations similar to the Systech episode; and where organization development practitioners and senior managers must make intervention choices in real time based on diagnosis and interpretations of what may be happening on both the literal as well as the symbolic levels. In short, we are suggesting that organizational actors read situations with an eye on group and organizational dynamics while simultaneously listening with an ear for discourse as situated symbolic action.

As an illustration from the Systech episode, let us consider how the silence of all participants except Grant and Collins could be interpreted and what the appropriate responses by the facilitator could be. If the silence was interpreted as literal silence from the participants (because they were introverted, or because they did not want to fight for air-time), then the standard intervention might be to attempt to draw out the silent participants and/or temporarily quiet down Grant and Collins: "OK, we've heard enough from you two for now, how about hearing what others may think?" If the silence was contextually interpreted as perhaps reluctance to speak openly in front of their boss, Sam Klein, or in front of each other, then an appropriate intervention might be more geared towards creating greater safety and openness: "Let's establish some ground rules for these discussions. First, everything said here will be confidential and there will be no retribution for anything said. Do we all agree? What else would you like to add?" Finally, if the silence by everyone except Grant and Collins was symbolically interpreted in the context as waiting to see the outcome of an archetypal form of single combat between the champions or heroes of the old and the new ways, then intervention choices might be focused more on ensuring a fair fight: "Let's summarize what each of you is saying. Grant's position is . . ., Collins' position is . . .; is that correct? What criteria are important in assessing this situation?"

As situated symbolic action, Grant's remark that, "Yes, things are different in Systech than in Consultco and maybe some responsibilities should be shared" becomes one of the critical moments in the episode. As such, the facilitator might initiate interventions to reinforce the concession and also ensure, if possible, that it was reciprocated by Collins in order to lead to a more "win-win" negotiation/ discussion: "Hmmm. So you, Grant, are saying that there are some differences here in Systech that need to be acknowledged by whatever business model is implemented; and you, Collins, are agreeing and suggesting that one possible way to share responsibilities is to . . . Can we all describe more specifically a shared responsibility model we can all agree upon?" If, on the other hand, the facilitator interpreted the statement as simply a comment from one of the more outspoken members of the group then an appropriate response could have been to ask others to add their inputs or perhaps to make no intervention at all. This might have led to more views being expressed or more silence, but the opportunity to underline the importance of the comment (in the symbolic context) and to get an immediate acknowledgement and reciprocal statement would have been missed.

Concluding Remarks

We offer our view of discourse as situated symbolic action as an additional perspective or lens in the emerging field of organizational discourse with the intention that it will help contribute to the field's vibrancy and promise. At the same time, we hope it will also help to address some of the field's current challenges, including encouraging more research that integrates a scholarly orientation with applied concerns, as we have sought to do through the action research orientation of this paper. Finally, we also hope that this perspective will contribute to the practices of action research and organization development while helping organizational actors interpret discourse and action in more contextually sensitive, symbolic ways, thereby improving their ability to assess situations and make appropriate interventions.

References

Alvesson, M., & Kärreman, D. (2000). Varieties of discourse: On the study of organizations through discourse analysis. *Human Relations, 53,* 1125-1149.

Argyris, C. (1996). Actionable knowledge: Design causality in the service of consequential theory. *Journal of Applied Behavioral Science, 32,* 390-408.

Aristotle. (1991). *On rhetoric.* Kennedy, G. A. (Trans.). Oxford: Oxford University Press.

Austin, J. L. (1962). *How to do things with words.* Cambridge, MA: Harvard University Press.

Bateson, G. (1972). *Steps to an ecology of mind.* London: Intertext.

Berger, P., & Luckmann, T. (1966). *The social construction of reality.* London: Penguin.

Blum-Kulka, S. (1997). Discourse pragmatics. In T. A. van Dijk, (Ed.), *Discourse studies: A multidisciplinary introduction,* Vol. 2 (pp. 38-63). Beverly Hills, CA: Sage.

Checkland, P., & Holwell, S. (1998). Action research: Its nature and validity. *Systemic Practice and Action Research, 1,* 9-21.

Cunliffe, A. L. (2001). Managers as practical authors: Reconstructing our understanding of management practice. *Journal of Management Studies, 38,* 351- 371.

Dash, D. P. (1999). Current debates in action research. *Systemic Practice and Action Research, 2,* 457-492.

Dickens, L., & Watkins, K. (1999). Action research: Rethinking Lewin. *Management Learning, 30,* 127-140.

van Dijk, T. A. (1977). *Text and context: Explorations in the semantics and pragmatics of discourse.* London: Longman.

Eden, C., & Huxham, C. (1996). Action research for management research. *British Journal of Management, 7,* 75-86.

Foster, M. (1972). An introduction to the theory and practice of action research in work organizations. *Human Relations, 25,* 529-556.

Gergen, K. J., & Thatchenkery, T. J. (1996). Organization science as social construction: Postmodern potentials. *Journal of Applied Behavioral Science, 32,* 356- 377.

Gill, A. M., & Whedbee, K. (1997). Rhetoric. In T. A. van Dijk, (Ed.), *Discourse studies: A multidisciplinary introduction,* Vol. 1 (pp. 157-183). Beverly Hills, CA: Sage.

Grant, D., & Hardy, C. (2003). Introduction: Struggles with organizational discourse. *Organization Studies, 25*(1), 5-13.

Grant, D., Hardy, C., Oswick, C., & Putnam, L. (Eds.). (2004). *Handbook of organizational discourse.* Thousand Oaks, CA: Sage.

Grant, D., Keenoy, T., & Oswick, C. (2001). Organizational discourse: Key contributions and challenges. *International Studies of Management and Organization, 31*(3), 5-24.

Gumperz, J. J., & Levinson, S. C. (1991). Rethinking linguistic relativity. *Current Anthropology, 32,* 613-623.

Hardy, C. (2001). Researching organizational discourse. *International Studies of Management and Organization, 31*(3), 25-47.

Heracleous, L., & Barrett, M. (2001). Organizational change as discourse: Communicative actions and deep structures in the context of information technology implementation. *Academy of Management Journal, 44,* 755-778.

Huxham, C., & Vangen, S. (2003). Researching organizational practice through action research: Case studies and design choices. *Organizational Research Methods, 6,* 383-403.

Hymes, D. (1964). Toward ethnographies of communication. *American Anthropologist,* *66*(6), part 2, 12-25.

Keenoy, T., Oswick, C., & Grant, D. (1997). Organizational discourses: Text and context. *Organization, 42,* 147-157.

Lewin, K. (1947). Frontiers in group dynamics: Channels of group life: Social planning and action research. *Human Relations, 1,* 143-153.

Marshak, R. J. (1998). A discourse on discourse: redeeming the meaning of talk. In D. Grant, T. Keenoy & C. Oswick (Eds.), *Discourse and organization* (pp. 15-30). London: Sage.

Marshak, R. J., Keenoy, T., Oswick, C., & Grant, D. (2000). From outer words to inner worlds. *Journal of Applied Behavioral Science, 36,* 245-258.

Morgan, G., & Smircich, L. (1980). The case for qualitative research. *Academy of Management Review, 5,* 491-500.

Perry, C., & Zuber-Skerritt, O. (1994). Doctorates by action research for senior practicing managers. *Management Learning, 25*(2), 341-365.

Peters, M., & Robinson, V. (1984). The origins and status of action research. *Journal of Applied Behavioral Science, 20,* 113-124.

Phillips, N., & Brown, J. L. (1993). Analyzing communication in and around organizations: A critical hermeneutic approach. *Academy of Management Journal, 36,* 1547-1576.

Samra-Fredericks, D. (2003). Strategizing as lived experience and strategists' everyday efforts to shape strategic direction. *Journal of Management Studies, 40,* 141- 174.

Schein, E.(1969). *Process consultation: Its role in organization development.* Reading, MA: Addison-Wesley.

Schein, E. (1987). *The clinical perspective in fieldwork. Qualitative research methods.* Thousand Oaks, CA: Sage.

Searle, J. (1975). Indirect speech acts. In P. Cole & J. Morgan (Eds.), *Syntax and semantics 3: Speech acts* (pp. 59-82). New York: Academic Press.

Searle, J. (1995). *The construction of social reality.* New York: Free Press.

Walker B., & Haslett, T. (2002). Action research in management-ethical dilemmas. *Systemic Practice and Action Research, 15,* 523-533.

18
Organizational Discourse and New Organization Development Practices

A new ensemble of organization development (OD) practices have emerged that are based more on constructionist, post modern and new sciences premises than the assumptions of the early founders. These include practices associated with appreciative inquiry, large group interventions, changing mindsets and consciousness, addressing diversity and multicultural realities, and advancing new and different models of change. We propose that the emerging field of organizational discourse offers sympathetic concepts and research that could add additional insights and theoretical rigor to the New OD. In particular, studies of organizational discourse based upon social constructionist and critical perspectives offer compelling ideas and practices associated with the establishment of change concepts, the role of power and context in relation to organizational change, and specific discursive interventions designed to foster organizational change.

Introduction

Recently, organizational change research has undergone a "metamorphosis," one that encompasses a pluralism of approaches and a strengthening of the links between organizational studies and the social sciences (Pettigrew, Woodman and Cameron, 2001, p. 697). We contend that one possible outcome of this metamorphosis is that there may now be an emerging set of new organization development (OD) practices – what we refer to collectively here as "New OD" (Marshak, 2006; see also Mirvis, 2006). Taken together, these practices emphasize a number of philosophical assumptions and associated methodologies that differ in varying degrees from key assumptions of those who founded the OD movement in the 1950s and 1960s. We further contend that the field of organizational discourse may offer sympathetic concepts, assumptions and approaches that could help advance thinking and practice in relation to these new/emerging aspects of OD.

This article is divided into four main sections. First, we briefly review and contrast some of the central philosophical assumptions and practices of "Classical OD" and an ensemble of newer OD approaches and techniques that have emerged over the last 20 years or so. In the second section we discuss the new academic field of organizational discourse. We examine the extent to which many of the assumptions and characteristics of this field of inquiry, in whole or in part, seem consonant with many of these New OD practices. In the third section we explore the capacity of organizational discourse to provide an emergent theory and research base that might help inform and expand New OD practices. In the final section we provide some concluding comments.

Marshak, R. J. & Grant, D. (2008). Organizational discourse and new organization development practices. *British Journal of Management, 19,* 7-19. Republished with permission.

Trends in OD

The future of OD, its present relevance and continued viability, have been the subject of considerable debate in recent years (Bradford and Burke, 2005). Much of this debate has focused on whether or not the more traditional humanistic values espoused by the founders of the field are still relevant or should be challenged by a set of more pragmatic business considerations (e.g., Worley and Feyerherm, 2003). There are also concerns that OD has become overly tool and technique oriented versus theory based (e.g. Bunker, Alban and Lewicki, 2004).

Lost in the discussions about traditional versus pragmatic values, or relevance and viability, however, is the possibility that OD may now incorporate a range of newer practices that are not necessarily different from a values or viability perspective so much as from an ontological and epistemological one. Put another way, there may now be an emerging set of OD approaches and techniques which emphasize philosophical assumptions and resulting methodologies about social phenomena and social reality that are somewhat different from several of the key assumptions propounded by its founders. None of these practices alone encompasses all the differing assumptions. Taken together, however, they accentuate how newer practices have emerged to challenge many of the key assumptions about change underlying "Classical OD." Table 18.1 summarizes the main differences of emphasis between Classical and New OD practices.

Table 18.1
Trends in OD

Classical OD (1950s onward)	New OD (1980s onward)
Based in classical science and modern thought and philosophy	Influenced by the new sciences and postmodern thought and philosophy
Truth is transcendent and discoverable; there is a single objective reality	Truth is immanent and emerges from the situation; there are multiple, socially constructed realities
Reality can be discovered using rational and analytical processes	Reality is socially negotiated and may involve power and political processes
Collecting and applying valid data using objective problem-solving methods leads to change	Creating new mindsets or social agreements, sometimes through explicit or implicit negotiation, leads to change
Change is episodic and can be created, planned and managed	Change is continuous and can be self-organizing
Emphasis on changing behavior and what one does	Emphasis on changing mindsets and how on thinks

Classical OD

The original formulations of OD included strong positivist orientations based in mid-twentieth century social science research methodologies. The whole idea of data-based change, e.g., action research (French, 1969; Lewin, 1947) and survey research methods (Cannell and Khan, 1984; Mann, 1969), presumes the existence and validity of an objective, discernable reality as contrasted with the subjective perceptions of organizational actors about that reality. This independent reality is then the subject of investigation or research so as to produce valid data and information that can be used to influence change. For example, one of Argyris's three core tasks of a change agent is the creation of valid data: "First, it has been accepted as axiomatic that valid and useful information is the foundation for effective intervention" (Argyris, 1973, p. 17). This theme is echoed by Chin and Benne (1976) in their classic discussion of general strategies for effecting change in human systems. In line with modernist thinking (Cooper and Burrell, 1988), they believe that objective knowledge is discoverable through the scientific method which has historically assumed a transcendent and knowable reality independent of subjective perception. Thus they assert that: "One element in all approaches to planned change is the conscious utilization and application of knowledge as an instrument or tool for modifying patterns and institutions of practice" (Chin and Benne, 1976, p. 22). Blake and Mouton also reflect this theme in their discussion of "catalytic" OD interventions, suggesting that these "assist the client in collecting data and information to reintegrate his or her perceptions as to how things are" (Blake and Mouton, 1976, p. 4).

Common to all of these formulations of Classical OD is a tendency to implicitly treat differences in how actors view a situation as "misperceptions" that may need to be corrected or integrated in new ways. In the remainder of this section, we show that this is an objectivist orientation that philosophically differs from treating such differences as alternative and competing realities, which is more typically the case in many of the newer OD practices.

New(er) OD Practices

From the 1980s onwards, constructionist and postmodern approaches have increasingly influenced the social sciences with ideas about multiple realities and the inherent subjectivity of experience (e.g. Hancock and Tyler, 2001; Linstead, 2004; Searle, 1995). Part of this movement includes the notion that if there are multiple realities then there can be no transcendent, objective truth to be discovered. Instead the issue becomes how agreements about the reality of a situation are negotiated among contending points of view (Cooper and Burrell, 1988). This also raises the issue of how power is used by proponents to help create or impose the resulting socially agreed upon or "privileged" version of things (Clegg, 1989; Knights and Willmott, 1989). In addition to constructionist and postmodern orientations, new ideas about change dynamics, including chaos theory and self-organizing systems (Wheatley, 1992), have begun to influence how people think about change in organizations.

Many of these ideas have been incorporated into aspects of OD thought and practice in recent years, although perhaps without the specific intent to create a "New OD." We argue that there are at least five contemporary OD related practices that are based on or influenced by newer theories and assumptions subsequent to the classical formulation of OD in the 1950s and 1960s. These include practices related to appreciative inquiry, large group interventions to seek common ground, changing mindsets and consciousness to achieve transformational change, addressing diversity and multicultural realities, and models of change, such as complex adaptive systems theory, that differ from the classical "unfreeze-movement-refreeze" linear change paradigm.

Appreciative inquiry. Initially developed by Cooperrider and his colleagues in the 1980s, appreciative inquiry seeks to effect change by focusing on organization members' positive experiences and appealing to their hopes and aspirations (Bushe and Kassam, 2005; Cooperrider and Srivastra, 1987). Interventions are based on constructionist assumptions and are intended to shift system member thinking to a more positive and generative consciousness in order to achieve transformational change.

Watkins and Mohr (2001), for example, contrast appreciative inquiry with traditional OD practices which they claim are based on a "modernist," objectivist and scientific orientation. They assert that appreciative inquiry is based instead on social constructionist premises where reality is at least partially, if not completely, a result of one's mindset. The power of socially constructed mindsets is reflected in the claims advocates of appreciative inquiry make about the impact of the "deficit-focused thinking" alleged to be part of traditional action research versus the "positive-focused thinking" that forms the core of appreciative inquiry.

Common ground and social agreements. Another example of New OD practices are large versus small group interventions (Bunker and Alban, 2005). These intend to seek "common ground" wherein the dominant approach is to get simultaneous agreement among multiple constituencies, all of whose points of view are considered legitimate versions of reality. While data are used in these approaches, the data are more for the purposes of representing multiple realities than for bringing objective "facts" to bear on a situation in order to discover the "best solution" or to correct "misperceptions." Instead, emphasis is placed on reaching new social agreements or adopting new mindsets, and therefore new realities, to guide future actions. "Future Search is designed to help the group arrive at agreements about the future they want and actions to achieve it" (Lent, McCormick and Pearce, 2005, p. 61). The underlying power and political dimensions involved in multiple constituencies reaching common agreements are also beginning to be recognized by some researchers, if not practitioners. Analyzing a case example of a search conference (SC), Clarke (2005, p. 42) comments that ". . . it was found that the most important outcome from the SC was its predominately political effects." Thus large group interventions pay less attention than Classical OD to objective diagnosis *per se* and more attention to processes that construct common social meanings and agreements necessary to effect change.

Changing mindsets and consciousness. In another stream of work, some OD consultants and academics advocate practices for promoting shifts in mindsets and/or consciousness as the principal method to address change dynamics rather than the more traditional focus on material processes, relationships, rewards and so forth (e.g. Adams, 2005; Senge et al., 1994). For them, organizational transformation requires a change in consciousness, often starting with the leadership and extending throughout the organization. This orientation ". . . understands transformation as being primarily driven by shifts in human consciousness" (Ackerman-Anderson and Anderson, 2001, p. 7). In these approaches there is greater emphasis on psychologically oriented methods that might transform a leader's or system's consciousness than on the more social-psychological methods found in Classical OD.

Diversity and multicultural realities. In addition to considering the influence of socially constructed realities, consciousness and mental models, there has been increased interest by some OD practitioners in diversity and multicultural realities, including how various groups establish or reinforce exclusionary standards, practices and paradigms that may favor their own interests and reality (e.g. Cross et al., 1994; Jackson, 2006). Miller and Katz (2002, p. 7) succinctly capture the essence of what is sometimes involved:

> Most organizations are filled with barriers – rigid structures, poor training processes, outmoded equipment, misguided incentive programs, and discriminatory promotion and assignment practices that keep people from contributing the full breadth of their skills, ideas, and energies to the organization's success. Expressed in conscious and unconscious behaviors, as well as routine practices, procedures, and bylaws, these barriers are typically rooted in the very culture of an organization.

Thus many New OD approaches to addressing diversity and multicultural dynamics include recognition of, and interventions to address, how power is used by dominant groups in the establishment of versions of reality and requirements that favor their group and interests over others. The emphasis on multiple realities and how power is used to privilege a dominant and often oppressive way of being helps to distinguish these approaches from more Classical OD.

Different models of change. Finally, and as several commentators have observed (e.g., Sturdy and Grey, 2003; Van de Ven and Poole, 2005), there has been an increasing interest in models of change that are based on assumptions quite different from those advanced in the early days of OD. They include, for example, shifting from thinking about change as being episodic to being continuous (Weick and Quinn, 1999); or even thinking in terms of continuous, transformational change rather than punctuated equilibria and episodic transformations (Marshak, 2002; Rindova and Kotha, 2001).

Some OD practitioners have also become more interested in ideas from the "new sciences," such as complexity theory and self-organizing systems. For example, Olson and Eoyang (2001, p. 19) suggest that a new change paradigm is needed in OD because "The use of rational planned change approaches, driven by leaders with the help of change facilitators, has fallen short even when bolstered by formal (and expensive) programs such as TQM and re-engineering." They go on to claim that "The emerging science of complex adaptive systems offers such a paradigm," and that "It establishes a foundation for a new theory of change. . . ." (2001, p. 19).

To sum up, New OD practices, in combination, place increased emphasis on socially constructed realities, transforming mindsets and consciousness, operating from multicultural realities, exploring different images and assumptions about change, and forging common social agreements from the multiple realities held by key constituencies. These emphases, *in toto*, tend to lead to interventions and approaches which deemphasize in varying degrees sequential, episodic and developmental change; objective diagnosis; and a focus on material processes, structures and rewards. Instead there is greater attention placed on transformational change achieved through shifts in individual and system consciousness, based in part on constructionist assumptions. The importance of power and political processes in establishing new realities is also implicitly part of New OD given its set of underlying assumptions. However, as we will discuss later and especially in our concluding comments, we believe the role of power and political processes needs to be much more explicitly recognized and integrated into New OD practices.

New OD practices all also share one other important characteristic. Instead of attempting to solely leverage techno-structural or human processes for change, they implicitly focus on meaning making, language and "discursive phenomena" as the central medium and target for changing mindsets and consciousness. In this regard they especially overlap with the new field of organizational discourse.

Organizational Discourse

In organizational studies the term *organizational discourse* connotes an eclectic variety of perspectives based on a range of disciplines where the central focus is the role of language and discursively mediated experience in organizational settings (Alvesson and Kärreman, 2000). A discourse in these instances is generally taken to comprise a set of interrelated "texts." These texts are regarded as the discursive unit of analysis (Chalaby, 1996) and may constitute, for example, conversations and dialogue or narratives and stories. These can be spoken or written or take the form of other more abstract types of media. Organizational discourse analysis focuses on the production, dissemination and consumption of such texts and is now used to study many aspects of organizational and managerial phenomena (Grant et al., 2004).

Although approaches to the study of organizational discourse encompass a range of ontological and epistemological positions, significant portions of the field embrace either or both a social constructionist and a critical perspective. We believe these two perspectives, in particular, resonate with many of the assumptions underlying New OD practices and could be used to extend their theoretical purchase and applied value. Specifically, they address the significance of language and other discursively mediated experiences in transforming social reality, influencing organizational behavior, and shaping organizational members' mindsets. They also emphasize postmodern thinking, focusing on the processes that construct common social meanings and agreements within organizational contexts while asserting that there is no single, objective reality; rather, there are multiple realities that might offer alternative understandings of organizational phenomena. Finally, they emphasize that power and political processes are often used to establish new realities as the established or favored view of the world, thereby advantaging the views and beliefs of some organizational members over those of others.

The Social Constructionist Perspective

The social constructionist orientation in organizational discourse places discourse at the center of sensemaking (Weick, 1995) and the ongoing social creation of reality. According to Mumby and Clair (1997, p. 181):

> Organizations exist only as far as their members create them through discourse. This is not to claim that organizations are "nothing but" discourse, but rather that discourse is the principal means by which organization members create a coherent social reality that frames their sense of who they are.

What any particular group believes is "reality," "truth" or "the ways things are" therefore is at least partially a social construct that is created, conveyed and reinforced through discourse in the form of theories, stories, narratives, myths and so on. This in turn reinforces or establishes organizational culture(s), structures and processes. Thus, how things are framed and talked about becomes a significant context, shaping how people think about and respond to any situation. Different groups or strata or silos of an organization might, of course, develop their own discourses about a particular issue through stories and narratives that define the way things are as they see and experience them. This can lead to competing versions of reality wherein no one version is "objectively" correct. Attention to the prevailing discourses within an organization, how they are created and sustained, what impacts they may have on perception and action, and how they may change over time becomes, as a result, a central aspect of organizational discourse theory and research. Naturally this implies the possibility that there may be potentially multiple realities (different stories, different narratives, different cognitive constructs, etc.) in any given situation (Boje, 1995).

The Critical Perspective

The critical perspective draws attention to the ways in which contending constituencies and players use power and power processes to create, privilege and affirm discourses that advantage their interests and preferred view of the world (Fairclough, 1995; Hardy and Phillips, 2004). "In this sense, organizations are conceived as political sites, where various organizational actors and groups struggle to 'fix' meaning in ways that will serve their particular interests" (Mumby, 2004, p. 237).

Changing consciousness or mindsets or social agreements – e.g., about the role of women in organizations, or about hierarchical structures, or even about how change happens in organizations – would therefore require challenging or changing the prevailing narratives, stories and so on that are endorsed by those presently and/or historically in power and authority. The critical orientation's emphasis on how power and interests intersect to create the privileged versions of things helps us to understand that more than just "awareness" may be necessary to find common ground or achieve a change in mindsets. Instead, power dynamics may be involved in establishing the story lines and alternative "texts" associated with a different worldview.

In sum, the power of discourse to shape and convey the concepts that organize how we experience the world is an essential aspect of the social constructionist orientation. In turn, the ways in which power dynamics help to shape the prevailing or privileged discourse is a central concern of the critical perspective in organizational discourse. These two orientations, combined with a focus on the central role of discourse in the processes of organizing and of organizations, create an emerging social science field of great potential value to the study of organizational change and specifically to New OD.

Potential Contributions of Organizational Discourse To New OD

It should be clear at this point that there is an overlap between the assumptions underlying the ensemble of approaches and practices labeled here as "New OD" and a significant portion of the emerging theories and research associated with organizational discourse. Some of the core components that both have in common, in whole or in part, include

- a turn away from the more classical, objectivist sciences of the mid-twentieth century towards newer and alternative theories and orientations;
- an interest in how narratives, texts, conversations and other forms of communication influence and shape organizational processes, behavior and change;
- attention to the influence of mindsets in shaping behavior, and the ways in which discourse in turn creates and reinforces mindsets;
- the potential existence of multiple socially constructed realities; and finally,
- a growing appreciation that power structures may need to be addressed in order to challenge and change the "story lines" that create and endorse the prevailing way things are experienced and understood.

Based on these areas of overlap, we believe organizational discourse can help inform New OD in three important and interrelated respects: first, by providing a related and supportive theory and research base concerning organizational change; second, by providing an understanding of the dynamics of power and discourse and how this impacts on change processes; third, by demonstrating and explaining how discursive practices create change by enabling participants to frame new shared meanings.

Theory and Research Base about Organizational Change

Organization discourse theories and approaches can be used to better understand the nature of organizational change in two significant respects: first, by drawing attention to the role of discourse in the social construction of our prevailing concepts about organization change, and second, by drawing attention to the role played by discursive contexts in organizational change (e.g. Marshak and Heracleous, 2005).

Change concepts. In the broadest sense, discursive practices and interactions bring certain concepts about change into being, such that they become the established way of thinking about change efforts (e.g., the need to first "unfreeze" before "moving"). As part of this process, discursive practices "rule in" certain ways of thinking and talking about organizational change while also "ruling out" other ways (Hall, 2001, p. 72). This can lead to outdated or constraining views of what change itself is and how it might be achieved. An example of this would be the difference between viewing change as a way to fix problems rather than as a way to cultivate new and affirming possibilities. To try to address this problem, some studies of organizational discourse have sought to move beyond conventional conceptions of change by proposing new language and metaphors that encourage alternative ways of thinking about the change process. For example, Marshak (2002) discusses change as "morphing" while Sturdy and Grey (2003) consider change as a form of stability.

Others meanwhile have examined the role discourse plays in the social construction of specific organizational change initiatives and how people conduct themselves in relation to these initiatives. For example, Doolin's (2003) study of change in a New Zealand hospital demonstrated how a new information system provided users with a technical vocabulary that determined the meaning ascribed to particular events and social relationships within the organization. This played a significant role in legitimizing the economic and management discourses that were used to justify the need for change. These new discourses came to dominate the thinking and behavior of organizational members. Doolin's study highlights how techno-structural and discursive interventions can interact in ways that help shape mindsets about specific organization changes.

Discursive contexts and change. Studies of organizational discourse and change demonstrate how the negotiation of meaning surrounding any particular change incident unfolds not as a rational systematic process but rather through the complex interplay of both socially and historically produced texts that are continuously unfolding in a non-systematic, iterative and recursive manner (Hardy, 2001). These types of studies challenge the more sequential, linear models of change associated with Classical OD while being more attuned to the thinking that underlies some of the New OD approaches and practices.

Many of these context-sensitive studies of change identify and analyze specific, micro-level instances of discursive action and then locate them in the context of other macro-level, "meta" or "grand" discourses that exist within or external to the organization (Alvesson and Kärreman, 2000; O'Conner, 2000). They also recognize that "discourses are always connected to other discourses which were produced earlier, as well as those which are produced synchronically and subsequently" (Fairclough and Wodak, 1997, p. 276).

Several studies of change help highlight the importance of taking these context related factors into account. For example, Heracleous and Barrett (2001) examine the implementation of electronic trading in the London Market over a period of five years, across multiple stakeholder groups and at different discursive levels of analysis. They analyze the competing discourses and dynamic negotiations that impact on the process of implementation at the micro- and macro- levels. This approach enabled them to identify the deep structures including both cognitive understandings and emotive feelings that key actors had about the role and expected use of electronic trading. Their study highlights the need in organizational change to pay attention to the underlying mindsets and discursive arguments of stakeholder groups as well as the passionate resistance and emotional responses from users as they "fear and distrust" the system and perceive a "loss of control."

In like fashion, Grant, O'Donnell and Shields (2004) consider the discursive contexts and dynamics associated with a major culture change project in the Australian Public Service. They show how a proposed culture change started first as a discursive concept among politicians and senior public servants, became a discursive object that was discussed and planned at the organizational level, and was then applied in the form of changed performance and reward structures. In this case, their findings showed that the proposed new motivational concepts and practices encountered significant barriers and had been counterproductive. Employees did not embrace the new discourse and its associated changes. Instead they constructed a counter discourse that played upon the perceived violations of their psychological contract, and procedural and distributive justice. This research demonstrates how change related discourses at the macro-level can influence and be linked to micro-level discourses. Further, it demonstrates the importance of taking the social, historical and political contexts in which change may be taking place into account and how this might be achieved.

The Dynamics of Power and Discourse and Its Impact on Organizational Change

Earlier we suggested that while New OD seems to implicitly recognize the role of power and political processes in organizational change, it needs to go further and explicitly recognize and engage with these important factors. Achieving this will involve an appreciation of the relationship between power and discourse and integrating this into New OD practices.

Several scholars have sought to examine the relationship between power and discourse in some detail (e.g. Fairclough, 1995; Hall, 2001). In doing so, they have drawn heavily on Foucault's (e.g. 1980) conception of discourse. However, perhaps one of the most informative ways of understanding the dynamics of this relationship and its effects on organizational change is to utilize a framework of analysis proposed by Hardy and Phillips (2004, p. 299):

> . . . power and discourse are mutually constitutive: . . . the power dynamics that characterize a particular context determine, at least partially, how and why certain actors are able to influence the processes of textual production and consumption that result in new texts that transform, modify or reinforce discourses. In other words, discourse shapes relations of power while relations of power shape who influences discourse over time and in what way.

Hardy and Phillips (2004, pp. 306–307) go on to assert that the ability of a particular group to produce and disseminate influential discourses will be impacted by whether members of the group are able to draw on

i. formal power (occupation of a formal hierarchical position that enables the holder to privilege their discourse);

ii. critical resources (the ability to use rewards, sanctions, expertise, access to organizational members higher in the authority structure, control of finances, etc., in order to promulgate a discourse);

iii. network links (social relationships and a capacity to constitute alliances with, incorporate, and win the consent of other groups that might otherwise oppose the discourse that is being promulgated); and

iv. discursive legitimacy (the ability to produce a discourse that is authenticated by other people who by virtue of their number or position validate its dissemination and extend its reach).

They also point out that multiple actors in a variety of positions are involved in establishing the extent to which a particular discourse comes to dominate the meaning attached to a particular issue. Often there is a considerable struggle among these actors to establish a dominant meaning, such that discursive "closure" is never complete, leaving space for the production of "counter" discourses that may in turn come to dominate.

This framework of analysis offers the potential to help provide theoretical and research-based models and practices addressing how mindsets and meanings get established or challenged through discursive events involving power processes. Several empirical studies have already gone some way to achieving this. For example, a study by Grant et al. (2006) of the implementation of new technology at three organizations demonstrates how key stakeholders (consultants, management, employees and vendors) deployed competing discourses. Consultants and vendors depicted the changes along technologically determinist lines suggesting that wholesale adoption would lead to cost savings, enhanced efficiency and more centralized management control. Drawing on a combination of formal power, critical resources, network links and legitimacy, these actors were initially able to deploy their discourse with considerable success. This dominant discourse was successfully challenged, however, by employees who by virtue of their own sources of power deployed a counter discourse that showed the new technology to be impractical and inefficient.

Studies such as these demonstrate that although some discourses related to a particular change initiative may seem to dominate, "their dominance is secured as part of an ongoing struggle among competing discourses that are continually reproduced or transformed through day-to-day communicative practices" (Hardy, 2001, p. 28). Where discourses related to the change process shift in this way, they are also indicative of shifting meanings and associated mindsets. This helps explain why in some instances change processes that seem to be proceeding relatively successfully are later derailed or suffer from "fade out." The importance of recognizing and managing power relations and the various discourses that surround them would seem to be essential to many of the approaches associated with New OD, such as work on diversity or forging common ground from among multiple stakeholders with different bases and relationships of power.

Discourse As a Means to Create Change

So far we have argued that organizational discourse could provide a useful theory and research base for aspects of New OD practices, and second, that it could enable those using these new practices to better recognize and engage the power and political processes inherent in organizational change. These are important contributions, but they do not acknowledge the potential to use discourse itself as a tool or method by which to effect change in organizations. We believe that the field of organizational discourse also has an important contribution to make with respect to discursive interventions and organizational change. Indeed, several commentators have already observed that engaging in discursive activity such as conversation, narrative and dialogue in order to frame new shared meanings and change mindsets is a principal means to create change in organizations (e.g. Ford and Ford, 1995).

A number of studies illustrate the potential for discourse to be used in this way. These include the work of Gergen, Gergen and Barrett (2004) who have explored the transformative capacity of dialogue in organizations. Dialogue can create space for new meanings and generate shifts in attitude and behavior among large or small groups of organizational members. This creates conditions conducive to effecting significant and beneficial organizational change. Gergen and his colleagues provide two examples of specific practices that can be used to facilitate such dialogue – the public conversations project and appreciative inquiry. In the case of the public conversations project (see Chasin *et al.*, 1996), opposing factions involved in the abortion debate in the USA were brought together in small groups over a period of time. Their dialogue was guided in specific ways to help ensure beneficial outcomes. At their first meeting participants were not allowed to discuss issues pertaining to abortion. In subsequent meetings their conversations with one another were allowed to focus on how and why they became involved in the issue, but not attempts to persuade or argue with the other side. They were also allowed to tell stories about events and experiences that had shaped their own views. Participants in this and similar projects reported that by following this method they were better able to understand the views of the opposing parties and not to over-react or be disparaging of those views.

In the case of appreciative inquiry, Gergen and his colleagues suggest that the success of this New OD practice largely rests on the ability to shape the dialogue among participants. This is done by carefully choosing the topic to focus on and the questions to be asked (see also Bushe and Kassam, 2005). The idea is to ensure that the dialogue focuses on positive processes, practices and other features of the organization, and to encourage participants to recount stories that embody and affirm these features. Barrett and Cooperrider's (1990) study of the Medic Inn case demonstrates the value of such an approach. The hotel's staff were given the task of transforming it from a one star facility to a four star facility. Although the hotel facilities were upgraded to meet four star standards, the service culture at the hotel did not change. To address the service culture appreciative inquiry was introduced which involved taking the entire staff at the Medic Inn to another four star hotel. Staff at the second hotel were asked to recount through stories and experiences what were the moments that led to their being energized, committed and most fulfilled in their jobs. Following this, staff at the Medic Inn interviewed each other and sought to identify similar defining and positive moments. These were then used to draw up a list of aspirations for the hotel's possible future and to generate an action plan. Within four years the hotel had achieved a four star rating from Michelin for its service.

Another discursive based intervention designed to alter mindsets has been proposed by Oswick and his colleagues (Oswick et al., 2000). This team of researchers advocates using "dialogical scripting" as a means to effect behavioral and attitudinal change among small groups. Dialogical scripting requires a group or team to select a key critical incident and then use it as a springboard for producing a fictionalized narrative (i.e., a script) through a collective interactive process. The emphasis is on the dynamics of discourse and narrative more than psychological factors as is found in psychodrama. This method offers a powerful and evocative means of enabling managers and professionals to reflect upon a common area of concern in order to develop new and deeper insights and understanding. In their study, Oswick and his colleagues applied this approach to a group of academics at a university who were finding it difficult to come to terms with a change in the leadership of their department and with it a change in workplace culture. In scripting a play around this issue, the group created a fictionalized reality and were thus able to detach themselves from the event in question. They also were asked to play the audience. This enabled them to see things from a different vantage point and become sensitive not only to their own role but to those of other key actors, notably the leader in question. Subsequently they were able to work with the new leader far more effectively than had hitherto been the case; they were better able to understand his position on a range of critical issues and were less inclined to over-react and be disparaging of him.

Finally, the work of Hardy and her colleagues demonstrates how conversation and narrative can be used to instigate changes on organizational strategy and behavior in the form of inter-organizational collaborations (Hardy, Lawrence and Grant, 2005). This work is particularly relevant to those New OD practices that seek to engender common ground and social agreement among contending stakeholders. Drawing on a number of studies, these researchers suggest that inter-organizational collaboration can be understood as the product of sets of conversations among representatives of various organizations that (i) lead to cooperative, inter-organizational actions, (ii) produce innovative, synergistic solutions, and (iii) balance divergent stakeholder concerns. Further, they assert that inter-organizational collaboration emerges out of a two-stage process in which new meanings about a key issue are established and existing mindsets are significantly altered. In the first stage, participants engage in conversations that are intended to establish a collective identity among themselves. The second stage involves participants translating this collective identity into effective collaboration through further conversations that produce common and private constructions of the key issue. These conversations involve both assertive and cooperative forms of communication. Effectively facilitating this two-stage conversational process requires a diversity of skills, structures and processes. It requires careful orchestration of the conversations so as to create the space and opportunity for collaborations to develop. It also requires facilitation that engenders cooperative styles of talk amidst conflict and legitimates assertive talk despite a group's desire to "get along." At the same time, those facilitating must ensure that no one group dominates the conversation.

These types of studies demonstrate the ways in which discursive processes that recognize power dynamics can be used to facilitate or engender change, especially transformational change, in organizational systems.

Concluding Comments

We believe there are important ways in which organizational discourse theory and research might be used to help create more informed and valuable practices consistent with New OD assumptions and approaches. Ideas and innovations from organizational discourse might be especially helpful in expanding understanding of the importance of conversation, context and contention as critical variables in socially constructing change. Incorporating theory and research from a discipline that is self-consciously focused on understanding discursively mediated experience as the core variable in organizational change would also add an important philosophical base to a set of practices that is still attempting to differentiate itself from more Classical OD assumptions and approaches. A brief review of some of the key ideas about organizational discourse and change discussed in this article may help underscore our point.

Create Change by Changing the Discourse

The application of New OD practices in many cases involves adopting a constructionist orientation. This orientation, in turn, requires change agents to be open to the possibility that a primary way to effect change in social systems is by changing the prevailing discourse. Changing the discourse involves changing the narratives, texts and conversations that create, sustain and provide the enabling content and context(s) for the way things are. This, in essence, adds "discourse" as an important target and lever for organizational change, in addition to, for example, strategies, structures, rewards and processes.

Create Shared Realities through Negotiated Narratives

From a social constructionist perspective, change agents applying New OD practices should also pay particular attention to ways to help the involved parties negotiate and socially construct new shared agreements and mindsets about the "reality" of a situation. This will primarily involve discursive interventions such as the inter-organizational collaboration project described above. They should also keep in mind that interventions to help negotiate agreement on a prevailing narrative may differ from interventions based on a more objectivist, educational orientation wherein more facts or information are provided to alter perceptions, create greater alignment and thereby reach agreement. Instead, and as noted next, power dynamics are involved and need to be explicitly recognized and managed.

Power Processes Are Central To the Creation and Change of Discourses

Drawing on aspects of the critical perspective, change agents need to understand how power is used to create, sustain and change the prevailing or privileged discourses or narratives guiding how situations are experienced. This means change agents who apply

New OD approaches should explicitly recognize and attend to the power and political processes underlying the situations they address, and the methods they employ. From this perspective, change methods assuming consensual processes among presumed "equals," facilitated by "neutral" consultants, will, at best, "misread" the underlying power dynamics. Instead, understanding how various forms of power and persuasion are used to help facilitate negotiated agreements becomes an ethical if not a practical imperative. This is true, even when the dominant approaches used by change agents are to help foster "power equalization" among the participants.

A New Professional Discourse Is Needed

Finally, and building on our last point, we also believe that further development of New OD such that it increases its influence and relevance may require a professional discourse that is more accepting, if not embracing, of power dynamics. Premises and practices related to the uses of negotiation, power and political processes to establish socially constructed realities, agreements and mindsets are in stark contrast to those prevailing in most current forms of OD. Instead, most OD practices and practitioners tend to embrace collaborative and generative assumptions about change in human systems. These assumptions reflect the strong values in both Classical and New OD against uses or abuses of most forms of power and in favor of using rational, fact-based processes (e.g., Argyris, 1973; Bennis, Benne and Chin, 1961).

Despite the ambivalence towards power that has been a hallmark of most forms of OD, the implicit emphasis on reality and mindsets being socially negotiated highlights the need for theories of power and discursive processes to be more explicitly incorporated into New OD practices. Exactly what forms of power can be used in the New OD and by New OD practitioners to help facilitate the establishment of social agreements from among contending realities? When and how should these forms of power be used? These questions are inherent in most or all forms of New OD, but those practicing and studying New OD are not paying as much attention to them as they should. In short, power has been neglected in favor of less confronting and more "optimistic" or "positive" approaches (e.g., Cameron, Dutton and Quinn, 2003). Aspects of the critical perspective in organization discourse could be especially helpful in drawing attention and legitimacy to the darker side of socially constructed change. This will be a crucial issue for proponents of New OD practices to confront and explore.

References

Ackerman-Anderson, L. A., & Anderson, D. (2001). Awake at the wheel: moving beyond change management to conscious change leadership. *OD Practitioner, 33*(3), 4–10.

Adams, J. D. (2005). *Transforming work*, 2nd ed. New York: Cosimo.

Alvesson, M., & Kärreman, D. (2000). Taking the linguistic turn in organizational research: Challenges, responses, consequences. *Journal of Applied Behavioral Science, 36*(2), 136–158.

Argyris, C. (1973). *Intervention Theory and method: A behavioral science view*. Reading, MA: Addison-Wesley.

Barrett, F. J., & Cooperrider, D. L. (1990). Generative metaphor intervention: A new approach for working with systems divided by conflict and caught in defensive perception. *Journal of Applied Behavioral Science, 26*(2), 219-239.

Bennis, W. G., Benne, K. D., & Chin, R. (Eds.) (1961). *The planning of change*. New York: Holt, Rinehart and Winston.

Blake, R. R., & Mouton, J. S. (1976). *Consultation*. Reading, MA: Addison-Wesley.

Boje, D. M. (1995). Stories of the storytelling organization: A postmodern analysis of Disney as Tamara-Land. *Academy of Management Journal, 38*(4), 997-1035.

Bradford, D. L., & Burke, W. W. (2005). *Reinventing OD*. San Francisco, CA: Jossey-Bass.

Bunker, B. B., & Alban, B. T. (Eds.) (2005). Special issue on large group interventions. *Journal of Applied Behavioral Science, 41*(1).

Bunker, B., Alban, B., & Lewicki, R. (2004). Ideas in currency and OD practice: Has the well gone dry? *Journal of Applied Behavioral Science, 40*(4), 403-421.

Bushe, G. R., & Kassam, A. F. (2005). When is appreciative inquiry transformational? A meta-case analysis. *Journal of Applied Behavioral Science, 41*(2), 161-181.

Cameron, K. S., Dutton, J. E., & Quinn, R. E. (Eds.) (2003). *Positive organizational scholarship: Foundations of a new discipline*. San Francisco, CA: Berrett-Koehler.

Cannell, C., & Khan, R. (1984). Some factors in the origins and development of the Institute of Social Research, the University of Michigan. *American Psychologist, 39*, 1256-1266.

Chalaby, J. K. (1996). Beyond the prison-house of language: Discourse as a sociological concept. *British Journal of Sociology, 47*(4), 684-698.

Chasin, R., Herzig, M., Roth, S., Chasin, L., Becker, C., & Stains, R. (1996). From diatribe to dialogue on divisive public issues: Approaches drawn from family therapy. *Median Quarterly, 13*(4), 323-344.

Chin, R., & Benne, K. D. (1976). General strategies for effecting change in human systems. In W. G. Bennis, K. D. Benne, R. Chin & K. E. Corey (Eds.), *The planning of change*, 3rd ed., (pp. 22-45). New York: Holt, Rinehart and Winston.

Clarke, N. (2005). Transorganization development for network building. *Journal of Applied Behavioral Science, 41*(1), 30-46.

Clegg, S. R. (1989). *Frameworks of power*. London: Sage.

Cooper, R., & Burrell, G. (1988). Modernism, postmodernism and organizational analysis: An introduction. *Organization Studies, 9*(1), 91-112.

Cooperrider, D. L., & Srivastra, S. (1987). Appreciative inquiry in organizational life. In R. W. Woodman & W. A. Pasmore (Eds.), *Research in organizational change and development*. Stamford, CT: JAI Press.

Cross, E. Y., Katz, J. H., Miller, F. A., & Seashore, E. W. (Eds.) (1994). *The promise of diversity: Over 40 voices discuss strategies for eliminating discrimination in organizations*. New York: McGraw-Hill.

Doolin, B. (2003). Narratives of change: discourse, technology and organization. *Organization, 10*(4), 751-770.

Fairclough, N. (1995). *Critical discourse analysis: The critical study of language*. London: Longman.

Fairclough, N., & Wodak, R. (1997). Critical discourse analysis. In T. A. Van Dijk (Ed.), *Discourse as social interaction*. London: Sage.

Ford, J. D., & Ford, L. W. (1995). The role of conversations in producing intentional change in organizations. *Academy of Management Review, 20*(3), 541-570.

Foucault, M. (1980). *Power/knowledge: Selected interviews and other writings,* 1972-1977. Brighton: Harvester Press.

French, W. (1969). Organization development: Objectives, assumptions and strategies. *California Management Review, 12*(1), 23-34.

Gergen, K. J., Gergen, M. M., & Barrett, F. J. (2004). Dialogue: Life and death of the organization. In D. Grant, C. Hardy, C. Oswick & L. Putnam (Eds.), *The Sage handbook of organizational discourse.* London: Sage.

Grant, D., O'Donnell, M., & Shields, J. (2004). The new performance paradigm in the Australian Public Service: A discursive analysis. In T. Duvillier (Ed.), *La motivation au travail dans le secteur public (The motivation of work in the public sector).* Paris: Harmattan.

Grant, D., Hardy, C., Oswick, C., & Putnam, L. (2004). Introduction - Organizational discourse: Exploring the field. In D. Grant, C. Hardy, C. Oswick & L. Putnam (Eds.), *The sage handbook of organizational discourse.* London: Sage.

Grant, D., Hall, R., Wailes, N., & Wright, C. (2006). The false promise of technological determinism: The case of enterprise resource planning systems. *New Technology Work and Employment, 21*(1), 2-24.

Hall, S. (2001). Foucault: Power, knowledge and discourse. In M. Wetherell, S. Taylor & S. J. Yates (Eds.), *Discourse theory and practice: A reader.* London: Sage.

Hancock, P. G., & Tyler, M. J. (2001). *Work, postmodernism and organization: A critical introduction.* London: Sage.

Hardy, C. (2001). Researching organizational discourse. *International Studies of Management and Organization, 31*(3), 25-47.

Hardy, C., & Phillips, N. (2004). Discourse and power. In D. Grant, C. Hardy, C. Oswick & L. Putnam (Eds.), *The Sage handbook of organizational discourse.* London: Sage.

Hardy, C., Lawrence, T. B., & Grant, D. (2005). Discourse and collaboration: The role of conversations and collective identity. *Academy of Management Review, 30*(1), 58-77.

Heracleous, L., & Barrett, M. (2001). Organizational change as discourse: Communicative actions and deep structures in the context of information technology implementation. *Academy of Management Journal, 44*(4), 755-778.

Jackson, B. W. (2006). Theory and practice of multicultural organization development. In B. B. Jones & M. Brazzel (Eds.), *The NTL handbook of organization development and change: Principles, practices, and perspectives.* San Francisco, CA: Pfeiffer.

Knights, D., & Willmott, H. (1989). Power and subjectivity at work: From degradation to subjugation in social relations. *Sociology, 23*(4), 535-558.

Lent, R. M., McCormick, M. T., & Pearce, D. S. (2005). Combining future search and open space to address special situations. *Journal of Applied Behavioral Science, 41*(1), pp. 61-69.

Lewin, K. (1947). Frontiers in group dynamics. *Human Relations, 1*(2), 143-153.

Linstead, S. (Ed.) (2004). *Organization theory and postmodern thought.* London: Sage.

Mann, F. (1969). Studying and creating change. In W. Bennis, K. Benne & R. Chin (Eds.), *The planning of change,* 2nd ed., (pp. 605-613). New York: Holt, Rinehart and Winston.

Marshak, R. J. (2002). Changing the language of change: How new concepts are challenging the ways we think and talk about organizational change. *Strategic Change, 11*(5), 279-286.

Marshak, R. J. (2006). Emerging directions: Is there a new OD? In J. V. Gallos (Ed.), *Organization development: A Jossey-Bass reader.* San Francisco, CA: Jossey-Bass.

Marshak, R. J., & Heracleous, L. (2005). A discursive approach to organization development. *Action Research, 3*(1), 69–88.

Miller, F. A., & Katz, J. H. (2002). *The inclusion breakthrough*. San Francisco, CA: Berrett-Koehler.

Mirvis, P. H. (2006). Revolutions in OD: The new, and the new, new things. In J. V. Gallos (Ed.), *Organization development: A Jossey-Bass reader*, (pp. 39–88). San Francisco, CA: Jossey-Bass.

Mumby, D. K. (2004). Discourse, power and ideology: Unpacking the critical approach. In D. Grant, C. Hardy, C. Oswick & L. Putnam (Eds.), *The Sage handbook of organizational discourse*. London: Sage.

Mumby, D. K., & Clair, R.P. (1997). Organizational discourse. In T. A. Van Dijk (Ed.), *Discourse as social interaction*. London: Sage.

O'Conner, E. S. (2000). Plotting the organization: The embedded narrative as a construct for studying change. *Journal of Applied Behavioral Science, 36*(2), 174–192.

Olson, E. E., & Eoyang, G. H. (2001). *Facilitating organization change*. San Francisco, CA: Jossey-Bass.

Oswick, C., Anthony, P., Keenoy, T., Mangham, I. L., & Grant, D. (2000). A dialogic analysis of organizational learning. *Journal of Management Studies, 36*(7), 887–901.

Pettigrew, A. M., Woodman, R. W., & Cameron, K. S. (2001). Studying organizational change and development: Challenges for future research. *Academy of Management Journal, 44*(4), 697–713.

Rindova, V. P., & Kotha, S. (2001). Continuous morphing: Competing through dynamic capabilities, form, and function. *Academy of Management Journal, 44*(6), 1263–1280.

Searle, J. R. (1995). *The construction of social reality*. London: Allen-Lane.

Senge, P. M., Kleiner, A., Roberts, C., Ross, R. B., & Smith, B. J. (Eds.) (1994). *The fifth discipline fieldbook: Strategies for building a learning organization*. New York: Doubleday.

Sturdy, A., & Grey, C. (2003). Beneath and beyond organizational change management: Exploring alternatives. *Organization, 10*(4), 651–662.

Van de Ven, A., & Poole, M. S. (2005). Alternative approaches for studying organizational change. *Organization Studies, 26*(9), 1377–1404.

Watkins, J. M., & Mohr, B. J. (2001). *Appreciative inquiry: Change at the speed of imagination*. San Francisco, CA: Jossey-Bass.

Weick, K. E. (1995). *Sensemaking in organizations*. Thousand Oaks, CA: Sage.

Weick, K. E., & Quinn, R. E. (1999). Organizational change and development. *Annual Review of Psychology, 50*(1), 361–386.

Wheatley, M. J. (1992). *Leadership and the new science: Learning about organization from an orderly universe*. San Francisco, CA: Berrett-Koehler.

Worley, C. G., & Feyerherm, A. E. (2003). Reflections on the future of organization development. *Journal of Applied Behavioral Science, 39*(1), 97–115.

PART IV
Insights for Organization Development Practitioners

Introduction
Robert J. Marshak

This section contains some of my earliest publications and a few very recent ones. They were all written for practitioner audiences about topics that concerned me primarily about the theory and practice of organization development. I have now spent close to 35 years as an organizational consultant; almost nine years as an internal consultant and executive in the federal government and the rest as an independent consultant with a global practice. Although I have become increasingly more scholarly in my orientation during the past dozen years or so, for most of my adult life my primary identity, (at least to myself,) has been as a practitioner. The articles in this section are primarily written in that voice and from that perspective, although the discerning reader will note the shifts over time related to experience and writing ability and styles.

In reviewing these articles in preparation for this volume I was surprised at how in even my earliest writings the themes of being on the edge looking out and looking in, contrasting ideal types, and noting how cognitive structures mediate experience were clearly present. I'll leave it to others to ponder what that might mean, but in some ways I suppose I have simply been learning how to better unfold some inner knowing or awareness that is part of who I am and how I experience and operate in the world.

Magicians and Shamans of OD in 1982 was my first publication and contrasted the difference between the organization development practitioner as purveyor of entertainment – tricks and illusions – versus real change. It was the first of what eventually became many commentaries – views from the edge – about the theory and practice of OD. At the time, however, I was delighted to prove (mainly to myself) that I could be published and had no real ambitions to ever publish anything else.

Around the same time, I had started teaching as an adjunct professor in a new graduate degree program in organizational development jointly sponsored by American University and NTL Institute (the AU/NTL program). Although an experientially- and practice-oriented program, the mandate given to me was to teach organization theory. Early on I found myself in discussions with fellow faculty members trying to explain how theories were really conceptual tools and that theories and concepts could be taught experientially. This led to my writing *Cognitive and Experiential Approaches to Conceptual Learning* where I explained what I tried to do in the classroom. It is also the earliest of what became many discussions of the power of cognitive structures and models to shape how we think and act.

Having written these two practitioner articles I essentially stopped writing for almost ten years. I had no real interest or motivation to write anything and my consulting practice and adjunct teaching kept me fully engaged intellectually. I am not sure what exactly motivated me to write again, maybe advancing age, maybe an accumulation of experiences from the edge, but I then wrote the first of several commentaries on OD and power and politics called *Politics, Public Organizations and OD*. This recalled some of my experiences during my years of government service and was an attempt to urge OD practitioners to pay more attention to the processes of power and politics. About ten years later I revisited this theme in *Claiming Your Power and Leadership as an OD Consultant* where, among other things, I commented on what I thought was a "profound ambivalence towards power by OD practitioners."

The discussion on *Generative Conversations: How to Use Deep Listening and Transforming Talk in Coaching and Consulting* was written as a way to present to an OD practitioner audience some of the ideas I had been writing about for a decade in more academic articles and book chapters. It was also a way to try to explain a little bit about some of "what I did" in my work, as people had heard I was interested in using language and metaphors in my consulting practice.

Throughout the late 1980s and 1990s, I collaborated with Judith H. Katz on a NTL workshop we called: Dealing with Covert Processes: The Hidden Dimensions of Individuals, Groups and Organizations. Over the years we communicated the theory and practices we were discovering in the workshop in a series of professional presentations and publications, two of which are presented here. *Keys to Unlocking Covert Processes: How to Recognize and Address the Hidden Dimensions of Individuals, Groups and Organizations* presented the model we developed to explain the existence and dynamics of covert processes along with some basic keys for dealing with them. *The Symbolic Side of OD* was a short discussion about how the modalities of metaphor, music, movement, and media could sometimes symbolically communicate information from the unconscious. It explained how practitioners could get additional insights into what might be going on covertly if they treated "symbolic messages literally and literal messages symbolically."

More recently, in what became part of a separate book on covert processes and organizational change, I wrote *Covert Processes and Organization Development* to expand practitioners' thinking about the multiple and often hidden dimensions involved in organizational change efforts. This selection explains the dynamics and impacts of five covert dimensions to organizational change that frequently exist in addition to the overt reasons usually relied upon to make the logical "case for change." Those covert dimensions are: politics, inspirations, emotions, mindsets, and psychodynamics. Often one or more of these five covert dynamics will block or undermine even the best planned and intended change effort. An expanded version of this selection is part of a separate book I wrote for practitioners called *Covert Processes at Work: Managing the Five Hidden Dimensions of Organizational Change*, published in 2006.

The final selection in this section is a very recent short article on *The Paradoxes of Sustaining Organizational Change*. It was an opportunity to raise some questions about the theory and practice of sustaining change in a world where there is both episodic and continuous change. In that regard it picks up on the theme of the differences between episodic and continuous change that I first wrote about in *Lewin Meets Confucius* published in 1993. A key paradox is, "How can we sustain a change (an episodic orientation) and at the same time sustain more changes (a continuous orientation)?"

So, in looking backward – from magicians with tricks and illusions to managing the hidden dynamics of covert processes; from never writing anything to publishing many articles and a book; from episodic to continuous change – all in all an intriguing quarter century of evolving practice and scholarship.

19
Magicians and Shamans of OD

Our profession is enchanted by magic. "Bring Back the Magic" was the theme of the Spring 1981 Conference. A few years earlier, "The Wizard of OD" was a keynote address. The "magic of Bethel" is part of our patois. Novices attend workshops to learn the "secrets of the trade" or to "fill their bag of tricks." The list can go on.

Reflecting on this imagery, I conclude that OD practitioners do well to distinguish between the magic of the magician and that of the shaman and to avoid the one while cleaving to the other. I mean that strongly.

To begin, a *magician* is someone who entertains with tricks of illusion and sleight of hand; one who practices the pretended art of producing effects beyond the natural human power; a practitioner of trickery and deception.

A *shaman* is someone else entirely, a priestly healer; a professional worker of magic who seeks to cure illness and counteract malevolent magical influences; one who enlists or possesses supernatural power.

If a magician succeeds, the audience is mystified and diverted. Since they know that the magician works within the framework of ordinary reality, using hidden secrets to create a fleeting illusion, members of the audience vacillate between wanting to be fooled and wanting to discover how the trick was brought off.

Your shaman is nobody's entertainer. His/her aim is to protect or cure a client, individual, family or community. If the shaman succeeds, the client advances to a healthier or safer condition. While performing magical acts, the shaman is believed to operate in the realm of the extraordinary. Acts performed and insights won in supernatural experience are aimed at producing lasting effects for the benefit of the client. The client's attention fastens on the help s/he is about to receive rather than on the technique for delivering it.

The magician manipulates; the shaman aids.

If that were their only choice, most OD practitioners would elect to be shamans; therapists, not exhibitionists, of course. But shaman is not necessarily the way consultants are regarded by clients, and there's the rub.

The Practitioner as Magician

Many an OD practitioner has been seduced by an appreciative audience into performing an unnecessary intervention. Often, an intervention or instrument (read trick) garnered at a trendy workshop is drawn out of a sleeve before a live audience. Well-worn

Marshak, R. J. (1982). Magicians and shamans of OD, *OD Practitioner, 14*(3) 8-9. Republished with permission.

interventions – old favorites – are routinely run out on the boards to guaranteed applause. We stuff the latest tricks (stress, socio-technical systems, MBTI, TA, OSP, NLP) into our repertoires before we've mastered the old ones lest they be featured first in someone else's show.

Here are some warning signals that you are being set up as a prestidigitator:

- A client bids you to repeat the act you did last month for another part of the organization, or a colleague or a boss.
- A client asks you to repeat an impressive intervention that makes no sense in the current situation.
- A client shows greater interest in your methods than in your results.
- You are invited for an encore performance by a group that seems to enjoy your sessions but doesn't seem to be going anywhere.
- A client wants to learn a technique to work on someone else, although the client's own system remains a snarl of problems.
- You notice passive-aggressive client behavior, like that of an audience that has been tricked and pushes to learn how you did it.

From what sources do these warnings spring?

Some clients expect the consultant to entertain, plain and simple. At a more subtle level, the warnings may signify client-consultant power and dependency issues; the client plays impresario and acts as if the consultant is a hired performer.

On the other hand, the consultant may actually *volunteer* to be a magician. Thus, the entire demeanor of the consultant may give evidence of a willingness to amuse and mystify. The consultant may stage situations that provoke applause, or linger at stage center. Sometimes a magician-consultant will strum out a theme that the client, too, can perform such wonders if s/he would attend this or that workshop, read these books, and practice, practice, practice.

The OD practitioner acting as magician will foster the client's interest in the tricks of the trade – intervention methodology – to the point where their conversation dwells more on *how* it is done than on the desired outcome. Nothing beats focusing on the trick. ("Let's do teambuilding!")

The Practitioner as Shaman

For the shaman, tricks and illusions are not ends in themselves but steps in preparing the climate for a beneficial action. In addition, the shaman uses supernatural powers, *real* ones.

For present purposes, supernatural or extraordinary reality means a *reality unlike everyday experience; moreover, a reality in which the laws, expectations and relationships which govern matter-of-fact life appear in uncustomary guises or not at all.*

Thus the shaman can *fly* since extraordinary reality does not bind him/her to the laws of gravity.

In the presence of a client, the shaman induces a trance-like state, enters the supernatural realm, and executes a therapeutic action. Afterwards, the shaman returns to ordinary consciousness with the hope of beholding a cured client waiting nearby.

The shaman then goes about his/her business the same as everyone else.

While you or I may wince at the idea that we've been tricked once or twice (or tricked ourselves) into acting as magicians while trying to please a client, still it may not be altogether clear what shamanism has to do with OD practice. Healers, yes ... that rings a bell. But what's this about supernaturalism and ... did you say *trances*?

Yet consider for a moment that you, like nearly all OD practitioners, have participated in T-groups. There you enter into a separate world in which normal behavior is suspended. Promptly, you acquire supernatural powers, such as the astonishing ability to unearth and disclose your deepest secrets, to trust others as if they were put on this world to care only for you, and to cherish them in turn as if they had become the children of your heart ... all in a space of a few days. And were not the insights that you gained during this extraordinary excursion benefits you carry back with you when you return to Monday morning?

Or think of your "trance-like" connections with notions of exfoliating human potential. In your far-out world of Theory Y managers, enriched jobs, self-actualized workers gladdened by their tasks, high-performance teams, and human institutions unsullied by racism or sexism, do you not enter into a realm utterly fantastical and foreign to normal experience?

The OD practitioner's ability – indeed *inclination* – to join with such extraordinary reality is a source of considerable power, and one not very different from the shaman's. The revelations glimpsed in your "trances" disclose possibilities undreamed of by clients whose feet are planted in the soil of everyday reality.

Some Confusions

Shamans do not mistake the supernatural for ordinary reality, nor do they attempt to mix the two states or to make one into the other. The realities are kept separate and distinct.

OD consultants sometimes fail to make these distinctions, however, and pay a high cost for their confusion.

When we seek to transform the workplace into an ongoing T-group, are we not failing to honor the separateness of the two realities? Is this not an attempt to transmute the humdrum into the supernatural?

Or, when we expose members of the client system to humanistic OD principles at training events and workshops, do we not mean to deny the ongoingness of prosaic reality in favor of a preferred extraordinary one?

As long as matter-of-fact organizations are what they are, they cannot also be T-groups and vice versa. To attempt to convert the one into the other is to ignore the properties of either. The commonplace cannot yield to the laws of the supernatural and still continue as commonplace.

The practitioner who seeks to whip an ordinary organization into a sustained state of exaltation ends up thwarted and embittered. S/he may seek to dull the pangs of disappointment by calling the members of the client system stupid. Or s/he may surrender more and more time to the supernatural world of personal growth workshops and such like. In extreme cases, the consultant may abandon our profession entirely for a better "real" world ... wherever that is. Thus do would-be shamans fall from grace.

Your true shaman, for whom the extraordinary is a tool not a goal, does not encounter these frustrations. His/her client is expected to remain in an ordinary state of consciousness and to reap the reward of the shaman's psychic adventure. In other words, the shaman guides the client to better his/her ordinary life, not to escape from it.

Good OD Shamanism

What we learn in our trances, our special knowledge of humankind, must be used to alleviate the maladies of teams and organizations. "The remedy for human ills," said Dr. Johnson (in 1773) "is ameliorative, not radical." We cannot really elevate a stable, humdrum bureaucracy into a company of gods enraptured with our sacred visions and we shouldn't try. We can help to heighten somewhat the quality and meaning of life for its members, and the quality and effectiveness of its operation for everyone. Not too humble for a shaman, I think, or for us.

20
Cognitive and Experiential Approaches to Conceptual Learning

One of the more difficult challenges facing trainers and instructors is communicating formal theories and concepts in ways that enhance internalization and use, rather than by rote memorization. The former leads to theory in action, while the latter often produces little more than recitation ability.

Despite considerable advances in training theory and methodology, the read-lecture-discuss method still tends to be the preferred vehicle for conceptual learning. This is particularly true when the concepts address collective versus individual or interpersonal behavior. Unfortunately, the result is too often people who can cite theories and concepts chapter and verse, but have difficulty finding any use for this knowledge beyond demonstrating that they are "educated."

There is an approach which confronts this challenge to internalize successfully formal theories and concepts, and it has proven to be a powerful vehicle for learning.

Theories as Conceptual Tools

As cognitive creatures, people think about the world around them. They do not just experience it. In conducting their thought processes, people order their world with beliefs about cause and effect relationships, assumptions about what is important and less important, and they create myriad categories to collect and store data. This ordering process is guided and influenced heavily by such factors as early value formation, socialization and education. The end result is people with fairly clear, but usually implicit, beliefs about the world in which they live. These beliefs guide or determine what people will see, how they interpret what they see and, therefore, how they will act. While perhaps not fitting the formal definition of a theory, these beliefs are nonetheless a person's "theory of how the world operates." Consequently, everyone, at all times, at some level, acts from theory. The only questions are: What theories are these, and how explicit are they?

Viewed in this manner, formal theories and concepts can become important tools for dealing successfully with the world around us. As with other tools, their effectiveness is enhanced if different types are available to meet a variety of needs and situations. The fewer tools available, the greater the likelihood for overuse, abuse or difficulty in getting the job done efficiently and effectively. As with many jobs, sometimes several tools need to be tried before the one that is most helpful in a particular situation is found.

Formal theories, for example, of organization, management, human behavior and social processes may be more explicit than everyday belief systems, but they are no different in complexity or use. Each is nothing more nor less than a conceptual system to understand

Marshak, R. J. (1983). Cognitive and experiential approaches to conceptual learning. *Training and Development Journal, 37*(5) 72-79. Republished with permission.

phenomena and guide behavior. The advantage of formal theories and concepts lies in their explicitness. This makes them easier to learn and understand than implicit beliefs. Their variety provides a diversity of possibilities for every occasion. Their liability, of course, is that like other belief systems, they may be inaccurate, incomplete or misapplied. The skilled user of tools, however, soon learns each instrument's particular strengths and weaknesses, while discarding outmoded or ineffective ones.

The value of learning formal theories and concepts is straightforward and utilitarian: They can be useful tools for effectively addressing daily life, its problems and situations. For illustration, consider the manager of a personnel department confronted with poor performance from one section. The manager can view and analyze this situation based on his or her implicit beliefs about human behavior, motivation, performance, productivity and so forth; reach a conclusion; and act from it. The resulting action may prove effective or ineffective, but it will always be limited by the single conceptual tool used by the manager.

On the other hand, the manager could view and analyze the same situation using a variety of conceptual tools, in addition to the implicit belief system. Use of several theories and concepts will provide a greater variety of perceptions to guide action than one theory or belief system alone. The resulting action may again prove effective or ineffective, but it will benefit from the greater opportunity to discover new insights and understandings. In fact, used in this way, some of the liabilities of formal theories – their proliferation and contradiction of each other – can be turned into assets. Each provides a different perspective and understanding of the same situation, creating a rounder and more complete view of the problem and the opportunities for action.

If theories and concepts are useful for their practicality, then it is essential that they be learned in ways which demonstrate utility and application. Reliance on the read-lecture-discuss method alone is unlikely to do this. Discovering the usefulness of theories and concepts requires putting them into practice, and that means experiential learning is needed in addition to cognitive learning.

Experiential Learning of Theories and Concepts

Experiential learning as a training methodology is not new, although it has suffered from a stereotype that it is non-rigorous and skill oriented, rather than concept oriented. In reality, the methodology is neutral. In its application to various learning objectives, it takes on rigorous or non-rigorous, skill- or concept-oriented characteristics. Limitations and opportunities are, therefore, related to how it is applied, not its inherent properties. In turn, how it is applied becomes more a question of the skill and creativity of the trainer or instructor than subject-based limitations.

The range of approaches to experience-based learning is broad, including: field projects, case studies, application exercises, simulations, role plays and structured experiences. All of these are valuable methods or serve as adjuncts to cognitive readings and lectures.

In conceptual learning, how experience-based means are used – rather than if they should be used – is the critical issue. There are two dominant ways cognitive and experiential processes are combined for conceptual learning. First, provide cognitive input followed by an experience, or create an experience followed by cognitive reflection. For example, participants might hear a lecture, followed by a case study application. Second, they might participate in a simulation and then reflect on the applicable theories or concepts through discussion, readings and/or lecture.

It is important to note that in both combinations, the different modes of learning are separate from each other, e.g., now cognitively, then experientially. This separation compels the learner to establish the linkages between the two. This, however, is made difficult by the linear sequence of the combinations, which creates a boundary – a separation of the two learning modes. The learner, then, has trouble establishing the necessary connections required for successful internalization. This problem is not a serious defect, as long as learners are able to bridge the gap. Unfortunately, learners are left to their own devices and, more importantly, must do so intellectually – they must think about how the two are related. This can be a particular problem in conceptual learning, since the contrast between conceptual abstraction and the richer texture of real life situations tends to be strong. When the contrast is too great, the ability to make the necessary connections will be impeded. The learner will be able to intellectualize about how the two are related, but without experiencing and internalizing the linkage.

Simultaneous Cognitive and Experiential Learning

One approach to this difficulty is a third process combination: simultaneous cognitive and experiential learning. In short, both learning modes occur at the same time. The advantages to this third combination are significant. First, it reduces the boundary between abstraction and specifics. Second, the two modes of learning are mutually reinforcing. Third, the process itself models the linkage between theory and action. Fourth, the learning is synergistic rather than linear. Fifth, different learning styles or preferences of participants are simultaneously addressed. Finally, participants not only think about the linkages, but directly experience them. Therefore, the probability of successful internalization and the ability to apply the theory or concepts are increased.

Designing a simultaneous cognitive and experiential learning event is not easy, but the difficulty may be associated more with the creativity and skills of the trainer than anything else. The principal design consideration is how to create a situation in which participants think about a theory or set of concepts cognitively while experiencing them. This can be done in three main steps:

- Identify the essence of the theory or concepts to be learned, leaving out the frills, flourishes and elaborations;
- Identify situations that will generate and highlight the phenomena described by the essence of the theory or concept identified;

- Merge the first two steps into a structured situation in which the task focuses on the conceptual content, while the process and dynamics replicate the phenomena described by the theory or concepts.

Emphasis should be placed on essence and simplicity to keep all data and dynamics highly focused on the main point(s) to be learned. The more complex the situation and theoretic point(s), the greater the likelihood that extraneous data and dynamics will be generated which will confuse the learning point and impede the desired connections. This may mean leaving out important, but secondary, aspects of a theory. If the design is successful, however, the simultaneous cognitive and experiential validation of a part of the theory will, through a halo effect, validate the rest of the theory for learners.

The following are examples of how such designs can be approached, if not achieved:

Impact of assumptions on organizational behavior. Douglas McGregor was one of the first theorists to draw attention to the impact that assumptions about human behavior have on managerial and organizational behavior. His Theory X and Theory Y have become part of the everyday lexicon in most organizations, yet remain difficult concepts to fully internalize and appreciate. The following design is intended to promote internalization by creating a structured situation in which participants experience the impact of assumptions about human nature on organizational behavior, while simultaneously performing a task that requires discussing and engaging McGregor's theory cognitively.

> ***Design.*** *Participants are divided into an even number of small (five- to seven-person) work groups and one evaluation group. The work groups are all given the same assignment: to develop a plan and management structure for evaluating the validity of McGregor's theory within a specified time frame. Their plan also must address how they will assure a complete, quality product delivered on time. Half the work groups then are told they must develop their plans consistently with Theory X assumptions about human behavior, while the other half are to develop their plans consistent with Theory Y assumptions. The work groups are informed further that after a specified preparation period, they will present their plans to the evaluation group, which will decide which plan is most likely to deliver the best product.*
>
> *While the work groups are developing their plans, the evaluation group is asked to develop the criteria and process they will use in determining the best plan. After the specified period has elapsed, the various plans are presented and evaluated. After the best plan is selected, the total experience is processed and discussed.*

Typically, X group plans end up radically different, in predictable ways, from Y group plans. All participants have engaged, in a cognitive way, the meaning and content of McGregor's theory. Simultaneously, they experienced the theory's implications, in terms of final product, as well as in how the groups organized and managed the assignments.

Impact of group size on group behavior. There is a significant body of literature that discusses the various impacts that size has on such group dynamics as leadership, participation, motivation, cohesion, task performance and satisfaction. This design is intended to highlight those impacts by creating a structured situation in which participants cognitively and experientially address the impacts of group size on group dynamics.

> ***Design***. *Participants are divided into pairs and asked to discuss the impact of group size on group dynamics. If the training situation includes pre-readings or lectures, participants can be requested to discuss a particular theorist's ideas.*
>
> *After a short discussion period, participants are asked to reflect individually and take notes on the two-person group discussion experience in terms of leadership, participation, motivation, cohesion, satisfaction, task performance and so forth. Pairs are then joined to form quartets, who are asked to continue the discussion of the impact of group size on group dynamics or to discuss a different theorist's ideas. Again, after a short discussion, participants individually reflect and take notes on the four-person group experience. This process of doubling the size of the group, followed by reflection, is continued until a total participant group is formed.*

The total group then discusses their earlier discussions, their reflections on what the different size groups were like in terms of the given aspects and the large group experience in which they are participating currently.

Individual versus organizational needs. One of the fundamental axioms underlying HRD is the belief that optimal organizational performance is achieved when organizational and individual needs are integrated. While a worthy goal in theory, this has proven elusive in practice. The following design highlights and dramatizes the issues and complexities involved by creating a structured situation in which participants cognitively and experientially face the difficulties of creating such organizations.

> ***Design***. *Participants are divided into several small (five-to seven-person) groups and asked to develop recommendations on how to create organizations which simultaneously can meet organizational and individual needs. The time period set to develop the recommendations is kept less than optimum, to create a sense of urgency. After the allotted time period has expired, the groups are given further instructions to: "Process how well your group met individual needs for participation, leadership, methods of working together and so forth, while simultaneously meeting the group's overall need to develop a quality set of recommendations within the specified time period." Following that discussion, they are to review and either modify or confirm their original recommendations.*

After the groups have "processed their process" and reviewed their recommendations, group presentations are given, and the whole experience is processed and discussed. Typically, the juxtaposition of the cognitive task with the process and emotions experienced in doing that task dramatically highlights the issues and dilemmas involved in integrating individual and organizational needs.

If the simultaneous cognitive and experiential learning event is well designed, it tends to highlight on its own accord the connections between conceptual abstraction and specifics. Thus, it lessens the need for the instructor to draw out these connections during post-experience processing and discussion and gives more attention to other aspects. One of those aspects is the communication of an understanding that theory and concepts are useful, practical tools. Other aspects which occur post-event are:

- Drawing out the feelings and emotions experienced by the participants during the event. This adds cohesion to the cognitive-experiential connections and aids internalization. Participants receive a conceptual overlay for a generic type of behavioral experience and identify the feelings and emotions associated with that experience. Understanding is reinforced, virtually simultaneously, at cognitive, process and feeling levels.
- Modeling the usefulness of theory or concepts as practical tools through post-hoc analysis of the event. This can be done, for example, by asking the question: "Before this event began, what would the theory or concepts have predicted would happen in such a situation?" followed by, "What did happen?"

If the concepts and design are good, predictive ability should be clearly demonstrated. Even in cases where this does not occur fully, the limitations of the theory or concepts will be identified. This may be as important as understanding how and when they apply.

While the simultaneous cognitive-experiential learning event has received the most attention in this discussion, it is not presented as the only way to learn theories and concepts. Learners benefit from a variety of stimuli, and any approach can be overdone. Instead, eclectic training designs using combinations of various learning methods are recommended. However, one of the methods considered in developing the overall design should include the simultaneous cognitive-experiential learning event.

Summary

Successful internalization and ability to use theories and concepts require more than cognitive knowledge of content. Instead, they need to be viewed as important tools for addressing and dealing with life in general, as well as specific situations. To help communicate and reinforce this understanding, learners must be presented with situations that permit application and/or experience of the theory or concepts in action. Experience-based methods are an essential part of conceptual learning. They provide the bridge from abstraction to specifics necessary for internalization and use.

The link between cognitive and experiential learning modes is an important aspect of the process, since the connection is one of the critical ingredients to internalization. One way to increase the likelihood of participants making desired connections successfully is by focusing explicitly on that aspect in learning design and methodology. The learning of theory and concepts through simultaneous cognitive-experiential learning events is offered as one way of doing this.

21
Politics, Public Organizations, and OD

In my experience most OD consultants treat politics and political processes as if they were an evil force operating in organizations. They are to be feared because they can do in you and your change effort. They are to be avoided because if you touch or engage in them, you will be contaminated and lost. They are rarely really talked about except in hushed, disapproving terms. The old superstition, it seems, is still strong: to say the name of an evil spirit is to evoke its presence.

The purpose of this discussion is to invite some new and potentially controversial ways of thinking about politics, political processes, and OD. Perhaps most disquieting to some will be an assertion that OD itself is inherently *political*. The discussion will focus on some of the political aspects of OD in all types of organizational systems, and then place particular emphasis on public organizations where the phenomena are most clear cut. In thinking about politics and OD it is useful to consider several dimensions:

1. The underlying political ideology of OD
2. The politics of organizational change
3. The interface of OD consultants, career bureaucrats, and political officials
4. The nature of change in governmental systems

To begin, let me offer a definition of politics: *Politics is the process of people using power to achieve their preferred outcomes*. This definition means, among other things, that the essence of politics and OD is the same: process. OD consultants should, therefore, be very adept at recognizing and working with political processes. Most, however, are not. Some would even argue that they should not be adept. Why the controversy? Part of the answer may lie in ambivalent or limiting beliefs and definitions about power and politics. Some may be associated with the underlying political ideology of OD itself.

The Political Ideology of OD

There are several ways to define ideology, but perhaps the simplest is to say an ideology is a logically related set of value based beliefs and assumptions that describe how things should be. Aspects of the underlying ideology of OD become clear when we consider the *a priori* OD answers to the following questions regarding a change effort. Because OD as a value based social technology has *a priori* answers, in general, to these questions, it can end up being ideologically opposed to other answers to the same questions. In short, opposed to other political ideologies. For example, reasoned people operating from a different set of beliefs and assumptions might answer the same questions quite differently, as illustrated in Table 21.1.

Marshak, R. J. (1992). Politics, public organizations, and OD. *OD Practitioner, 24*(4) 5-8. Republished with permission.

Table 21.1
Political Answers about Change

Political Dimension	An OD Answer	Another Non-OD Answer
What *Process(es)* should we use?	Democratic, participatory, consensual, win-win	Only use the chain-of-command or majority vote
Which *People* should be involved?	Anyone involved or impacted by the decision; all levels; representative cross-sections	Those with legitimate authority to decide based on election or appointment to a position with defined responsibilities
What type(s) of *Power* should we use?	Expert, referent, moral, data-based	Positional, rewards & punishments, coercive, institutional
What are our *Preferred Outcomes*?	To realize the best interests of people, in general, and the total organization. Humanistic and social outcomes are as important as economic ones	The ends and interests of the people one represents (my function, my set of stakeholders, my group, etc.)

Thus a whole range of OD practices, based on underlying values and beliefs, will frequently confront and challenge many leaders' and managers' normal beliefs about the "right way to do things." This act of confrontation becomes, among other things, a political act since the desired outcome is to change the manager's underlying beliefs about processes, people, power, and preferred outcomes. At that moment of confrontation OD consultants are clearly and inevitably involved in a political interaction. If a conservative confronts a liberal about if and how a program or policy should be carried out we would certainly describe that interaction as political. Accordingly, it is just as surely political when an OD consultant requests participatory, consensual processes of a manager who believes only those in official decision-making roles should be involved.

The Politics of Organizational Change

Not only is the process of *how to change* an organization political, but the content of *what to change* is also inherently political. Here, some additional ideas about the nature of change and choice in organizations are useful. The disciplines of Political Science and Economics distinguish between *public goods* and *private goods*. In brief, private goods may be purchased, consumed, and/or used separately by an *owner* based on preference and ability to pay. Public goods, on the other hand, are consumed, used, and/or impact everyone *regardless* of individual preference or ability to pay. The air quality in Los Angeles is an example of a public *good* (or in this case, *bad*) for the people who live there. In classical economic and political theory, the supply and distribution of private goods is determined through markets and market processes, while the supply and distribution of public goods is determined through political processes.

Because there can be only *one* set of any given system, structure, or practice in an organization, and everyone in that organization must operate under that specific choice (even if the choice is to have many rather than one option), organizational choices and changes inevitably involve public goods and political processes. For example, whatever the given structure of an organization, everyone in that organization is expected to work within it. No one is usually permitted to have their own *private* structure, and everyone who works there is impacted by it. If the city of Los Angeles decides to build two new parks, everyone in the city gets two parks whether they wanted none, or one, or twenty. The decision is made through formal and informal political processes including: voting, legal appeals, lobbying, use of the media, advocacy campaigns, leaks, threats and deals. When an organization decides to reorganize, everyone is subject to the reorganization whether they want it or not. Because an organization's structure is a public good, formal and informal political processes, including lobbying, appeals and threats, should be expected to become part of the decision making process.

In addition, whatever the process, there will be some people, units, and stakeholders who end up more or less advantaged or disadvantaged by the reorganization decision. That means those people, units, and stakeholders have vested interests in the outcome. They therefore become active or latent actors with particular interests to pursue. The pursuit of those interests, the formal and informal means and methods selected, and the resulting interactions naturally create a political dynamic to any reorganization decision-making process. Consequently, OD consultants need to understand that: 1) the intervention processes they propose have political dimensions, and 2) the content of what they address (the public goods of the organization) also has political dimensions.

The Interface of OD Consultants, Bureaucrats, and Politicians

In terms of dealing with the political dimensions of OD, consultants also need to be aware of the differing orientations of the people they deal with who are clients or significant actors in the change effort. In public organizations this is particularly true for the differences in orientation and agenda among the OD consultant, career bureaucrat, and political official (elected or appointed). Some of these differing views are reflected in Table 21.2 and result from the position, orientation, and underlying beliefs of the actors, i.e., whether they operate from a political, bureaucratic, or humanistic change perspective.

Table 21.2
OD, Bureaucratic, and Political Perspectives on Organizational Change

Dimension	Consultant	Careerist	Political Official
Who Decides:	"Everyone involved should collaborate"	"We are responsible for the decision based on our technical judgment and the best interests of the program"	"We do, because we won the election. To the victor go the spoils"
Decision-making by:	Participatory and consensual processes	Reasoned analysis and conclusions of the experts	Majority vote; then implement the winner's agenda
Time Frame:	5-7 years	Next budget cycle	Next election
Change is:	Good. Positive. Improvement	Threatening to fiduciary responsibility to provide stability and take care of the program in the public interest	Opportunity to advance one's own political policy agenda; and/or undo opponents' agenda
Purpose of Change:	Enhance human and organizational potential	Enhance program and organizational ends	Enhance political agenda, influence, and electability
How Others are Seen:	"Neither careerists nor politicians consider the best interests of the people and the total system"	"Neither politicians nor consultants consider the best interests of the program"	"Neither careerists nor consultants consider the best interests of the electorate and the winning political agenda"

As is readily apparent from a review of Table 21.2, there are many points at which the different actors could be predictably at odds. Who should be involved? How will decisions get made? What is the time frame? What are the purposes of the change effort? These are just some of the questions for which there are likely to be different answers. This means each actor is likely to be more concerned with their own *interests* while viewing the other actors with some suspicion. Consequently, the OD consultant needs political skills and judgment to be able to create the working contracts, conditions, and alliances necessary to position a change effort for success. In so doing, OD consultants should never forget that the other parties will likely view them as having their own perspective and agenda that they bring to the table.

Changes in Governmental Systems

To understand and effectively bring about change in public organizations, the OD consultant needs to understand that public organizations are, at their core, governmental, not economic agencies. As an integral part of the official political system, all aspects of public organizations, including what they do and how they do it, are both instruments and objects of the political policy process. Because public policy emerges from complex interactions within the political system, real change must recognize and deal with that system. In most cases this means that significant change requires interventions that ultimately must impact on, or at least acknowledge, the power and preferred outcomes of a myriad of stakeholders and players including: organizational careerists, political appointees, legislative committees and staffs, executive agencies, elected officials, judicial bodies, other political jurisdictions, interest groups, the media, and so forth. To ignore the potential of any one of these stakeholders in a complex change initiative in a public organization is to place the success of the change effort in peril. Remember also that every action and expenditure of a public organization manager is potentially subject to scrutiny by higher political officials, legislative oversight committees, lobby groups, and the media for political as well as managerial, organizational or economic reasons. This naturally creates an atmosphere where everything involves an aspect of politics, from deciding on a new regulation to holding a team building session. Wait a minute, you say, "How can a team building session be an aspect of politics?" Well, consider the following:

1. Just asking for team building may give ammunition to political opponents who object that the manager's program or organization is "out-of-control" or poorly managed.
2. What about potential objections that could be raised in the media that it is a "boondoggle" at taxpayers' expense? Better not go too far away, for too long, to too nice a place, nor pay too much for a consultant.
3. You say you want to do data collection and feedback? You can; just remember that your report, prepared at taxpayer expense, could be considered a public document and might be requested by almost anyone. Better yet, it can be leaked with allegations of a cover-up and create calls for an outside investigation. See what that does to trust, openness, and honesty.

These and other concerns are part of the climate of change that must be considered in planning and conducting OD change efforts in public organizations. Therefore, OD consultants need to be especially alert to both political and organizational processes if they hope to be successful.

In sum, politics and OD are clearly linked, especially in public organizations. The political dimensions involving OD include: its underlying ideology of values, beliefs, and assumptions; the public goods nature of change in organizations; the differing orientations of OD consultants, career bureaucrats, and political officials; and the political system surrounding change efforts in organizations, especially public agencies. As OD consultants we cannot afford to regard politics and political processes as if they were an evil force to be kept at distance. Instead we need to extend and develop our awareness and skills to include the political as well as organizational dimensions of change.

22
Claiming Your Power and Leadership as an OD Consultant

Over the years I have worked with a great many established, new or aspiring Organization Development (OD) consultants. I have been impressed with their sense of purpose and enthusiasm for the field. I have also been struck by what appears to me to be a profound ambivalence or even antagonism towards power by many of them. This is not entirely surprising to me. I have written previously about the tenuous relationship between OD practitioners and political processes. What is surprising to me, however, is the seeming lack of clarity or conviction that effective use of power is a necessary component of OD practice, especially if you wish to exercise leadership as an OD consultant. The purpose of this article is to explore this ambivalence, offer a model of the use of power to support leadership as an OD consultant, and discuss some of the particular things I do in my practice.

What Is Power and Leadership?

People often confuse what power is with how power is used. In terms of what power is, there are many definitions available. For our purposes, power will be defined as *the ability to develop and use sources of strength, vitality, force, potency, and so forth*. In terms of how power is used, there are primarily two dimensions to consider:

- Power may be used aggressively against or in defense of someone or something, e.g., coercion, attack, abuse, and also defensiveness, protection, resistance.
- Power may also be used synergistically with someone or for something, e.g., collaborate, harmonize, partner, align.

When power is implicitly or explicitly defined as aggression, then the focus often becomes how to neutralize, combat or defend against it. This leads to anti-aggression or anti-power orientations and actions. When one has an anti-power orientation one tends to see uses of power as negative. This often leads to behaviors and actions intended to stop the use of power, sometimes including one's own. Paradoxically, power is used to negate power, resulting in a less power-full system overall.

There are also two planes of power: one horizontal, the other vertical. Power operating in a horizontal plane is the power of *doing*. It involves moving towards or away from someone or something. Horizontal movement evokes images and emotions associated with territoriality and turf, advance and retreat, war and surrender, and so on. Horizontal power can be perceived to be or is aggression.

On the other hand, power operating in a vertical plane is the power of *being*. It involves aligning oneself in the context. It evokes images and emotions associated with being centered, congruent, knowing what one stands for, and so forth. Power used in the vertical plane can be perceived as being a beacon, standing tall, providing support.

Marshak, R. J. (2001). Claiming your power and leadership as an OD consultant. *OD Practitioner, 33*(4), 35-40. Republished with permission.

In its simplest form, leadership means *providing guidance or direction*. Power, or sources of strength, vitality, potency, etc., is needed for the exercise of leadership. Put another way, power in some form is required to inspire, command, demand or draw enough attention, acknowledgement, acceptance or acquiescence for the guidance to be followed.

Powerful Confusions

For whatever reasons, it seems to me that many OD consultants tend to approach the question of power, and therefore leadership, from an anti-power orientation. Power is implicitly defined as aggression and the role of the OD consultant is to combat or neutralize its abuse in organizations. This also often leads to anti-top management orientations, since top managers are typically seen as the ones possessing power in organizations. The danger of this orientation is that rather than helping to lead an organizational change effort, the OD consultant may attempt to "save" the organization "victims" from their "abusive" or "oppressive" top management. While some situations might actually fit this description, many or most would not, thereby leading to inappropriate or unhelpful behavior on the part of the OD consultant.

An additional twist to the tale comes when you ask some OD practitioners if they want power. After the initial gleam in their eye thinking about the possibility, the answer is often a variant of "Well, yes… I mean no… I mean I'd like to have some *influence*, but not power." Here the profound ambivalence towards the term power and its implicit meanings becomes clear. Yes, influence is desired, but not power, presumably because if one had real power one would, by definition, become an aggressor, oppressor or abuser. The dilemma unfortunately is that by psychologically staying in an anti-power stance one also ends up negating one's own power and leadership potential. Thus, for example, the opportunities for an OD consultant to use her or his power and leadership as a beacon or synergistically in alignment with the entire organization, including top management, may be missed for fear of being seen as a transgressor.

Without power, however, you lack the potency to really help a system, or are vulnerable to being used or abused by the competing factors, forces and personalities in the system. How can one expect to be a change agent or co-leader or facilitator of change without using considerable power? Some deal with this difficulty by avoiding direct uses of power and leadership in favor of indirect or behind-the-scenes uses of influence and persuasion. Among the dangers with that approach is that indirect uses of influence and persuasion can be perceived as manipulation. There can also be a retreat to the false assertion that OD practitioners are neutral facilitators of processes, forgetting our roles as humanistic change agents and leaders. Consequently, one's power as an OD consultant must be accepted, developed, balanced and used along several dimensions to be an effective change agent and leader.

A Mandala of Power for OD Consultants

Most uses of power by OD consultants are based in four dimensions: 1) their role, 2) the purpose(s) of the work, 3) professional practices and 4) use of self. Each dimension also has polar aspects that are the actual bases of power to support leadership by the OD consultant. The dimensions and aspects of power are described below.

1. Role as an OD Consultant:

- *Authority as an OD Consultant.* Here, Max Weber's definition of authority as legitimate power is employed (Weber, 1947). This aspect represents uses of power and leadership that are considered legitimate to your role as an OD consultant. By the nature of your professional role you are legitimately entitled to ask, press, even "demand" certain things. It is expected that you will ask for the involvement of people, seek an action research mode of inquiry, request confidentiality, and so on. Not because you personally like those things, although that might be true, but because your role gives you the authority to ask for them.

- *Responsibility as an OD Consultant.* This aspect of power and leadership is based on your contractual, professional and moral rights, obligations and duties as an OD consultant. It is not an abuse of power or leadership to confront a client system about failing to fulfill a contractual obligation, whether psychological or logistical. One also has a responsibility and therefore a right to raise professional or moral issues. These responsibilities not only give you the right to raise or press an issue; they also give you contractual, moral or professional bases of power to assert your point of view.

2. Purpose(s) of the Work:

- *Contract.* Related to your responsibility and leadership as an OD consultant is the power associated with contracting and your contract with the client system. This is power based on written and psychological agreements governing what you, and others, can/can't or should/should not do. Your contract gives you a legitimate source of power to request that agreements be carried out, to confront misunderstandings, and to assert your position as a co-leader or partner in the change effort. Ambiguous, unclear or one-sided contracts, of course, are not very potent sources of power. This is another reason why contracting is especially important in OD consulting.

- *Professional Values & Ethics.* This aspect of power and leadership is based on professional, organizational and societal standards about how one should/should not behave and why (see for example, Gellerman *et. al.*, 1990). These are not personal values that one might fear imposing on a system, but moral and ethical principles that have been recognized and legitimated by others. Organization Development is a humanistic, value-based field of practice. Some may see this as a weakness when dealing with bottom-line driven managers. It is also a source of power and strength. Remember, using your power and leadership does not automatically mean

Collected Papers of Robert J. Marshak

aggressively imposing values on others. It can also mean being a beacon or moral compass by embodying those values and ethics in your day-to-day behavior.

3. Professional Practices:

- *Theories & Principles.* A well-recognized source of power and leadership is your ability to apply relevant concepts that guide thought, action and interpretations of behavior. This form of expert power not only legitimates your leadership as a consultant, but also empowers you to see and size up situations with insight and clarity, while being open to a range of possibilities. The broader and deeper the knowledge of theories and principles about people, teams, organizations, change, etc., the greater the range of possible intervention choices and therefore the greater your power to impact a client system.

- *Methods & Skills.* Knowledge of theories and principles alone, however, does not make for a powerful OD consultant. You must be able to exert leadership based on your knowledge and ability to design and facilitate behavioral change processes. The power one exerts when facilitating a group or team is well known, if not always claimed and owned. The power exerted by selecting a particular intervention(s) or intervention methodology is not always recognized, but can be equally powerful. As with theories and principles, the greater the range of methods and skills, the greater the potency of the OD consultant.

4. Use of Self:

- *Self-Awareness.* This is power based on knowing and reflecting on who you are and how you typically act, react and why, including competencies, blind spots, reactive patterns and emotional responses. Leadership comes not only from what you learn, and presumably address, but also from role modeling self-awareness and learning for the client system. The power of demonstrating how to be open about learning about one's own patterns offers guidelines to others about what is possible and how change in human systems can occur.

- *Degree of Self-Realization.* Being self-aware is important and powerful, but so too is manifesting one's full potential. This is power and leadership based on authenticity, congruence, sincerity, alignment and fulfillment of who one is and what one does. The ability to bring your full self to any situation is a source of considerable power and leadership that need not be aggressive or abusive. One can "command" a situation by one's presence and being, not just by orders and demands.

Graphically organizing the four dimensions and eight polar aspects into a single holistic framework produces a mandala of power for OD consultants (see Figure 22.1).

Figure 22.1
Mandala of Power for OD Consultants

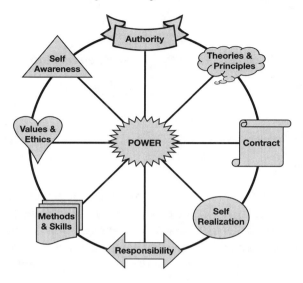

You can also assess yourself, or be assessed by others, by turning the mandala into a scale. If the center of the mandala is "zero," and the outer circumference indicates full manifestation of a particular aspect of power, then you can assess your power and leadership potential graphically. Consider Figure 22.2, which is an example of such an assessment. The enclosed space in Figure 22.2 represents the boundaries of one's current limits of power and the remaining space in the mandala represents the opportunities to expand one's potency and power.

Figure 22.2
Mandala of Power Assessment

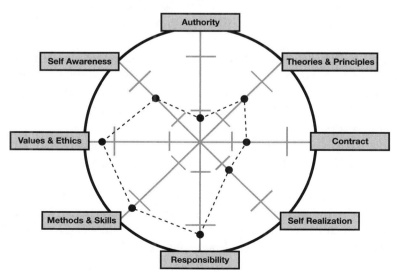

Because the eight aspects are polarities of the four dimensions (see Table 22.1 below), this way of graphing your power and potential as an OD consultant may also suggest areas of imbalance and therefore tendencies to watch or avoid.

Table 22.1
Balancing Your Power and Leadership

Dimension	Balancing Aspects		
1. Role	Authority	....	Responsibility
2. Purposes	Contract	....	Values & Ethics
3. Professional Practices	Theories & Principles	....	Methods & Skills
4. Use of Self	Self-Realization	....	Self-Awareness

As shown in Table 22.2, any one of the eight aspects of power that is not balanced by its polarity can lead to excessive use of that aspect, and therefore an imbalance in your leadership. Test these tendencies for yourself. Where might you be unbalanced in your use of power as an OD consultant? Do people say you sometimes act like a "caretaker?" If so, maybe you need to enhance your use of authority to balance your potency in responsibility.

Table 22.2
Unbalanced Power and Leadership

When Aspects are Unbalanced ...	You Can Appear To Be:
Authority	*Autocratic*
Responsibility	*Care Taker*
Contract	*Legalistic*
Values & Ethics	*Moralistic or Ideologue*
Theories & Principles	*Academic or Ivory Tower*
Methods & Skills	*Technician*
Self-Realization	*Closed or Rigid*
Self-Awareness	*Self Absorbed or Narcissistic*

Notice the idea is to enhance the balancing polar aspect, not to reduce an aspect such as responsibility. If you reduce an aspect, you are reducing your power! By adding more of the balancing aspect, you increase your total potency and leadership potential. In an ideal sense, you strive to enlarge and complete the total mandala of power in all its dimensions and aspects.

My Ways of Manifesting Power and Leadership as an OD Consultant

Each of us has our own way of manifesting our mandala of power as an OD consultant. No two ways need be identical. Over the years I have discovered what works and resonates for me given who I am and my particular gifts as a practitioner. Here I'd like to share five ways of manifesting my power and leadership (see Table 22.3). Some might call them principles or secrets or keys. I prefer to say they are simply "what I do."

Table 22.3
Ways to Enhance Your Power and Leadership as an OD Consultant

1. Clarity
2. Multi-Level, Multi-Dimensional, Multi-Modal Seeing and Doing
3. Use Tracking to Discern What is Core
4. Be Political and Leverage Yourself
5. Find, Form, Frame Reality

Clarity. I have always found clarity to be critical in manifesting my power and leadership as an OD consultant. First, clarity is about my purpose(s) in the engagement. What are the intended outcomes? What is the explicit or implicit contractual purpose(s)? Second, it is about my principles, in the form of both theories and values. What ways of thinking about the situation seem most relevant? What are the core values that guide what I am doing? Next is my philosophy of consulting and organizational change. What are my beliefs about how change occurs and what is relevant or important in this situation? Finally, there is clarity about my power. What are the aspects of power that are my strengths and how do I attend to those that are less potent? What are my thoughts and feelings about using my power and leadership, in this situation and with this client? I have always found that the clearer I am about my purpose, principles, philosophy and power, the easier it is to simply assert my leadership without need to move into or away from someone or something. When I am thrown off balance, the first thing I try to do is re-check my clarity. Everything else comes from that.

Multi-Level, Multi-Dimensional, Multi-Modal Seeing and Doing. This way of working has been greatly influenced by my work with covert processes. It is an orientation that I aspire to more than realize on an on-going basis. Put simply, it means I seek to see/diagnose and do/intervene in multiple ways. Those ways include seeing/doing at multiple levels of system, including individual, group, organization, industry, society, etc. Seeing and doing at multiple levels can be very powerful and provides leadership, especially when working with people or a system that tend to stay focused on one level alone. As a "rule of practice" I generally look one level up and one level down no matter what the presenting situation. I also try to see and address how different dimensions may be impacting the situation. Those include rational, political, inspirational, emotional, mental (mind sets), and psychological dimensions. Each is assumed to be a potential source and/or solution for the situation the client system is experiencing. Finally, in discerning the different levels and dimensions, I assume both literal and symbolic data are valid sources of information (Marshak & Katz, 1992).

Use Tracking to Discern What is Core. Along with multi-level/dimensional/modal seeing and doing goes tracking. This refers to trying to discern out of the mass of data presenting itself, on multiple levels and in multiple ways, what is central or core. Tracking requires several things. First, continuous data collection, both literally and symbolically, throughout an engagement. This can involve continuous questions and interventions in-the-moment, noting responses, followed by assessing what the responses might mean and then more questions and interventions. Such an approach is partially a continuous, real-time application of Lewin's famous dictum "If you want to understand a system, try to change it." Finally, in discerning reactions and responses, the idea is to "track" recurring patterns and themes that may be expressed by the system (Marshak & Katz, 1997). These usually reflect the core dynamics that are most centrally impacting the system. The ability to see and intervene with respect to core themes and patterns is itself a form of power and leadership, and also allows one to most powerfully impact the system or systems in question.

Be Political and Leverage Yourself. As I mentioned at the beginning of this discussion, I realize that it might be unwise to use the term "be political" with an OD audience. If "be political" just doesn't work for you, try "be influential" and read on. Being political means thinking about organizations in terms of systems of power and power relationships, and then consulting accordingly. It also means thinking of oneself as a change leader or political actor in such systems, meaning that OD consultants have power and intervene in ways that impact or influence the existing power structure. Key aspects of this orientation include anticipating who the stakeholders and political players might be in any particular change effort, as well as knowing or learning their mindsets, needs, interests and potential agendas. It also means understanding the organization's political system and political culture. Finally, it means using your power as an OD consultant to be an agent or leader of change, not just a facilitator of processes. It is an orientation that accepts power and political processes as inherent aspects of organizations and therefore of effective organization development.

Find, Form, Frame Reality. Meaning makes reality. Yes, there may be objective, empirical events, but it is the interpretation or meaning that is given to those events that creates social reality for individuals and organizations. "The glass is half empty or half full" is the classic example of meaning making in action. An organizational example might be a proposal to change existing reporting relationships. Is this put forward to increase competitive advantage, improve coordination and communication, cut costs, politically advantage/disadvantage certain players, demonstrate the power of a new boss, or what? The proposal itself is simply a presenting event. People then ascribe meaning(s) to the event. This creates the "reality" from which subsequent thoughts and actions follow. This orientation towards organizational reality guides me to do three things:

- Learn others' reality by understanding their meanings or how they interpret events. "I understand you believe the reorganization proposal is an attempt to cut costs at the expense of the workers."
- Invite new realities by creating new meanings or interpretations. "Maybe the reorganization is a way to deal with the communication problems between Departments A, B and C." Or, "Maybe it could serve as a step towards transforming the organization."
- Present alternative realities by re-framing meaning(s) or interpretations. "Yes, I understand the reorganization proposal is an attempt to cut costs at the expense of the workers. I wonder if it might also be a way to increase competitive advantage by removing organizational barriers and costs."

Such interventions are a form of "in-the-moment consulting" that can help people see possibilities beyond the limitations of what is perceived to be current "reality." Of the five things that I try to do, finding, forming and framing reality, when successful, is the most powerful and the most direct form of leadership. Yet it must be guided, informed and aided by clarity, multi-level/ dimensional/modal seeing and doing, tracking to discern what is core, and being political and leveraging yourself. Otherwise you cannot find the current reality, nor have enough purposeful intent and power to help form or frame a new reality.

Concluding Remarks

I am not sure if this discussion has convinced anyone to become "pro-power," or "pro-leadership" as an OD consultant, but I do hope my fellow practitioners will seek to avoid being "anti-power" in the future. Effective organizations and organizational development require uses of power and leadership, no ifs, ands, or buts. It's time for all of us to unambiguously claim our power and leadership as OD consultants.

References

Gellerman, W., Frankel, M. S., & Landenson, R. F. (1990). *Values and ethics in organization and human systems development*. San Francisco: Jossey-Bass Publishers.

Marshak, R. J., (1992). Politics, public organizations, and OD. *OD Practitioner, 24*(4), 5-8.

Marshak, R. J., & Katz, J. H. (1992). The symbolic side of OD. *OD Practitioner, 24*(2), 1-5.

Marshak, R. J., & Katz, J. H. (1997). Diagnosing covert processes in groups and organizations. *OD Practitioner, 29*(1), 33-42.

Weber, M. (1947). *The theory of social and economic organization*. New York: The Free Press.

23
Generative Conversations: How to Use Deep Listening and Transforming Talk in Coaching and Consulting

The purpose of this article is to introduce a subtle and powerful method that coaches and consultants can use to help clients address limiting assumptions and create new possibilities. The term *generative conversations* is used to capture the essence of this approach. Generative conversations are based on the premise that the way people see and respond to the world is determined by out-of-awareness cognitive structures that may be identified and addressed during everyday conversations. How to listen for these unspoken but powerful organizing structures and how to intervene to challenge or change them is also presented. The discussion first addresses some of the underlying premises about cognitive structures and the role of language in reinforcing and revealing what they are. The key ideas associated with generative conversations, including how to diagnose (*deep listening*) and intervene (*transforming talk*), are then discussed. This is followed by a case example to illustrate a generative conversation in action.

Premises about Cognitive Structures and Language

For many years now, I have been asked by colleagues, clients and students what I do that is special or different as a consultant or coach. Invariably I respond that, "I consult to the structure of reality of individuals, groups and organizations." Because this response is too cryptic, I'd like to elaborate here on what I mean and what is involved. I begin my work with the premise that people as individuals, groups, and organizations experience the world through nonconscious cognitive structures that mediate or "organize" both what is experienced as well as any resulting comments, behaviors and actions. These internal structures or frameworks (in the form of assumptions, images, mindsets, metaphors, unconscious archetypes, etc.) help create and reinforce "reality" for the individual(s) by organizing how data and events are interpreted, categorized and related. This is represented in Figure 23.1.

Figure 23.1
Mediating Role of Cognitive Structures

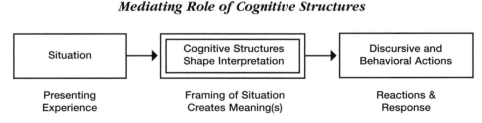

It is further presumed that if these internal, mediating structures can be modified in some way, then transformational change may be possible. A short example will help to make the point. The classic question of whether a glass is half full or half empty is not based on the physical quantity of water and the size of the glass. Instead it is a question of meaning making or interpretation that is determined by a person's internal ways of categorizing and interpreting the world.

How people talk about things, the words, phrases and images they use, is further assumed to be a primary means whereby these internal cognitive structures are created, reinforced, revealed and modified. In short, what is reality for a particular person is based on a world mediated by internal structures of beliefs and ways of seeing the world that are created, conveyed and reinforced through language. Furthermore, if one listens carefully one can hear cues and clues in what is being said that may reveal the underlying cognitive structures operating in a particular situation. One may then be in a position to implicitly or explicitly challenge, reinforce and/or modify those structures, even if they remain nonconscious. Thus, when working in this mode, I address the way reality is cognitively structured for the individual or system I am working with in order to create greater awareness and options for action. I do not address what is said; I address the cognitive structures that frame what is said. These premises about cognitive structures and language are summarized in Table 23.1.

Table 23.1
Premises about Cognitive Structures and Language

- Nonconscious cognitive structures mediate experience and response for individuals, groups and organizations.
- Cognitive structures (assumptions, images, mindsets, metaphors, archetypes, etc.) help organize how someone interprets and experiences the world.
- Changing internal cognitive structures can stimulate increased awareness, greater choice and transformation.
- How people talk about things both reinforces and reveals underlying cognitive structures.
- It is possible to listen for, address, and modify unspoken cognitive structures during normal conversations.

A Symbolic and Constructionist View of Language

All coaching and consulting is based in conversations carried out between two or more people. Typically participants in these exchanges don't think very much about the language they are using. Consequently, except when there are misunderstandings or confusion, the actual words and phrases are listened to less than the presumed rationally intended messages. Another view of what is going on in such exchanges, however, assumes that the words and phrases are not simply literal, but also symbolic and constructive. When we assume that language conveys implicit meanings and symbols and not just explicit, rationally intended statements, we are led to wonder what the specific words and phrases being used by a client signify about how that person is experiencing the world (Marshak, Keenoy, Oswick & Grant, 2000). We might ask ourselves:

What is the structure of beliefs, orientations, and ways of interpreting the world that is leading this person to describe things in this particular way or to use those specific word images? What words and phrases might we use in return to get "in sync with," or confront, or alter the client's inner perceptions and assumptions that may be limiting their choice(s), and are often deeply held and nonconscious?

We as coaches and consultants can use the insights provided by a symbolic and constructionist view of language to aid us with "in-the-moment" diagnosis and intervention with our clients. Our conversations with clients can be *generative* as well as informational; they have the potential to construct and reinforce meanings and therefore perceptions and possibilities (Anderson, 1995; Schön, 1993). Generative conversations are in-the-moment interactions where the coach or consultant is intentional about using the symbolic and constructionist aspects of language to help clients better assess the ways they are conceptualizing and addressing their situations, dilemmas and difficulties.

Generative Conversations in Coaching and Consulting

There are two main aspects to generative conversations between coaches or consultants and clients – Deep Listening and Transforming Talk.

Deep Listening

Deep listening is diagnostic. The coach or consultant listens to the client and develops hunches and hypotheses about unspoken mindsets, presumptions and orientations based on the explicit and implicit language used by the client. This is called deep listening because it calls for listening to overt metaphors, themes and narratives as well as unspoken, but underlying frameworks contained in unconscious and/or conceptual metaphors (Lakoff & Johnson, 1999; Siegelman, 1990). It also invites paying attention to what is emphasized and omitted in what someone is saying (Marshak & Katz, 1997).

The term deep listening emerged spontaneously several years ago during a workshop I was leading on "how to leverage language for change." The participants began referring to the way I was asking them to listen to their clients as "deep listening." The term has been used ever since. In contrast to "active listening" where the listener seeks to draw out the speaker while also acknowledging and responding to the emotions behind the words, in deep listening attention is placed on discerning and responding to the possible mindsets and cognitive frameworks behind the words and the emotions. There are four main aspects to deep listening.

First, one listens for the information the client(s) seems to be overtly trying to convey. What is the situation? What is desired? What is or is not happening? This alone would simply be good listening. Deep listening adds three additional aspects.

Second, one listens for *explicit* metaphors, analogies, word images, and themes in what the client is saying. For example, if the client describes a situation as "like a pressure cooker," and later that they are "under a lot of pressure" or that something got them "hot and boiling mad," then a compelling theme emerges that potentially reveals how they are experiencing their situation. This theme may be suggestive of their mindset about this and possibly similar situations even if they have not explicitly stated: "I am under intense pressure and am constrained in what I can do or where I can go. If the pressure continues, I may explode or boil over."

Third, one listens for *implicit* metaphors and images, in addition to listening for explicit expressions. In cognitive linguistics these are referred to as image schematics or conceptual metaphors and indicate the cognitively unconscious ways we tend to organize and experience the world (Lakoff & Johnson, 1980, 1999). For example, if someone talks about their life in terms of "starting out in humble origins, getting over a number of obstacles, sometimes getting detoured, but now on the right path," then it is possible that the unconscious image schematic "Life is a Journey" is implicitly organizing their experience and therefore the choice of words for how to describe that experience: *starting, getting over obstacles, detoured, right path.* One could also listen from a psychoanalytic perspective and assume the metaphors and word images are the symbolic way the repressed unconscious expresses itself (e.g., Jung, 1964). Regardless of orientation, however, one listens for the implicit symbolic framing(s) as a potentially legitimate clue or indicator of the way the client is interpreting and experiencing the world.

Finally, one listens not only for what is said or emphasized, but also for what is not said or deemphasized. If a client leaves out seemingly relevant information or topics, this may suggest a blind spot or something hidden for presently unknown reasons. Similarly, if the client emphasizes "X" it may indicate that "Y" is being intentionally or inappropriately ignored or repressed. For example, a conflict averse client who, after describing his unit's organization structure, was surprised to discover that a key office had been omitted from the discussion. It also turned out that the head of that office and my client had a history of conflict that had never been addressed.

Deep listening requires the consultant or coach to listen simultaneously for what the client is explicitly stating, while also listening for what is being expressed implicitly and symbolically, and for what is being omitted or emphasized. This is a tall order, but deep listening can be learned and developed much like group facilitators must learn to simultaneously follow both task and process. The consultant or coach must also listen from the frame of reference of the client, in order to intuit the unspoken mindset or framework that is behind the particular word choices and expressions. A critical error of some beginning deep listeners is to unintentionally impose their own metaphors or framings on the situation, as if they were guessing what the client was thinking or experiencing by assuming it must be what they would think or experience in the same situation. This might be a way to empathize with the client, but it is not deep listening for the unspoken ways the client may be framing and experiencing the situation. A summary of what is involved in deep listening is provided in Table 23.2.

Table 23.2
Summary of Deep Listening

In order to develop hunches and hypotheses about client mindsets and assumptions: • Listen for the information the client is overtly conveying. • Listen for explicit metaphors, analogies, word images, themes, and so on. • Listen for implicit metaphors and images in addition to explicit expressions. • Listen for what is said or emphasized and also for what is not said or is deemphasized.

Transforming Talk

Based on the insights and hypotheses emerging from deep listening, the coach or consultant has the opportunity to address the explicit and implicit world view(s) of the client and/or client system. This is the intervention aspect of generative conversations. Because this aspect is intended to alter or change the way a present situation is conceived by the client, it is referred to as transforming talk. Transforming talk occurs primarily through reflecting and reframing interventions.

During "reflecting interventions," the coach or consultant helps clients become more aware of their present worldview and how it may be limiting their options and choices. This is done primarily by reflecting or mirroring back to clients their own word images and themes that may be suggestive of how they are currently interpreting and experiencing a particular situation. Reflection interventions allow clients the opportunity to make conscious choices about critical and possibly limiting assumptions that might previously have been out of their awareness. For example, after hearing repeated images and phrases such as: "I am confined in what I can do," "I am watched carefully," "I better not step out of line," or "I wish they would just turn me loose," the coach or consultant might reflect back something like, "As I listen to you describe your situation it almost sounds like you are in jail. Is that true? Are you really that confined?" This form of transforming talk might help the client reflect on and modify an implicit and potentially limiting framing of a situation.

"Reframing interventions," on the other hand, go beyond reflecting back to the client hypotheses about themes and frameworks. They also include testing out or suggesting alternative assumptions or framings with the client. Thus the consultant or coach intentionally reframes the situation to see if an alternative framing might provide greater opportunities or choice for the client. For example, a client might describe in a variety of ways that the present situation is "like going down with a sinking ship." Clearly this framing of the situation offers few positive options and invites potentially debilitating emotional associations. The coach or consultant could, in-the-moment, reframe the situation and wonder if "perhaps you are simply leaving one type of ship to get to another so as to have greater mobility and choice for your next destination?" The client can then accept or reject the reframing. Whatever the response, however, it will provide more data to the coach or consultant to develop further hypotheses to guide reflecting and reframing interventions. A summary of transforming talk is provided in Table 23.3.

Table 23.3
Summary of Transforming Talk

- **Reflect** back to the client images, themes and assumptions revealed by deep listening in order to:
  - ○ Test hunches and hypotheses.
  - ○ Get in sync with the client's way of experiencing the world.
  - ○ Bring to awareness ways of seeing things that may be limiting possibilities and choices.
- **Reframe** potentially limiting mindsets and assumptions by offering alternative ways to see and experience a situation (e.g. could the glass be half full instead of half empty?).

Case Example

The following example is offered to demonstrate how an in-the-moment, generative conversation might unfold. The example comes from a situation where the author was providing shadow consulting/coaching to an internal OD consultant. Information provided in italics conveys scene setting information, commentary or the internal thoughts of the consultant/author at the time.

> *Background: Jane is an internal OD consultant working on a difficult change initiative. Bob is working with her as a shadow consultant/coach. The following abbreviated excerpt is from a conversation they had near the beginning of their working together.*

BOB: So Jane, tell me more about this new change project you are working on.

JANE: Well, it's a very challenging and difficult assignment. There isn't much support for the change; I am really out there on my own.

BOB: Is there a sponsor for the change? Who are you working for on the change?

JANE: I'm working for John C. and I don't want to let him down. I need to get out there and lead the way despite all the resistance.

BOB: You sound alone in this…?

JANE: Yes, I'm very much alone. I'm kinda out there ahead of everyone else, dealing with all the resistance and attacks from everyone opposed to the change. It's a very lonely position, but someone has to do it.

> *Bob is now starting to hear a theme and images that sound similar to someone out on a military reconnaissance patrol deep into enemy territory and who is "on point" – out in front of everyone – in a dangerous and vulnerable position. Bob has heard military type themes many times in the past but more typically from men, so he is tentative about this initial hunch and decides to seek more background information.*

BOB: By the way, Jane, have you ever worked in a military organization?

JANE: Well, if you count my family, then yes, of course. I come from a military family; both my father and older brother are in the army.

> *Knowing that Jane has some military background, Bob now seeks to draw out more information about how she is experiencing her assignment by asking questions that might elicit more insights into her ways of seeing things.*

BOB: Thanks for the additional background. I understand that you are out on this difficult assignment. Tell me, how did you get this assignment?

JANE: I got it from John C.

BOB: Yes, well, hmmm, did John C. call you in and give you the assignment, were you recommended by others? Did you volunteer? How did it happen?

JANE: I knew someone needed to do it, so I went to John and told him I would be willing to take the lead to be out in front and take whatever fire or heat might happen because his change initiative is so very important.

> *Bob is now more confident that Jane may be operating from some kind of "on point," or "out in front of the troops" unconscious or semi-conscious organizing imagery. He begins to test this hypothesis by trying to "get in sync" with her way of seeing and experiencing the world and also to begin testing possible reframings that might give Jane more options and choices in this assignment.*

BOB: Wow, it must be pretty scary to be out in front of everyone; that's a pretty vulnerable position.

JANE: (*pausing*) It is. It is very scary, but I don't think about it because it needs to be done and someone has to do it.

BOB: So you have more or less volunteered to be out on point on this assignment?

JANE: Yes, pretty much so. I just figured I was the best person to do it and I didn't want to let John C. down – that I owed him my loyalty and the change initiative is very important.

> *Bob decides now to be more direct and also to test one possible way the situation might be reframed to give Jane more choices or more support. He also decides that for now his approach will be to see how Jane reacts to a reframing of the possible "on point" military image without directly confronting or changing the image entirely. Bob also makes a mental note to see how extensively this image, or military images in general, may be influencing how Jane sees and experiences the world. At some future point this image may be reflected back to Jane to see if and how it may be unconsciously limiting her options and choices.*

BOB: You seem to describe yourself as out in front all alone. Do you have any help or support? Have you asked for any?

JANE: Well, no, it's my job to take the lead in this.

BOB: Couldn't you ask John C. for support to back you up or provide better cover? After all you are on a mission to advance his agenda.

JANE: Well, I volunteered…

BOB: …for a suicide mission?

JANE: (*frown*) Well no… (*now smiling*) although sometimes it feels that way!

> *At this point Bob suggests a specific reframing to see if asking for support or setting up the situation in a more favorable way is a possible option for Jane in this situation.*

BOB: I don't know John C., but it seems to me that if you are on an important mission for him it would be OK to ask for as much support and help as possible…

JANE: …even if I volunteered? Wouldn't that be "pushy" or out-of-line?

BOB: Again I don't know John C., but I think it is more than appropriate to tell him what is needed for a successful change project and ask for everything you think you need to make his change initiative a success and to ensure you are as effective as possible. You know, he has some obligation and loyalty to you too. You are advancing his initiative. If it's something he wants, then it should be something he is willing to provide strong support for.

JANE: (*tentatively*) Hmmm…Well, maybe I could ask him for some help. I could really use it.

BOB: If you did ask him for help or more support what would you want or need?

JANE: (*laughing*) Lots! For starters I need …

> *At this point the conversation was reframed into what was needed for a successful "mission" and that it was acceptable to request it from John C. A different and more confrontational reframing would have been to challenge the military imagery that seemed to be framing how Jane was experiencing her situation and choices. In this instance, that occurred in a later meeting when "dangerous military mission" imagery continued to pervade her descriptions of her work on the change initiative and seemed to frame how she experienced the situation and what she saw as her options and choices.*

There are, of course, other possible interventions that could have occurred in this shadow consulting/coaching relationship. There are also other possible interpretations of what might have been going on with Jane and why she seemed to see the situation the way she did, including, perhaps, non-military interpretations. The purpose of presenting this case is not to suggest exactly what should be done or how certain phrases should be interpreted, but to give a realistic example of a generative conversation where deep listening is used to inform intentional transforming talk to get in sync with the client and provide more options and choices.

Concluding Comments

Consultants and coaches using a constructionist and discursive orientation always have the opportunity to enter into generative conversations with clients and client systems for the purpose of facilitating or inducing change. Interventions can occur in-the-moment and do not have to rely on or wait for more programmed or scheduled interventions. This orientation requires skills in deep listening and transforming talk to be able to hear implicit and symbolic messages indicative of internal mindsets and to be able to reflect back and/or reframe those messages in order to create new options and choices for the client. It also requires a good sense of timing, ability to hear the world through someone else's words, and the ethics to use this social technology with positive intent and with the ambition to always keep the client in a position of choice.

References

Anderson, H. D. (1995). Collaborative language systems: Toward a postmodern therapy. In R. H. Mikesell, D. D. Lusterman, & S. H. McDaniel (Eds.), *Integrating family therapy: Handbook of family psychology and systems theory*, (pp. 27-44). Washington, DC: American Psychological Associates.

Jung, C. G. (1964). *Man and his symbols*. New York: Doubleday.

Lakoff, G., & Johnson, M. (1980). *Metaphors we live by*. Chicago: University of Chicago Press.

Lakoff, G., & Johnson, M. (1999). *Philosophy in the flesh: The embodied mind and its challenge to Western thought*. New York: Basic Books.

Marshak, R. J., Keenoy, T., Oswick, C., & Grant, D. (2000). From outer words to inner worlds. *Journal of Applied Behavioral Science, 36*(2), 245-258.

Marshak, R. J., & Katz, J. H. (1997). Diagnosing covert processes in groups and organizations, *OD Practitioner, 29*(1), 33-42.

Schön, D. A. (1993). Generative metaphor: A perspective on problem-solving in social policy. In A. Ortony (Ed.), *Metaphor and thought* (2nd ed., pp. 137-163). Cambridge UK: Cambridge University Press.

Siegelman, E. Y. (1990). *Metaphor and meaning in psychotherapy*. New York: Guilford.

24
Keys to Unlocking Covert Processes: How to Recognize and Address the Hidden Dimensions of Individuals, Groups and Organizations

In order for consultants and change agents to be able to address complex organizational issues they need to be able to identify and deal with the hidden dimensions of the individuals, groups and organizations with whom they work. Without this ability, they may find themselves less effective in facilitating change or confused by the behavior of others.

The Covert Processes Model™

To help people understand the hidden dimensions that impact all social systems, we developed *The Covert Processes Model™* (Marshak & Katz, 1991, 1999), which shows the fundamental dynamics and sources of covert processes for individuals, groups and organizations. (See Figure 24.1) Although the model draws from a wide range of behavioral science theories, for example, analytic, cognitive, gestalt, and transpersonal psychology, we intentionally present it in everyday language using almost universal imagery (e.g., "What's going on under the table?"). This imagery facilitates use of the model in everyday discussions.

Figure 24.1
The Covert Processes Model™

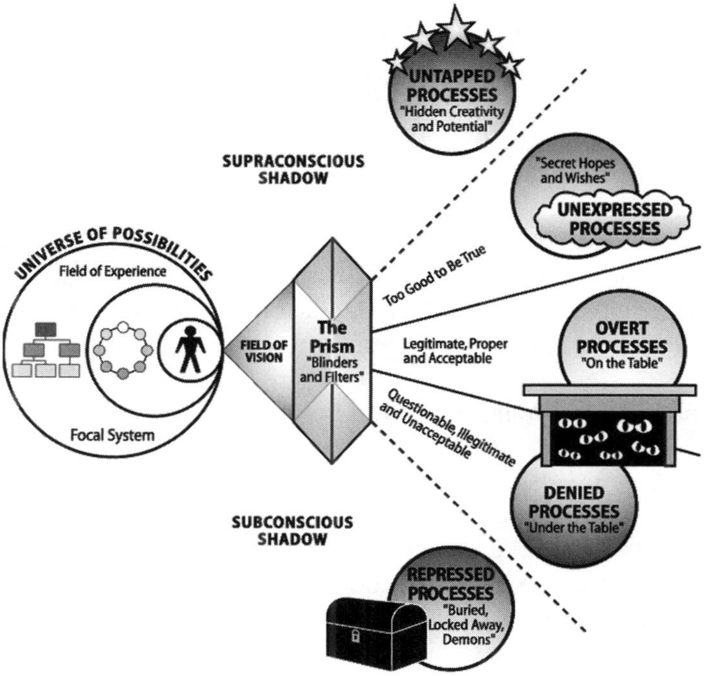

Marshak, R. J., & Katz, J. H. (2001). Keys to unlocking covert processes: How to recognize and address the hidden dimensions of individuals, groups and organizations. *OD Practitioner, 33*(2), 3-10. Republished with permission.

Included in the model is the premise that all social systems have conscious, unconscious, and out-of-awareness dimensions that impact perception and behavior. The unconscious and out-of-awareness dimensions are, of course, normally "hidden" or covert to the system. Meanwhile the conscious dimension includes both overt and covert areas. Following is a brief description of the major aspects of the model.

The Context or Field Of Experience

The first step in understanding covert processes is to consider the overall context of the focal system. Every individual, group and organization exists within a universe of possibilities. However, no individual, group or organization can know, experience, or comprehend all that there is to know. By definition then, the field of experience becomes a subset of all that there is in the universe and is impacted by life experiences. For individuals this can include their age, education, race, gender, sexuality, socioeconomic status, professional identity, family experiences, etc. For groups and/or organizations analogous factors include: age; type of business; demographics; type(s) of products or services provided; the group and/or organization environment; and history and experience with change, competition, forms of organization, technology, leadership styles, and so on. The limits provided by the context or field of experience begins the process of determining what may be open (overt) and closed (covert) to consideration by the system.

> *For example, a work group with a long history of autocratic bosses may find it difficult to even conceive of working with an alternative leadership style. Another example is an organization with a 125-year history in a regulated industry initially finding the realities of deregulation and market competition literally inconceivable. In both of these examples something may be "missing" or "hidden" from consideration because it is beyond the experience of the focal system.*

The Prism

What we actually perceive and how we make sense of the world is further filtered through a *prism* composed of individual, group, organizational and societal lenses (Bennett, 1987). There is a wide range of elements that exist within the prism. Each aspect plays a part in defining reality and response for the individual, group and/or organization. Each also serves to "interpret" and/or provide meaning to data and events.

The content of the prism includes, but is not limited to:

- *Childhood lessons learned* including "tapes" and introjections from parents, teachers, and other authority figures about what is right and wrong, how one should behave, what it means to be a "good little boy or girl," and so on. Also included are the ways one learns to navigate and cope with the world. Often these early lessons learned remain unexamined in one's prism to influence later adult behavior.

- *Beliefs, assumptions, and values* including the broadest array of concepts that order, judge, link, or otherwise explain events. They include biases and prejudices, habitual thought patterns, proverbs, sayings, and learned or assimilated ways of thinking carried forward from childhood, and those of current or recent origin. All have the impact of both organizing and limiting experience and response.

- *Formal theories and systems of thought* including all aspects of what one learns through formal education, as well as training and/or exposure to religious, philosophical, and/or professional ideals and concepts. These theories and systems of thought help shape how one looks at the world and how things are believed to be associated and/or related to each other.

- *Paradigms* that are often out-of-awareness conceptual schemas that guide how one organizes and thinks about some class of phenomenon. Formal theories and systems of thought usually develop and exist within the framework of a particular paradigm. It is virtually impossible to "see" something that does not exist within the viewer's operating paradigm. A change in paradigm can be so powerful that it is revolutionary or transformational.

- *Organizational and societal cultures* that represent taken-for-granted assumptions about the most basic aspects of life in the organization and society, e.g., the nature of people, how one survives and prospers, proper relationships between people as well as with the environment, the meaning of life and work, the concepts of time, space, causality, etc. Until one encounters another culture or society these aspects of one's prism are usually assumed to be "givens" i.e., the "natural" way the world operates.

Significantly, the existence of the *prism*, its many lenses and facets and its powerful influences, is itself covert; that is, it remains out of the awareness of most individuals, groups and organizations. It is through our prisms that a range of overt and covert processes takes shape. Those behaviors and beliefs that the contents of our prism define as *legitimate, proper, acceptable,* and *reasonable* become overt and open to view. Those behaviors and beliefs that are defined as illegitimate because they are either *unacceptable* or *too good to be true* become covert and hidden from view. In short, the content of our prisms help us to interpret and deal with the world, but also can serve as blinders and filters that prevent us from considering certain possibilities because they don't fit our current ways of thinking about and seeing things.

> *For example, if the prevailing norms of a group prohibit open discussion of emotions, then feelings will need to be disguised, denied, or otherwise expressed covertly. Likewise an organization's culture may imply that "win-win" collaborative relationships between the union and management or with key suppliers is only "pie-in-the-sky." If so, in that organization contrary beliefs or courses of action would likely become covert or not even considered.*

Overt Processes

What becomes overt or *on the table*, therefore, will include topics and issues that the individual, group or organization defines as *acceptable, proper, reasonable* and *legitimate*. These topics and issues will be open to view and public discussion. The range of what's permitted on the table will vary from group to group and organization to organization depending on what is valued in the system, its norms, culture, and the tacit agreements among the members of the system.

> *For example, in many organizations discussions related to "the bottom line" are always out on the table, but discussions about visions and values are often considered too "airy fairy" to be discussed.*

Covert Processes

Behaviors and beliefs that are not, or cannot be, put out on the table for open discussion and view become hidden or covert to the system. Recognizing their multidimensional and complex nature, there are four principal manifestations or places to "look for" covert processes:

- Denied or *under the table* processes. What gets hidden under the table are those behaviors and beliefs seen as illegitimate or perceived as too risky to openly address. People in a group may easily refer to "skeletons in their closet," but not feel safe enough to openly talk about the issues the skeletons represent.

> *For example, in an organization where top leadership is supposed to "have all the answers" elaborate processes may evolve to keep spontaneous issues off the table and thereby protect senior managers from ever appearing stupid or lacking answers, e.g., no surprises, advance briefings, working things out before meetings, and so on.*

- Repressed or *unacceptable to see* processes (the subconscious shadow). At a deeper level, hiding in our "shadow" are those aspects that seem unacceptable to acknowledge or see. Freud and Jung described the shadow as those powerful aspects of our psyche that are usually out of our consciousness, that have been repressed, buried and locked away, yet have a strong hold on our behavior (Zweig & Abrams, 1993). These repressed processes are seen by many as a somewhat mysterious aspect in which powerful emotions, fears, responses and memories of traumatic events lie. They are often the source of projections and other compensatory behaviors.

> *For example, the undesirable characteristics attributed to another work group ("they are selfish, and only out for themselves") may be nothing more than a defense mechanism wherein an unacceptable to acknowledge aspect of one's own group is projected onto another entity. In reality it may be our group, not the other, who has needs for power and competitive victory at all costs.*

- Unexpressed or *too good to be true* processes. A third often overlooked dimension of covert processes takes place in the realm of our secret hopes and wishes. For many individuals, groups or organizations it is illegitimate to express desires to reach new heights, or to openly admit pride in one's accomplishments and talents, or to express altruistic values and/or hopes for great achievements or contributions. Our hopes and wishes and those things that seem too good to be true are kept covert out of fear of others' ridicule or being labeled as a stargazer, too naive, or unrealistic.

    For example, in many work teams and organizations attempts to create and express inspirational visions and values routinely fail because they are considered to be "too far out" or "not grounded in reality."

- Untapped or *unacceptable to imagine* processes (the supraconscious shadow). Often out of our awareness and sense of reach are those aspects of our creativity, talent and as yet undiscovered potential that help us realize our spiritual and higher selves. Locked away in these untapped processes, a part of our supraconscious shadow, is unleashed creativity, synergy and the outer limits of our abilities, inventiveness and possibilities (Ferrucci, 1982). These processes and possibilities are unavailable to many individuals, groups, and organizations because they are simply unacceptable to imagine.

    For example, the possibilities for creating collaborative, synergistic alliances between producers and suppliers, supported by just-in-time inventory systems, were unimaginable not very many years ago.

In sum, The Covert Processes Model™ provides a multidimensional framework to help understand the sources and manifestations of hidden dynamics in individuals, groups and organizations. Importantly, we wish to also emphasize that in this model covert processes simply "are," and refer to anything that is not overt, for whatever reasons. No negative value judgment is automatically implied or negative intent assumed. Things may be hidden for good, bad, or unknown reasons.

Keys to Unlocking Covert Processes

Clearly, change can be thwarted by the fears, untested assumptions, filters and under-the-table dealings of organizational members. Change may also be facilitated by unleashing hidden or repressed creativity, removing unspoken blocks and barriers, and giving voice to "unspeakable" visions of potential and greatness. In our work, as we developed a more complete understanding of the hidden forces that may be blocking successful change efforts, we found ourselves searching for keys to unlock the covert processes. What we discovered was that unlocking covert processes is no easy task, but is possible when guided by the following seven fundamental keys. (See Table 24.1)

Table 24.1
Keys to Unlocking Covert Processes

1. Safety First
2. Be Clear and Selective
3. Seek Movement not Exposure
4. Assume People are Intendedly Competent
5. Remember Covert Processes Protect Against Threat
6. Look in the Mirror
7. Intervene Consistent with Your Contract

© 2001 Robert J. Marshak, Ph.D. & Judith H. Katz, Ed.D

Key #1: Safety First. Most things are, or stay, covert due to fear and/or perceived risk. It is, therefore, critically important to create a safe environment in order to address covert processes. To enter the world of covert processes we must recognize that things are often hidden when people feel there is a risk. We must also remember that safety is in the eye (prism) of the beholder. In short, all types of fears, thoughts, needs, motives, and even hopes, dreams, and wishes will remain hidden until individuals feel safe. Therefore, a primary intervention in all covert process work is to create a safe environment for further work.

Creating a safe environment involves efforts to establish, re-establish, or emphasize a context where people feel there is trust and that they have some control. People will not share their secret hopes and dreams, nor fears and failings, if they believe this information will be used against them, hold them up to ridicule, punish them, or the like.

They must trust that what is revealed will be treated with care and respect. They must trust they will not suffer retribution for "letting the cat out of the bag." They must trust what will be put on the table will be used towards important and meaningful ends, not simply to satisfy someone's curiosity.

People also need to feel that they have (at least some) control over what happens: How much to reveal, when, in what way(s), to whom, etc. An environment where people feel they will be forced, coerced, or bullied to do something they might not wish to do is also an environment where covert processes will be well protected, defended, and/or denied. Creating norms and ways of working that make clear people have choices and (at least some) ability to control the pace, process, and purpose(s) are important aspects of helping to set an environment where people feel safe enough to put things out on the table.

Key #2: Be Clear and Selective. Multiple covert processes are always present and result from a variety of complex dynamics. This means we must follow a four-part process in our approach to intervening.

- First, we must be continually alert to all types of covert processes that may be operating at individual, group, and organizational levels simultaneously. This requires diagnostic skills and abilities as well as clarity about one's own covert processes that may filter and/or distort the information.

- Second, we must maintain a stance of non-judgmental inquiry and curiosity about the possible reasons for the covert processes we suspect may be at work in any particular situation. If we begin to judge what we suspect, either positively or negatively, we are likely to close off inquiry. Worse, we may become tempted to violate the safety of the situation as perceived by one or more participants because "what's going on is not so bad (to us)," or "it's really terrible and he/she/they deserve to be exposed."
- Third, we must be clear as to the outcomes we (and the system) wish to achieve. Without some clarity as to what we wish to achieve, we run the risk of revealing and/or opening up covert processes just for the sake of it. This might, through happenstance, help create the desired effect, but runs the risk of violating people's trust and sense of control over what is revealed and for what reasons.
- Fourth, we must be selective in what we do, based on our non-judgmental diagnoses and the outcome(s) desired in the situation. We cannot bring all covert processes out into the open, nor put everything onto the table. We must select what to do and when to do it based on our best assessments of what is most likely to help achieve the desired outcome, given our diagnosis, the particular situation, and the context.

Key #3: Seek Movement Not Exposure. The purpose of addressing a covert process is to facilitate desired movement, not to uncover or expose as an end to itself. We must remember that the desired outcome is to increase individual, group, and/or organizational effectiveness, not to prove our abilities to diagnose or to expose or raise issues that either cannot be addressed or are not ready to be addressed. The intention behind what you say and do is critical on several dimensions.

- First, because it helps to keep you clear and focused as to what you are doing and why you are doing it.
- Second, because individuals in the system will be sensitive to your intentions, no matter what you publicly say. If they sense you are likely to expose someone or something, without good cause and/or safeguards, then trust will be low and little will be accomplished.
- Finally, remembering that you are trying to achieve movement, not exposure per se, is important in "measuring" the effectiveness of your interventions.

At a very basic level, if there is movement your interventions (or non-interventions) can be interpreted as on-track and effective, even if nothing has been publicly revealed, exposed, or brought to light. The same would not be true if your purpose was to expose, regardless of movement. It does little good to pry a "secret" out into the open if you have not also prepared the system to deal with it. Worse, the inability to deal with it could end up convincing everyone that they were right in keeping it a secret.

Key #4: Assume People Are Intendedly Competent. In working with covert processes we assume that most people are doing the best they can, and are intendedly competent. This helps to do three things that are critical aspects of setting the stage for effective intervention(s).

- First, the assumption of intended competence is an important aspect of developing hypotheses about the contents of an individual's, group's, and/or organization's prism. What beliefs, assumptions, values, and so on would likely exist to lead the system to behave in a certain way, assuming the system was doing the best it could? This is a diagnostic prerequisite to effective intervention and helps insure that actions are taken from the frame of reference of the system not the change agent.
- Second, the assumption of intended competence is a stance that communicates to the system (both overtly and tacitly) an invitation to be proactive, and that the system is also competent enough to work on changing itself.
- Third, assuming the system is doing the best it can encourages us to stay open, empathize with the system, and invites inquiry rather than judgment. This stance helps to create a setting that is more conducive to disclosure and exploration, rather than defensiveness.

Key #5: Remember Covert Processes Protect Against Threat. The intent of most covert processes is to protect the individual, group, and/or organization from real or perceived threat. While an observer might not agree that a particular covert process is a very useful or effective protection, nor perhaps that the threat is very real or serious, we must remember that the system is doing the best it can from the frame of reference of its *field of experience and prism*. Consequently we must be alert to danger as defined by the system and the particular methods and processes used to guard against the danger.

If we operate only from our frame of reference without awareness of the system's experience and prism we are likely to be perceived as "blind to realities," "foolhardy," and therefore dangerous. Thus, when we ignore the system's perspective we run the very real risk of violating the primary conditions of trust, safety, and sense of control ourselves. Instead, interventions must recognize the sense of threat inherent in revealing what has been hidden, concealed or disguised.

Key #6: Look In the Mirror. We must constantly be alert to the possibility that our own covert processes may be distorting our observations and diagnoses. Some examples include:

- Believing the system cannot change without our help because we have a (secret) need to be seen as a powerful helper.
- Choosing to avoid or ignore angry exchanges in a group because we are uncomfortable with anger.
- Not seeing how the larger system is impacting the specific setting because the primary theories and models we use to interpret events mostly address individual and group dynamics.
- Convincing a system to pursue a particular approach or intervention because it will meet their needs when, in reality, it is really advocated because we like the intervention, or we want to try a new method, or we feel especially comfortable with that particular method.
- Disguising and/or concealing our experience and even competence because we want the opportunity to work on a particular project or with a particular system.

To ameliorate the potential of one's own covert processes distorting perception and judgment it is helpful to have a high degree of personal awareness. We cannot "get rid" of all of our own covert processes, but we can be aware enough of many of them to recognize when our own patterns are being reflected back to us from whatever system we are working with. It is also very helpful when working with covert processes to team with someone else. This provides a professional colleague who can help track the complexities of the covert processes in the system, provides another view through a different prism, and can also be a mirror to help you see if any of your "stuff" is being confused with their "stuff." We must always be open to the possibility that the covert process blocking the movement of the system is our own, and aware, experienced, and confident enough to make the judgment about whose covert process is at work in a particular situation.

Key #7: Intervene Consistent With Your Contract. Finally, one should only intervene when it's indicated that the system wants or needs to work a covert process, and such interventions are consistent with your "contract" and/or relationship with the system. Thus, helping to raise issues related to repressed anger about a manager's recent promotion may not be appropriate, especially if your presence was requested to help the manager's team plan a ten-year celebration. Despite how clear the underlying issue might be to you, it would or could violate the necessary components of trust and control if you unilaterally helped to bring such feelings out into the open. At the same time you must also be responsible for paying attention to the spirit as well as the specifics of your presence. Were you asked to be involved because they needed your help on the ten-year celebration or because they wanted your help on being a better team? Such questions remind us that clear understandings and expectations are just as important in dealing with covert processes as with any other type of consulting work.

In sum, there are seven keys that help provide the orientation needed to begin to unlock covert processes in a system. They are: 1) safety first; 2) be clear and selective; 3) seek movement not exposure; 4) assume people are intendedly competent; 5) remember covert processes protect against threat; 6) look in the mirror; and 7) intervene consistent with your contract.

Concluding Comments

The Covert Processes Model™ evolved as a way to help us access and work with the hidden dimensions of individuals, groups and organizations. We found ourselves needing to develop a framework that moved beyond familiar change models, skills and practices. It has helped us to explore in a multidimensional and holistic way the conscious and the unconscious; the literal and the symbolic; the spoken and the unspoken; a system's hopes, aspirations and dreams with its fears, resistances and traumas. The seven keys, in combination with our knowledge of other intervention theories and methods, have been surprisingly helpful in guiding and reminding us as to what is essential when attempting to address covert processes. Both have made us better diagnosticians and interventionists. We are pleased to be able to put the model and the keys "on-the-table" for consideration by OD practitioners.

References

Bennett, H. Z. (1987). *The lens of perception*. Berkeley, CA: Celestial Arts.

Ferrucci, P. (1982). *What we may be*. Los Angeles, CA: J. P. Tarcher.

Marshak, R. J., & Katz, J. H. (1999). A look at the hidden dimensions of group dynamics. In A. Cooke et al. (Eds.) *Human relations reading book, 8th edition*, (pp. 251-257). Alexandria, VA: NTL Institute.

Marshak, R. J., & Katz, J. H. (1994). *The covert processes workbook: Dealing with the hidden dimensions of individuals, groups and organizations*. Dealing with Covert Processes Workshop workbook.

Zweig, C., & Abrams, J. (Eds.) (1993). *Meeting the shadow: The hidden side of human nature*. Los Angeles, CA: J. P. Tarcher.

25
The Symbolic Side of OD

This article focuses on the use of symbolic data as an integral part of OD diagnosis and intervention, especially regarding issues that might otherwise remain hidden. As we begin, we need to point out that working issues as described here could be seen as counter to the implicit rules of OD that you need to be able to publicly "collect data," "publish it," and "own it," before "working it." The dilemma, as OD practitioners know, is that even if pertinent data is collected, published, owned and worked, much remains hidden. We know too, that it is often these hidden aspects that have the greatest impact on change efforts, are the more difficult to surface, and that the likelihood of real change decreases dramatically if they are not addressed.

In our work with complex cultural change we found that not everything would or could be openly presented for rational analysis or verbal discourse. Other means and methods were needed to recognize, surface and address the more hidden, sometimes out-of-awareness issues that might be blocking change. This led us to develop The Covert Processes Model™ (Marshak & Katz, 1988, 1990, 1991a, 1991b) as a way to see the multiple levels that operate simultaneously within any given context: the overt and covert; the conscious and out-of-awareness; the verbal and nonverbal; the literal and symbolic. The more we worked with hidden issues, the more we found ourselves needing to expand and fine tune our abilities to gather data from multiple levels of communication, especially symbolic modes. As a result, our diagnostic insights and range and effectiveness of interventions increased dramatically as we recognized and worked with the issues conveyed through various symbolic modes of communication.

While the skills and abilities needed to recognize and address hidden dynamics are varied, knowing why, when, and how to use symbolic communications is a prerequisite for success. We, therefore, turn our discussion to a brief introduction to symbolic communication.

Symbolic Communication

Learning how to understand and work with symbolic aspects of diagnosis and intervention takes the ability to focus on several levels of information simultaneously. To assist our understanding of this process, we have identified some key beliefs and an overriding principle that guide our work:

1. Communication is complex and expressed through multiple modalities. All messages contain literal, verbal, and conscious components, as well as symbolic, nonverbal dimensions which may be out-of-awareness.

Marshak, R. J., & Katz, J. H. (1992). The symbolic side of OD. *OD Practitioner, 24*(2), 1-5. Republished with permission.

2. Messages conveyed through nonverbal, symbolic expression communicate real and legitimate issues, just like those conveyed through verbal, literal language.

3. Symbolic, nonverbal communication provides a way to express aspects of ourselves and situations about which we may not be consciously aware, or which we may not be able to express analytically and/or verbally.

4. We "know" more than what is in our conscious verbal minds and communicate nonverbally and symbolically regardless of what we consciously say or think.

With these beliefs reminding us to constantly pay attention to symbolic communications, a paradoxical principle informs our diagnostic processes: *Explore literal messages symbolically, and symbolic messages literally.* This principle tells us always to stop, look, and listen at least two ways, and to be open to the potential multiple meanings that may be conveyed by a seemingly single communication.

When symbolic communications are looked at, or listened to, for their literal as well as symbolic meaning a wider range of diagnostic speculation and/or inquiry is revealed. For example, if someone in an off-handed comment says: "This office is like a prison," it can be heard as a symbolic way of expressing the range of feelings and thoughts they have about their work place. In this instance they may be conveying a sense of little or no freedom, confinement, isolation, punishment, and the like. Pursued literally, however, would mean following up on the symbolic comment as if it were actually true. Therefore, appropriate diagnostic follow-up could include data collection as to: How exactly is this place like a prison? Who are the inmates, guards, and the warden? Why are you here? All of these, and other inquiries, serve to expand understanding of the original symbolic communication by treating it as if the person were literally telling you: "I am in prison."

Conversely, seemingly literal verbal statements should also be looked at or listened to symbolically. For example, if people talk about how "You can't tell the truth around here because too many people would get hurt," or "You can tell the boss the truth, but only if you are willing to take your lumps," or "We need to be brutally honest," it is appropriate to hear that telling the truth can be painful and to also speculate about what may be being communicated symbolically. Do these people, or the system, symbolically experience truth as a weapon, or that honesty brutalizes people? If so, what are the implications of such a message? Needless to say, it would be difficult to imagine much honesty in a system that consistently evokes such strong images and feelings.

In sum, to receive the full range of data and messages available to us, we need to tune ourselves to hear, see and experience both the literal and symbolic levels of communication. The essential issue becomes how do you tune into these symbolic and nonverbal messages? We next turn to four modalities through which symbolic communication is commonly expressed.

The 4M's of Symbolic Communication: Metaphor, Music, Movement and Media

To be able to tune fully into symbolic levels of communication involves tracking multiple sources of data including sounds, images, feelings and movements. As practitioners we must become more aware of the messages that are being conveyed through means other than literal, oral and written language. Because data are being sent both literally and symbolically it means we must tune ourselves to receive it both literally and symbolically. Below we have identified four dominant modes through which symbolic and nonverbal communication is most often expressed. For purposes of alliteration we have defined them as the "4M's" – metaphor, music, movement, and media. Remember, to find the clues and cues of symbolic meaning you must listen, look, feel and experience between the lines of literal meaning.

1. *Metaphor* – includes figures of speech, similes, puns, parables, myths and other forms of word imagery. Although the representational expression is through language, the focus is on the symbolic meaning, picture or image that is painted verbally. For example:
   - Do people describe their group as a family? A team? Solo performers? A feudal system?
   - Is the culture described as sink or swim? May the best person win? Only the strong survive? or We're all in this together?
   - As you watch and listen to people work in a group what metaphor or image comes to mind? Do they seem repetitive like a broken record? Like kids on a jungle gym? Are they moving full steam ahead?
   - Do certain themes and/or expressions occur regularly in discussions? For example: "It's hard to tell the truth," "The facts can be cruel," "Honesty hurts," in contrast to "The truth is freeing," "The facts are our friends," "Honesty is a help."

2. *Music* – includes all forms of auditory expression conveyed through voice, tone, pitch, tempo, volume, speed, rhythm, harmony, beat, melody, tune, as well as themes in song and music. For example:
   - As you listen to a group, do their discussions sound like an orchestra? A jazz band? A quartet? A reggae group?
   - Are all voices in tune? Heard? In harmony? Dissonant? Counterpoint? Is the sound shrill? Soothing? Sharp? Flat?
   - Is the rhythm of the group fast or slow? Is everyone in the same rhythm? What's the beat? The pace? The pitch? The tempo?
   - As you listen to a group's discussions do you hear a funeral march? A joyful tune? A melancholy refrain? A wedding song?

3. *Movement* – includes all forms of kinesthetic expression such as gestures, facial cues, posture, position, spatial relations, dance, and of course, "body language." For example:
   - How are people sitting or standing? Are key people sitting in opposition to one

another? Lined up in support? How close or far apart are they? Are they looking down? Looking up? Are individuals or groups sitting together? Apart? Scattered?
- Do people touch one another? Shake hands? Hug? Avoid contact? What does their posture and positioning convey? Warmth? Distance? Comfort? Formality?
- Do gestures and body language seem to display openness and support, or displeasure and judgment?
- If you were to describe the movement or dance of this group – is everyone in step? Moving at a snail's pace? Frolicking? Jumping? Dragging their feet? Are they moving in circles? Taking three steps forward and one back?

4. **Media** – includes all forms of artistic techniques and expression such as pictures, painting, drawing, sculpture, photography, collage, three dimensional forms, slides and other representational media. For example:
   - If you were to take a snapshot of a group at a given moment is anything missing from the picture? Are certain aspects over-emphasized? Minimized? What color, size, shapes do they suggest? Do they remind you of an abstract painting? Impressionist? Realism? Modern Art?
   - As you look at an organization's logo, brochures, reports, graphics, do they suggest an organization that's lined up? Boxed in? A network? Disconnected or blurred lines? Open-ended? Two-dimensional? Stuck in the past? Unclear about the present?
   - If someone draws an organizational chart what office(s) seems most central? Peripheral? Is anyone/anything "not in the picture?" Who's on top? Is everyone who needs to be in the picture?

By tuning ourselves to receive data expressed through these four modalities – listening to tone, pitch, and pace; recognizing the metaphors and images being verbally painted; alerting ourselves to the underlying songs and melodies, picking up the dance steps; noticing the different postures and positions, experiencing the impact of space; and seeing the pictures and portraits – we can better recognize and diagnose hidden or covert issues which may exist. With this understanding of the cues and clues of symbolic communication, we next present some examples of interventions using symbolic communication.

The 4M's in Action

The following vignettes, drawn from our experiences, are examples of symbolic communications in the context of OD interventions:

Metaphor. During a planning meeting with a task force charged with designing and implementing a new way of doing business that could ultimately impact the existing organizational structure, technology, reward system, accounting system, and career paths, certain phrases kept coming up throughout the discussion. "Look, if it ain't broke, let's not fix it." "Remember, we have to minimize down time and get this up and running quickly." "Maybe we only need to tinker with what we're doing." "That's been running well for twenty years, I don't see why we need to fix it now." The consultant listened to these remarks listening not only for the literal meaning being conveyed but also what was being expressed at a more symbolic level. It appeared through the statements that the group members were operating from an implicit shared metaphor that the organization was some kind of machine. This was consistent with their discussions which seemed more focused on making small incremental changes (tinkering), rather than the more fundamental shifts that seemed to be called for in the situation. Concluding that the group might be constrained by an unexpressed limiting belief ("We're here to fix the machine") the consultant intervened by reframing the suspected underlying metaphor. "You know, maybe what you are designing is a fundamentally new model of the organization that incorporates the latest technology and achieves higher performance standards." The invitation to think in terms of designing a higher performance machine rather then trying to repair an old outdated one worked as different members of the task force began seeing their assignment in a new way. Soon they were talking about making fundamental changes in aspects of the organization that they had earlier not considered because those aspects were "still functioning and therefore did not need fixing."

Music. During an executive planning session to consider organizational changes, the group's discussion kept getting bogged down as people debated how much change was really needed and how that would or would not help the business. The consultant noticed that one of the participants was humming a tune and asked her what it was. She responded, "For whatever reason the theme song to the movie, 'Gone with the Wind,' keeps playing in my head." When asked to reflect on what that might mean, she said, "As the movie opens there is the theme song and an introductory narrative that ends with the words, '… And an entire way of life was gone with the wind.'" Soon the group began talking about their fears of how drastic the changes might have to be and what that would mean to them and the rest of the people in the organization who were used to the "old way of doing things." The rest of the planning session became the most intense they ever had on the subject of organizational changes.

Movement. During a team building session with a group of men and women, one of the men got up and said, "I want to make a point." At the same time, he moved a flip chart such that it blocked the view of the team leader and ended up standing on the same side of the table as the rest of the men, "looking down" at the women. Thus, the consultant was well prepared to help create the necessary conditions of trust, safety and legitimacy that enabled the man to later reveal his secret, "That I feel more aligned and comfortable with men than women and sometimes I feel competitive with our team leader." Obviously, this message had already been conveyed through his nonverbal symbolic communication – he had made more then one kind of point when he got up to move the flip chart!

Media. During a meeting related to implementing a new organizational vision, a group of middle managers drew pictures representing what the organization and its people would look like when the vision was fully implemented. After group members described their pictures in ways that seemed rationally consistent with the vision, the consultant working with them asked why some of the people drawn in the pictures had no eyes while some others did. The initial response was, "Because we are poor artists." However, as the consultant continued to explore who the people with no eyes were, the somewhat hesitant response that came back was, "Top management." When asked about the people with eyes the response was, "The rest of the organization, especially the people in this room." This opened the way for a very candid discussion of group members' perceptions and feelings about top management and their leadership. "They are blind to what's really going on around here." "It's the three blind men describing the elephant, but we're the ones who end up having to take care of it." "They have walked into this vision thing with their eyes shut and they don't know what they've gotten us into." "They have their heads in a cloud and can't see the road ahead of us ... we're going to crash." Once the deep mistrust of top leadership and their vision had been surfaced it was much easier to begin a more "rational" discussion of the merits and potential problems of the vision, how it might make a positive difference, and why it might be needed and appropriate. The meeting concluded with a decision to seek a face-to-face meeting with top management to discuss how best to achieve the vision, gain a better understanding of the "view from the top," and perhaps "open their eyes a little."

Closing Comments

Finally, we'd like to highlight some important considerations we keep in mind when working with symbolic communication:

1. Potentially covert or hidden blocking factors are often presented openly on a non-verbal symbolic level by one or more people in the group.
2. When symbolic messages are noted or acted upon, important additional insight and data to guide diagnosis and intervention are provided.
3. Significant movement can occur when symbolic messages are treated seriously and recognized as a non-spoken, covert invitation to address the concerns they raise.
4. Recognizing and commenting on symbolic messages in a non-threatening manner can make previously hidden issues available to be put on-the-table for open discourse.
5. Addressing the theme(s) of symbolic messages is not done as an end unto itself, but as a way to potentially raise and address previously hidden obstacles.
6. Interventions related to symbolic communications may occur in their own right (e.g., "everyone draw a picture representing your group.") and/or as described above, in the context of another explicit overt process (e.g., team building, change planning, etc.)
7. Working with messages sent symbolically requires an ability to receive messages symbolically, as well as trusting one's intuition, one's inner voice, and developing skills to respond creatively and artistically.

We find it crucial to remember that our role as practitioners is not to serve as a "mind reader," trying to conclude what the covert issues are within the group, or one of confronting group members with "hidden truths." This will likely create defensiveness and scare the issues into deeper hiding. Rather, our role is to create a context of safety, trust and legitimacy to enable participants to explore the covert issues that may be blocking them from achieving their desired outcomes.

The more we work with symbolic modalities, the more we find a wealth of data available to us. Hearing someone humming a tune, as in the "Gone with the Wind" example above, provides equally potent data for exploring real issues and concerns as does an overt verbal statement, "I'm fearful we could lose everything in this change." Furthermore, because symbolic communications also provide a powerful link between the unconscious and the conscious they help provide a bridge between what is often censored and that which is openly discussed. Consequently, the more we are able to tune into symbolic communications the more we enhance our abilities to identify real (but normally hidden) issues and discover new ways to uncover and remove potential obstacles to the effectiveness of individuals, groups, and organizations.

References

Marshak, R. J., & Katz, J. H. (1991a). Keys to unlocking covert processes. In M. McDonald (Ed.), *Building ourselves ... Our work ... Our organizations ... Our world: Organization Development Network Conference Proceedings* (pp. 65-71). Portland, OR: Organization Development Network.

Marshak, R. J., & Katz, J. H. (1991b). Covert processes at work. *Chesapeake Bay Organization Development Network newsletter, 6*(2), 1, 4-5.

Marshak, R. J., & Katz, J. H. (1990). Covert processes and revolutionary change. In M. McDonald (Ed.), *Forging revolutionary partnerships: Organization Development Network Conference Proceedings* (pp. 58-65). Portland, OR: Organization Development Network.

Marshak, R. J., & Katz, J. H. (1988). *The Covert Processes Model™*. Unpublished manuscript.

26
Covert Processes and Organization Development

All Organization Development practitioners understand that organizational change involves multi-faceted dynamics, some of which may be covert or hidden. This discussion reviews six broad types of overt and covert processes that routinely manifest themselves during an organization change. The reader is invited to consider prior experiences with these processes, and especially to reflect on how well prepared you are to deal with each of them in your work. To begin, consider the following scenario.

You are working with an executive team. During a change planning meeting Pat, the VP for Product Division Beta, keeps challenging the proposed organization changes that are intended to increase efficiency of operations. Pat continues to raise concerns and objections no matter what the CEO or others say. Pat appears animated, agitated and sometimes angry during these interactions, but never really goes "over the line."

Keeping this brief scenario in mind, let's now look at the overt and covert dynamics that typically occur during organization change initiatives.

Overt Rational and Analytic Logic

When all is said and done, most organization change efforts begin and sometimes end with "making the case for change." The case for change is invariably a well documented, logical analysis of the compelling reasons why the organization and the people in it must do something slightly or dramatically different. For example, in the scenario it might be explained to Pat that:

"Due to increased worldwide competition, we must a) change our strategy, b) reorganize, c) create a new reward system, d) transform our corporate culture, e) downsize, right size, contract out, off-shore, etc., or, f) all of the above. If we do these things then we will once again be a global leader."

The unspoken part of this message, of course, is that:

"Pat, we expect everyone to be logical and rational and accept the compelling reasons for what has to be done and therefore not only understand and go along with the changes, but embrace them."

Especially for executives, the case for change tends to be the most central and overt dimension of organizational change initiatives, but is actually only one of multiple dimensions involved. Another five are "non-rational" and include hidden or covert dynamics. Separately, and in combination, these play a critical role in all organizational

Marshak, R. J. (2006). Covert processes and organizational development. *Seasonings, 2*(3). Republished with permission.

change efforts. Unless attended to they may become covert traps and surprises that can block or detour any change initiative.

Covert Politics: Individual and Group Interests

The possibility that individuals and sub-groups might have their own needs and interests that will be expressed or acted upon is usually guarded against by admonitions that people should act in the best interests of the organization not themselves. To act based on one's own interests is to be "political," and being political is considered inappropriate behavior in most organizations. Instead one is supposed to operate only from objective logic and reason based on the best interests of the overall collective.

Actually, however, people and groups do have their own needs and interests that they do, in fact, take into consideration in how they assess and react to organizational change. It would be unwise or unrealistic to assume otherwise. Such needs and interests may at times be considered "selfish" or "self serving," but in many instances simply reflect that people of good will operate from a calculus rooted in their own experience and perspectives. In the scenario perhaps based on Pat's experience or point-of-view the "resisting" behavior is a well-intentioned attempt to keep the organization on the right track or to preserve the accomplishments of Pat's Product Division and people. Additionally, perhaps the proposed changes are the result of "political dealings" involving the other executives who did not include Pat in their deliberations. This way of thinking suggests a model of organizations where it is assumed that people and groups act based on their own needs and interests, and where a combination of political as well as managerial processes is how organizations really operate.

The general distaste with which many OD consultants view the possibility that they may have to engage in or deal with uses of power (other than the power of expertise) as well as political processes (other than checking things out with obvious stakeholders) is often evident in change efforts. In my experience, this is mostly associated with attempts to avoid or downplay the need to think in terms of politics and political interests or to engage in substantive change planning and implementation from political as well as managerial perspectives. To do so is somehow either inappropriate or to stoop to what others might do, but we should not. As a consequence, when political processes of one kind or another emerge to challenge or disrupt a change effort, change planners are sometimes surprised or unprepared to deal with what is experienced as "covert politics."

Covert Inspirations: Values-Based and Visionary Aspirations

Most change efforts include some kind of vision statement intended to capture the essence of the desired future state or change goal. "We will be the best (biggest, smartest, fastest) company in the world." These statements often are a shorthand version of the conclusion of the case for change analysis: "And, therefore because of globalization, we need to become the best company in the world." The difference between these kinds of vision statements and employing values-based and visionary aspirations is the difference between head and heart. Many vision statements are a projection of the rational analysis and logic used to develop the case for change. They are intended to help people think about the end state of the change effort and to become convinced to work towards it. Invoking values-based and visionary aspirations, on the other hand, is intentionally inspirational. It seeks to strike a chord in people, compelling them to work towards the desired change, sometimes despite rational logic, because strongly held values or aspirations have been evoked. Perhaps for Pat, the "greater efficiency" advocated in the scenario is not an inspiring goal, or worse, may push against strongly held values that currently inspire everyone in Beta, such as developing superior products.

Enlisting positive values and aspirations is the province of the inspirational leader not the analytic manager. Think in terms of Dr. Martin Luther King's "I Have a Dream" speech, an inspirational statement to enlist people in a change effort by evoking powerful shared values and aspirations, regardless of a rational analysis of the prevailing conditions. Imagine the same speech if it were filled with an analysis of the number or percentage of discriminatory events in the past year and the trends and market forces both for and against a more just society. What is precisely powerful about the use of inspiration in a change effort is that it does not directly appeal to reason and logic, the same reason and logic that can present multiple rationales not to implement the change. Inspiration speaks to the parts of people that want to do good things, want to be part of something bigger than themselves, and want to see their values, hopes and dreams fulfilled.

Despite the power of inspiration, it is not always fully utilized and often becomes an untapped covert dynamic in organizational change. Worse, as noted, change efforts sometimes fail because they work against the strongly held but unexpressed or covert values and aspirations of key executives and employees. The power of heart over head in organizational change is explained by Kotter and Cohen (2002) in their book, *The Heart of Change*. They strongly advocate greater use of inspiration and emotion over reason and analysis in organizational change efforts. Engage the heart; not just the head.

Covert Emotions: Affective and Reactive Feelings

Similar to but different from inspiration is the role of emotions in organizational change. Historically, in Western thought emotions are generally viewed as the enemy of logic and reason and must be overcome or suppressed. This extends into the organizational world where decision-making by logic and analysis, not emotion, is extolled as a virtue. Although emotions and feelings are an integral part of human and organization life they are still generally considered to be anathema in the workplace. Consequently, whatever feelings and emotions exist related to a change effort they are supposed to be suppressed or ignored in favor of a reasoned, rational discussion. Once again we are back to the bias towards making and discussing the rational case for change. It would not be unfair to say that many leaders and managers of change who lack emotional intelligence (Goleman, 1995) are reluctant to participate in open meetings or forums because the sessions might become too emotional. It's almost as if these leaders are saying, *"If people are going to be emotional about these changes, then I don't want to deal with them. When they are ready to discuss things rationally then I'll meet with them."*

The desire for reason and logic in organizational matters and avoiding dealing with anyone who is too mad, glad, sad, excited or afraid insures that emotions – an integral part of change in human systems – will have mostly covert effects on change initiatives. Take for example the extension of Kübler-Ross (1973) on the stages of death and dying to human reactions to organizational change and endings. Most organizational change consultants would assert that people will react to change in ways similar to the stages of death and dying: denial, anger, bargaining, depression, acceptance, and finally adaptive behavior. This model makes perfectly clear that there will likely be initial anger by a broad range of people to the announcement of an organizational change of any significance and that this is normal, predictable and expected. In fact, it would be unreasonable and illogical to expect otherwise. Nonetheless, leaders and managers often act as if they should be able to make a change announcement and then immediately enter into rational and reasoned discussions with affected employees about how to implement the changes. If the employees show any anger or its variants, they are labeled as irrational, too emotional, or resisting the change, not that they are having normal human reactions that need to be worked through. Perhaps Pat's agitation and anger are simply showing normal emotional reactions to the proposed changes, or the rest of the executive team is suppressing their emotions and thereby ignoring important data that could influence implementation efforts.

Covert Mindsets: Guiding Beliefs and Assumptions

All change initiatives, even those driven solely by rational analysis, are also guided by tacit and usually untested assumptions, beliefs and premises that are collectively referred to here as mindsets. Because people generally don't think about the underlying assumptions and frameworks that guide how they reason and interpret the world, mindsets have a profound but covert impact on the ways in which people react to change possibilities. The term mindsets is used to embrace a broad array of concepts that explain how our experience is affected by underlying beliefs, assumptions, and cognitive structures. These include: mental models, paradigms, worldviews, and organizational and societal cultures (Schein, 2004). All guide how we think and can also prevent people from imagining possibilities if left unexamined or untested.

Dramatic organizational change is only possible when prevailing mindsets are made overt, challenged, and modified in some way. Without a change in mindsets people will continue to see situations in the same way and develop the same responses no matter how much they say they wish to change (Argyris & Schön, 1974). It is not unusual, therefore, for those involved or affected to be limited in their thinking by unspoken, covert mindsets that prevent truly transformational initiatives. It's not that such results are not wanted or intended, it's simply that covert assumptions and beliefs are preventing people from thinking much differently from the ways things have always been. Perhaps Pat has a different mental model than the other executives about organizational success or failure that is blocking how the proposed change is understood. Stop and consider how many of the new management initiatives or organizational forms that are accepted practice today were almost or actually unthinkable some twenty years ago. The shift from the capacity driven, certainty oriented, mass production, industrial age paradigm to the more customer-oriented, flexible, and customized paradigm of the current information age requires both a revolution in information technologies as well as a revolution in mindsets. And, as more than one organization attempting transformational change has discovered, installing transformational technologies is sometimes much easier than changing prevailing beliefs, assumptions, paradigms and cultures.

Covert Psychodynamics: Anxiety Based and Unconscious Defenses

Politics, inspirations, emotions and mindsets may all be hidden or covert dimensions of organizational change, but no dimension is more covert or less addressed than the psychodynamic aspects of organizations and organizational change. This is partially related to the fact that by definition we are dealing with unconscious and speculative phenomena. It is also related to the widespread taboo about dealing with unconscious dynamics in a workplace setting. That's for employee assistance programs or outside of work counseling. As a manager once remarked to me during a team building session when people were sitting in a circle and asked to share their perceptions of each other, "Is this going to become a shrink session?" Addressing the overt, rational, logical case for change is always a requirement for an organizational change effort. Considering and possibly even trying to address the covert, unconscious reactions and dynamics fueled by the anxieties the change initiative might have triggered in individuals and groups is almost always considered off limits in the workplace setting.

Despite the general taboo about openly speculating about or attempting to deal with unconscious phenomena in workplace settings, there has been a great deal of attention to the topic among more psychoanalytically oriented organization theorists and consultants (e.g., de Board, 1978; Hirschorn, 1991; Kets de Vries, 1991). Generally speaking, various unconscious reactions to and defenses against anxiety are considered to be a primary cause of psychodynamic phenomena at work. Because the processes associated with organizational change from the initial perceived need for change through implementation of new ways of working are likely to be anxiety producing, being alert to the possibility of unconscious reactions is yet another covert dimension to consider during change efforts. Yes, some reactions may be consciously calculated resistance; but some may also be unconscious reactions or defenses against the anxieties triggered by the organizational change or organizational life in general.

Consequently, from a psychodynamic point of view we should not be totally surprised if during an initial meeting to discuss a change initiative someone, or even the whole team, exhibits various unconscious defense mechanisms. Maybe the team, instead of rationally working on how to implement the change, will engage in unconscious "dependency" or "fight or flight" behavior. In the scenario, maybe Pat is involved in "transference" and has started to act as if the team leader was Pat's father or mother telling Pat how to behave as a teenager. Maybe the leader is "repressing" feelings of anxiety about having to downsize fellow workers and is "compensating" by acting overly logical and cool at a time when some warmth and emotions may be needed. This does not mean that we should become organization therapists, but we do need to understand the potential ways unconscious dynamics may manifest themselves during change efforts, and not be surprised or incapable of at least minimally dealing with them.

Conclusion

In order to help facilitate an organization change, we need a clear understanding of both overt and covert dynamics and how they manifest themselves during change efforts. OD consultants must be able to help leaders and managers to consider and manage both the overt, rational aspects of change, and also the more covert, non-rational dimensions that invariably will be involved. Developing ways to recognize and work with the overt and covert dimensions of organizational change becomes, therefore, a critical competency for OD practitioners.

References

Argyris, C., & Schön, D. A. (1974). *Theory in practice*. San Francisco: Jossey-Bass.

De Board, R. (1978). *The psychoanalysis of organizations: A psychoanalytic approach to behavior in groups and organizations*. London: Routledge.

Goleman, D. (1995). *Emotional intelligence*. New York: Bantam Books.

Hirschorn, L. (1991). *The workplace within: Psychodynamics of organizational life*. Cambridge, MA: MIT Press.

Kets de Vries, M. F. R. (1991). *Organizations on the couch: Handbook of psychoanalysis and management*. San Francisco: Jossey-Bass.

Kotter, J. P., & Cohen, D. S. (2002). *The heart of change*. Boston: Harvard Business School Press.

Kübler-Ross, E. (1973). *On death and dying*. New York: Macmillan.

Schein, E. H. (2004). *Organization culture and leadership, 3rd edition*. New York: Wiley.

27
The Paradoxes of Sustaining Organizational Change

One of the ongoing concerns in the theory and practice of organization development has been "how to sustain organizational change?" Historically this has involved inquiry into ways to maintain changes after the initial implementation "push" has subsided.

The tendency of systems to revert back to initial proclivities a few years, or even months, after a major change effort is well known. This is often attributed to the lack of effective and sustained follow through; or, in terms of the Lewinian model of change, a triumph of restraining forces over driving forces once the initial pressure has been reduced.

This orientation to the question of sustaining organizational change, however, seems based in the episodic, *start-stop*, punctuated equilibrium models of change of the late twentieth century, for example, the stages of "unfreezing – movement – refreezing" (Marshak, 2004). The present concerns with continuous change (Weick & Quinn, 1999) have now introduced a new context and set of considerations to the question and in so doing have raised a number of paradoxes. The purpose of this brief paper is to outline the dimensions of the issues and paradoxes involved in the question of "sustaining organizational change" depending on whether we are considering episodic or continuous models of change.

We will first consider some of the issues associated with sustaining episodic change. The discussion will then raise the issues associated with sustaining continuous organizational change and the paradoxes that emerge in that context.

Sustaining Episodic Changes

The questions and issues associated with sustaining episodic change tend to center on how to keep or maintain a change once initiated. This picks up on the dictionary meanings of the word "sustain" associated with "to keep in existence; keep up; maintain or prolong." The primary resulting questions and issues include:

- What is needed to maintain a change and/or prevent "organizational recidivism?"
- Are there some types of change that are easier or harder to maintain, for example, changes in culture or subcultures, structures, relationships, processes, technologies?
- Are there some change processes that contribute to higher rates of "organizational recidivism," for example directed changes versus participatory changes?
- Given today's rapidly changing world, how long must a given change continue to exist to be considered sustained?

Slightly edited from: Marshak, R. J. (2008). The paradoxes of sustaining organizational change. *OD Practitioner, 40*(2), 61-63. Republished with permission.

Sustaining Continuous Change

Once the model of change shifts from episodic to continuous the question of sustaining organizational change takes on new meanings that lead to some paradoxes in our traditional ways of thinking about the question. Here some of the other dictionary definitions of "sustain" come into play: "to provide for the support of; to strengthen the spirits; courage, etc; to bear up against, endure, withstand."

First, let's look at how our thinking shifts when we consider continuous versus episodic change. Some of the key questions and issues now become:

- Are we primarily concerned with how to sustain an episodic change or rather how to sustain ongoing, continuous changes?
- How well do most of our theories and expectations based on our historic models of change fit concepts of continuous change; for example, is there ever a stage in continuous change that we are attempting to refreeze, or otherwise maintain?
- What do we know about successful and sustained continuous change given how recently we have begun to deal explicitly with this phenomenon?
- As we shift our perspective we also shift our assessments of what is happening, for example, are rapid changes considered to be mistakes being corrected (a more episodic view), or indicators of successful sustained change (a more continuous change view)?

Next, we consider the effect on organizational members of sustaining change in a continuous versus episodic context. Now instead of stabilizing a change, we become more concerned about keeping the change process open. This can lead to requests to stop all the changes because we are now dealing with change fatigue. Instead of being primarily concerned with how to *unfreeze* and *refreeze* an organization and its members, we become more concerned about strengthening the spirits of organizational members so they can endure and withstand continuous movement. Some of the key questions and issues from this point of view are:

- What affects people's ability to sustain continuous change, for example, different types of change, different types of change leadership?
- What are the characteristics of change fatigue? Does it really exist? What is it associated with? Are there things that especially help or hinder, for example dealing with change alone or within a (support) group?
- Are human systems capable of sustained, continuous change? What are the costs and benefits? What should be done in the short and long term if the competitive environment now "demands" it? Do we have any theories and research to guide our thinking and actions?

Some Paradoxes

The paradoxes associated with "sustaining organizational change" come from the multiple meanings of the term in a world that includes both episodic and continuous change. The three dominant meanings in this multi-dimensional context include: 1) How to sustain an episodic change once initiated; 2) How to sustain continuous changing; and 3) How to sustain people in dealing with continuous change. These lead to a set of circular paradoxes that change agents must explicitly or implicitly deal with in today's organizations:

- The more we seek to sustain (keep or maintain) a change, the harder it is to sustain (keep) changing.
- The more we keep changing, the harder it is to keep people engaged and capable of changing.
- The less we are able to keep people engaged and capable of changing, the harder it is to create and then sustain (another) change.

These paradoxes are more than just turns of a phrase. Instead they reflect the changing nature of change and the demands for organization development and change theories, research, and practices to keep up with a world that now involves both episodic and continuous change.

References

Marshak, R. J., (2004). Morphing: The leading edge of organizational change in the twenty-first century, *Organization Development Journal, 22,* 8-21.

Weick, K. E., & Quinn, R. E. (1999). Organizational change and development. *Annual Review of Psychology, 50,* 361-386.

INDEX